Method and Appraisal in Economics

Method and Appraisal in Economics

EDITED BY

SPIRO J. LATSIS

CAMBRIDGE UNIVERSITY PRESS

CAMBRIDGE

LONDON · NEW YORK · MELBOURNE

Published by the Syndics of the Cambridge University Press
The Pitt Building, Trumpington Street, Cambridge CB2 1RP
Bentley House, 200 Euston Road, London NW1 2DB
32 East 57th Street, New York, NY 10022, USA
296 Beaconsfield Parade, Middle Park, Melbourne 3206, Australia

First published 1976

Printed in Great Britain at the
University Printing House, Cambridge
(Euan Phillips, University Printer)

Library of Congress Cataloguing in Publication Data
Main entry under title:
Method and appraisal in economics.
'Results from the Economics Sessions of the
Nafplion Colloquium on Research Programmes in
Physics and Economics held in Nafplion, Greece,
2–14 September, 1974.'
Includes index.
1. Economics–Congresses. 2. Economic research–Congresses.
I. Latsis, Spiro J., 1946–
HB21. M45   330   75–44581
ISBN 0 521 21076 3

Contents

	page
Preface	vii
A research programme in economics	1
S. J. LATSIS	
Economics and psychology: the death and resurrection of a research programme	43
A. W. COATS	
Schools, 'revolutions' and research programmes in economic theory	65
A. LEIJONHUFVUD	
Anomaly and the development of economics: the case of the Leontief paradox	109
N. DE MARCHI	
From substantive to procedural rationality	129
H. A. SIMON	
Kuhn versus Lakatos *or* Paradigms versus research programmes in the history of economics	149
M. BLAUG	
On the history and philosophy of science and economics	181
T. W. HUTCHISON	
'Revolutions' in economics	207
J. R. HICKS	
Index	219

Preface

This collection of essays results from the Economics Sessions of the Nafplion Colloquium on Research Programmes in Physics and Economics held in Nafplion, Greece, 2–14 September 1974. A separate volume, entitled *Method and Appraisal in the Physical Sciences*, edited by Colin Howson, contains the papers arising from the Physics Sessions of the Colloquium.

The idea of holding this Colloquium was first conceived by my friend and teacher, Imre Lakatos, Professor of Logic at the University of London until his death in 1974. Its central purpose was a synoptic examination of Lakatos's new and provocative methodology of scientific research programmes (MSRP) to developments in the physical sciences and in economic theory.

The papers by Coats, Latsis, Leijonhufvud and de Marchi were read during the meetings of the Colloquium and have been modified in the light of the discussions they provoked. Those by Hicks, Hutchison and Simon, on the other hand, were prepared after the Colloquium and arose from exchanges at the Sessions and informal discussions between the Sessions. Blaug's paper was circulated during the Colloquium and was later revised.

The central problem that binds together the contributions in this volume is the problem of theory-appraisal in economics. When is one economic theory better than another? Are there objective criteria for assessing the cognitive value of theories and what is the status of such criteria? Are there pragmatic temporary criteria? Or are there no articulable criteria at all?

Hicks, for instance, inclines to the view that our criteria are pragmatic and can at best be valid for brief historical periods and relative to the social and economic problems prevalent in them. Hutchison, on the other hand, concludes that the criterion of falsifiability transcends particular periods in the history of economic science and should be applicable to good science across the board. The papers by Blaug, Coats, Latsis and de Marchi are more or less straightforward attempts to discover the extent of the applicability of Lakatos's MSRP to the development of economic analysis.

MSRP, though closer in spirit to Hutchison's view than to Hicks's, insists that the recognition of 'goodness' in a theory is a complex matter and that no single criterion is capable of demarcating good from bad theories. The criteria made available by MSRP supplement the usual logical and empirical adequacy criteria: MSRP adds new dynamic criteria for assessment of the process of theory-change as distinct from assessment of the end results. In terms of MSRP, if we are comparing the ith version of some research programme – RP_1 – with some other research programme – RP_2 – it becomes important for our relative appraisal to know how RP_{1_i} and RP_{2_i} have been arrived at. The logical and empirical status of the isolated competing hypotheses h_1 and h_2 – which form parts of RP_{1_i} and RP_{2_i} respectively – are no longer sufficient data for appraisal. MSRP provides the apparatus required to judge the way in which a hypothesis h_1 embedded in a research programme RP_{1_i} has been arrived at. Although several of the papers in this volume are suggestive of the power of the approach in one social science, the desirability that more work should be done is evident.

In most of the papers in this volume a backward look is taken at economic theory and there is heavy reliance on hindsight. This is in line with Lakatos's methodological strictures according to which we should be careful to demarcate *appraisal* from *advice*. Lakatos insisted (although some of his earlier work bordered on the psychology of discovery) that the proper domain of philosophy of science is the appraisal of past achievements and *not* the rendering of heuristic advice. In particular, the descriptive apparatus and the criteria of appraisal offered by MSRP were designed to answer questions of the type 'Why is theory A better than theory B?' and *not* questions of the type 'Should I work on theory A rather than theory B?' or 'Will theory A be corroborated and theory B not?'

The papers by Herbert Simon and Axel Leijonhufvud are different from the others in that they include forward-looking elements. Simon examines a fundamental concept of the neoclassical research programme in economics – the assumption of '*substantive*' *rationality*. He argues that this concept has become progressively inappropriate. But he also points into the future when he suggests that in the next few decades a different concept of rationality – *procedural rationality* – will take over. Leijonhufvud's paper examines and appraises the fundamental assumptions in the hard core of neoclassical economics not only with a view to past performance but also with regard to future prospects.

I would like to thank the participants in the Colloquium, the administrative staff – especially Mrs Daisy Mavratzioti – and my fellow members on the organising committee – Hans Albert, Erwin Hiebert, Paul Feyerabend, John Watkins and Basil Yamey – for their continued help and support. I am indebted to Mrs Diana Radsma for her help in the organisation of the Colloquium and the preparation of the manuscript, and to Mrs Barbara Lowe for the compilation of the index.

S.J.L.

A research programme in economics[1]

SPIRO J. LATSIS

HARVARD UNIVERSITY AND BOSTON UNIVERSITY

I Alternative methodologies of economics
  a Apriorism
  b Falsificationism
  c Conventionalism
II The methodology of scientific research programmes
  a Situational determinism as a research programme
  b Single- and multiple-exit decision situations
  c Perfect competition and monopoly
  d Monopolistic competition
  e Duopoly and oligopoly
  f Limit price theory

I *Alternative methodologies of economics*

A seemingly liberal adequacy requirement may be employed to test the applicability of any methodological framework to economic theory. That is, on the basis of the proposed methodological criteria, (i) *not* every putative economic theory should automatically qualify as economic science and (ii) *not* every economic theory whatever should be banished as pseudo-science.

Unless the first requirement is satisfied, the criteria would obviously be too *lax*: unless the second is satisfied they would equally obviously be too *restrictive*. Both extremes defeat their purpose, which is to organise and appraise some subject matter. The first extreme opens the floodgates of confusion while the second legislates the subject out of existence.

Yet most economists and methodologists would feel uncomfortable if these adequacy requirements were effectively imposed. And this is not surprising. Most methodological frameworks transplanted from the natural to the social sciences fail to fulfil even these minimal adequacy requirements when applied to economic theory. More specifically, where the subject matter is the history of economic theory, *apriorism* is too *lax*, while *falsificationism* is too *restrictive*.

[1] This is an extended version of a paper read at the Nafplion Colloquium on Research Programmes in Physics and Economics in Nafplion, Greece on 8 September 1974. Sections (*d*) and (*e*) in Part II of this paper are reproduced unchanged from my [1972]. I would like to thank Peter Bauer, Peter Clark, Kurt Klappholz, John Watkins and Basil Yamey for helpful criticisms.

My thesis will be that there is however, a comparatively new methodology, the methodology of scientific research programmes (MSRP), which fares better than any of the hitherto available methodologies of economics for the description and appraisal of developments in economic analysis. I am not seeking to argue that it solves all outstanding problems in the methodology and history of economic theory; merely that it appears better equipped for description and appraisal than alternative currently available methodological frameworks.[2]

MSRP is applicable to economics only if there are research programmes in economics. In the latter part of this paper I shall indicate why I think there are research programmes (or at least one research programme) in economics, and why the development of economic analysis may be fruitfully described and appraised in terms of MSRP. I shall also provide detailed examples from the development of the neoclassical theory of the firm.

I would now like to discuss three alternative methodologies which have gained wide currency, if not among economists, at least among methodologists of economics in recent decades: they are, *apriorism, falsificationism* and *conventionalism*.[3] Although I hold that these approaches have weaknesses, I also believe that each highlights important aspects both of the nature of economic analysis and of the nature of the criticism to which it has been subjected. Indeed, I shall be arguing that it is the chief merit of MSRP that it captures the advantages of these three methodological approaches without sharing some of their disadvantages. I note that I shall be selective in my account of these three methodologies. That is, I shall be highlighting those aspects which have counterparts in MSRP.

Apriorism claims that the assumption of rationality is an absolute prerequisite for describing and explaining human actions and, in particular, economic actions. The reluctance to give up the rationalistic approach in the explanation of economic action is mirrored in the elevation of the assumption of rationality to the status of an *apriori true* postulate. *Falsificationism*, on the other hand, with its emphasis on bold hypotheses and 'deadly' evidence, reflects the need to impose stringent empirical requirements on the acceptability of hypotheses; and it bars *ad hoc* hypotheses introduced to accommodate counter-evidence. *Conventionalism*, though apparently unduly defensive, has some merit of its own. We

---

[2] The methodology of scientific research programmes was put forward by Imre Lakatos in his [1968] and his [1970]. It was applied extensively by Lakatos and others to the history of physical theory but Lakatos himself doubted the applicability of his methodology to the social sciences. In applying MSRP to economics I have adopted a slightly modified version of the Lakatoshian framework. For instance, I shall not require that appraisal only be *relative* to a competing programme. Rather I shall claim that a research programme may progress, or indeed degenerate, in isolation. Finally, I shall often not require that, to be *non ad hoc*, a theory be 'empirically progressive'.

[3] This is not an exhaustive list of the available methodologies of economics. But it is, I hope, representative of the intellectually respectable ones.

should be prepared to put up with counter-intuitive and implausible hypotheses if they are explanatorily and predictively adequate and we may be justified in defending and developing an anomaly-ridden theory.

I shall argue that the MSRP captures the advantages of these approaches under a single methodological framework. With its reluctance to give up the fundamental postulates and methods of a research programme, it combines a tolerance of anomalies and refutations, and it also insists on a stringent bar on *ad hoc* hypotheses. I hope to clarify these points as I go along.

But before I proceed I should stress two important preliminary points.

One of these I have already hinted at: I shall take it that the task we set the methodologies under discussion is description and appraisal. While recognising that the problem of heuristic advice is a central one for methodology, and that methodological theories of appraisal may contain tacit heuristic advice, for the present purposes, I shall demarcate appraisal from advice and deal mainly with the former.[4] In other words, I shall be concerned with the problem, 'Is theory A better than theory B?' rather than the problem, 'How should one proceed if one wants to construct a theory that is better than an existing one?'

Secondly, I shall assume in what follows that the structure of any satisfactory explanatory/predictive schema in economics must be deductive. I take it that most economic theorists would not object to this requirement.

(a) Apriorism

I turn first to apriorism. Apriorism, as a methodological approach to economics, had been entertained by Nassau Senior in the early nineteenth century, but only gained wide currency in the first half of this century through the work of von Mises and Robbins.[5] According to this approach the fundamental propositions of economic science are 'true' or 'hold' independently of the vagaries of experience. Indeed, they are the means which allow us to experience economic actions and economic phenomena. Paraphrasing Mises, no *meaningful action can be performed without them and therefore no action would contradict them.*

According to von Mises the fundamental apriori category is that of *purposeful action.* He writes: 'Human action is one of the agencies bringing about change...As it cannot be traced back to its causes it must be considered as an ultimate given'.[6]

Concerning the apriori categories which constitute the springs of action, he adds, 'Every attempt to prove them [the apriori categories] must presuppose their validity. It is impossible to explain them to a

---

[4] For my views on the problem of heuristic advice see Latsis [1976].

[5] Robbins [1932]; von Mises [1949].

[6] Von Mises [1949], p. 18.

being who does not possess them on his own account...They are ultimate unanalyzable categories. The human mind is utterly incapable of imagining logical categories at variance with them. No matter how they may appear to superhuman beings, they are for man inescapable and absolutely necessary. They are the indispensable prerequisites of perception, apperception and experience.'[7]

We may, in my view, distil from von Mises' somewhat cryptic and grandiose text the fundamental presuppositions underlying the approach of neoclassical microeconomics. In my opinion when von Mises talked of 'ultimate' and 'unanalyzable' prerequisites for experience, what he had in mind was in part the *rationalistic approach* to explanation and prediction in the social sciences.

The rationalistic approach takes it for granted that the actions of an economic agent are not to be viewed as random or haphazard, or as not capable of being explained. Rather it assumes that economic actions, like other events, follow general principles, and that specific actions involve the application of such general principles to particular cases.

We may ask, what is the status of these general principles? Are they physical laws? Are they psychological laws? Or are they social laws? The rationalistic approach gives a sharp and perhaps somewhat unexpected answer to this question, namely, that the general principle involved in the explanation of action is *neither a physical law nor a psychological law nor a social law*. It is rather a *synthetic apriori principle*, i.e., the *rationality principle*. This principle says that human actions *are adequate or appropriate to the situations in which they occur*. I am purposely leaving the formulation of the principle vague and open to different interpretations. I shall suggest later that in the explanation of economic behaviour it takes a more definite and criticisable form.

I now turn to a brief discussion of the metaphysical underpinnings of the rationality principle not only because it occupies a central role in the methodologies under discussion but also because it lies in the central core of an important research programme in microeconomics.

When von Mises defends the apriori nature of the category of human action he is, in my view, arguing for the synthetic apriori character of the assumption of rationality. Von Mises is quite explicit. He argues that the fundamental category of action is teleology and that it does the job that causality does in the physical sciences. Behaviour, according to von Mises, becomes action if it is teleological, i.e., goal-directed. The criterion of the purposefulness of behaviour closely mirrors the rationality principle. Whether an action is purposeful or not depends on whether or not it aims 'at the attainment of definite ends'.[8]

This aspect of von Mises' aprioristic methodology, namely, his explicit

---

[7] Von Mises [1949], p. 34.
[8] Von Mises [1949], pp. 26 and 21–5.

4

and forceful adherence to methodological separation of social from natural sciences (which he terms 'methodological dualism') and the rationalistic approach of the latter, has since been tacitly adopted by most economists and methodologists of economics.[9]

I have referred to von Mises' methodological dualism and to the adherence of other writers to this principle. I shall now give a rough and ready account of what I understand by these terms. The position of *methodological dualism* may be contrasted with that of *causalism*. According to causalism our approach to explanation and the substance of our explanatory accounts are the same in both the natural and the social sciences. The laws involved in our explanations and predictions should ultimately be reduced to psychological and eventually to deeper physiological and physical laws. Nevertheless we may temporarily operate with more superficial laws for the purposes of explanation and prediction while remaining alert for opportunities of reduction to deeper laws.

According to methodological dualism, both our approach and the results we should expect to obtain are different in kind in the social sciences. Although we may and often do adopt the deductive approach to explanation in the social sciences, the components of the explanation schema differ in kind; i.e. they are not empirical laws carrying nomic necessity. Rather, they are synthetic apriori principles carrying a different kind of necessity. An important role they fulfil is to bridge the conceptual gap between mentalistic and activistic concepts; or, to put it in other ways, the gap between nature and convention, between events (such as decisions and actions) and the mental processes which give rise to them.

One may justifiably ask, why should we go to all this trouble? We could, after all, tentatively accept laws connecting mental and physical events and processes for the purposes of explanation and consider them both empirical and nomically binding as we do the laws of physics. But by doing so we would be skating over a problem which the rationalistic approach faces head on. According to the individualistic–rationalistic approach, if we are to offer explanations of social phenomena we must,

[9] The centrality of the rationalistic approach for economic theory was already analysed by Pareto in his [1909] classic. Pareto points out that although it is fruitful to apply the rationalistic approach to the explanation and prediction of economic actions and phenomena, we should recognise that a great deal of our everyday behaviour is not rational in the sense postulated. At the same time, Pareto notes, we do tend to correct our actions mainly through learning by trial-and-error and as we repeat the same type of decision or action over and over again we tend to reduce the gap between our actual and the optimal decisions. That is, our series of decisions converge to rationality or optimality, and it is this last element in the series of economic decisions that economic theory seeks to analyse. And it will not do to say, as some have done, that learning and decision processes are ignored because neoclassical partial equilibrium analysis predominantly considers static models. It is rather because neoclassical theory considers a model of the *last* in a series of decision processes converging to optimality that the learning and decision processes themselves may be left out of theoretical consideration.

in part, account for the fact that agent A performed action X rather than Y. But if the relevant laws and conditions are known in advance the action would then seem to be predetermined in a causalist way.

For the causalist there is no problem: given the complete picture of the internal state of the agent and the state of the environment, the fact that agent A will do X is predetermined and carries nomic necessity. To put it another way, once the appropriate laws and the relevant initial conditions have been accurately ascertained, we can explain why A did X rather than Y; and, in view of the symmetry thesis (namely, that the logical structure of a scientific explanation is the same as that of a scientific prediction), we can predict it as well if the relevant conditions are known in advance.

It is the dualist-libertarian who is in trouble: for him behaviour does not qualify as 'action' unless the agent in question has the choice of actually *not doing X*, although if follows from his explanation schema that he *should do X*.

One way of attempting to avoid this difficulty is to call the explanation schema a 'decision schema', and to claim that it merely singles out the decision that the agent will arrive at even though he may not execute it. But then the same problem can be reformulated. Does it follow with nomic necessity that the agent in question will *decide* to do X? The libertarian is again bound to say *no*! After all, decisions are mental acts, and it is no good having the mental acts predetermined while their physiological accompaniments are 'free'. For the libertarian, a particular action X may follow from the agent's decision schema and yet, at the last moment, weakness of will or a change of heart might prevent him from actually doing X.

The trouble with this dualist-libertarian position is that in making the actions of a free agent unpredictable it also makes them inexplainable.

Several methods may be seen to reconcile libertarianism with deducibility:

(i) We may claim that in the social sciences] both explanation and prediction are essentially incomplete and that therefore the requirement of deducibility should be relaxed.

(ii) We may employ the *rationality principle* as do von Mises, Popper, Watkins and others.

(iii) Finally, we may deny the symmetry thesis. We may then be prepared to offer a deductively complete explanation of an action *but only after* the action has occurred. We cannot predict it in advance, and on this view we should abandon efforts in this direction.

The second position – and the one von Mises subscribes to – combines adherence to *deducibility* and the *symmetry thesis* with the doctrine of *free will*.

The rationality principle bridges the logical gap between mentalistic and activistic propositions while *not* necessitating (in the same way as a natural law would necessitate) that the predicted action will take place. This explains Popper's puzzling remarks about the falsity and yet indispensability of the rationality principle.[10]

It may be false because a 'free' agent may falsify it by not acting in accordance with it. But it is indispensable because it bridges a conceptual and deductive gap.

By stressing von Mises' defence – via his aprioristic methodology – of the rationalistic approach I hope to have humanised some aspects of his strongly worded but weakly argued aprioristic methodology. I have done this by showing how the two apparent alternatives to this approach may appear frightening to a libertarian economic theorist. On the one hand there is monism and the shadow of physicalism, on the other the abandonment of any hope and indeed effort at scientific explanation and prediction of social phenomena. An important merit of von Mises' methodology has been to alert us to the fact that some position on these problems, whether explicit or implicit, must be adopted even before we embark on the explanation and prediction of economic and social phenomena. Our stance, for example, on the problem of rationalistic explanation influences our selection of the explananda and explanantia as well as the interpretation we place on them. Decisions on these questions are often prerequisites for theory construction.

(b) Falsificationism

Falsificationism contrasts sharply with apriorism. Its purpose is to expose maximally theories to the logical possibility of empirical counter-examples. The criterion of goodness of a theory is a function of its falsifiability together with its success in withstanding attempts to falsify it. If, other things being equal, theory A is more falsifiable than theory B and has survived non-trivial efforts to falsify it, then theory A is better than theory B.

Falsificationism was introduced into the methodology of economics by Hutchison,[11] and reflected the growing impatience with the apparent lack of exacting critical standards in economics. Hutchison pointed out that empirical criticism could not be directed against the theoretical propositions in economics because these were interpreted in a tautological or near tautological way.

What distinguishes an empirical statement from a tautology is the former's falsifiability. But what do we mean when we say that hypothesis H is falsifiable? We mean that H must have 'potential falsifiers', i.e., H together with initial conditions and observational theories must give rise to an observation statement e. The negation of e would then be a potential falsifier. That is, if realised, it would falsify the system of state-

[10] Popper [1967], pp. 142–50.
[11] Hutchison [1938].

ments including the hypothesis H. This means that *at least one* of the system of statements from which we validly deduced proposition e must be false.[12]

There are *degrees* of falsifiability and of two falsifiable but unfalsified theories, that which is more falsifiable is the better. Consider two falsifiable hypotheses h_1 and h_2 and suppose that h_2 is a consequence of h_1 and h_1 has additional falsifiable content h_3. Clearly then h_1 would be more falsifiable than h_2. Finally, other things being equal, the one of the two hypotheses with the greater specificity is the more falsifiable (i.e., the more specific the hypothesis the more observation statements would qualify as potential falsifiers).

Unfortunately, in economics the degree of specificity that may be attained is limited by the kind of predictions economists strive for. Neoclassical economists have tended to subscribe, explicitly or tacitly, to the testing technique of qualitative comparative statics developed by von Mises, Robbins and Samuelson.[13] According to this method a simplified and idealised economic model is considered at some equilibrial position. One of the parameters of the model is altered. The model by some specified mechanism moves to a new equilibrial position. This new position is then compared with the previous one in terms of the direction but *not* the amount of change. This means that *any amount* of change, *provided it is in the right direction*, would corroborate the hypothesis.

Thus the range of potential falsifiers is severely reduced and the possibility of 'severe testing' – in the sense of exact quantitative specification of the potential falsifier – becomes very remote. Moreover, it is often the case that no unambiguous prediction of the direction of change is available.

Space does not permit me to go into the fine points of falsificationism but what I have said is, I hope, sufficient to suggest the direction towards which falsificationism would urge economic theorists. It would recommend that economists should try and derive from their theories empirical propositions of a high degree of specificity describing conditions the non-occurrence of which would falsify the entire theory. The message of falsificationism is not *mere* testing but *severe* testing, and the adoption of the techniques of qualitative comparative statics makes severe testing practically impossible.

No extensive historiographical research is required to reveal that the development of economic analysis would look a dismal affair through falsificationist spectacles. Moreover, to a large extent, neoclassical economists appear unable and unwilling to specify even potential *qualitative*

[12] According to Popper it is possible under very special conditions to single out the guilty component. Such conditions he attempts to specify in a footnote in his [1957]. Unfortunately, Popper's argument is not convincing. Cp. Popper [1957], p. 132n.

[13] See Archibald [1961] for a lucid exposition.

falsifiers. Consider an example from the theory of the firm: suppose that there is an exogenously-induced, marked rise in cost in a perfectly competitive industry. Suppose the theory predicts that, *ceteris paribus*, some firms will leave the industry. What if no firm leaves? Will the *modus tollens* be guided to the fundamental assumptions of the model? I doubt it very much. The theorist will probably suspect that the situation to which the model was applied did not fulfil the minimal conditions for perfect competition. Or he would blame the 'refutation' on the *ceteris paribus* clause.

The problem then arises: how do we sort out the genuine (or justified) defence manoeuvres from the *ad hoc* ones? Falsificationism may be very useful here. For instead of attempting to knock out theoretical systems by furnishing empirical counter-examples we may employ falsificationist criteria to rule out defensive manoeuvres that are unacceptable on these criteria.

(c) Conventionalism

This brings me to the *conventionalist* methodologies of economics. Conventionalism grew out of Kant's apriorism. Early conventionalists agreed with Kant that the human mind categorises experience with a framework: but they claimed that the human mind is *creative*, that it is not imprisoned in Kant's eternal categories, but can freely choose its framework and then, by imaginative adjustments, adjust it to accommodate all experience.

This 'voluntarism' was applied to the philosophy of the natural sciences in the late nineteenth and early twentieth century by Le Roy and Milhaud and – in a less extreme form – by Poincaré.[14]

Conventionalism almost at its birth was introduced to economics by Vilfredo Pareto in his [1909] book. With acknowledgements to Poincaré, Pareto writes:

The same facts may be explained by an infinity of theories, equally true, because they all reproduce the facts to be explained. It is in this sense that Poincaré could say that from the very fact that a phenomenon allows one mechanical explanation, it allows an infinity of them...The theory of universal gravitation does not have a real absolute content to oppose to 'the error' of the theory which assigns to each heavenly body an angel who regulates its movements. Moreover, this second theory may be made as true as the first one by adding that the angels, for reasons unknown to us, make the heavenly bodies move *as if* they were attracted to each other in direct proportion to the masses and inversely to the squares of the distances.[15]

More recently, conventionalist methodologies of economics were put forward in the forties and fifties primarily by Machlup and Friedman.[16]

[14] Cp. Milhaud [1896], Le Roy [1899] and Poincaré [1902]. According to Poincaré, conventionalism applied to geometry and the laws of mechanics but to *nothing else*. The theory of gravitation, electrodynamics and heat theory were *induced* from experience.

[15] Pareto [1909], pp. 31 and 36.

[16] Machlup [1946], [1952] and [1955], Friedman [1953].

Machlup and Friedman did not wish to apply peculiar standards to the social sciences. They wanted what I call the neoclassical research programme to come out as satisfactory when judged by *general* methodological standards; at least it should not be impatiently rejected at the behest of Utopian norms.

In this more recent literature, conventionalism has appeared in the guise of the following two subtheses:[17]

(i) Qualitative indirect testability is an adequate and effective criterion of appraisal and one which rules favourably in the case of neoclassical microeconomics.

(ii) The narrow ideal type of a mechanical optimiser is indispensable for neoclassical microeconomics because it brings order to the otherwise chaotic diversity of isolated economic decisions and actions.

With regard to the first subthesis the crux of the matter was this: falsificationism requires the economic theorist to specify in advance potential empirical falsifiers, not just for the parameters of his theory but for his fundamental assumptions; but neoclassical economists were unable and unwilling to specify such potential falsifiers for the hard core of their theoretical system (or, as I would call it, their programme); and they wanted to justify their attitude. They also tried to argue that the unit of intellectual appraisal should not be an isolated *hypothesis* but rather an organic unit, i.e., though they did not use this term, a research programme. Most of the obscurities in the so-called 'assumptions controversy' in the mid-sixties disappear once we regard it as conventionalist defence of a research programme against falsificationism.

Machlup, for instance, repeatedly argues that counter-intuitive and apparently refuted assumptions may nevertheless be valuable for explanation and prediction in neoclassical microeconomics.

He adds that 'the test of the pudding lies in the eating and not in its ingredients. If we find no better theory to explain or predict changes in prices, outputs, etc., etc., and if our present theory does no worse than it has been doing, we may consider our Assumption warranted.'[18]

Two questions remain open:

(i) What is success apart from an occasional lack of failure?

(ii) What conceivable circumstance could seriously undermine the theory?

Machlup attempts answers to both questions.

The gist of his answer to the first question is that neoclassical partial equilibrium theory provides qualitative answers to qualitative questions about mass reactions to drastic changes in the economic environment. Such indirect verifications should count as successes of the theoretical system used. But have such indirect verifications been obtained? I shall

---

[17] Machlup [1967].
[18] Machlup [1956], p. 489.

try to show in Part II of this paper that the principal assumptions and problem-solving techniques of the neoclassical theory of the firm are inappropriate for the analysis of an important segment of market situations to which they are nevertheless applied. They are inappropriate in the sense that they do *not* lead to in principle testable (let alone 'verified') models.

Machlup's answer to the second question reflects the defensive attitude of conventionalist methodology. He writes:

When there is an apparent conflict between observations and the theory they are supposed to test, the observations can usually be disqualified as of uncertain reliability; and where this will not do the conflict can usually be reconciled by means of auxiliary hypotheses.[19]

Machlup's interpretation of the neoclassical theory of the firm generates built-in defence mechanisms enabling the reconciliation of almost any recalcitrant evidence with the theory. Examples of this abound. Consider, for instance, the following passages:

the effects of changes in wage rates, interest rates, tax rates and so forth, are, if there is *effective* competition, essentially independent of the relations among the various levels in the managerial hierarchy of the firm [my italic].[20]

Competition...is sometimes called 'heavy', 'vigorous', or 'effective'. The simplest meaning of these adjectival modifiers is this: ...if the firm is kept under continuing pressure to do something about its sales and its profits position...the firm will not be able to pursue any objectives other than the maximisation of profits – for the simple reason that anything less than the highest obtainable profits would be below the rate of return regarded as normal at the time... There can be no doubt about the fact that competition is not effective in many industries and that many, very many firms are not exposed to vigorous competition.[21]

Machlup's adjectival qualifications tell us nothing about the limits of applicability of the perfectly competitive model; they only tell us that the perfectly competitive model is only applicable where it can be applied.

The crucial question is the following: Is all awkward evidence to be regarded as either unreliable or reconcilable or can it serve a serious critical role?

According to Machlup, 'Where the observations can neither be dismissed as unreliable nor reconciled with the theory on the basis of special circumstances, then at last, "negative empirical evidence" against the theory exists.'[22]

'But', Machlup adds, 'since the theory merely expresses tendencies, this adverse evidence should not be taken as a final refutation'. More generally, since Machlup and other neoclassical economists are either reluctant or unsuccessful in spelling out in advance the specific circum-

---

[19] Machlup [1952], p. 73.   [20] Machlup [1967], p. 15.
[21] Machlup [1967], p. 18.   [22] Machlup [1952], p. 73.

stances in which their models are applicable, any adverse evidence what-soever can be attributed to 'special circumstances'; and even the weak disconfirmation favoured by Machlup would not be achieved in practice.

Friedman's distinctive contribution to conventionalist methodology seems to consist of what Samuelson has called the 'F-twist'[23] – that 'to be important...a hypothesis must be descriptively false in its assumptions'.[24] This, I take it, is a rather provocative formulation of the truism that a powerful theory often (though not necessarily) over-simplifies.

I now turn to the second conventionalist subthesis.

Explicit in the case of Machlup and implicit in the case of Friedman is the thesis that the ideal type of an *economically efficient decision-maker* more than makes up for its implausibility by its impressive explanatory power. The explanatory and predictive success refers to the prediction of *mass reactions* to *pronounced changes in conditions*.[25]

The conventionalist's use of the typological method goes hand in hand with the antipsychologism of Pareto, von Mises and Robbins. That is, conventionalist methodologists of economics have tended to subscribe to what may be called (paraphrasing Machlup) the *psychologically anonymous ideal type*. The 'psychologically anonymous' type is a theoretical construct which concentrates on a decision-maker with a minimal internal structure and minimal characteristics. The decision-maker, far from being a 'black box', is a 'transparent box'[26] which allows a full view of the simple internal decision-making structure. Propositions concerning the decision-maker's internal characteristics do not commit the theorist to any particular tradition in psychological theorising. The economic theorist is guided by what may be called the method of single-exit reduction. We should seek to reduce economic situations in which human decisions and actions are to be explained to 'single-exit' situations, i.e., where the agent's situation, as well as his appraisal of it, is such that it 'singles out' one best course of action open to him (or indeed to any other agent in the same environment regardless of the specific characteristics or psychology of the agent). In Part II of the paper I shall suggest that this approach has provided the building blocks for the dominant research programme in microeconomics.

Yet the adoption of the ideal type or zero-method in the explanation of social phenomena surely *does not* imply the adoption of the neoclassical conception of an empty, transparent economic man. This latter is surely

---

[23] Samuelson [1963], p. 232.

[24] Friedman [1953], p. 15.

[25] According to Machlup, 'In the analysis of mass action where each individual actor counts only a little, we need not know them intimately in order to explain the combined result.' (Machlup [1952], p. 418). For theoretical reasons we concentrate 'only on the effects of the hypothetical reactions of numerous hypothetical reactors' (Machlup [1967], p. 9).

[26] This term was suggested to me by John Watkins.

one ideal-type model. There may be fruitful alternatives. For instance, a 'satisficer' may serve as an ideal type, as can a 'bankruptcy avoider'.[27] We would not have to bring in idiosyncratic peculiarities and reduce ourselves to analysis 'from case to case' if we decided to reject the perfectly informed optimiser. At the same time the method of ideal types does not stand or fall with neoclassical maximisation. It is neutral towards the particular behavioural traits with which we choose to endow the typical economic agent.

Another conventionalist tactic has been to start with an idealised, 'pure' assumption which can be falsified in isolation, and to proceed to qualify or 'weaken it' in the process of making it more realistic and widening its applicability. The trouble is that in the process a criticisable proposition is often turned into a virtually uncriticisable one. A good instance of this is the erosion of the assumption of profit maximisation. I shall illustrate this by contrasting Cournot's simple and sharp assumption of the maximisation of money profits with Fellner's definition given over one hundred years later.

I start with Cournot. Cournot in his [1838] classic considers the case of a monopolist who has no cost of production and then the case of a monopolist who faces production costs. Then 'it will no longer be the function $pF(p)$, or the annual *gross receipts*, which the producer should strive to carry to its maximum value, but the *net receipts* or the function $pF(p) - \phi(D)$, in which $\phi(D)$ denotes the cost of making a number of liters equal to D'.[28] Joan Robinson in her [1933] writes briefly: '(the seller) is assumed always to choose the output which will maximise his net receipts'.[29]

This simple postulate contrasts sharply with Fellner's [1949] definition which follows after an intricate discussion of the applicability of the assumption of profit maximisation to markets with monopolistic elements:

Competitive groups of producers tend towards the maximisation of the joint profits of the group and towards division of these profits in accordance with:

(a) Long-run consequences of violating accepted value judgments.

(b) The immediate political consequences of a stalemate in the relations between the parties concerned.

(c) The ability of the parties to take and to inflict losses during stalemate.

(d) Toughness in the sense of unwillingness to yield in a range in which the other party is expected to yield if one fails to do so.[30]

Such interpretations of the assumption of profit maximisation make it very difficult indeed to submit theories incorporating it to empirical test.

[27] Machlup recognises this in his [1967] but does not seem to draw the correct conclusions from it. He seems to believe that the alternative to the neoclassical cypher is to abandon theoretical explanation altogether. Cp. Machlup [1967], p. 28.

[28] Cournot [1838], chapter 5.

[29] Robinson [1933], p. 33.

[30] Fellner [1949], pp. 24–9, italic in original.

Any empirical criticism may be immunised by a suitable reinterpretation of the vague terminology employed in the definition. And it seems to be a crucial shortcoming of the conventionalist approach that it facilitates such evasive tactics.

II *The methodology of scientific research programmes*

Conventionalist methodology is, as I have indicated, peculiarly suited to account for the appraisals of economists. Direct empirical confrontation of the theory's postulates with lower level statements is excluded. Empirical anomalies, i.e., clashes between the theory's consequences and experiential statements, are accommodated by means of a battery of conventionalist stratagems. Finally, those empirical successes, if any, which the theory secures are hailed as triumphs and used as arguments for putting up with its intuitive implausibility and its empirical deficiencies. The conventionalist ethic is: use the theory where it is applicable. Different theories may be required for different problem situations within the same problem area. The question of their truth or falsity, or even truthlikeness, does not arise. Theories are tools for predictions.

The falsificationist ethic contrasts sharply with that of the conventionalist. Theories should be tested to destruction. Sincere attempts should be made to refute them rather than to try to delimit their range of applicability. The tests to which we submit the theory should be the severest we can devise. Theories, though false, tell us something about the real world, and of two false theories one may be more 'truthlike' than another.[31] Ability to pass severe tests – especially if these same tests refute a competing hypothesis – is the hallmark of respectability according to the falsificationist's criterion of appraisal.

The reason for briefly restating these methodological approaches is to contrast them with the methodology of scientific research programmes.

A central distinction between the methodological approaches discussed above and MSRP concerns the *unit of appraisal*.[32] Instead of appraising isolated hypotheses or strings or systems of hypotheses, as we would do within a falsificationist or conventionalist framework, we now appraise an organic unity – a research programme, or, still better, two competing research programmes.

A research programme is *not* a single hypothesis or theory or even a string of hypotheses or theories. It is an organic unity which contains both rigid and flexible components – essential, structural components as well as non-essential ones. The essential structural features of the programme Lakatos has called its 'hard core' and its 'positive heuristic'. Giving them up means abandoning the research programme we have been

---

[31] Also see Popper [1963], p. 397.
[32] Cp. Lakatos [1968], [1970], [1971 a] and [1971 b].

using to investigate an entire problem area. Yet a research programme does contain or generate, components which could be given up or replaced without abandoning the particular approach advocated as an instrument for explanation and prediction. Non-essential, replaceable components of a research programme belong to what Lakatos has called the programme's 'protective belt'.

One criterion of appraisal which occupies a central role in falsification-ism is also central to MSRP, namely that auxiliary hypotheses in the protective belt should, in the face of empirical anomalies, be replaced progressively if the modification is to have cognitive value. To put it another way, changes in the 'protective belt' of a research programme are favourably judged only if they are progressive. And they may be *theoretically progressive*, i.e., the modification has independently testable content; and they may also be *empirically progressive*, i.e., at least part of the excess testable content is corroborated. But if the criterion of empirical progressiveness is nothing more or less than Popper's 'third requirement', where does the novelty of this new methodological framework lie?

The criterion of empirical progressiveness is indeed one more version of Popper's so-called 'third' criterion which by itself is of little help in appraisal. It is designed for the comparative static appraisal of alternative theories. For instance, if T_1 has T_0 as a consequence and additional corroborated content and no discorroborated content, we seem to be justified in making the judgment that 'T_1 is better than T_0'. One of the difficulties is that for any theory T_0 it is very easy to devise a T_1 such that T_1's excess content is corroborated. For instance T_1 may be T_0 & h_1, where h_1 is any corroborated hypothesis. Various methods have been proposed to get over this problem. Popper has had to add to it the sub-jectivist 'first requirement' that 'the new theory should proceed from some simple, new, and powerful unifying idea'.[33] But it is not my purpose to discuss them in this paper.

The criterion of excess testable (or corroborated) content plays an important role in the falsificationist and conventionalist methodologies of economics, but its application leads to difficulties because both method-ological approaches are restricted to comparative static appraisal. That is, their criteria are intended to apply to contemporary alternative hypo-theses independently of how these have been arrived at (though not independently of whether the corroborating evidence was known before-hand or only came to light when testing the theory).

The major innovation introduced by the MSRP is that the appraisal of successive modifications of a research programme is *not a comparative static* but a *dynamic* one. The process by which a falsified auxiliary hypo-thesis is replaced by a new one becomes an important criterion of apprai-sal. This is possible because a research programme is more than a series

[33] Popper [1963], p. 242.

of hypotheses, characterising assumptions and initial conditions. Apart from its *descriptive hard core* which specifies its fundamental characteristics, each programme has a *normative hard core* or, as Lakatos has called it, a 'positive heuristic'. This is a set of imperatives which contain guidance as to how the programme should unfold, how it should be defended, what falls within and what falls outside its scope. The 'positive heuristic' is quite as 'hard' as the 'hard core': it cannot be given up without giving up the programme itself. Moreover, the positive heuristic may help to resolve the difficulties encountered by the criterion of independent testability without adducing Popper's dubious 'first requirement'. This is so because it enables us to judge not only the excess content of the hypothesis but also how it was arrived at. For we may add the requirement that the new auxiliary hypothesis should be in line with the positive heuristic of the programme. And this brings the 'dynamics' of theory-change into the appraisal of isolated or competing research programmes.

(a) Situational determinism as a research programme

The rationalistic conception of action, as briefly sketched in Section (*a*) of Part I, does indeed serve to explain a certain sort of action that has been the central concern of the neoclassical theory of the firm. It is the kind of action that does not reflect genuine decision or choice but rather *highly constrained reaction*. Yet this reaction is determinate, apparently voluntary and the best the agent could have done in the circumstances.

In Sections (*a*) and (*b*) I shall investigate the structure and content of *situational determinism* which has been the dominant research programme of neo-classical microeconomic theory. This investigation will be restricted to the very general characteristics of the programme. Its specific applications to the theory of the firm and some of its special features will be described in Sections (*c*), (*d*), (*e*) and (*f*) below.

The main purpose of this section and the next will be to distinguish between *single-exit situations* (i.e., situations where the actor's choice is uniquely determined by situational considerations) and *multiple-exit situations* (i.e., situations where the actor's choice is *not* narrowly delimited by situational considerations), and to suggest that as we move away from single-exit situations it becomes more difficult to account for action rationalistically. In multiple-exit situations the agent's internal environment, i.e., his decision and information-gathering rules, his psychological and social psychological characteristics etc. become central components in the explanation. We have a rather paradoxical situation: single-exit situations are best explainable in terms of the libertarian-rationalistic model. In multiple-exit situations explanation of actions may require a model where the psychologistic components may well have a more central role in the explanans. To put it crudely, it appears that the more 'free' the action, the more deterministic the explanans.

16

One excuse for the descriptive and evaluative exercise undertaken in this part of the paper is the persistent and serious misunderstandings and misappraisals that plague the history of economic theory. In Section (d) I shall be arguing that the so-called 'monopolistic competition revolution' was not a revolution at all but merely a timid extention of the single-exit methods of perfect competition to a problem area where they could not be fruitfully applied. Another fundamental misunderstanding lies in the frequent attribution of psychologism to the neoclassical programme: 'The extreme emphasis on psychology and the individual, kept the marginalists from the really practical economic problems. Economic theory was reduced to an aspect of psychology dealing with the economic individual, primarily a consumer.'[34]

The main thesis of Part II is the contrary of this view. I shall argue that the development of marginalism in the theory of the firm (and most other areas of microeconomics) gave rise to the research programme of situational determinism whose central characteristic is the autonomy of economic decision-making and the deliberate exclusion of the decision-maker's inner environment from explanations of economic behaviour.[35]

Before proceeding it may be useful to clarify what I mean by the decision-maker's inner environment. I mean hypotheses relating to decision rules, information-gathering rules, learning procedures and psychological or social psychological theories which substantially concern the decision-making process. But we should tread carefully here. The rationalistic approach does *not* exclude a variety of rules and habits which may form part of the agent's situation. What it does preclude is that such rules and habits should overrule the tendency towards rational behaviour. Thus on the rationalistic approach, rules, habits, routines, etc., may be followed by an agent who is conscious of them and subjects them to constant critical appraisal as indeed he does to other components of his situational picture. But such components *do not determine* a rational agent's decision – it is the agent who determines his decision having appraised these components.

Viewing economic actions as highly constrained reactions has provided a research programme for the neoclassical theory of the behaviour of the firm. That is, the approach to the explanation of the decisions and actions of sellers in all the diversity of market structures is handled in a unified way, in accordance with certain principles and certain problem-solving rules. This research programme, which goes back to Adam Smith, has had a measure of success, at least relative to other economic and social theories. This early success is followed by a period of stagnation and it now seems that the programme has run out of steam. In subsequent sec-

[34] Sachs [1973], p. 16.
[35] The useful distinction between the 'inner' and the 'outer' environment is due to Simon [1969].

tions I shall be giving examples from the history of economic theory to support these claims.

It should be noted that the research programme in question does not restrict itself to explanations of economic action, but can also often be applied with success to historical and psychological explanation.[36] Popper writes in his *Open Society*: (As a matter of fact) 'most historical explanation makes tacit use, not so much of trivial sociological and psychological laws, but of what I have called,...the *logic of the situation*; that is to say, besides the initial conditions describing personal interests, aims, and other situational factors, such as information available to the person concerned, it tacitly assumes as a kind of first approximation, the trivial general law that sane persons as a rule act more or less rationally'. And he adds: 'in history we have no such unifying theories; or rather, the host of trivial universal laws we use are taken for granted; they are practically without interest, and totally unable to bring order into the subject matter'.[37]

The economic theory of the firm views the actions of economic agents in market situations in very much the same way. More recently Herbert Simon gave an example of an analogous *physical* situation which illustrates well the type of social situations envisaged by *equilibrium models in economics*.

'Suppose we were pouring...molasses into a bowl of very irregular shape...How much would we have to know about the properties of molasses to predict its behaviour under the circumstances? If the bowl were held motionless and if we wanted only to predict behaviour in equilibrium we would have to know little, indeed, about molasses. The single essential assumption would be that molasses, under the force of gravity would minimise the height of its centre of gravity. With this assumption, *which would apply as well to any other liquid*, and a *complete knowledge of the environment* – in this case the shape of the bowl – the equilibrium is completely determined...equilibrium behaviour depends only on its goal and its environment, *it is otherwise completely independent of the internal properties*.'[38] Analogously, if an individual wishes to get to the other side of the road, whatever his reasons and motivation, he will typically elicit a motor response within *certain narrow limits*. This response will be largely determined by the relevant environmental characteristics and not by the actor's inner environment (which may vary widely while his overt responses remain substantially the same). For instance, in certain situations the *suspension of a vehicle* and *a parachutist's legs* both behave as *shock absorbers*. Yet the internal environments that generate this activity are of very diverse structure and complexity.[39]

---

[36] Herbert Simon applies it to cognitive psychology (Simon [1969], chapter 2) and Hempel and Popper to historical explanation (see Hempel [1942] and Popper [1957]).

[37] Popper [1945], pp. 264, 265.

[38] Simon [1959], p. 255.

[39] Cp. Simon [1969], chapter 1.

(b) Single- and multiple-exit decision situations

Situations where one best course of action is uniquely prescribed by the structure of the situation according to some liberal conception of rational behaviour, I shall call *single-exit* situations. The phrases 'uniquely determined' or 'straight-jacket' situations come to mind. I, however, opted[40] for the phrase single-exit situations so as to avoid the idea that the actor's behaviour is on this view uniquely or largely determined in terms of external physical constraints. Of course, this may well be the case: we may consider various environments which, though physically constraining may be viewed as 'situationally open'. Similarly, 'physically open' environments may be 'situationally open' or indeed 'situationally closed'. Although physiological and physical states and processes are involved in descriptions of human behaviour they are not, in the present state of knowledge, major components of the available explanatory accounts of human actions.

In trying to elucidate what I mean by single- and multiple-exit situations I shall consider examples from relevant neighbourhoods of a spectrum ranging from complete causal determinacy to physical and situational openness, and then locate within this spectrum that type of situation that is characteristic of situational determinism.

Consider for instance an individual agent wired up to a computer which is in turn programmed to supply periodic stimulation to parts of his brain in order to elicit certain overt responses. Suppose, moreover, that while this procedure is in operation the computer suspends all mental and physical processes other than those required to carry out the instructions of the programme. This would then be a paradigm case of extreme causal determinacy of an 'agent' in a 'situation'. We would, of course, agree: (i) that this is not a genuine case of 'agency', and (ii) that the 'situation' in which the agent finds himself is not representative of the type of situations one encounters in social life. Nonetheless, if this imaginary case could be actualised and the 'agent's' overt responses constituted our explanandum, we could have provided a causally complete explanation and indeed accurate predictions concerning the agent if we had advance knowledge of the 'agent–computer' set-up.

Consider another type of explanandum: a spectator at a football game left the stadium by gate K. Let us slightly elaborate on this spectator's physical environment and suppose that he is seated near gate K and that the stadium is packed with thousands of spectators. Let us further suppose that gate L (the only other exit from the stadium) is situated at the opposite end of the stadium and that the spectator in question must vacate his seat to enable other occupants to leave the stadium after the end of the game.

A host of behavioural alternatives remain *logically possible* and (in principle) open to the spectator even if we make the motivational assump-

[40] At the suggestion of John Watkins.

tion that he genuinely wishes to leave the stadium. For instance, he may stubbornly refuse to get up from his seat until at least some of the spectators have left. He may get up, stumble, fall and get trampled by the masses vacating the stadium. He may attempt to overcome an almost insuperable adverse current of thousands of spectators in order to reach the other end of the stadium and use gate L. No ingenuity is required to devise any number of such outcomes. Yet if any of the above outcomes actually materialised we would be tempted to ask in puzzlement: 'Why didn't he leave by gate K?' The reason for this question is that the physical and social situation in which the spectator finds himself seems to be compelling towards a specific kind of overt activity. Though a host of logical possibilities exist, the environment seems *physically and situationally constraining*. Deviations from this particular course of action raise questions either about the internal make-up of the agent in question or about unknown situational factors which happened to be relevant to the agent's situational picture. But as the situational picture (including his articulable preferences) becomes more complete one would expect deviations to be almost exclusively attributable to the agent's internal environment.

Let us now consider still another sort of explanandum more relevant to the type of situation we shall be considering. Agent x decides to produce output z. Suppose that agent x, having considered his preferences and the economic and social conditions in which he finds himself decides that, given the situation, output z and no other would be economically viable. Any deviation from output z would be met with severe economic penalties. Now this situation has two main characteristics: it is (i) *physically open* and (ii) *situationally closed*. We can offer no physical or physiological reasons for predicting output z. Moreover, it seems that *the economic situation remains closed under a variety of emotional, psychological or social psychological characteristics and conditions*. The environment though *physically open* is *situationally closed* because economic conditions uniquely determine the appropriateness of producing output z given some fairly weak assumption such as 'the removal of extreme (economic) uneasiness' which is *neutral* with respect to a considerable variety of alternative psychological and social psychological theories.

Let us now switch to a different kind of economic environment: consider a small investor's decision to invest his money. Suppose that the investor in question has just inherited this sum of money, that he has little or no understanding of the stock market and indeed of most other markets, and that he cannot articulate his preference map. He knows, however, that unless he does something with his money, it will depreciate at a yearly rate of about 30 per cent. How can we predict his subsequent behaviour? Or how can we explain it a week or a month later? It is clear that by reconstructing the *agent's appraisal* of his preferences and his situation we shall not get very far. Adding the assumption that he wants to maximise his returns from his outlays will be little help: there may still be a large number of alternative ways of investing open to him, and the logic of his situation is unlikely to single one of them out. Whether he chooses to buy land rather than investing in shares the consequences will probably not be disastrous, although he has no knowledge of the precise outcome of either action. There is a conscious belief on the part of the agent that not every decision is as good as any other, while at the same time no course of action stands out as obviously the best. Even with the help of expert advice, though he may be able to eliminate possibly disastrous alternatives, he will be left with an unmanageable variety of others.

We are confronted here with what may be called a *multiple-exit decision situation*. Of course, this need not deter us from applying the usual single-exit methods of analysis. We may say that the knowledge of the situation on the part of the agent, though not perfect, is tolerable, and that by taking account of his preferences and the objective market conditions we may narrow down the set of alternatives very considerably. We may then arbitrarily impose further situational constraints until one alternative stands out. But in *fluid* and partially known situations this is unlikely to be much good. We might be successful in 'cooking-up' the situational constraints so that a *known* explanandum will be derivable from them. But it is unlikely that we will succeed in prediction.

The above example of a multiple-exit decision situation describes an environment which is both *physically and situationally* open. It is physically open because the subsequent action does *not* appear to be narrowly circumscribed by available physical or physiological laws and conditions, and it is situationally open in the sense that the socioeconomic environment does not (given the decision-maker's aims, interests and objectives) uniquely determine any particular course of action. Yet economic agents do take decisions and do engage in actions under such conditions. That is, they typically seem to have ways of bridging their cognitive gaps and making-up for their limited knowledge.

When faced with the problem of explaining an actor's behaviour the heuristic of the single-exit approach tells you: *Look at the situational constraints and the preferences of the actor in question. Look at the institutional, technological, or structural obstacles, given his goal. Given that the actor correctly perceives all these, they will uniquely determine his course of action. Then, using the rationality principle as the trivial animating law, you will be led to an explanatory argument which suggests why the actor in question did x rather than not x.*

It is, for instance, quite easy to predict the approximate behaviour of a driver of a car moving in heavy traffic when the vehicle in front of him reduces speed suddenly. The explanation of this behaviour will contain a considerable amount of information about traffic rules, about constraints imposed by the structure of the road, by other cars and their relative speeds and positions etc., as well as a rough picture of the driver's explicit preferences.[41] Very little information will be required about the driver's information-gathering rules, character, psychology, decision-making procedures etc. To put it another way, the major components of the explanans would in this case be the situational components.

There appear to be considerable advantages in adopting the *single-exit* approach: (i) We do not have to commit ourselves to any particular psychological or social psychological theory, because what we use is so weak that it is consistent with widely divergent views on psychology and social psychology. (ii) One can claim autonomy for one's discipline: a description of the situation in the terms used by one's particular discipline is all that is needed to explain the phenomenon in question. (iii) Situational descriptions appear to be, and often are, more easily empirically checkable than psychological hypotheses about the agent. (iv) The 'single-exit' approach often makes the application of powerful mathematical techniques easier.

My claim will be that the approach described in this section has provided a research programme for the neoclassical theory of the firm with an identifiable 'hard core' and 'positive heuristic'.

The hard core of the neoclassical programme may be put forward in the following four propositions:

(i) Decision-makers have correct knowledge of the relevant features of their economic situation.

(ii) Decision-makers *prefer* the best available alternative given their knowledge of the situation and of the means at their disposal.

(iii) Given (i) and (ii), situations generate their internal 'logic' and decision-makers *act appropriately to the logic of their situation*.

(iv) Economic units and structures display stable, coordinated behaviour.

The positive heuristic of the programme may be expressed in terms of the following maxims:

(i) 'Construct static models.'

(ii) 'Minimise and if possible completely eliminate psychological and, in general, non-economic content from the model.'

(iii) 'Set up the situational assumptions in such a way that a determinate equilibrium issues.' ('Set up "single-exit" situational models').

(iv) 'Where possible construct functions which are suitable for the application of the procedures of the calculus.'

(v) 'If the model yields no determinate equilibrium, modify the situational assumptions until such a solution becomes possible.'

(vi) 'When the model yields a determinate equilibrium, attempt to refine it by introducing more realistic situational assumptions.'

The 'protective belt' of a research programme is developed by the clash of the research programme's structural components ('hard core' and

---

[41] That is preferring *not* having accidents to having them!

'positive heuristic') with its major current anomalies. The protective belt may consist of various types of propositions from specific auxiliary hypotheses, accounting for predictive failure, to redefinitions of the conceptual apparatus.

(c) Perfect competition and monopoly

Perfect competition is the paradigm case for the application of single-exit methods of analysis. Indeed, this was probably the example Popper and Hayek had in mind when they put forward situational analysis as a fruitful method for the explanation of social phenomena.[42]

The analogues of the hard-core postulates for the perfectly competitive model are as follows:

(i) Profit maximisation.

(ii) Independence of decisions.

(iii) Complete relevant knowledge.

In addition to the hard-core postulates, further situational assumptions are required to characterise the perfectly competitive market situation. It is further required that:

(i) The sellers deal in a perfectly homogeneous commodity.

(ii) The number of sellers is very large.

(iii) The existing sellers may freely leave the market and new sellers may enter.

Most of these assumptions and the mode of reasoning go back to Adam Smith although, of course, he never held a fully-fledged theory of perfect competition.[43]

One of the consequences of the situational assumption of large numbers is that under perfectly competitive conditions each seller takes prices as given. For suppose that the ruling price is P_0 and suppose that one of the sellers reduces his sales by half. What will be the change in price? Because of the large number of sellers, what is considered a drastic reduction in output

---

[42] Cp. Popper [1945], p. 96 and Hayek [1948].

[43] The assumptions proposed by Adam Smith have been transferred almost unchanged to the neoclassical programme. Smith assumed:

(1) That there is a very large number of sellers in the market.

(2) That each seller takes decisions independently of every other.

(3) That there is free entry of new sellers in the market and free exit of existing sellers.

(4) That buyers and sellers have a tolerable knowledge of market opportunities.

(Cf. A. Smith [1776], chapter 7 and chapter 10, Part 1.) For a fuller discussion of the emergence of perfect competition theory see Stigler [1957].

Adam Smith was not entirely consistent in his adherence to these assumptions, and at times explicitly noted the presence or even the prevalence of concerted action both among sellers and buyers. (Cf. A. Smith [1776], chapter 7.) However, these assumptions represent the *main* strand of Smith's thought; see, for example, Stigler [1957].

Subsequently, this programme developed with Cournot's introduction of the infinitesimal calculus (Cournot [1838]) and Marshall's detailed discussion of the model. Marshall also discussed its limitations (Marshall [1890]) such as 'decreasing costs'. Marshall's strongest doubts concerning the theory of the firm are voiced in his [1919] but there are also traces in his *Principles of Economics* [1890] (see pp. 374–5 and p. 458, footnote 1).

for each one individually is minute in relation to the industry's total output. It follows that sellers under perfectly competitive conditions cannot influence price *individually*, however drastic their variations in output.

Apart from price, the situational information the seller has at his disposal is his cost schedule. According to economic theory the average cost schedule has a U-shape: for small quantities the average cost of production is high; at greater quantities, the average cost is smaller; and beyond a certain point it increases again because of diseconomies of scale.

Consider a situation where the sellers' minimum average cost is less than the ruling price. Profits will ensue which will attract new entrants and this will in turn drive the price down to a level such that P_0 equals the minimum average cost. The alternative situation, i.e., where minimum average cost is higher than the ruling price, leads to symmetrical results. Losses will be incurred by at least some sellers which will cause the exit of some sellers until price equals minimum average cost.

Therefore at equilibrium, the price P_0 is equal to minimum average cost and there are zero profits. It should be noted that in equilibrium (and also out of it) each seller chooses output q such that the marginal cost of q equals P_0.

At equilibrium then each seller is faced with the following choice: either to sell q or go bankrupt. Whether he maximises profits or is content simply with satisfactory profits, whether he is an optimist or a pessimist, a risky or a cautious personality will make no difference to his decision. There is only one policy he can adopt if he wants to remain in business. Indeed the assumption that firms maximise profits is very often defended on the grounds that it is the best thing to do. There seems to be a persistent failure to notice that the behaviour of the seller under perfect competition is over-determined and that a weaker assumption could do the same job: namely, the assumption that the firm avoids bankruptcy. In areas such as monopoly theory, where profit maximisation is present in a stronger version, economists are ready to retract it and allow for security motives and cautiousness to play a role in determining a seller's decisions.

Von Mises was often at pains to indicate that the economic agent's role is not so much that of engaging in complex decision-making following a process of careful deliberation but that of *reacting* to changes in economic conditions over which he has no control. No complex psychological or social psychological knowledge of any aspect of the agent's inner environment is required. It is sufficient here to 'assume...nothing other than that the acting man wants to remove uneasiness... To buy in the cheapest market and to sell in the dearest is, other things being equal, not conduct which would presuppose any special assumptions concerning the actor's motives and morality. It is merely the necessary offshoot of any action under the conditions of market exchange'.[44]

---

[44] Von Mises [1949], p. 241.

Fritz Machlup is in the habit of declaring that the economic theory of the firm does *not* seek to explain economic *actions* but merely economic *reactions*.[45] The only sense I can make of his distinction between actions and reactions is the following: reactions are highly constrained actions; to put it another way, reactions are actions which can be explained by the single-exit method. But as we have indicated, only a few, special kinds of actions lend themselves to single-exit analysis. Moreover, this use of the word 'reaction' offers an escape route: what we can explain we call 'reaction'; what we find awkward and unmanageable we call 'action'. The danger is avoided if we abolish the distinction.

We have seen how under the conditions characterising perfect competition the decision-maker's discretion in choosing among alternative courses of action is reduced simply to a choice between whether or not to remain in business. The decision is seen as a strictly determinate process. The price which the firm can secure is a datum and so are consumer preferences and technological conditions. In equilibrium, average costs of all producers are at their minimum, and there are no profits beyond the minimum rewards required to enable the entrepreneur to continue operations. Thus in this approach such activities of the entrepreneur as decisions on prices, the search for information, the organisation of decision-making, the choice of method of production and appeal to buyers and also the psychology of decision-making, are either taken as given or assumed away. The neoclassical approach may perhaps fairly be termed as envisaging entrepreneurs without entrepreneurial functions or, to put it another way, *decision-makers without decision procedures*. In this programme the internal structure and characteristics of the decision-making unit constitute merely irrelevant noise.[46] Any disturbance to the system triggers off negative feedback which restores its initial state of 'zero profit' equilibrium. Moreover, the mere fact that the firm survives in the perfectly competitive industry is 'proof' that its behaviour is – relatively[47] – optimal, since it would otherwise have been eliminated by a 'natural selection' procedure.

Under perfect competition entrepreneurs do not really *compete* with *each other*. The situation may be compared to that of a player in an *n-*

---

[45] Machlup [1967], p. 8.

[46] Higgins, in his [1939], struggling with the anomalies arising from indeterminate solutions, suggests that if we further specified the entrepreneurs' motivation, unambiguous equilibrium solutions could be found even in cases of indeterminacy. Rothchild [1947] also recognises that the dependence of neoclassical analysis on environmental factors is one sided. Enke, in his [1951] argues that Chamberlin's monopolistic competition theory (which according to Enke is a long-run theory of aggregate competitive behaviour) is situationally determinate while J. Robinson's theory of monopoly is not.

[47] According to the weakened view (in the sense that the perfect knowledge assumption is relaxed) of neoclassical optimisation theory, expounded by Machlup, it is subjective costs which are minimised and equalised with marginal revenue. It is therefore only in relation to other producers that a perfect competitor's behaviour is optimal. Cp. Machlup [1946].

person game where n is very large. Such games are reducible to one-person games against nature where the opponent has no objectives and no known strategy. The 'nature' of perfect competition is unusually strict in allowing a choice between following a single strategy or going under.

Pure monopoly, usually regarded as the exact opposite of perfect competition is in fact its heuristic twin. The 'hard-core' postulates remain intact. The monopolist maximises on the basis of his knowledge of the market conditions and the application of the simple optimising rule. As with perfect competition, so with monopoly the 'rational' decision-maker will arrive at the uniquely determined optimal decision by a simple calculation. (The 'solution' to the calculation is formally the same in the two models: the firm selects that output at which the additional costs of an additional unit equal the additional revenue occasioned by the sale of that unit, that is, the output at which marginal cost equals marginal revenue. The only difference in this respect is that while marginal revenue equals price in perfect competition, marginal revenue is lower than price in monopoly.)

(d) Monopolistic competition

Chamberlin's celebrated book *The Theory of Monopolistic Competition* illustrates very well the attachment of neoclassical economists to situational determinism. And so does its reception.[48]

In a recent paper assessing the impact of Chamberlin's book, Samuelson writes: 'Marshall's crime is to pretend to handle imperfect competition with tools only applicable to perfect competition'.[49] But I suggest that it is more appropriate to say that, if a so-called crime was committed,

[48] The wide and immediate acceptance of Chamberlin's monopolistic competition theory may have been partly due to its apparent ability to resolve the protracted 'cost controversy' about the compatibility of decreasing costs and competitive conditions. This controversy was set off by J. H. Clapham's [1922] article on 'Empty Economic Boxes' and extended at least to the symposium on 'Increasing Returns and the Representative Firm' in the *Economic Journal* in June 1930. The alleged high point of this controversy consists of Sraffa's [1926] which is a skilful recantation of Marshall's (and indeed Cournot's) doubts concerning the monopoly-perfect competition package. Two major anomalies in the Marshallian programme were highlighted; (i) the inconsistency of perfect competition with falling costs; (ii) the glaring unrealism of a perfectly elastic demand curve. Chamberlin's [1933] classic appeared to solve both problems while, at the same time, not demanding the wholesale abandonment of Marshallian orthodoxy. An excellent short review of the controversy is given in R. Robinson [1971], pp. 17–23.

Although it contributed little to our understanding of entrepreneurial behaviour under competitive conditions, the theory of monopolistic competition is sometimes claimed to have produced incidental benefits. One is the recognition of the concept of marginal revenue. Another is the emphasis on the distinction between one firm and the collection of firms called an industry.

On the concept of marginal revenue there is little to be said. Admittedly it furnishes a unified way of describing the maximising conditions in neoclassical models. However, these conditions may be described in all cases without employing the marginal revenue concept at all. The concept has been neither heuristically nor empirically fruitful.

[49] Samuelson [1967], p. 112.

it was Chamberlin's crime to pretend to handle imperfect competition with tools only applicable to perfect competition.

Even a casual inspection of what Chamberlin terms his 'large group' case reveals its obvious kinship with perfect competition. In both there is 'atomistic competition': the number of firms is so large that no action of any single firm can affect the price of the product and that no coalition is possible. In both, the producers have identical cost curves and face identical demand curves. In both, entry is free and prompt and continues as long as profits are above minimum. In both, firms maximise profits by producing the quantity at which marginal cost and marginal revenue are equal. The firms under monopolistic competition produce goods which are different in the eyes of the consumers but which do not demand any special knowledge or advantage (if the model is to be consistent) on the part of the producer who is responsible for their differentiation. Thus the only difference between perfect and monopolistic competition consists in a slight modification in the situational description; the hard core and the analytical machinery of the perfectly competitive paradigm are preserved intact. In both cases, in equilibrium the individual firm's demand curve is tangential to its average cost curve. This means that only this one particular price–output combination will keep the firm in business. If the demand curve cuts the average cost curve, this means that profits will be made which will attract entry, thereby shifting the individual demand curve leftwards until it is again tangential to the average cost curve (at which point there will again be no incentive to entry). In both cases, the situational description is such that optimising behaviour (yielding merely normal or subsistence profits in equilibrium) is the only way of avoiding elimination from the industry.

Thus perfect and monopolistic competition share the common neoclassical 'hard core'; monopolistic competition results from a slight modification of the situational assumptions of perfect competition, and in both cases the assumption of profit maximisation is trivial.

The question I should now like to raise is whether, during the last few decades, the neoclassical programme of the theory of the firm has been theoretically progressive or degenerating. To answer this question we must pay special attention to the theory of monopolistic competition. It is widely held among economists that this theory was an important advance within the neoclassical framework. I shall argue that it actually was a degeneration from Marshall. But let us start with the evaluation of the perfectly competitive model.

The perfectly competitive model represents the most impressive application of situational determinism. This model, in its simplest, static form is logically impeccable; and it has some explanatory, predictive power: for instance, exogenously-caused changes in costs can be expected to result in corresponding changes in prices and in influx or exit of firms from the industry (until equilibrium is restored). Yet the simplicity and ideal character of the model makes it difficult to locate and identify anomalies; for the fundamental assumptions and the initial conditions which have to be fulfilled if the model is to be tested are never exactly realised. There is little guidance to indicate how much divergence is tolerable.[50] For instance, it has been found empirically that firms in highly competitive industries sometimes fail to behave in the predicted way in the face of large changes in cost. There may be substantial changes in costs *without* substantial entry or exit of firms.[51] The programme can however attempt to accommodate such difficulties: the blame can be put on the auxiliary situational assumptions (such as the instantaneity of entry and exit or the U-shaped cost curve) and the hard core can thus be saved. But these accommodations have not led to anything but *ad hoc* adjustments. For many this has come as no surprise. After all, it can easily be seen that the perfectly competitive model, by virtue of its construction, can deal only with a narrow range of questions of a 'comparative static' type.

But one useful heuristic function is certainly left to this idealised model. If its analytical techniques can be fruitfully extended to different market situations, then it may be claimed that it has accomplished the valuable task of serving as a testbed for the development and application of analytical methods to the theory of the firm. To me this represents a certain kind of theoretical progress.

Unfortunately, the extensions of situational determinism to monopolistic competition and oligopoly do not have even this merit. Chamberlin's introduction of product differentiation is a rather radical step towards executing the heuristic of situational determinism. Instead of using the argument of product heterogeneity as an escape clause (to indicate that whenever heterogeneity is present, the theory of perfect competition is only imperfectly applicable), he incorporates product differentiation into his model itself.

The solution to several problems was expected from this modification, for instance, the problem of selling costs and that of the decreasing-cost equilibrium which were both excluded from the theory of perfect competition. It was also expected that the modified theory would lead to a wealth of testable consequences. But Chamberlin himself was quite uninterested in the derivation of testable predictions, and later efforts by Kaldor, Demsetz and Archibald have shown that – on the qualitative

[50] 'The reason for not stating the weakest assumptions...for competition is that they are difficult to formulate and in fact are not known precisely' (Machlup [1967]). For a brave attempt to state the limits of applicability of monopolistic competition theory, see Machlup [1952], pp. 315–16.

[51] See for instance Bauer [1945]. This example refers to the rubber producing industry in Malaya which appeared to fulfil the initial conditions for perfect competition unusually well.

comparative static level – the model is even poorer than that of perfect competition. The reason for this poverty is common to monopolistic competition and to monopoly theory: if we vary a parameter (demand), the change of the variable we wish to predict (price) may be construed as either an increase or a decrease, depending on the relevant quantitative information in the model. However, no such quantitative data are available; and in their absence one cannot deduce even qualitative predictions.

The only novelty offered by Chamberlin is, then, the excess capacity theorem: equilibrium must occur at a point where average costs for the firm are decreasing. Yet serious doubts have been cast on the validity of this theorem.[52] The first serious difficulty was highlighted by Kaldor who pointed out that Chamberlin's large-numbers case with zero profits and free entry converges to perfect competition. For as newcomers enter the industry in an initial disequilibrium situation, they simultaneously reduce profits and render the individual demand curves more elastic. Admittedly, equilibrium may occur while profits are still being made if the situation is such that the entry of one additional firm would convert minute profits into losses (even if we accept Chamberlin's 'heroic assumptions' of symmetry and uniformity). But Chamberlin dismisses these small profits which could ensue from product differentiation; he calls them zero profits because they are so small. Nevertheless, he claims as a major result of his theory that, in equilibrium, average costs diverge from the minimum point on the average cost curve. But both divergences are of the same order of magnitude. We cannot choose to disregard one without also disregarding the other. And if both are dismissed, we are back to perfect competition. If, on the other hand, we are prepared to admit small monopoly profits (as seems reasonable) in a monopolistically competitive situation, then the equilibrium is analytically identical with that of pure monopoly. In both cases the novelty of the tangency equilibrium is lost.[53] Another serious criticism of the decreasing-cost equilibrium came from Demsetz. He claimed that if we include in the firm's cost function any demand-increasing costs whatsoever and allow them to vary optimally with output – as indeed we do in the case of production costs – then decreasing-cost equilibrium is no longer assured: it may occur and it may not.[54]

The only remaining way of testing the theory is to attempt to observe the equilibrium conditions. Yet such attempts are beset with difficulties. If, for instance, we want to test zero profits as an equilibrium prediction

---

[52] Kaldor [1935] and [1938], Archibald [1961], Demsetz [1964].

[53] For a critical discussion of the tangency equilibrium see also Machlup [1952], chapter 10. When the 'heroic assumptions' are relaxed it no longer follows that there should be a decreasing-cost equilibrium with zero profits. See also, Chamberlin [1966], p. 195. Under monopoly we may have equilibrium with decreasing costs and positive profits but whether or not this is the case depends on the position of the cost and demand curves.

[54] Cp. Demsetz [1964]. Also see Dewey [1958]. He showed that mergers between two 'sub-optimal' monopolistic competitors would remove the 'excess capacity'.

we have to decide how small profits must be to be considered 'zero'. Then, of course, we are still left with the problem of the reasonableness of our convention.

Finally, there are serious logical difficulties with Chamberlin's notion of a product differentiating group. These difficulties were first intimated by Triffin.[55] He pointed out that the assumption of free entry was inconsistent with that of product differentiation, and that there was no criterion to delineate a product differentiating group or 'industry' from the multitude of firms competing in an economy.

It appears therefore that the Chamberlinian 'large numbers' case fails to fulfil the testability criterion. It is, therefore, less criticisable even than perfect competition. It also fails, as we have just seen, the requirement of logical coherence.

In the light of all this it is amusing to look at a few quotations from 'specialists' in the field: J. S. Bain writes of Chamberlin's theory: 'in "Monopolistic Competition" Chamberlin really introduced a new price theory with a vastly greater empirical relevance than that of preexisting theory and with an immensely increased immediate or latent power to generate hypotheses concerning enterprise behaviour'.[56] P. A. Samuelson calls monopolistic competition: 'the best current model of price theory';[57] and Robert Bishop writes: 'As I judge the consensus of economists Chamberlin's "Theory of Monopolistic Competition" and Mrs Robinson's "Economics of Imperfect Competition" are acknowledged to have touched off, in 1933, a theoretical revolution whose relative importance in the microeconomic area was comparable to that of the Keynesian analysis in macroeconomics.'[58]

I have suggested that the dominant research programme in the theory of the firm is 'situational determinism' and that some of the major debates, especially the Chamberlin–Chicago controversy, are mere family quarrels between slightly different variants within the same programme. I have also suggested that this programme after its initial progress in the theory of perfect competition, was overextended into fields in which it failed.

---

[55] Triffin [1940], pp. 88 and 118.　　　　[56] Bain [1967], p. 149.

[57] Samuelson [1967], p. 112.

[58] Bishop [1964], p. 33. These appraisals are invalid and the sociologist of knowledge will be interested why they were made. Irrational appraisals can be explained by 'external' causes. (For this 'internal–external' distinction cp. Lakatos [1971a] and Kuhn [1971].) One such 'external' explanation could be that if capitalism contains many instances of large-numbers monopolistic competition, then it would be shown to involve social waste through excess capacity.

Excess capacity under monopolistic competition was at times instanced as a defect of the market system as it actually works. Chamberlin thought that excess capacity in his sense was not necessarily wasteful, and that within his model it represents the price that consumers were willing to pay for product differentiation. Unfortunately, this explanation does not carry conviction since, in Chamberlin's model, differentiation is more or less imposed on the consumers. Nicols [1947] has criticised Chamberlin for requiring a rather perverse consumer theory in order to carry through the analytics of his large-number case.

(e) Duopoly and oligopoly

Traditionally, the problem posed by oligopoly has been to analyse and explain economic behaviour in a market situation where there are few sellers and many buyers. The distinctive characteristic of oligopolistic models is not numerical fewness as such, but 'fewness' in the idiosyncratic sense that decisions are interdependent.[59] In oligopolistic market situations the awkwardness of a single-exit model is most apparent. In such situations, sub-optimal behaviour is still viable, and the guesses and counter-guesses about competitors' decision processes are crucial factors in the determination of price–output behaviour: we are confronted with genuine multiple-exit decision-situations. This being the case, one might assume that further psychological and social psychological considerations would have to be introduced to supplement the basic model. However, a very different picture emerges when we look at classical and neoclassical oligopoly theory. Psychological or behavioural considerations often do not come in at all. And when they do come in, as in the Cournot–Bertrand model, they are dragged in in order to mould the oligopolistic situation into a shape amenable to the yielding of a single-exit situation: the situational or cognitive assumptions are tampered with minimally but in such a way as to reduce the oligopoly problem to a kind of monopoly problem with a single-exit solution.

Traditionally, the question *why* there are 'few' sellers has not been closely investigated by oligopoly theory. The theory simply assumed that entry is barred by institutional or physical means (for instance, by law, by significant economies of scale or by privileged access to primary factors of production). The type of questions raised by oligopoly theory are typically of the traditional classical and neoclassical variety, notably questions relating to the determinateness of equilibrium and of the effects on the variables of changes in the parameters. Indeed, the Cournot–Bertrand type model of oligopoly, reflects again the principal heuristic characteristics of the general neoclassical programme.[60]

Let us first look at a *difference*. In oligopoly each decision-maker is involved in guessing the other's expected behaviour; and if perfect knowledge on both sides is assumed, we should be led to an infinite regress. Thus even when the assumption of perfect knowledge is retained concerning all other aspects of the market situation, oligopoly theorists have to admit one qualification, namely, that the decision-makers have incomplete knowledge about each others' states of mind. But if perfect knowledge is impossible, does situational determinism not break down? Is not the oligopolistic situation then necessarily a multi-exit one? Traditional

---

[59] In this idiosyncratic conception of 'fewness' it is important that industries with quite a large number of firms may nevertheless qualify for treatment in terms of an oligopolistic model, and that, in general, the analysis of oligopolistic phenomena has wide applicability in the domain of market behaviour.

[60] Cournot [1838] and Bertrand [1883].

oligopoly theory has tried to avoid reaching this unwanted conclusion. Taking the case of duopoly, one way has been to restrict each seller's knowledge to the assumption that the other will go on producing the same amount whatever the first does. Now a single-exit solution is forthcoming. For now the first duopolist can subtract his rival's output from the output indicated by the market demand curve at each price, and thereby obtain his own demand curve. He will then (by the usual marginalist calculation) set his output so as to maximise as a monopolist. But since the other duopolist, by assumption, proceeds on the same cognitive assumptions (and he too maximises), his output will change. So the first will be maximising on (knowingly) false assumptions, and so on. A process of trial-and-error adjustments *may* lead in due course to a situation where each duopolist's assumption about the other's output is correct, and then neither will have an incentive to change his output.[61] (Of course, the process of trial-and-error might not be convergent, and then no equilibrium would result.) It is clear from this brief account of the Cournot-type theory of duopoly that the qualification of the assumption of perfect knowledge while not departing from the hard core of the programme enables a unique price–output decision which may be calculated on the basis of objective market data. There is no empirical justification for the modification; and none has been claimed.

Chamberlin's contribution to the analysis of the oligopoly problem is even more in the tradition of situational determinism. He attempts to solve the oligopoly problem while closely adhering to the hard core postulates and the neoclassical positive heuristic. His 'solution' is that with symmetry, product homogeneity and the maximisation motive, the participants in an oligopoly are inevitably led to collusion and hence to a joint monopoly price. The outcome of collusion will be the monopoly price only if its selection is accompanied by acceptability to each of the oligopolists of the resultant profits accruing to each of them; that is, that the monopoly price is combined with a 'fair' division of profits. But no convincing reason is given by Chamberlin or by anybody else why we should expect such a coincidence of outcomes.[62] Thus Chamberlin's 'solution' adds nothing to the theoretical armoury of the oligopoly theorist, since it does not go beyond the analysis of pure monopoly theory avoiding the additional difficulty posed by oligopoly situations. In this application of situational determinism the big difference between a single decision-maker and a coalition of two or more is concealed by an appropriately constructed situation. The interesting problems of oligopoly

[61] The Bertrand–Edgeworth solution of the duopoly problem is only trivially different from Cournot's: according to Bertrand, the cognitive assumption refers to the constancy of price of the other duopolist; not to his quantity. This, Bertrand argued, led to a 'price undercutting' process and eventually to a 'zero profit' equilibrium.

[62] More recently Fellner [1949] has dealt with the problem of collusion mainly on the analytical level.

namely, 'why and on what terms would oligopolists collude?' are accommodated *ad hoc* by being transferred into the premises.[63] The structure of the Chamberlinian situation leaves the question of the division of the joint profit undetermined and implies that it is irrelevant to the stability of the equilibrium.[64]

Chamberlin's writings in price theory from 1933 onwards reflect the belief that a satisfactory theory of the firm can be developed simply by inserting elements of monopoly into a theory of market behaviour according to which firms operated under situational determinism.

(*f*) *Limit price theory*

Economists writing on monopoly pricing have often suggested that the monopolist will have regard to potential competition and will take it into account when setting the price for his product. Thus J. B. Clark puts it graphically: 'Let any combination of producers raise the prices beyond a certain limit, and it will encounter this difficulty [of new entry]. The new mills that will spring into existence will break down prices; and the fear of these new mills, without their actual coming, is often enough to keep prices from rising to an extortionate height. The mill that has never been built is already a power in the market'.[65]

Until recently no attempt was made to integrate in a formal theory the effect of potential competition or of potential entry on the determination of price and output. However, J. S. Bain and P. Sylos-Labini have now come forward with a theory designed to incorporate this effect.[66]

They have introduced the concept of the 'limit price', i.e., that price at which entry will not take place, but above which entry will take place. I shall argue that in their analysis of the limit price Bain and Sylos follow the heuristic of situational determinism to arrive at a single-exit situation in which the factors which are crucial to the determination of the equilibrium limit price lie outside the decision-making units.

Their treatment of the theory of limit pricing need not have been placed in the context of oligopoly. It will be seen that, in fact, the analysis of limit pricing could proceed independently of the treatment of the more traditional question of pricing in oligopoly. Bain's and Sylos's eagerness to present their analysis of limit pricing as an oligopoly model reflects the pervasiveness of the neoclassical positive heuristic in the theory of the firm.

[63] Chamberlin [1933], pp. 100–4 of the sixth edition [1966].

[64] In his later work, collected in his [1957] *General Theory of Value*, Chamberlin tried to minimise the central role of the 'large group' monopolistic competition case and shifted the emphasis on his small-group situation. Yet his approach still does not come to grips with the oligopoly problem since he still cannot free himself of the blinkers of situational determinism.

[65] Clark [1901], p. 13. See also Marshall [1919], pp. 396–7.

[66] Sylos-Labini [1956] and Bain [1956]. A recent publication following this mode of analysis is Dewey's [1969].

The results of the theory of limit price as presented by Sylos and Bain may be viewed in two ways:

(i) According to the theory, the limit price is determinate in the sense that the limit price and output possess equilibrial characteristics.

(ii) According to the theory, oligopoly price is indeterminate within bounds with the limit price as an upper bound and the competitive price as a lower bound.

The second view (ii) is, in a way, an admission that oligopolistic situations are indeterminate and that the most that can be predicted by the consideration of purely economic aspects of the situation is an upper and a lower bound. This answer is far from satisfactory not only because of its indeterminacy but also because most students of business behaviour (and common sense too) would agree that an oligopolistic price is higher than the competitive but lower than the monopolistic price. The first view (i), according to which equilibrium is determinate, is more challenging and we shall therefore confine our attention to it, after having briefly considered the second view.

Sylos-Labini's strictly determinate solution was elaborated in Modigliani's [1958] and it is advisable to retain Modigliani's expository schema since it has gained wide acceptance and usage.[67] At first sight the approach of Sylos-Labini and Bain seems quite straightforward. They consider a *homogeneous oligopoly model* where all firms face the same cost and demand conditions, and may thus be analysed in terms of a *typical* firm. The members of the oligopoly group are assumed to act collusively. However, they face the threat of entry into the industry by potential entrants whose actual entry would reduce their profits. Sylos and Bain avoid assumptions about interdependence both as among the existing firms, on the one hand, and a potential entrant, on the other.

As regards the group of existing firms, such questions as the strength of collusive bonds or the stability of collusion are not discussed. Sylos writes characteristically: 'The elements of price determination are the following: (*a*) the absolute size of the market; (*b*) the elasticity of demand; (*c*) the technologies; and (*d*) the price of the variable factors and of machines which, together with the technologies, determine the total average cost of the firms.'[68] Brems, in his review of Sylos-Labini notes: 'The merit of this book lies in its insistence that...oligopoly theory does not need conjectural reaction curves but may be based upon objective firm unit-cost curves and *industry* demand curves to be observed empirically'.[69]

Both Sylos and Bain claim that their price–output solutions depend on the internal structure of the industry, i.e., basically, the size distribution of the firms in it. This is in contrast with other neoclassical oligopoly

---

[67] The entire reconstruction of the Sylos–Bain theory depends to a large extent on Modigliani's lucid review of the two books. See Modigliani [1958].

[68] Sylos-Labini [1956], p. 50.　　　　　[69] Brems [1963], pp. 189–90.

theories where the particular oligopolistic structure makes no difference. Sylos writes: 'In all cases the initial structure of the industry affects the final equilibrium situation'.[70] He further complicates the picture by describing the determination of the limit price and output in terms of an oligopolistic group composed of three discreet subgroups distinguished by size and technology. However, the internal architecture of the industry turns out to be completely irrelevant to price and output determination. Limit price and output have the same value in Sylos's model whether the industry is composed of three distinct subgroups producing some total output or a single group composed of firms of identical size producing the same total output. The reason for this is that the limit price and output are determined (cp. below pp. 36–7) by the demand curve facing the industry and the cost curve facing the most advantageously placed potential entrant.

Thus, the problem of interdependence among existing producers is assumed away, and it becomes debatable whether we have a theory of oligopoly at all. By placing restrictive situational assumptions we have reduced the assumed situation of oligopoly with free entry to one of monopoly with free entry.[71]

We now turn to the determination of the limit price. At this point departure from the 'hard core' of the neoclassical programme seems to take place. This is the adoption of the so-called Sylos postulate in the place of the 'decision independence' assumption which is characteristic of situational determinism. For the Sylos postulate specifies a particular kind of interdependence assumed to exist between existing producers and potential entrants. It will be shown, however, that as in the case of Cournot's duopoly solution, the Sylos postulate fulfils the role of avoiding the infinite regress of guesses and counter-guesses by turning the rival's expected reaction into a stable situational constraint, and thus of allowing decision making to conform to the usual neoclassical pattern.

The necessity of the Sylos postulate is evident only when we envisage the operation of the assumed market situation. Existing producers are assumed to act collusively. Potential entrants are assumed to be attracted to entry by the possibility of profits. However, the 'possibility of profits' as seen by potential entrants, depends on their expectation about the reaction of the existing producers to their entry. In order to specify the nature of the assumed interdependence between existing firms and potential entrants, an assumption is required about the way in which the decisions of potential entrants are affected by their expectations about

---

[70] Sylos-Labini [1956], p. 50.

[71] In his discussion of Bain's [1949], Machlup [1952] does not seem to agree with this. See especially pp. 562–3. The main distinction according to Machlup between pure monopoly and monopoly with potential competition is that in the latter case the producer fears both 'insiders' and 'outsiders'. However, my main point is that in the Sylos–Bain model the 'insiders' do not matter for analytical purposes.

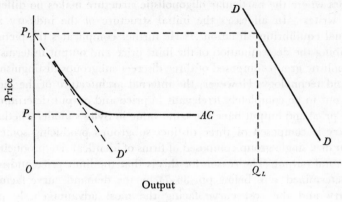

Fig. 1

actual producers' behaviour after entry. But without some further restriction, the unqualified assumption of perfect knowledge may lead to a chain of guesses and counter-guesses (as with the Cournot model). For instance, it may be advantageous for the existing producers to change their pricing strategies in accordance with some behaviour rule or random device so as to foil any attempts of potential entrants to guess the patterns in their behaviour. If a determinate solution is sought, some strong assumption about the cognitive status of potential entrants is required. This need is filled by the *Sylos postulate*:[72] potential entrants assume that existing producers will adopt *the most unfavourable strategy open to them with respect to a new entrant, namely that of maintaining output.*

The standard requirement of profit maximisation is interpreted by Sylos as long-run maximisation. This weaker interpretation of maximising motivation is, as we shall see, necessary for a determinate equilibrium.

The postulate of quasi-perfect knowledge is necessary here, as it is in Cournot's duopoly theory, in the sense that without *total relevant knowledge* the proposed price–output solution would not hold. For instance, if a potential entrant held a different view of the industry demand conditions from that of the existing producers, a determinate equilibrium would not be obtained. The same also holds for the assumption of a perfectly functioning market.

On these assumptions each oligopolist charges the same price for his product, and it includes a *premium* on the competitive price (P_c in Fig. 1) which latter price corresponds to the minimum point of the average cost curve, AC. The premium is in turn determined as the maximum entry-preventing mark-up on the competitive price.

[72] This is Modigliani's terminology. Cp. Modigliani [1958], p. 217. Bain does not recognise the need for such a postulate and Sylos-Labini himself does not discuss it at any length.

The geometry of price determination rests on two basic situational assumptions:

(i) product homogeneity

(ii) market economies of scale represented by an L-shaped average cost curve.

Consider the demand curve, DD facing the industry, and suppose that each firm faces the average cost curve AC, as in Fig. 1.

Draw $P_L D'$ parallel to DD at a position just to the left of the AC curve. At price P_L, the output of the industry is OQ_L. Suppose an additional firm enters the industry, and the established firms continue producing OQ_L. The new firm is left with a segment of the market represented by $P_L D'$ (i.e., DD less OQ_L). By construction the new firm's average cost for any output is above the price at which it has to sell that output. According to the Sylos postulate, the potential entrant is endowed with the situational belief that the established firms will maintain their pre-entry output. Accordingly entry does not take place. P_L is thus an entry-forestalling price – the 'limit price'.

The determinacy of the limit price and output is achieved at the expense of several restrictive assumptions.

One assumption which is implicit in the derivation of the equilibrium conditions is that entry takes place instantaneously on the occurrence of an opportunity for profit (i.e., if the actual price is above the limit price). Should this assumption be dropped, lags in entry would be introduced. Profit-maximising oligopolists might then find it profitable knowingly to set price above the limit price and to allow some entry to take place. It should be profitable to do so provided the (discounted value of the) profits earned during the lag period exceed the (discounted value of the) subsequent reduction in profits resulting from entry. The optimum price in such circumstances would be determinate only if further assumptions were introduced about the relationship between the level of price and the speed and rate of new entry; and the limit price itself would be of little, if any, significance.

The explicit assumption of product homogeneity also is necessary if the theory is to remain manageable. Without this assumption, the determination of the limit price would require that the established firms have perfect knowledge of the nature of the differentiated product which each potential entrant would introduce if he were to enter the industry and of the effect of the price of their own variety of the product on the demand for the new variety of product. It should be noted, further, that 'entry' which is the distinguishing feature of the Sylos–Bain model cannot be sharply defined unless the time-honoured problem of defining a 'group of product-differentiating firms' is solved satisfactorily.

Thus any attempt to weaken the assumptions on which the formal solution rests, and thereby to give empirical relevance to the model is likely to rob the solution of its determinacy. It is therefore no accident that Sylos's treatment is almost exclusively theoretical, and that the empirical material which is deployed in it does not bear in any way on his theory of limit price.[73]

Further difficulties arise with limit price theory. These difficulties reflect the fact that the theory attempts to get round or avoid problems of strategic rivalry (between the established firms and the potential entrants) by the adoption of more elaborate situational assumptions according to the dictates of an optimistic positive heuristic, which in fact, in the context of situations of small numbers, seems to have run out of steam.

Thus the theory does not explain why a potential entrant should not call the bluff of the established firms by entering the industry when the limit price is being charged. The theory can give no reason why the established firms would continue to produce the limit quantity in the changed circumstances, since their profits might well be larger if they reduced their output and co-existed peacefully with the new entrant, particularly if it were clear that the new entrant was prepared to endure a long period of unprofitable operations. If it were to be inferred from the theory that the established firms would be prepared to suffer losses in order to force out the new entrant rather than accommodate him in their industry, a further question is raised. Without setting their price at the level of the limit price, the established firms could communicate the threat that they would deal with the problem of new entry by enforcing losses on any new entrant who enters their industry. The theory does not explain why the communication of such a threat should be ruled out,[74] nor why the only effective communication of a threat is that implicit in the adoption of the limit price.

Indeed, more generally, the motivation of the existing producers is not clear in the theory of limit pricing. The trivial Sylos postulate does not provide us with the answer. If we retain the standard assumption of profit maximisation we may find that under a wide range of circumstances it conflicts with the Sylos pricing policy. Further specifications of the decision-maker's knowledge and motivation is required. It is characteristic of the tenacity and the pervasiveness of situational determinism that neither Sylos-Labini nor Modigliani recognises the opportunity open to them to investigate alternative assumptions concerning the motivation, cognition and decision procedures of interacting potential and actual

[73] In the appendix of his [1956] Sylos tries to refute the view that the United States industry has become less concentrated since the turn of the century. As far as I can see this can, at best, have a very weak impact on limit price theory. Bain seems to have realised most of the potential defects of the formal model and has been more cautious. Instead of attempting to refine the model, he has been content to describe the divergences between the situational conditions assumed by the model and the actual ones in different oligopolistic industries.

[74] This point is voiced by several writers. See, for instance, Stigler [1940], p. 533; Fellner [1949], p. 162; and Machlup [1952], p. 538.

competitors. According to Modigliani: 'it is both to Bain's and Sylos's credit that [they have moved] us away from conjectural variations and similar subjective notions and [focussed] instead on objective market and technological data'.[75] By 'subjective notions' he presumably means both the interdependence of decisions among existing producers and also the interaction – by means of threats and counter threats[76] – between existing producers and potential entrants that are excluded from the Sylos model.[77]

References

Archibald, G. C. [1961]: 'Chamberlin *versus* Chicago', *Review of Economic Studies*, **29**, pp. 2–21.

Bain, J. S. [1949]: 'A Note on Pricing in Monopoly and Oligopoly', *The American Economic Review*, **39**, pp. 448–64.

Bain, J. S. [1956]: *Barriers to New Competition*.

Bain, J. S. [1967]: 'Chamberlin's Impact on Microeconomic Theory', in R. E. Kuenne (ed.): *Monopolistic Competition Theory: Studies in Impact*, pp. 147–76.

Bauer, P. T. [1945]: 'Notes on Cost', *Economica*, N.S., **12**, pp. 90–100.

Bertrand, J. [1883]: Review of Cournot's *Reserches*, *Journal des Savants*, September 1883.

Bishop, R. L. [1964]: 'The Theory of Imperfect Competition After Thirty Years: The Import on General Theory', *The American Economic Review*, **54**, pp. 33–43.

Brems, H. [1963]: '*P. Sylos-Labini, Oligopoly and Technical Progress*', *Journal of Political Economy*, **71**, pp. 189–90.

Chamberlin, E. H. [1933]: *The Theory of Monopolistic Competition*.

Chamberlin, E. H. [1957]: *Towards a More General Theory of Value*.

Chamberlin, E. H. [1966]: *The Theory of Monopolistic Competition*, 6th edn.

Clapham, J. H. [1922]: 'Of Empty Economic Boxes', *Economic Journal*, **32**, pp. 305–14.

Clark, J. B. [1901]: *The Control of Trusts*, 2nd edn, 1912.

Cournot, A. A. [1838]: *Recherches sur les Principes Mathématiques de la théorie des richesses*. References are to the English translation by N. T. Bacon, 1927.

[75] Modigliani [1958], p. 222. Modigliani adds that in doing this 'they provided us with theories rich in empirical content and capable of being disproved by evidence' ([1958], p. 222). As indicated above, this claim is incorrect. Difficulties in subjecting the Sylos model to actual tests are described by Osborne [1964]. Recent efforts to improve the theory have been made by Pashigian [1968], without however enriching its empirical content.

[76] It is unfortunate, though hardly surprising in view of the dominance of situational determinism, that economists persist in ignoring psychological literature on bargaining behaviour under conditions of 'threat'. See, for instance, Deutsch and Krauss [1960] and Kelley [1965].

[77] The oligopoly model recently proposed by Stigler [1964] also seems to lie within the scope of the positive heuristic of situational determinism. Stigler assumed that the group-profit maximising price will be charged if there is no scope for secret price-cutting; but that, if there is such scope, the effective price will vary inversely with the difficulty of detecting secret price-cutting. In turn, the difficulty/ease of detecting secret price-cutting depends on situational factors such as the number of sellers, the number of buyers, the rate of entry of new buyers and the 'loyalty' of buyers. Sellers are endowed with profit-maximising motivation stretched to include a propensity to cheat if they can cheat undetectedly, i.e., if 'cheating pays'. For a critical appraisal see Yamey [1972].

Demsetz, H. [1964]: 'The Welfare and Empirical Implications of Monopolistic Competition Theory', *Journal of Political Economy*, **74**, pp. 623–41.

Deutch, M. and Krauss, R. M. [1960]: 'The Effect of Threat upon Interpersonal Bargaining', *Journal of Abnormal and Social Psychology*, **61**, pp. 181–9.

Dewey, D. [1958]: 'Imperfect Competition no Bar to Efficient Production', *Journal of Political Economy*, **66**, pp. 24–33.

Dewey, D. [1969]: *The Theory of Imperfect Competition*.

Enke, S. [1951]: 'On Maximising Profits', *The American Economic Review*, **41**, pp. 566–78.

Fellner, W. [1949]: *Competition Among the Few*.

Friedman, M. [1953]: *Essays in Positive Economics*.

Hayek, F. A. [1948]: *Individualism and Economic Order*.

Hempel, C. G. [1942]: 'The Function of General Laws in History', *The Journal of Philosophy*, **39**, pp. 35–48.

Higgins, B. [1939]: 'Elements of Indeterminacy in the Theory of Non-Perfect Competition', *The American Economic Review*, **29**, pp. 468–79.

Hutchison, T. W. [1938]: *The Significance and Basic Postulates of Economic Theory*.

Kelley, H. H. [1965]: 'Experimental Studies of Threats in Inter-personal Negotiations', *Journal of Conflict Resolution*, **9**, pp. 79–105.

Kaldor, N. [1935]: 'Market Imperfection and Excess Capacity', *Economica*, N. S., **2**, pp. 33–50.

Kaldor, N. [1938]: 'Professor Chamberlin on Monopolistic and Imperfect Competition', *Quarterly Journal of Economics*, **52**, pp. 513–38.

Kuhn, T. S. [1971]: 'Notes on Lakatos', in R. C. Buck and R. S. Cohen (eds): *Boston Studies in the Philosophy of Science*, vol. 8, pp. 137–46.

Lakatos, I. [1968]: 'Criticism and the Methodology of Scientific Research Programmes', *Proceedings of the Aristotelian Society*, **69**, pp. 149–86.

Lakatos, I. [1970]: 'Falsification and the Methodology of Scientific Research Programmes', in I. Lakatos and A. Musgrave (eds.): *Criticism and the Growth of Knowledge*, pp. 91–195.

Lakatos, I. [1971a]: 'History of Science and its Rational Reconstructions', in R. C. Buck and R. S. Cohen (eds.): *Boston Studies in the Philosophy of Science*, **8**, pp. 91–136.

Lakatos, I. [1971b]: 'Replies to Critics', in R. C. Buck and R. S. Cohen (eds.): *Boston Studies in the Philosophy of Science*, **8**, pp. 174–82.

Latsis, S. J. [1972]: 'Situational Determinism in Economics', *The British Journal for the Philosophy of Science*, **23**, pp. 207–45.

Latsis, S. J. [1976]: 'The Limitations of Single-Exit Models: Reply to Machlup', *The British Journal for the Philosophy of Science*, **27**, pp. 51–60.

Le Roy, E. [1899]: 'Science et Philosophie', *Revue de Métaphysique et de Morale*, **7**, pp. 375–425, 503–62 and 706–31.

Machlup, F. [1946]: 'Marginal Analysis and Empirical Research', *The American Economic Review*, **36**, pp. 519–54.

Machlup, F. [1952]: *The Economics of Seller's Competition*.

Machlup, F. [1955]: 'The Problem of Verification in Economics', *Southern Economic Journal*, **22**, pp. 1–21.

Machlup, F. [1956]: 'Rejoinder to a Reluctant Ultra-Empiricist', *Southern Economic Journal*, **22**, pp. 483–93.

Machlup, F. [1967]: 'Theories of the Firm: Marginalist, Behavioural, Managerial', *The American Economic Review*, **57**, pp. 1–33. Also reprinted in D. Needham (ed.): *Readings in the Economics of Industrial Organisation*, pp. 3–31.

Marshall, A. [1890]: *Principles of Economics* (7th edn, 1916).

Marshall, A. [1919]: *Industry and Trade* (3rd edn, 1932).

Milhaud [1896]: 'La Science Rationelle', *Revue de Métaphysique et de Morale*, **4** pp. 280–302.

Mises, L. von [1949]: *Human Action*.

Modigliani, F. [1958]: 'New Developments on the Oligopoly Front', *Journal of Political Economy*, **66**, pp. 215–32.

Nicols, A. [1947]: 'The Rehabilitation of Pure Competition', *Quarterly Journal of Economics*, **62**, pp. 31–63.

Osborne, D. K. [1964]: 'The Role of Entry in Oligopoly Theory', *Journal of Political Economy*, **72**, pp. 396–402.

Pareto, V. [1909]: *Le Manuel d'Economie Politique*, references are from the English translation by Ann S. Schwier, 1972.

Pashigian, B. P. [1968]: 'Limit Price and the Market Share of the Leading Firm', *Journal of Political Economy*, **16**, pp. 165–77.

Poincaré, H. [1902]: *La Science et l'Hypothèse*.

Popper, K. R. [1945]: *The Open Society and its Enemies*.

Popper, K. R. [1957]: *The Poverty of Historicism*.

Popper, K. R. [1963]: *Conjectures and Refutations*.

Popper, K. R. [1967]: 'La Rationalité et le Statut de Principe de Rationalité', in E. M. Classen (ed.): *Les Fondements Philosophiques des Systèmes Economiques: Texte de Jaques Rueff et Essais Redigés en son Honneur*.

Robbins, L. C. [1932]: *An Essay on the Nature and Significance of Economic Science*. References are to the 2nd edn, 1969.

Robinson, J. [1933]: *The Economics of Imperfect Competition*.

Robinson, R. [1971]: *Edward H. Chamberlin*.

Rothchild, K. W. [1947]: 'Price Theory and Oligopoly', *Economic Journal*, **57**, pp. 299–320.

Sachs, I. (ed.) [1973]: *Main Trends in Economics*.

Samuelson, P. A. [1963]: 'Comment on Ernest Nagel's "Assumptions in Economic Theory"', *The American Economic Review*, **53**, pp. 231–36.

Samuelson, P. A. [1967]: 'The Monopolistic Competition Revolution', in R. E. Kuenne (ed.): *Monopolistic Competition Theory: Studies in Impact*, pp. 105–38.

Simon, H. A. [1959]: 'Theories of Decision-Making in Economics and Behavioural Science', *The American Economic Review*, **49**, pp. 253–83.

Simon, H. A. [1969]: *The Sciences of the Artificial*.

Smith, A. [1776]: *The Wealth of Nations*.

Sraffa, P. [1926]: 'The Laws of Returns Under Competitive Conditions', *Economic Journal*, **36**, pp. 535–50.

Stigler, G. J. [1940]: 'Notes on the Theory of Duopoly', *Journal of Political Economy*, **48**, pp. 521–41.

Stigler, G. J. [1957]: 'Perfect Competition Historically Contemplated', *Journal of Political Economy*, **65**, pp. 1–16.

Stigler, G. J. [1964]: 'A Theory of Oligopoly', *Journal of Political Economy*, **72**, pp. 44–61.

Sylos-Labini, P. [1956]: *Oligopolio e Progresso Technico*.

Triffin, R. [1940]: *Monopolistic Competition and General Equilibrium Theory*.

Yamey, B. S. [1972]: 'Notes on Secret Price-Cutting in Oligopoly', in M. Kooy (ed.): *Studies in Economics and Economic History*, pp. 280–99.

Economics and psychology: the death and resurrection of a research programme

A. W. COATS
UNIVERSITY OF NOTTINGHAM

I

Imre Lakatos originally conceived his methodology of scientific research programmes (MSRP) as a procedure for analysing and appraising developments in the natural sciences. Yet he deliberately designed the Nafplion Colloquium as an opportunity to test its applicability to the history of economics, and thereby to encourage an assessment of its wider implications. In so doing he undoubtedly gave hostages to fortune, for there was every likelihood that MSRP would be interpreted too loosely and applied to circumstances to which it is scarcely appropriate. Some members of the Colloquium did not hesitate to suggest that these deficiencies were exemplified in the present case, and in revising my paper for publication I have endeavoured to take account of their legitimate misgivings.[1] While confidently predicting that it will not be long before Imre's spirit cries out, in the manner of its illustrious antagonist: 'Je ne suis pas Lakatosiste!' I have no desire to hasten that evil day, for this essay is designed as a constructive contribution to the collective effort to assess the value of MSRP as a research tool for the historian of economics.

As a rule, historians are notoriously reluctant to commit themselves to any specific theory or interpretative framework, preferring instead to concentrate on small- or medium-scale problems for which, so they imagine, no general theory is required. On those comparatively rare occasions when they feel compelled to venture on to a broader plane of discourse they tend to resort to intuition or implicit theorising, rather than exposing their habitual loose, unsystematic, and possibly subconscious patterns of explanation. Such an evasion of responsibility is profoundly unsatisfactory to the philosopher or historian of science or any intellectual discipline.

[1] The subject-matter of this paper has undergone several metamorphoses which may be worth recording, for the sake of future devotees of Lakatosiana. It originally formed part of chapter 3, entitled 'Economics and Psychology' of Coats [1953]. Twenty years later, after an appearance at Imre's LSE seminar, he persuaded me to produce an abbreviated version, which was published [Coats, 1974]. A more extended treatment, prepared for Nafplion, was already obsolete by the time it was presented to the Colloquium in a substantially modified form. The present, and I trust final, version owes much to the ideas and examples encountered during that memorable gathering, and to Mark Blaug's brilliant essay printed elsewhere in this volume. I have also benefited from constructive comments by Spiro Latsis, John Maloney and Ian Stewart.

The quest for an adequate explanation may be doomed to disappointment, but it is a challenge to be faced; and in the present imperfect state of our knowledge MSRP offers the best hope of success for the historian of economics who is seeking to understand the general development of his field. MSRP is assuredly more promising than T. S. Kuhn's suggestive 'structure of scientific revolutions', which was too rigid and monolithic in its original form, and in subsequent versions seriously lacking in precision and specificity, largely owing to the vagueness of such key terms as 'paradigm', 'crisis', 'revolution' and 'normal science'.[2]

As the Nafplion discussions revealed, it is still much too early to pronounce a definitive judgment on the value of MSRP as applied to the natural sciences, let alone economics and her softer sister disciplines. There is still much solid historical research to be done, and the precise nature and interpretation of MSRP is still not yet clear. Yet, paradoxically enough, herein lies much of its promise for the historian of economics, for while MSRP is more precise, specific and subtle than Kuhn's theory, it nevertheless possesses a measure of flexibility that prevents it from hardening into a rigid dogma, even in the hands of its most unimaginative exponents. In one of his last writings, Imre himself described MSRP as 'a new and perhaps a bit too elaborate philosophical framework',[3] for he was fully aware that historical facts are notoriously messy and recalcitrant, and that efforts to pour them into preconceived moulds fashioned by philosophers of science might prove neither intellectually nor aesthetically pleasing. In the present instance it is undeniably difficult to resist the temptation to adapt MSRP to fit the facts while trying to remain tolerably faithful to the author's original conception. The protracted controversy in the USA concerning the relations between economics and psychology, which is the subject of this exercise, falls so far short of the strict requirements of the 'paradigm' case of MSRP, i.e., Newtonian physics, that it hardly constitutes a suitable test. Yet here, as elsewhere, the proof of the pudding must be in the eating. MSRP does not only apply to success stories; it also affords insights into 'budding' or 'emergent' programmes.[4] The attempt to infuse psychology into economics manifestly failed in the period under review; it was premature, as well as abortive – so much so that one may be unduly straining the gynaecological metaphor in suggesting that the subsequent renaissance of interest in these matters constitutes a resurrection. Yet the resulting controversy was serious, intense, protracted, and wide-ranging, and almost all the leading American economists entered the lists. The issues included most of the fundamental questions about economics and psychology which have arisen either before or since; and the discussion formed part of a larger debate en-

---

[2] Kuhn [1970]. A revealing account of the successive shifts of Kuhn's position is contained in Toulmin [1972] pp. 98–117.

[3] Lakatos and Zahar [1973], p. 16.   [4] Latsis [1972], pp. 208, 229.

compassing many of the perennial problems of the methodology of the social sciences, such as: the epistemological status and functions of theory; its explanatory and/or predictive value; the realism of assumptions; and the methodological similarities and differences between the social and the natural sciences.[5] The controversy was therefore substantial enough to provide at least a preliminary test of MSRP as a tool for the historian of economics; and an incidental, more practical advantage is the existence of close parallels with the example presented by Latsis,[6] the first serious attempt to apply MSRP to that discipline. Whereas Latsis dealt with the theory of the firm, I am concerned with aspects of the theory of consumer's demand which, Latsis maintained, was based on 'a very similar, if not identical programme'.[7] Yet the two cases were not exactly parallel either with respect to the sequence of events, the details of the controversy, or its outcome. During the period under review, from the early 1880s to the late 1920s, repeated efforts were made to discredit the subjective theory of value which underlay the theory of demand formulated during the so-called 'marginal revolution' of the 1870s.[8] Unlike the theory of the firm, in the present case the principal stimulus to efforts to launch a new research programme came from developments in the neighbour discipline of psychology. The innovators' intentions were clear enough, even though as a group they were generally disunited, unable to define or comprehend the target of their attacks, and quite incapable of formulating an effective rival programme. Yet their efforts did not go unheeded, for the defenders of the received tradition of economics were sensitive to the limitations of the subjective theory of value; and in the process of defending their position they succeeded in refining and strengthening the 'neoclassical' research programme.

In the ensuing pages a brief review of the critical attacks on the 'orthodox' theory of consumer's demand to be found in the American economic literature of the period is followed by an account of the defence and reinterpretation of the received doctrine put forward by its proponents; an assessment of the consequent gains and losses to economic 'science', in the light of recent discussions of these same issues; and some concluding remarks on the value of MSRP as a tool of research for the historian of economics. In the interests of brevity, attention will be concentrated on the bare essentials of the story while endeavouring to minimise the unavoidable oversimplifications involved in this, or indeed any, attempt to 'rationally reconstruct' a complex episode in the history of ideas.

II

The intellectual background to the American discussion of the psychological foundations of economic theory can be depicted very briefly.

[5] Coats [1953]   [6] Latsis [1972].   [7] Latsis [1972], p. 208n.
[8] For a recent review of this episode see Black, Coats and Goodwin [1970].

During the second half of the nineteenth century the development of new ideas and experimental methods in psychology led to the formulation of three major new approaches in the USA, each of which seemed directly applicable to economics: namely, William James's conception of the physiological and biological determinants of human behaviour; William McDougall's instinct theory; and John Broadus Watson's behaviourism.[9] At about the same time, the new 'subjective' theories of value commonly associated with the so-called 'marginal revolution' of the 1870s[10] were being assimilated, not without difficulty, into the central corpus of economic theory. In retrospect it seems hardly surprising that the trend towards objectivism in psychology should clash with an apparently contradictory trend in economics. As the critics of economic orthodoxy never tired of reiterating, economics is a social not a natural science, and must necessarily take account of new knowledge of human behaviour provided by the psychologists and other social scientists.[11] This seemingly obvious commonsense contention was not unduly shaken by the conspicuous disagreements among the psychologists. Admittedly some over-enthusiastic advocates of a marriage, or at least more intimate relations between the two disciplines committed themselves to support of one or other versions of the new psychology only to find it subsequently discredited by even newer ideas or research findings. But they were usually undismayed, presumably concluding that such were the inevitable risks of research in new and hitherto uncharted fields of inquiry.

The variety of responses to the challenges offered by the new psychological ideas makes it difficult to summarise the various and occasionally conflicting positions adopted. A broad distinction between 'critics' and 'defenders' of the received tradition is not seriously misleading, although some of the participants appeared to change sides during the course of the debate,[12] but there is some danger of implying that the received tradition

[9] James [1890], McDougall [1908], Watson [1914].

[10] Black, Coats and Goodwin [1970].

[11] Although, as noted below, some of these critics favoured the adoption of natural science methods in economics.

[12] For example, Herbert Davenport, having declared in 1894 that 'we need to reconstruct the psychological basis of our science...no shirking of psychological difficulties will suffice', added in 1908 that 'the next line of advance in economic theory will be distinctly psychological in character, and that further progress awaits its new impulse at the hands of the psychologists'. Yet he subsequently maintained that economics was the 'science that treats phenomena from the standpoint of price', a position implying that psychology was irrelevant. Davenport [1894], pp. 562–3; [1908], p. 312; and [1913], p. 25. In fact the change in his views was less real than apparent. Coats [1953], pp. 240–6.

Wesley C. Mitchell frequently advocated the importance of psychology for economics and repeatedly warned his fellow economists of the danger of relying on false psychological premises. Yet he conceded that 'for many purposes of economic theory it does not matter for what people want their dollars...in many cases little does lie behind the dollars; the symbols have become the real thing'. He drew attention to the influence of the use of money on the growth of rationality in economic affairs, but while stressing the evolution of habits and institutions, in a manner reminiscent of Thorstein Veblen, he

of economics was sufficiently well established and unified to be recognised without difficulty. Indeed, one of the constructive outcomes of the discussion, as will be shown later, was a more precise and systematic formulation of the 'orthodox' position. Nevertheless, it is reasonably safe to subdivide the responses to the new psychology into three broad categories. Some economists flatly denied that any psychology whatsoever was relevant to economics, arguing that economists should concentrate their attention on catallactics, the science of exchanges, in which the only elements of value to be included were exchange values, or prices, without reference to the motives of those entering into exchanges.[13] At the other end of the spectrum were those who held that the recent developments in psychology had so undermined the subjective theory of value that it was necessary to undertake a wholesale reconstruction of the foundations of economic theory.[14] Finally, in an intermediate position, were those who maintained that the new ideas could be assimilated, either wholly or in part, without undue difficulty, so that only minor changes in terminology, shifts in theoretical formulation or interpretation, or modifications in the conclusions of economic theory, were required.[15]

Generally speaking, critics of the subjective theory of value focused their attention on the marginal utility variant which, they contended, presupposed the hedonistic theory of motivation which had been utterly discredited by professional psychologists.[16] In the economic literature, Thorstein Veblen's devastating satirical portrayal of the hedonistic conception of man as responding passively to external stimuli was especially persuasive when juxtaposed against the positive, actively intelligent interpretation of human nature presented in William James's well-known work.[17] Veblen's attempt to formulate an alternative 'evolutionary' research programme for economics failed completely,[18] and his wholehearted commitment to a pre-McDougall version of the instinct theory of psychology has often been regarded as a particular weakness of his system.[19] Nevertheless, he exerted a considerable influence on the younger

actually devoted his main research efforts to the statistical study of business cycles, a field in which psychology played virtually no part whatsoever. For his earlier views on economics and psychology see, for example, Mitchell [1910] and [1937].

[13] For example, Davenport [1913], p. 99; Hadley [1893]; Fisher [1892].

[14] Veblen [1932], especially pp. 73, 157, 141.

[15] Fetter [1915] endeavoured to take account of these new developments. Cf. his earlier text, Fetter [1904]. For a careful critical analysis of the attempt see Whittaker [1916].

[16] Of the three co-founders of the marginal utility revolution, one, W. S. Jevons, adopted the language of hedonism, thereby revealing his intellectual links with the Benthamite utilitarian tradition. See, for example, Black [1970].

[17] Veblen [1932], p. 73; the hedonist conceived man as 'a lightning calculator of pleasures and pains, who oscillates like a homogeneous globule of desire of happiness under the influence of stimuli that shift him about the area, but leave him intact...Self-imposed in elemental space, he spins symmetrically about his own spiritual axis until the parallelogram of forces bears down upon him, whereupon he follows the line of least resistance'. [18] Coats [1954]; for a more favourable view see Gruchy [1947].

[19] For a different interpretation see Ayres [1958].

fin de siècle generation of American economists, spreading doubts about the psychological and methodological foundations of the orthodox doctrines. When the defenders denied – as most did – that marginal utility presupposed hedonism, the critics merely shifted their ground and attacked the 'hard core' of economic theory, in particular the conception of the 'economic man'. Economic theory, it was said, assumed that the individual consumer possessed a stable and consistent scale of preferences, and was able and willing to make the requisite rational calculations of satisfactions depicted in the marginalists' conception of equilibrium – that he possessed, in J. M. Clark's words, an 'irrationally rational passion for dispassionate calculation'.[20] These assumptions were flatly in conflict with the findings of recent psychological research, which demonstrated that human behaviour was seldom rational, and often impulsive, instinctive, inconsistent, and in other respects unstable. By contrast with the economists' static and passive view of human nature, psychologists (and also the pragmatist philosophers Peirce, James and Dewey, who were becoming increasingly influential in the United States) stressed the active, dynamic, and constructive aspects of human behaviour.[21] The economists' theory was not only unrealistic and demonstrably unscientific; it was also too restrictive, since it was incapable of explaining relevant past and contemporary phenomena – for example, how consumers respond to new commodities or situations, how preferences are formed and changed; and how effective are advertisers' efforts to influence sales.

A related, though not wholly consistent set of arguments focused attention on the stabilising, and presumably non-rational influence of habit and the social determinants of behaviour, such as custom and social emulation. Some critics conceded that earlier economists had made passing reference to these factors; but their true significance had been neglected, for the conventional individualistic theories of consumer's behaviour could neither explain the origins nor assess the role or the effects of changes in these social forces.[22] Moreover, they claimed that economic theory was based on discredited subjective and unscientific notions such as introspection, whereas the new trends in psychology were based on the objective and measurable aspects of human behaviour. In its most

[20] Clark [1936] considered that this criticism was subsidiary to the main charge that marginal utility analysis assumed a static view of human nature. Whether economic theory actually presupposed the notion of an 'economic man' or rational calculator of pleasures and pains is not the issue here. As will be indicated below, the 'fundamental assumption' underlying demand theory had not yet been fully and unambiguously specified.

[21] For a careful effort to take account of these views see Stuart [1896a], [1896b] and [1917].

[22] There were at least two distinct motives underlying these efforts – to enhance the realism of economic theory, and to enable economists to take account of welfare considerations. See, for example, the essays in Clark [1936] and his [1946]. Other contributions in this vein include: Anderson [1911], Cooley [1913], Fetter [1920] and [1923], Haney [1914], Viner [1925], Wolfe [1924].

extreme form this view presupposed that 'science is measurement', and that the social sciences should be modelled on the methodology of the natural sciences.[23] Not all the critics went this far; but they were generally agreed that if economists would acknowledge the validity and relevance of recent advances in psychology they would not only become more sensitive to the limitations of their theories, but would also discover hypotheses and methods that would enable them to establish their discipline on a more scientific foundation.

Viewed from the perspective of MSRP, this miscellaneous ragbag of assertions and complaints does not amount to much. Apart from some valid and pertinent criticisms of the received economic doctrine about the most one can discern, even on a generous interpretation, are a few elements which might form part of the hard core of an embryonic rival research programme, and some statements constitutive of a positive and a negative heuristic. The proposed new psychology-based theory of consumer's demand was really no more than a preliminary declaration of intent; and regrettably, even its most persistent proponents contributed nothing more constructive than a few well-directed critical articles or passages in elementary textbooks. There was, in other words, no sustained effort to devise or test an alternative economic theory. Moreover, notwithstanding their confident pronouncements about the proper method of developing economic science, none of the leading critics ever undertook any detailed empirical studies of the type required to advance their programme. They preferred the easy path of destructive criticism to the painstaking uphill task of constructive economic research.

Nevertheless, with some stretch of the imagination, it is possible to spell out the ingredients of this abortive rival research programme. The following items are presented schematically, for they can be reformulated or reinterpreted in a variety of ways.

Broadly speaking, the critics' proposals included the following assumptions and procedures:

(i) Employ methods similar or identical to those used in the natural sciences.

(ii) Adopt 'realistic' fundamental assumptions, i.e., assumptions compatible with observed behaviour or consistent with the findings of other scientific disciplines (especially psychology).

(iii) Derive assumptions from the study of psychology (and other disciplines) and empirical research into the actual behaviour and motivations of consumers.

(iv) Abandon efforts to formulate abstract, general theories and concentrate on the development of more specific, low- or middle-level, empirically grounded theories.

(v) Develop empirically testable theories which will serve as a basis for scientific explanation, prediction, and/or control.

[23] For example, Tugwell [1922] and [1924], Copeland [1931].

(vi) Undertake systematic empirical studies (and draw upon any relevant studies undertaken by scholars in related disciplines) as a basis for formulating sound empirical generalisations and for testing and, if necessary, reformulating established theories.

(vii) Wherever possible, replace static theories by empirically grounded dynamic theories (e.g. to take account of changes of income, tastes, new commodities, etc.).

(viii) Broaden the scope of economic theory to take account of the social forces influencing economic behaviour (e.g. habit, custom, social emulation, advertising, etc.).

(ix) Go beyond prices and exchange values to examine the influence of market and non-market forces on economic and social welfare.

As already noted, this 'rational reconstruction' is inevitably somewhat speculative – the more so as the research programme was so ill-formed. Yet it may be suggested that the first three (or perhaps even the first five) propositions constituted the hard core, since they could not have been given up without abandoning the entire programme.[24] Propositions (vi)–(ix), on the other hand, comprised the positive heuristic, i.e., the presciption how to develop the programme both theoretically and empirically. And propositions (viii) and (ix) may be said to illustrate the kind of problem-shift entailed by this novel programme.

III

On the whole, the defenders of the orthodox tradition experienced comparatively little difficulty in dividing, defeating, or simply dismissing the opposition. As might be expected, given the strength and durability of the central corpus or economic theory, they were less disunited than their opponents, and they found it easy to expose the gaps and inconsistencies in the critics' contentions. They dismissed as irrelevant suggestions that the boundaries of economics should be systematically broadened to take account of matters which had been conventionally regarded as belonging to other disciplines and indeed, as with the marginal revolution, the general effect of the controversy was to narrow the accepted interpretation of the scope of economics.[25] But above all, the defenders were able to point to their critics' failure to develop a viable alternative theory.

During the debate two general themes emerged, and despite the considerable area of disagreement there was undoubtedly some convergence towards a consensus of opinion on certain essentials.[26] Firstly, virtually all parties agreed in repudiating hedonism as a valid psychological theory,

---

[24] As the Nafplion discussions revealed, even with a well-developed programme in physics it is sometimes difficult to decide whether a specific statement should be regarded as part of the hard core or the positive heuristic.

[25] Winch [1970].

[26] Boucke [1922], Clark [1921], and Parry [1921].

the defenders adding their denial that it had ever constituted an essential foundation for marginal utility analysis. Secondly, there was a marked, albeit by no means unanimous, shift of opinion in favour of a more 'objective' approach to human behaviour, though the nature and significance of this shift was variously interpreted. Some, especially certain critics, advocated the wholesale adoption of behaviourism as the only appropriate psychological basis for economic theory,[27] whereas others merely regarded objective methods as sources of specific hypotheses, generalisations, and relevant data. Curiously enough, the critics who were most receptive to behaviourism in one form or another eventually found allies among those defenders who argued that psychology, as a discipline, had no relevance to economics, the science of prices (or the logic of choice, as it has subsequently been termed). And yet, at the same time, subjective interpretations of consumer's behaviour continued to figure prominently in the textbooks, sometimes with modified terminology designed to purge them of psychological overtones.

Without entering into the details of the matter it is sufficient to illustrate the formulation of the strict constructionist defence of the orthodox hard core by quoting the views of two leading American economic theorists, Irving Fisher and Frank H. Knight. In his doctoral dissertation, published in 1892, Fisher endeavoured both to delineate the scope of economics and to define the type of explanation appropriate to it, by asserting 'this foisting of Psychology on Economics seems to me inappropriate and vicious...to fix the idea of utility the economist should go no further than is serviceable in explaining *economic* facts. It is not his province to build a theory of psychology.'[28] For the purpose of price theory it was sufficient to adopt the postulate that '*Each individual acts as he desires*', for questions about the antecedents of desire lay 'completely within the realm of psychology'. Discussions of subjective states of mind should be avoided, for 'while utility has a 'common sense' meaning relating to feelings, when economics attempts to be a positive science, it must seek a definition which connects it with objective and commodity.'[29]

Some thirty years later Knight adopted broadly the same position, but he specified the methodological implications in a much more extreme and detailed manner. He welcomed the economists' tendency to view the psychology of their subject as behaviouristic on the paradoxical grounds that behaviourism was 'less a psychology than a dogmatic repudiation of everything to be called by that name'.[30] Many of the critics' contentions were valid from a psychological standpoint, but they

[27] For example, Tugwell [1922], p. 332 and, from a very different point of view, Knight, *infra*. A balanced interpretation of the relevance of behaviourism to economics was presented in Dickinson [1922].

[28] Fisher [1892], pp. 5, 11. Italic in original.

[29] Fisher [1892], pp. 11, 17. Italic in original.

[30] Knight [1931*a*], p. 64.

were irrelevant to economics as a science, for '...the basis of a *science* of conduct must be fixed principles of action, enduring and stable motives. It is doubtful, however, if this is fundamentally the character of human life.'[31] Indeed, the essential distinction between the natural and the social sciences was that the latter must take account of 'the facts of consciousness and mental communication. In human behaviour we have a kind of direct knowledge of motives, whereas we only infer the existence of physical forces from observations of the changes specific to each. Hence the irresistible urge to treat motives as real.'[32] It was therefore necessary to recognise the severe limitations of economics as a science and, with reference to economic theory, to grasp that 'there are no laws regarding the *content* of economic behaviour, but there are laws universally valid as to its *form*'.[33] The critics had failed to offer any constructive proposals and they had 'made little headway in bringing forth substitute principles.' I do not believe that they ever will. The strictures are valid as *limitations* on the familiar reasonings, not as negations. The principles of the established economies are partial statements, but sound as far as they go, and they go about as far as general principles can be carried.'[34]

It would be quite wrong to suggest that Knight's interpretation of the proper relationship between economics and psychology was generally accepted in all its details by defenders of the orthodox tradition, most of whom were far less subtle and less interested in methodological and philosophical issues. Nevertheless, Knight's austerely restrictive conception of the scope of economic science, and his pessimistic view of the potentialities of economic theory pointed the way that subsequent studies of utility and demand analysis were to follow. By the end of the 1920s it was already clear that the more ambitious efforts to infuse psychology into economics, or to reconstruct basic economic theory in terms compatible with the new psychologies, had manifestly failed. And the development of the Slutzky–Hicks–Allen indifference curve analysis a few years later seemed to confirm that psychology had little or nothing to contribute to the theoretical apparatus.[35]

[31] Knight [1921*a*].   [32] Knight [1931*a*], p. 67.
[33] Knight [1924].
[34] Knight [1921*b*].

It would be inappropriate to discuss here Knight's epistemological views, which involved the assertion that scientific knowledge was ultimately inferior to knowledge derived from intuition, emotion and common sense, for this would take us too far afield. See Knight [1924], [1925*a*] and [1925*b*].

[35] For example, Robbins [1935]: 'It is difficult to overstress its importance. With one slash of Occam's razor it extrudes from economic analysis for ever the last vestiges of psychological hedonism.' This is not in fact the case, for economists still employ the notion of 'hedonic indexes', though in a somewhat different context. For further comment on the limitations of indifference curve analysis cf. *infra.*, p. 55, footnote 40.

It is worth noting that in his outstanding pioneer article of 1915, 'On the Theory of the Budget of the Consumer', E. V. Slutzky had begun by asserting that 'if we wish to place economic science upon a solid basis, we must make it completely independent of

Yet this does not mean that the controversy was futile or unimportant, even from the most severely orthodox standpoint. During the debate the hard core of economic theory was not merely preserved intact; it was also reinforced, as its key terms were more carefully specified. Moreover, the protective belt of auxiliary hypotheses was strengthened by the elimination of unnecessary and suspect propositions. The fundamental assumption, which had earlier been identified with the popular notion of the economic man, was reformulated in less objectionable terms as the abstract concept of rationality,[36] or the logic of choice – what Veblen and his followers had scathingly dismissed as the 'pecuniary logic'. It is important not to underestimate the significance of this development. At the time the general level of methodological sophistication in economics was undeniably low, not only in the USA, and there was insufficient recognition of the nature and limitations of the conventional analysis. Restoration of confidence in the basic theory was an essential prerequisite to its subsequent elaboration, an observation that applies not only to the theory of consumer's demand but also to other related areas of microeconomics.

By the end of the 1920s the essential components of the hard core of orthodox demand analysis had emerged, by implication if not explicitly, in roughly the following form:

(i) Basic economic theory is necessarily abstract, static and general in form.

(ii) The fundamental assumptions must therefore be simple, uniform and constant; they can neither be 'realistic' nor subject to falsification.

(iii) It is assumed that consumers aim to maximise their satisfactions (total utility).

(iv) They have limited incomes.

(v) They have unlimited wants in general, but normally experience eventually diminishing marginal utility from consuming successive units of a given commodity.

(vi) They have full (or perfect) knowledge of relevant market conditions, for example, prices, the range of available goods and services, etc.

(vii) They make rational calculations of alternative uses of their income, especially by adjusting their expenditures at the margin.

(viii) The individual's decisions are independent of those of other individuals.

psychological assumptions and philosophical hypotheses'. Later, however, he acknowledged the complexities arising from the *factual* interdependence between economics and psychology, leaving 'a more profound investigation' of 'the manifestations of utility in the consciousness of the individual' to 'future studies'. Cf. Ekelund, Furubotn and Gramm [1972], pp. 189, 215, 216–18.

[36] For example, as Z. C. Dickinson put it: 'The "rationality" which we do assume is merely some ability to learn connections between present goods or situations...and future final utilities, which faculty everyone...has always known to be lamentably imperfect.' Dickinson [1922], p. 86.

This list is, of course, necessarily debatable, for assumptions can be specified in a variety of ways and in more or less detail. (For instance, is it necessary in the present case to specify zero costs of information, or to assume that the individual consumer knows in advance that a given commodity or service will fulfil his expectations?) Yet by adding the positive heuristic implied by the orthodox demand analysis we increase its resemblance to a full Lakatosian MSRP – though it still falls far short of that ideal type. If the positive heuristic is defined as a series of suggestions or instructions for improving the theory and testing its implications, it may be said to have included the following:

    (i) construct static models;

    (ii) reduce the number of postulates to a minimum (including psychological postulates);

    (iii) develop general theories;

    (iv) concentrate on the analysis of prices or exchange values (ignoring, as far as possible, such questions as the origin and nature of wants and satisfactions, the structure and stability of preferences, processes of valuation, etc.);

    (v) reinterpret the theory to take account of discrepancies between the assumptions and the facts (as revealed by casual empiricism).

IV

It is now time to consider the significance of this controversy both from the broader standpoint of the history of economics and, more narrowly, in terms of the applicability of MSRP to the discipline. This is no easy undertaking, given the philosophical, methodological, and substantive problems of interpretation involved.

As already indicated, the victory of the orthodox research programme was virtually complete. Both during and after the debate marginal utility theory continued to dominate the economics textbooks – admittedly often in a supposedly objective, quasi-behaviouristic form – until it was supplemented or displaced by indifference curve analysis and, very recently, by 'revealed preference' theory. In the process the majority of economics students were effectively immunised against contamination by psychologists.[37] Yet whatever the pedagogical advantages of this practice the results were obviously by no means costless in terms of the progress of the subject. As might be expected, interest in the theory of value; economic motivation; the formation, structure, and stability of consumers' preferences, and indeed almost all aspects of economic psychology, de-

[37] As Spiro Latsis has said elsewhere in this volume, in the usual treatment by economists the consumer is 'psychologically anonymous' and can therefore be endowed with any traits we wish. See his essay 'A Research Programme in Economics,' pp. 1–41.

clined sharply, as revealed by an analysis of leading economics journals.[38] On the other hand, the slow adoption of utility analysis as a tool of research,[39] and repeated expressions of concern about its theoretical limitations – from respectably orthodox, as well as heterodox economists[40] – are somewhat more unpredictable and disquieting. And the recent resurgence of economists' complaints about the isolation of their subject from other social sciences, including psychology, and the serious neglect of important theoretical and empirical problems in economic psychology,[41] suggests the need for a fresh historical and methodological appraisal of the whole episode.

As is well known, methodological controversy is seldom, if ever, confined to purely methodological issues. But even if space permitted, it would be inappropriate for the present purpose to consider the wider economic and social context of the debate, even the professional academic context. In the Lakatosian MSRP this 'externalist rubbish' (as one Naf-plion participant described it) has only a subordinate place, if indeed that. Nor is it necessary to examine the contending philosophical convictions underlying the critics' and defenders' views, although some of the contro-versialists were certainly sensitive to this level of discourse.[42] We cannot, however, ignore the fact that MSRP embodies criteria for the normative appraisal of scientific theories, and it is accordingly necessary to attempt an exposition of the criteria of 'good' scientific theories to be found, or implied in the literature of economics. Some of these criteria differ from, and may even conflict with MSRP, and they will perhaps seem somewhat bizarre to conventional philosophers of science. But there is no single, universally agreed set of evaluative criteria,[43] and the following list seems not only pertinent to the present case but also to the general history of economics.

The criteria of 'good' theories, as seen by economists past and present, include the following elements:

[38] This is evident from an analysis of articles in the American Economic Association's *Index of Economic Journals*. Coats [1971]. In MSRP terms this represents a substantial problem-shift.

[39] See Stigler [1970].

[40] As Mark Blaug observed, 'the attitude of the utility theorists was that utility theory was merely a matter of systematic common sense', citing Stigler's view that the long labours of many able economists working in this field had merely buttressed the view that all demand curves have negative slopes, which they 'had known all along'. E. J. Mishan has extended the same general criticism to indifference curve and revealed preference analysis, advocating the abandonment of all these theorems since 'there is nothing the practising economist can take away with him to help him come to grips with the complexities of the real world'. Blaug [1968], p. 359; Mishan [1961], especially p. 327. For other criticisms see footnotes 45–49.

[41] *Infra.*, pp. 57, 58 and references in footnotes 48 and 49.

[42] Knight [1931*b*].

[43] See, for example, the list of 70 criteria ranked in 24 subdivisions by S. C. Dodd, reproduced in Zaltman, Pinson and Angelmar [1973], pp. 92–3. Criteria (*c*), (*e*) and (*f*) were considered by Stigler in a context directly relevant to this essay. Cf. his [1950] reprinted in Stigler [1965].

(a) consistency;

(b) simplicity;

(c) generality;

(d) fruitfulness, i.e. adaptability, extensibility;

(e) manageability, i.e. amenability, in terms of available techniques;

(f) congruence with reality, i.e. capacity to explain part of the available empirical knowledge;

(g) testability, i.e. capacity to generate falsifiable predictions;

(h) relevance to the expectations of the scientific community.

The individual items can, of course, be formulated and interpreted in a variety of ways. Not all the criteria can necessarily be fulfilled simultaneously, and they are unlikely to be valued equally.[44] Indeed, the need for some trade-off between them is one of the most familiar sources of irreconcilable methodological disagreements. In the present case, the critics of the orthodox research programme generally emphasised the importance of criteria (f), (g) and (h); and they construed 'relevance' so as to include not only 'internal' criteria of scientific importance but also, like many other economists, 'external' criteria of relevance to social policy. To this end they were prepared to forgo a considerable measure of generality and simplicity, whereas these criteria, together with (d), (e), and (f), ranked very high among the defenders.

To present-day economists, and advocates of MSRP, the most striking feature of the orthodox programme was the comparatively low valuation its proponents placed on criterion (g), testability. As George Stigler, himself no ardent defender of economic heterodoxy, concluded:

Had specific tests been made of the implications of theories, the unfruitfulness of the ruling utility theory as a source of hypotheses in demand would soon have become apparent. Had these economists sought to establish true economic theories of economic behavior – that is, to isolate uniformities of economic events that permitted prediction of the effects of given conditions – they would not long have been content with the knowledge that demand curves have negative slopes... [Whereas in fact] Not only were such specific implications not sought and tested, but there was a tendency, when there appeared to be the threat of an empirical test, to reformulate the theory to make the test ineffective.[45]

When viewed in relation to the long-term progress of economic science, the essential question here is: how much explanatory power and predictive efficiency should be sacrificed for the sake of preserving a theory possessing considerable simplicity, generality, fruitfulness, and manageability? This problem was recognised towards the close of the controversy by another highly respected economist, Jacob Viner, who deplored the

[44] The weight attached to particular criteria will vary according to whether one is evaluating a single theory or an entire research programme. In MSRP Lakatos was essentially concerned with sequences of theories. I owe this point to Mr J. Maloney.

[45] Stigler [1965], pp. 155, 153. Blaug concurs, concluding that 'the long and tortuous history of utility theory presents a disheartening picture' (Blaug [1968], p. 359).

all-too-prevalent methodological fanaticism which prefers the accurate but super-ficial to the approximate but fundamental, and which makes adaptability to its special technique of investigation, rather than importance, the standard for the selection of problems and the delimitation of the scope of the inquiry.[46]

Of course the criteria of 'importance' were at the very heart of the dispute, for the contending parties had entirely different conceptions of the fundamental purposes of economic theory (for example, whether its function is purely explanatory and/or predictive and/or a device for solv-ing immediately practical problems) and they could not agree as to the relative importance of the various theoretical and empirical problems requiring solution.

Differences of this kind also underlay the disagreement about the proper scope of economics, a species of demarcation dispute which is all too common among social scientists, and probably much less so among physi-cal scientists.[47] It would be pointless to try to resolve the issue here; but if there is indeed a resurrection of the heterodox research programme which was so roundly defeated before 1930, it is largely due to the re-surgence of interest in a set of problems which the orthodox theory of consumers' demand is incapable of handling. And it must be stressed that these include theoretical, as well as empirical problems. As Herbert Simon noted more than a decade ago,

economics has been moving steadily into newer areas where the power of the [orthodox or, as he terms it, 'classical'] model has never been demonstrated and where its adequacy must be considered anew...Classical economics was highly successful in handling small-maze problems without depending on psychology. Labor relations, imperfect competition, uncertainty, and long-run dynamics encase the decision-maker in a much larger maze than those considered in classical short-run static theory. In these areas the economist and the psychologist have numerous common interests in cognitive theory that they have not shared previously.[48]

Much more recently, as the result of persistent, widespread and growing dissatisfaction with the theoretical refinements and empirical limitations of available theories of demand and consumer's behaviour there has been a swelling chorus of demands for new research into a wide range of prob-lems recognised as relevant and important by the critics of half a century ago. Current complaints about the existing theory have an inescapable quality of *déjà vu* to those familiar with the literature reviewed in Section II of this paper, and it is not only the ignorant or the methodological fana-tics who voice them. Criticism extends from the fundamental assumptions

---

[46] Viner [1925], p. 212.

[47] This is doubtless because natural scientists disagree less markedly about the social purposes and relevance of their work.

[48] Simon [1963], pp. 709, 711. A somewhat similar range of problems was mentioned forty years earlier by Dickinson [1922]. For further statements of Simon's views see his [1959] and his essay 'From Substantive to Procedural Rationality', in this volume, pp. 129–48.

of maximising behaviour to the economists' failure to examine the process of individual decision-making, the neglect of the relationship between individual and household behaviour, the problems posed by new goods, changes of income and tastes, advertising, social interaction, and so on;[49] and there is considerable evidence of research designed to develop new theories to deal with these unsolved problems and to provide data to fill gaps in existing knowledge. Whether this amounts to a new research programme, rather than a disconnected series of *ad hoc* hypotheses and empirical generalisations it is still too early to say. But if it does, it will surely be legitimate to regard it as the resurrection of a departed spirit of fifty years ago.

What conclusions can the historian of economics draw from this experience? Would it be true to suggest that the successful defence of the orthodox tradition has retarded the development of economics? There is certainly some justification for Latsis' view that 'the adoption of antipsychologism as a heuristic canon is not only unnecessary but, by restricting permissible types of explanatory generalisation, may halt progress in microeconomics',[50] yet it is very doubtful that any viable alternative course was available in the 1920s. Despite the scientific status of the new empirical findings in psychology, that discipline was still in a highly unsettled state, and the efforts to infuse psychology into economics at that time were over-ambitious, premature, sometimes confused, and generally lacking in persistence and clarity of focus. Moreover, it must be remembered that the methodological foundations of economics were weak, and the discipline was under severe and repeated attacks from those who were hostile to all theory and who favoured either descriptive studies or extensions of scope that threatened to convert economics into encyclopaedic sociology. While the desire to facilitate the application of mathematical and statistical techniques[51] and the preference for analytical convenience over testability and descriptive complexity may be regarded as 'temptations'[52] they were by no means easy to resist.

MSRP is helpful in evaluating this episode for Lakatos fully appreciated the difficulty of deciding whether a research programme is degenerating and if so whether it is likely to recover in the foreseeable future. The orthodox programme was not progressing empirically, and in certain respects it was degenerating theoretically as economists reinterpreted the established theory, and added fresh terminological refinements and *ad hoc*

---

[49] For a comprehensive review of the literature see 'The State of Contemporary Demand Theory' by the editors in Ekelund, Furubotn and Gramm [1972], pp. 57–93. Shubik [1970] is an especially devastating and witty critique of the pretensions of recent demand theory. Two further articles should be noted: Tobin and Dolbear [1963] and Ferber [1973].

[50] Latsis [1972], p. 229.

[51] For a balanced statement of the economists' need to draw on available quantitative work in psychology see Dickinson [1924].

[52] Latsis [1972].

assumptions in an effort to protect it from refutation.[53] As one later commentator remarked, even when economists admitted the importance of psychology they recognised it as a 'theoretical obstacle' and therefore 'it is small wonder that psychology gets such summary treatment in most modern texts on economic theory.'[54] Yet it would surely have been wrong to abandon the degenerating orthodox programme in the absence of a viable alternative; and, as we have seen, the critics manifestly failed to provide one. It is therefore appropriate to credit the pre-1930 defenders of economic orthodoxy for their efforts to preserve the intellectual capital which had been accumulated by several previous generations. It may, indeed, be the right way to protect scientific traditions from disintegration, especially when one recalls the dictum that 'the exact sciences have won some of their earlier successes by avoiding the kind of problems still too difficult for their undeveloped powers'.[55]

V

What light does the foregoing account shed on the value of MSRP to the historian of economics? Obviously no general conclusions can be derived from a single case study, but it is worth recording a few provisional impressions for the benefit of future investigators.

It is seldom easy to reconstruct the principles and processes that scientists actually adopt in developing and testing their theories, and it is surely more difficult to do this in economics than in physics. As some Nafplion participants observed, MSRP is based on the 'paradigm' case of Newtonian physics, and there is no precisely comparable paradigm or exemplar in economics. It is therefore correspondingly more difficult to devise acceptable standards (whether in MSRP or other terms) for judging scientific performance in economics, and this helps to account for much, though by no means all, of the perennial philosophical and methodological disagreements in the discipline. These circumstances may constitute an argument for applying exogenous, rather than endogenous criteria of appraisal; but even if this were conceded it would not necessarily follow

---

[53] The slow revival of criticism after the 1920s is surely due in part to the decline of interest in microeconomics. The orthodox explanatory models seemed less unsatisfactory when applied to group or aggregative problems as contrasted with individual behaviour.

[54] Hayes [1950], p. 293. This valuable survey article reveals the continuity between the earlier and later critics of economic theory. Cf. his argument that: 'If further psychological assumptions promise to improve prediction and control...it would be absurd to exclude psychology from economics on the grounds either that it seems *a priori* to be unimportant, or that its inclusion would destroy the distinctiveness of the economic discipline...The crux of the matter is whether or not psychological data, principles, and research techniques promise to increase substantially our capacity to understand, predict and control economic behavior, and this question can only be answered after the fact, not before it.' (*Ibid.* p. 303.)

[55] Deutsch [1958], pp. 9–10. Also Neumann and Morgenstern [1944], pp. 6–7; Medawar [1967], p. 7. The reluctance to abandon the scientific gains of the past has been dignified as the 'principle of tenacity'.

that MSRP was an appropriate source of such criteria. It is difficult to find satisfactory examples of theoretical progressiveness (involving new and unexpected predictions) in economics, let alone empirical progressiveness (i.e. corroborated predictions) although economists have produced numerous *ad hoc* empirical generalisations. Considerations of this kind have led some critics to conclude that economics is not a science at all – or, at least, not a developmental science;[56] but this view is obviously unacceptable to the present writer since it would render pointless any attempt to apply MSRP to the subject.

Nevertheless, these warnings must be heeded, and MSRP must be applied to economics with due caution. Much depends on how literally it is interpreted. For example, it may be said that the entire history of economics constitutes one massive unitary research programme, and that the methodological disagreements among economists are merely 'family quarrels'.[57] To the present writer this view seems a drastic over-simplification; yet even if it were true, it would not necessarily destroy the value of MSRP as a tool of methodological and historical appraisal. As the foregoing paragraphs show, MSRP is a valuable tool for analysing the methods by which an established research programme or scientific tradition is preserved, and the changes it undergoes in the process at the hands of its proponents. The great difficulty in economics is not so much to decide whether there are many research programmes or only one, but how to decide whether a given programme is degenerating, static, or progressing. For as noted above, clear-cut examples of theoretical and empirical progressiveness are hard to find. Too often, it seems, research programmes in economics are preserved long after they have entered their degenerative phase, while new programmes are too readily adopted, and too casually abandoned. And if this judgment is accepted, it raises the intriguing question: what leads economists, or indeed any scientists, to espouse one research programme rather than another?[58] This is a problem that Lakatosians need to tackle in relation to the history of physics and other natural sciences, as well as the social sciences.

This leads us directly to a further general observation about the applicability of MSRP to economics. Derisory references to 'externalist rubbish' notwithstanding, it is clear that Imre Lakatos acknowledged the presence of psychological, sociological and other extra-scientific influences on the history of science. His aim in developing MSRP was not to ignore these

[56] Latsis [1972], p. 207.

[57] As some methodologists have noted, theories in economics are as often complementary or overlapping as competitive, a point that helps to explain their survival value.

[58] As Kuhn recognised, the allegiance to one paradigm or research programme rather than another – at least in its early stages – is a matter of 'promise' or expectations, rather than performance. Kuhn undoubtedly exaggerated the non-rational elements in such attachments, and especially in cases of paradigm-switching. But it is doubtful whether an internalist explanation can provide a satisfactory solution to this problem.

factors but to relegate them to a subordinate place, so that they would not be brought into the account until the internal influences had been fully explored. This approach is even more valuable for the history of economics than for the history of the natural sciences, for although external factors have undoubtedly played a larger part in the former[59] it is all too easy to fall back on them – for example, environmental[60] or ideological influences – as a substitute for detailed historical research. In other words, MSRP represents a sound approach to an explanatory model for the history of economics, even though it will probably take us less far in that field than in physics.

In the end, the value of MSRP to the historian of economics will depend on the correspondence between its component parts (including the logical relationships between them) and the historical facts. The crucial question is: how far is it possible to identify research programmes in the literature of the subject, with their hard cores, protective belts, positive and negative heuristics, progressive and degenerate phases, and so on? To the historian, MSRP is essentially a practical tool which will ultimately be judged by its results. At this early stage of its application it seems to possess considerable promise.

References

Anderson, B. M. [1911]: *Social Value.*
Ayres, C. E. [1958]: 'Veblen's Theory of Instincts', in D. F. Dowd (ed.): *Thorstein Veblen: A Critical Reappraisal*, pp. 25–37.
Black, R. D. C. [1970]: 'W. S. Jevons and the Foundation of Modern Economics' in Black, Coats and Goodwin [1970], pp. 98–112.
Black, R. D. C., Coats, A. W. and Goodwin, C. D. W. (eds.) [1970]: *The Marginal Revolution in Economics, Interpretation and Evaluation.*
Blaug, M. [1968]: *Economic Theory in Retrospect*, 2nd edn.
Blaug, M. [1970]: 'Was there a Marginal Revolution?', in Black, Coats and Goodwin [1970], pp. 3–14.
Boucke, O. F. [1922]: 'A Unique Situation in Economic Theory', *The American Economic Review*, **11**, pp. 598–605.
Clark, J. M. [1921]: 'Soundings in Non-Euclidean Economics', *The American Economic Review, Supplement*, **11**, pp. 132–43.
Clark, J. M. [1936]: *A Preface to Social Economics.*
Clark, J. M. [1946]: 'Realism and Relevance in the Theory of Demand', *Journal of Political Economy*, **59**, pp. 347–53.
Coats, A. W. [1953]: 'Methodological Controversy as an Approach to the History of American Economics, 1885–1930', Unpublished PhD thesis, Johns Hopkins.
Coats, A. W. [1954]: 'The Influence of Veblen's Methodology', *Journal of Political Economy*, **62**, pp. 529–37.
Coats, A. W. [1970]: 'The Economic and Social Context of the Marginal Revolution of the 1870s', in Black, Coats and Goodwin [1970], pp. 37–58.

[59] For a stimulating discussion of the influence of 'lay images' in the social sciences see Lammers [1974].
[60] On environmentalist explanations in economics see Coats [1970].

Coats, A. W. [1971]: 'The Role of Scholarly Journals in the History of Economics: An Essay', *Journal of Economic Literature*, **9**, pp. 29–44.

Coats, A. W. [1974]: 'Situational Determinism in Economics: The Implications of Latsis's Argument for the History of Economics', *The British Journal for the Philosophy of Science*, **25**, pp. 285–8.

Cooley, C. H. [1913]: 'The Institutional Character of Pecuniary Valuation', *American Journal of Sociology*, **18**, pp. 543–55.

Copeland, M. A. [1931]: 'Economic Theory and the Natural Science Point of View', *The American Economic Review*, **21**, pp. 67–79.

Davenport, H. J. [1894]: 'The Formula of Sacrifice', *Journal of Political Economy*, **2**, pp. 561–73.

Davenport, H. J. [1908]: *Value and Distribution: A Critical and Constructive Study*.

Davenport, H. J. [1913]: *The Economics of Enterprise*.

Deutsch, K. W. [1958]: 'Scientific and Humanistic Knowledge in the Growth of Civilization', in H. Brown (ed.): *Science and the Creative Spirit, Essays in Humanistic Aspects of Science*.

Dickinson, Z. C. [1922]: *Economic Motives, A Study in the Psychological Foundations of Economic Theory, with some Reference to other Social Sciences*.

Dickinson, Z. C. [1924]: 'Quantitative Methods in Psychological Economics', *The American Economic Review, Supplement*, **14**, pp. 117–26.

Ekelund, R. B. Jr., Furubotn, E. G. and Gramm, W. P. (eds.) [1972]: *The Evolution of Modern Demand Theory*.

Ferber, R. [1973]: 'Consumer Economics', *Journal of Economic Literature*, **11**, p. 1332.

Fetter, F. A. [1904]: *The Principles of Economics*.

Fetter, F. A. [1915]: *Economic Principles*.

Fetter, F. A. [1920]: 'Price Economics versus Welfare Economics: Contemporary Opinion', *The American Economic Review*, **10**, pp. 719–37.

Fetter, F. A. [1923]: 'Value and the Larger Economics, II, Value Giving Way to Welfare', *Journal of Political Economy*, **31**, pp. 790–803.

Fisher, I. [1892]: 'Mathematical Investigations in the Theory of Value and Prices', *Transactions of the Connecticut Academy*, **9**.

Gruchy, A. G. [1947]: *Modern Economic Thought: The American Contribution*.

Hadley, A. T. [1893]: 'Recent Tendencies in Economic Literature', *Yale Review*, **3**, pp. 251–60.

Haney, L. [1914]: 'The Social Point of View in Economics, I and II', *Quarterly Journal of Economics*, **28**, pp. 115–39, 292–321.

Hayes, S. P. Jr. [1950]: 'Some Psychological Problems of Economics', *Psychological Bulletin*, **47**, pp. 289–330.

James, W. [1890]: *Principles of Psychology*.

Knight, F. A. [1921a]: *Risk, Uncertainty and Profit*.

Knight, F. A. [1921b]: 'Traditional Economic Theory: Discussion', *Tke American Economic Review, Supplement*, **11**, pp. 143–7.

Knight, F. A. [1924]: 'The Limitations of Scientific Method in Economics' in Tugwell [1924], pp. 229–67.

Knight, F. A. [1925a]: 'Economic Psychology and the Value Problem', *Quarterly Journal of Economics*, **39**, pp. 372–409.

Knight, F. A. [1925b]: 'Fact and Metaphysics in Economic Psychology', *The American Economic Review*, **15**, pp. 247–66.

Knight, F. A. [1931a]: 'The Relations of Utility Theory to Economic Method in the work of William Stanley Jevons and Others', in S. A. Rice (ed.): *Methods in Social Science: A Case Book*, pp. 59–69.

Knight, F. A. [1931b]: 'Marginal Utility Economics', *Encyclopedia of Social Sciences*, **5**, pp. 357–63.

Kuhn, T. S. [1970]: *The Structure of Scientific Revolutions*, 2nd edn.

Koch, S. (ed.) [1963]: *Psychology: A Study of a Science*, vol. 6.

Lakatos, I. and Zahar, E. [1976]: 'Why did Copernicus's Programme Supercede Ptolemy's?' in R. Westman (ed.): *The Copernican Achievement*.

Lammers, C. J. [1974]: 'Mono- and poly-paradigmatic developments in natural and Social Sciences' in R. Whitley (ed.): *Social Processes of Scientific Development*, pp. 123–47.

Latsis, S. J. [1972]: 'Situational Determinism in Economics', *The British Journal for the Philosophy of Science*, **23**, pp. 207–45.

McDougall, W. [1908]: *An Introduction to Social Psychology*.

Medawar, P. [1967]: *The Art of the Soluble*.

Mishan, E. J. [1961]: 'Theories of Consumer Behavior: A Cynical View', *Economica*, reprinted in Ekelund, Furubotn and Gramm [1972], pp. 327–37.

Mitchell, W. C. [1910]: 'The Rationality of Economic Activity', *Journal of Political Economy*, **18**, pp. 97–113, 197–216.

Mitchell, W. C. [1937]: *The Backward Art of Spending Money and other Essays*.

Neumann, J. von and Morgenstern, O. [1944]: *The Theory of Games and Economic Behavior*.

Parry, C. E. [1921]: 'A Revaluation of Traditional Economic Theory', *The American Economic Review*, Supplement, **11**, pp. 123–31.

Robbins, L. C. [1935]: *The Nature and Significance of Economic Science*.

Shubik, M. [1970]: 'A Curmudgeon's Guide to Microeconomics', *Journal of Economic Literature*, **8**, pp. 405–34.

Simon, H. A. [1963]: 'Economics and Psychology', in S. Koch (ed.): *Psychology: A Study of a Science*, vol. 6, pp. 685–723.

Simon, H. A. [1959]: 'Theories of Decision-Making in Economics and Behavioral Science', *The American Economic Review*, **49**, pp. 253–83.

Slutzky, E. V. [1915]: 'On the Theory of the Budget of the Consumer', translation reprinted in Ekelund, Furubotn and Gramm [1972].

Stigler, G. J. [1950]: 'The Development of Utility Theory', *Journal of Political Economy*, reprinted in G. J. Stigler (ed.) [1965]: *Essays in the History of Economics*, pp. 66–155.

Stigler, G. J. [1970]: 'The Adoption of the Marginal Utility Theory', in Black, Coats and Goodwin [1970], pp. 305–20.

Stuart, H. W. [1896a]: 'The Hedonistic Interpretation of Subjective Value', *Journal of Political Economy*, **4**, pp. 64–84.

Stuart, H. W. [1896b]: 'Subjective and Exchange Value', *Journal of Political Economy*, **4**, pp. 208–39.

Stuart, H. W. [1917]: 'The Phases of the Economic Interest', in *Creative Intelligence: Essays in the Pragmatic Attitude*, pp. 282–353.

Tobin, J. and Dolbear, F. T. Jr. [1963]: 'Comments on the Relevance of Psychology to Economic Theory and Research', in S. Koch (ed.): *Psychology: A Study of a Science*, vol. 6, pp. 677–84.

Toulmin, S. [1972]: *Human Understanding*.

Tugwell, R. G. [1922]: 'Human Nature and Economic Theory', *Journal of Political Economy*, **22**, pp. 317–45.

Tugwell, R. G. [1924]: 'Experimental Economics', in R. G. Tugwell (ed.): *The Trend of Economics*, pp. 371–42.

Veblen, T. [1932]: *The Place of Science in Modern Civilisation and other Essays*.

Viner, J. [1925]: 'The Utility Concept in Value Theory and its Critics', I and II, *Journal of Political Economy*, reprinted in his collected essays, *The Long View and The Short*, 1958, pp. 177–212.

Watson, J. B. [1914]: *Behavior: An Introduction to Comparative Psychology*.

Whittaker, A. C. [1916]: 'Fetter's Principles of Economics', *The Political Science Quarterly*, **31**, pp. 430–44.

Winch, D. [1970]: 'Marginalism and the Boundaries of Economic Science', in Black, Coats and Goodwin [1970], pp. 59–77.

Wolfe, A. B. [1924]: 'Functional Economics', in Tugwell [1924], pp. 452–82.

Zaltman, G., Pinson, C. R. A. and Angelmar, R. [1973]: *Metatheory and Consumer Research*.

Schools, 'revolutions', and research programmes in economic theory

AXEL LEIJONHUFVUD
UNIVERSITY OF CALIFORNIA

I met Imre Lakatos only once. I will not soon forget him. I still do not know how much economics he knew, but he was not lacking for very definite ideas about the paper he wanted me to write. The script that he ordered was to retell my version of the Keynesian revolution story,[1] attempt to make the issues comprehensible to a largely non-economist audience, reassess my earlier work with the benefit of hindsight, and discuss whether the story can be told to advantage as one of a Kuhnian revolution or as a shift from one Lakatosian research programme to another. I did not want to rehash my views on Keynes again. But the 'Growth of Knowledge' literature holds fascination also for economists – even as the lack of social science case studies as inputs into this philosophical debate leaves us unsure about what exactly we can learn from it. Lakatos felt the time was ripe for philosophers of science to move into the study of the evolution of the social sciences. Economists would have to help out with supplying the case studies. He made a good case. But, mainly, he was simply a hard man to refuse – as those fortunate enough to have known that remarkable man for a longer time will, I am sure, well recall.

So, this paper will attempt what I understood Imre Lakatos to want. Part I deals in general terms with some of the problems in the way of applying recent Growth of Knowledge theories to the history of economics.[2] Part II draws on the Keynesian revolution 'case' for somewhat more concrete illustrations of these problems.

I

I.1

The new Growth of Knowledge theories combine the philosopher's traditional preoccupation with epistemology and the historical study of the actual evolution of the sciences. Methodology of the old, sternly

---

[1] Cf. Leijonhufvud [1968], [1969].

[2] Part I is obviously philosophically amateurish. It cannot be overlooked, but I trust it will be forgiven. It is, in any case, the price philosophers will have to pay for cooperation of economists.

normative brand never did have much appeal to scientific practitioners.[3] The recent Growth of Knowledge literature has gained a wider audience. One may conjecture that it is chiefly the efforts to explain the actual evolution of knowledge, and less the modifications in methodological prescriptions that such inquiry is producing, that accounts for the renewed interest among scientists in the philosophy of science. This is so, at any rate, in my own case. Could these new theories be used to structure an account of the history of economics that would give it a more readily intelligible, more instructive pattern? That is the most interesting question. To the economist, it also appears to have logical primacy, for his appraisal of any methodological prescriptions that the theory advances will be heavily influenced by the answer.

The problem is that philosophers of science tend to combine epistemology and historical analysis so as to make it exceedingly difficult, at least for philosophical dilettantes, to disentangle the normative from the positive aspects of their Growth of Knowledge theories. One starts out reading an often spell-binding historical tale – for they tend to have the merit of writing well – that ends up by degrees as a morality play. The outsider is apt to be similarly captivated by the skillful cut, thrust and parry of the critical debates and controversial exchanges among philosophers of science – but not apt to be helped in this regard. Economists, in particular, who have themselves always to be on guard against mixing normative and positive statements, will be bothered by the Growth of Knowledge discussion's apparent 'drunkard's walk' along and across this sacred line.

Lakatos's methodology of scientific research programmes (MSRP) presents one with this problem in its most difficult form – albeit for reasons that economists (themselves addicted to 'rational reconstructions' of observed behavior) can well appreciate. Science history, in Lakatos, is 'rationally reconstructed' – i.e. explained with the use of the assumption that scientists make the methodologically correct decisions. To the practitioner this may be an on the whole welcome change from those chastizing accounts of how science ought to be done whose stringent criteria not even the 'best' work done in one's field ever seemed to meet. But it would seem to put in prospect much the same predicaments as those produced for economists by their use of the 'maximizing behavior' postulate.

Consider, for example, what attitude to take towards apparently dis-

[3] When I was a child, the itinerant knife-grinder was still a common figure in Sweden. He would show up at the kitchen door and ask: 'Want to have any knives sharpened?' Most often he was told: 'No, thank you, we're all right'. They tended to be persistent characters. Another knock: 'Bet your knives are in bad shape. I know they are. People shouldn't be allowed to use knives like that...' And you would say: 'We are busy today. Please go away'. But soon he knocks again and there he is, demonstrating: 'Look, with my knives you can split hairs!' Some farmers, it was said, would set their dogs on people like that. Some philosophers of science may of course, feel that, without the grindstone always in evidence, charges of vagrancy without visible means of support are inevitable.

confirming empirical evidence. Should the constitutive hypotheses of the rational reconstruction theory all be retained in the 'hard core'? If so, the behavior of scientists in the apparently anomalous historical episode was 'appropriate' to their epistemological situation and the account given of that situation should therefore be reconstructed so as to eliminate the anomaly.[4] Or else, Lakatos's theory – regarded as a positive theory of the evolution of scientific knowledge – should be taken as falsified for the case in question. If rational reconstruction is truly in the hard core, the normative preoccupations of philosophers become superfluous – for scientists act in accordance with methodological prescription 'whether they know it or not'. If, on the other hand, the theory is to be taken as falsifiable, the strictly 'internalist' Lakatosian position is imperilled. The assumption that the history of science can be rationally reconstructed serves the same function of keeping 'externalist rubbish' beyond the pale as does the maximizing behavior postulate in defending the economist from the threat of having to admit psychologists and sociologists to share in his enterprise.[5]

I.2

The philosophical layman reading Kuhn or Lakatos, Hanson or Toulmin finds analogies to, or illustrations from his own field coming to mind in rich profusion. The temptation is strong to rush ahead and dress up one's account of, say, the history of economics in the same terminology. The exercise can be both exciting and genuinely stimulating – but it prejudges the applicability to economics of Growth of Knowledge theories developed to 'fit' physics and biology.

Economists could benefit from the perspectives provided by a theoretically structured account of the history of their field. Philosophers of science, one presumes, would like to draw on the history of the social sciences for independent 'test'-cases for Growth of Knowledge theories originally developed with reference to the natural sciences. If philosophers and economists are to cooperate to mutual advantage, the economists' end of the bargain must include the obligation so to present our doctrine historical episodes that anomalous characteristics calling for further work on the part of philosophers are brought out – or so that 'falsification' (if admitted) is a possibility. Use of the concepts of philosophy of science theories so loose and impressionistic that the history of economics will automatically be made to 'fit' will then not do.

Traditionally, the history of economic doctrines has for the most part been written as a 'straight' historical narrative – as a chronological story of 'progress' by accumulating analytical improvements in a field of inquiry of more or less stable demarcation and with a largely fixed set of questions.

[4] Compare Latsis' discussion of 'situational determinism' in economics, in Latsis [1972]. I have discussed the status of the Maximizing Behavior postulate in economics at length – and using Lakatosian terminology – in *Maximization and Marshall* (forthcoming).
[5] Cf. the papers by H. A. Simon and S. J. Latsis in this volume.

Such narratives are not structured in accordance with any explicit Growth of Knowledge theory[6] – and one cannot presume, therefore, that the categories in terms of which it has been found convenient to organize them will serve the task that Imre Lakatos had in mind.

Consider, for example, the various 'schools' in the history of economics: the French Physiocrats, the British classical, German historical and Austrian schools, the Lausanne, Stockholm, Cambridge, and Chicago schools and several others. Were these associated with distinct Kuhnian paradigms? Do the labels denote Lakatosian research programmes?[7] We also have labels of wider coverage: Marxian economics, Keynesian economics, neoclassical economics. Are these, perhaps, better candidates? The division and subdivision of economics into fields and areas of inquiry cuts across these classifications into 'schools'. Do the cells of the resulting matrix provide more appropriate objects of analysis?

Similarly, the term 'revolution' has become attached to certain developments in economics: the 'marginalist revolution', the 'imperfect competition revolution', the 'Keynesian revolution'. But since these were coined well before T. S. Kuhn and since Kuhn has no such social science episodes in the 'sample' he worked with, there are no strong reasons to presume that our revolutions are of the Kuhnian class. Nor do we have a *prima facie* case for taking them to be shifts from degenerating to progressive research programmes.[8]

The 'doctrines' and 'schools' of economics are not all animals of the same species as, say, Ptolemian and Copernican astronomy or the Phlogiston and Oxygene theories of combustion; nor, moreover, do they very often succeed each other in such clear-cut fashion. In short, the basic objects and events in economics to which we might seek to apply the Growth of Knowledge theories developed for the natural sciences are not defined for us by previous work in the history of economics.

[6] One might perhaps take such accounts of economic doctrine history as 'progress' as reflecting a Growth of Knowledge theory akin to the 'absolutist' epistemology for which Toulmin chooses Gottlieb Frege as representative. Frege was primarily concerned with mathematics and, as a latter-day Platonist, took it as a model for the sciences in general: 'Often it is only after immense intellectual effort, which may have continued over centuries, that humanity at last succeeds in achieving *knowledge of a concept in its pure form,* by stripping off *the irrelevant accretions which veil it from the eye of the mind.*' (Quoted by Toulmin [1972], p. 56.) Economic doctrine histories that concentrate heavily on the history of 'pure' economic analysis (which is essentially mathematical in nature) will tend to read as variations on this theme.

[7] Is the designation of 'schools' by city or country of origin a practice that tends to disappear with the maturation of a science?

[8] Latsis [1972] denies the Theory of Imperfect Competition the status of an independent research programme. He treats it as a branch, degenerating from the start, of the neoclassical Theory of the Firm. I think his judgment of Imperfect Competition theory entirely justified. Note, however, that what he has to say about 'situational determinism' applies as well to the neoclassical theory of Consumer Behavior. It is this approach to the analysis of the behavior of agents in general, rather than just to firms, that may qualify as a research programme.

Economists are, of course, quite capable of enumerating the characteristic features of economic models and used to distinguish between various theories through point-by-point comparisons of such properties. Although a necessary preliminary to the definition of paradigms or research programmes, such lists of model properties do not by themselves accomplish the task. They do not necessarily convey the essential *pattern* of theories nor yield criteria for deciding whether 'different' economic models belong to distinct research programmes or the same programme.

The newer Growth of Knowledge theories emphasize the gestalt of clusters of theories. It is indeed largely this emphasis that is earning them so much attention outside philosophical circles. They address problems of genuine concern to scientific practitioners about which the older, more normatively oriented philosophy of science had relatively little to say. Scientists will on occasion be forced to reflect on the arational gestalt of their more basic beliefs – on the, as it were, 'Gödelian' pattern that is not to be rationalized within the theory itself. From it flows the stuff of which hard-to-settle controversies are made: views on what questions a theory is and is not obliged to answer and on what does and does not constitute evidence; persistent adherence to a theory in the face of falsification of some of its hypotheses; translation-difficulties between 'paradigms'; and Kuhnian (or Frankian) losses.

With these sometimes disturbing aspects of scientific work economists may be more thoroughly acquainted than most. Economics is a controversial subject and our controversies drag on. But controversies may rage within as well as between research programmes. Persistent controversy does not necessarily indicate to us a struggle between contending gestalt-conceptions of what the economic world is like; even if it did, the record of the arguments used by participants may not instruct us in how accurately to characterize the essentials of the two contending programmes.

Learning to do so will have to be the first order of business if we are to make the history of economics one of the proving grounds for Growth of Knowledge theories. But that is not an easy task. There is no – can be no – 'canned programme' for how it is to be performed. In the absence of fixed rules, attempts so to characterize economic theories will themselves be controversial. Professional agreement on the adequacy of such gestalt-characterizations is apt to emerge, if at all, only through successive rounds of 'conjectures and refutations'.[9]

[9] We need to consider such questions as (i) whether two (or more) of the 'schools' traditionally recognized in the history of economic doctrines may not have the same 'hard core' and thus belong to the same research programme, and (ii) whether one and the same 'school' may not over time have shifted some of its main tenets from the 'protective belt' to the 'hard core' (and *vice versa*) and thus in effect transformed itself into a new research programme.

A. LEIJONHUFVUD

I.3

One of the virtues of MSRP is that Lakatos gives us somewhere to start. Given a 'list' of the characteristic properties of an economic model (or of the features that distinguish it from some alternative model), we should ask whether they derive from 'hard core' propositions or from propositions belonging in the 'protective belt'. If all the distinguishing features of two models are of the 'belt'-variety, the models belong in the same family; if some are found lodged in the 'hard cores', we have distinct research programmes to contend with. Now, having the Lakatosian distinction between 'hard core' and 'belt' in hand does not, of course, give us an automatized 'routine' for identifying research programmes in economics. The relevant judgments will often be hard to make. But clear-cut cases should be common. There will be propositions such that, if they are negated, one finds it impossible to 'patch up' the model at all, etc.

Unfortunately, the matter will not end there for examination of economic models will never yield a full description of the corresponding research programmes. The formal structure of the model does not tell us anything about the 'positive heuristic' of the programme. It does not, for example, define the scope claimed for the theory. Statements belonging to the positive heuristic must be regarded, Lakatos tells us, as part of the programme's hard core. But we will not get them off a 'list' of characteristic model properties.

Trying to identify the research programmes of economics from such 'lists' will miss some boats also for another reason. Economists are in the habit of using 'theory' and 'model' as synonymous terms. For the remainder of this paper, I will use them in distinct senses. With 'theory' I will mean a 'patterned set of substantive beliefs' about how the economic system works. (In Lakatosian terms, we can take 'theory' to be what remains of a research programme if we exclude the 'positive heuristic'.) A 'model' is the formal representation of a 'theory', or of a subset of it, or of some aspect of it. We will seldom, if ever, have a 'model' that gives an exhaustive account of the hard core of the corresponding theory. We may miss quite essential characteristics of research programmes, therefore, if we approach the problem only by inference from 'lists' of distinctive model properties.

An example may be more helpful than further disquisition in general terms at this point. The long-lived 'monetarist' controversy is illustrative. Is it the case that 'monetarist' macroeconomics and 'Keynesian' macroeconomics belong to distinct research programmes or are they to be regarded as competing theories fighting it out in the 'protective belt' of the same one? A comparison of models commonly employed to represent the two theories will show, *inter alia*, that the magnitudes hypothesized for certain functional 'elasticities' differ. If that is all there is to it, we should

70

plainly consider them as belonging to the same research programme. Conclusive empirical evidence for the range in which the values of these coefficients actually fall may be hard to come by, but in principle – or so it would seem – both models should attach the same 'meaning' to that evidence when and if obtained. And that should settle the matter.[10] It is as if we had two contending Newtonian theories that differ by the value assumed for the coefficient of gravitation. But, as it turns out, this is not all there is to it. Monetarist 'theory' differs from Keynesian also in including the 'belief' that the economic system will exhibit strong tendencies to converge relatively rapidly to the equilibrium values of its 'real' variables and that the equilibrium values, most specifically of employment and 'real' interest rates, are (to a first approximation, at least) independent of general monetary and fiscal stabilization policies. Now, this qualifies, in my judgment, as a distinct gestalt – the entire 'vision', to use Schumpeter's term, of how the economic system works is at variance from that underlying 'Keynesian economics'.[11] We should recognize the monetarist controversy as involving two distinct research programmes, therefore. But the standard models in terms of which much of the debate has been conducted are static and incorporate no statements about convergence tendencies, adjustment velocities and the like.

In dealing with economic theories, therefore, we have to recognize that, in addition to those hard-core propositions that appear in (or may be directly inferred from) the formal model structure, there are likely to be additional hard-core 'beliefs' belonging to the theory. The former set of hard-core propositions have been through the purgatory of incorporation in (more or less) rigorous formal models; the language in which they are

[10] The most widely known 'monetarist', Professor Milton Friedman, has for a long time consistently voiced the position that 'monetarists' and '(neo)-Keynesians' share essentially the same theory and that their differences all derive from contrasting hypotheses concerning certain crucial empirical magnitudes. (He has also, however, persistently denied that the issues can be defined as a 'simple' matter of the magnitude of the interest-elasticity of the excess demand for money – an otherwise oft-repeated contention in the debate.) In his recent attempts to provide an explicit representation for his theory, accordingly, Friedman chose to use the 'Keynesian', so-called 'IS-LM' framework as his language of formal discourse. Cf. Friedman [1970], [1971].

In my opinion, as indicated in the text, there are 'hard core' differences between the two theories and ones, moreover, that the 'IS-LM' framework will not help us define. Not only are these differences at the 'cosmological' level not accurately represented by the models used, but they will also lead to divergent interpretation of empirical results.

The September/October 1972 issue of the *Journal of Political Economy* was devoted largely to a debate on Friedman's 'monetary framework' between Friedman and five distinguished critics. Professor Tobin opened his critical commentary by thanking Friedman for having '...facilitated communication by his willingness to express his argument in a language widely used in macroeconomics, the Hicksian IS-LM apparatus.' Yet, this round of the debate did little to clarify old issues and settled none. It did provide still more evidence of mutual misunderstandings.

[11] The alternative 'visions' afoot with regard to the efficacy of the system's self-regulating mechanisms will be the main substantive theme pursued in Part II below. Cf. also Leijonhufvud [1973a].

formulated has been honed to fulfil requirements of mathematical consistency with other propositions; they are precise. When an economic theorist uses them, we can know exactly what he is *saying* – although we may be uncertain what he is *talking about* (if ignorant of the hard-core beliefs of his theory that may not appear explicitly in his model). The latter set, however, will – if ever made explicit – be less precisely, more informally stated. The scientific collective may show considerable uncertainty about 'how best to put it'. They are 'hard core' in the minimal sense that they cannot be given up in the face of anomalies while preserving the research programme, but not in the stricter sense that their statement simply cannot be tampered with. They may be apparently quite wooly 'grand generalities', somewhat in the nature of cosmological beliefs.

It will be useful, here, to have a distinct term for these informal and, in modelling contexts, implicit propositions. I will use 'presupposition',[12] and reserve Lakatos's 'hard core statement' for propositions appearing in formal model structures.

I.4

Arriving at a definition of the research programmes of economics by acceptable characterizations of their essential gestalt-conceptions may be the first order of business, but it is far from being the only conundrum in the way of extending the application of Growth of Knowledge theories to economics. Economics is less mature as a discipline – especially as an empirical discipline – than are the natural sciences. It has to cope with a different and in many respects more recalcitrant subject matter. It is only to be expected that the Growth of Knowledge process observed in economics, will exhibit features, some of them methodologically problematical, that are without close analogies in the history – or, at least, 'modern' history – of the physical and biological sciences. Whether these 'atypical' characteristics of the collective learning process pose basic, novel problems to philosophers of science coming to economics[13] from the natural sciences will be a debatable question and is not to be prejudged here.

Two of these problematical features of the Growth of Knowledge process observed in economics are put to the fore in Sir John Hicks's essay in this volume. The first concerns the always controversial question of what role must be accorded 'external' factors in a theory of the development of science. The second relates to the difficulty discussed in Section I.3 above as well as to other problems of 'substance *versus* form' in economic theory which will occupy the rest of Part I.

[12] This is Collingwood's term. Cf., again, Toulmin [1972], where Collingwood is made to serve as the 'relativist' pendant to the portrait of Frege, the 'absolutist'.
[13] Hesitant souls may perhaps want to consult my [1973b] before taking the plunge.

I.5

The universe that is the object of economic inquiry, Hicks points out, is not unchanging, but evolves. The evolution of the economy and the development of economic knowledge occur, moreover, on the same time-scale. Hence, the oft-quoted Einsteinian reflection that 'The Lord is subtle, but not mean' will carry little comfort to economists who have to recognize that, by the time the subtle 'laws' governing the economic system at some particular date have been found out, the system is apt to have undergone institutional transformations that will dictate the renewal of the quest.[14] This, by itself, will suffice to give 'external' factors a role in the history of economics that they lack in the natural sciences and, by that token, render suspect historical accounts structured according to severely 'internalist' Growth of Knowledge theories.[15]

Further considerations might be brought in to buttress the argument, but its point appears indisputable as it stands. One may still question, however, whether conceding the point compels one to renounce 'internalist' epistemological theory constructions altogether.

The incorporation of all 'external' factors, that may be found relevant to the chronological reconstruction of the history of economic doctrines, into a systematic theory of the collective learning process in economics seems an objective beyond reach. The alternative to attempting it would be analogous to what economists routinely do in their own field, namely, to search for some classification of all the relevant explanatory factors into 'exogenous' and 'endogenous' variables such that a useful theory of the 'open' system comprising the relationships among the endogenous variables may be formulated. Models of this sort will be ahistorical in the straightforward sense that the values of the exogenous variables at different dates must be supplied in order to make explanations of observed historical processes feasible.

A well-known metaphor of Knut Wicksell's may be converted to our purposes here. Consider the task of 'explaining' and/or 'predicting' the motion of a rocking-horse. Suppose the strength, timing, etc., of the forces impinging on it obey no known 'laws' – 'you never know what those brats will do next'. Predicting its motion becomes a fool's game. (Here the analogy to economics is a bit too close for comfort.) But from the curvature of its runners, the distribution of its weight, etc., it will be possible to construct a model explaining the response to any given shocks. That is

[14] This is only to say, of course, that the economist's theory tends to take much of the institutional setting as 'given' and thus fails to comprise the 'laws of change' for the institutional framework of economic activity. (I am not denying that some worthwhile exploration has begun into these problem areas.) The Good Lord may not be mean, but if he is too subtle for you, the result is pretty much the same. The problems arising from the (so far) unmanageable complexity of the economist's subject matter we postpone to the subsections to follow.

[15] MSRP is, of course, 'severely internalist' and in this respect, to my mind, in clear line of descent from the Vienna Circle via Popper.

about what macroeconomists could hope to accomplish in the way of a 'general theory' – except for the added complication that their horse is 'live' and grows and develops. One might set a similarly limited ambition for theories of the Growth of Knowledge. They would then be 'internalist', in a sense,[16] and relevant 'external' factors would have to be brought in *ad hoc* in explaining the particular timing, and so on, of historical episodes.

The pursuit of such a goal will be based on an 'ultimate presupposition', the adoption of which is an act of faith, namely, that 'there exists a horse', i.e., that there exists a potentially identifiable subsystem, with stable rules of interactions among its elements that may be studied separately from remaining relevant factors. What this requires in the present context is that 'internalist' criteria are in fact the predominant determinants of the survival probability of concepts and ideas and of economists' allegiance to research programmes. If political expedience, ideological advocacy or other, more honorable, 'external' considerations significantly bias the selection among intellectual mutations, it will not work. We need be alert, therefore, to the possibility that even if an 'internalist' theory of the Growth of Economic Knowledge appears to do well in 'reconstructing' developments of recent decades, it may be entirely inadequate in dealing with the evolution of doctrines in periods ante-cedent to the academic 'professionalization' of the field.

In Part II, we deal only with recent decades. The remainder of this paper will be governed by the 'internalist presupposition'. Note that this does not entail the fusion of descriptive and normative theory discussed in Section I.1. I will assume that the collective selection of ideas, concepts, models, etc., for survival and development is governed by the 'internal logic' of economic inquiry as perceived by a largely academic corps of professionals. But the question whether the internal criteria used by economists are also 'epistemologically rational' in the sense of Lakatos (for example) is left open. A 'rational' reconstruction is necessarily 'internalist', but the converse must not be assumed to hold.

I.6

Professor Hicks also stresses the necessarily simplified structure of useful economic theories, i.e., their selectivity with regard to the 'facts' and relationships included. The economist's models are but schematic or 'partial' representations of the system he studies; the complexity of the economy is of an order that makes 'general' representation impossible.[17]

---

[16] 'In a sense' because the defense of concentration on internal factors – at least as a temporary strategy – essayed here demands that the definition of the line between 'internal' and 'external' factors be determined, not on *a priori* grounds, but according to whatever division between 'endogenous' and 'exogenous' variables is found to be feasible in theory construction.

[17] The ultimate ambition of 'economics' is similarly limited – the basic notion of an 'economic system' is that of a particular set of interactions abstracted (by procedures never clearly specified) from the totality of interactions among individuals in the more complex

External events will from time to time cause the focus of professional attention to shift from one family of models, one type of representation, to another. But such shifts in the concentration of research do not signify the victory of one research programme over another. There will be problems and policy-issues – for a time less pressing but apt to recur – for which the models in decline provide a better engine of analysis than do the models in ascendancy. The Kuhnian losses in prospect were one analytical tradition to be promoted to the exclusion of all others are seen to be prohibitive.[18] Hence, in economics, we find several analytical traditions surviving side-by-side.

Economic models 'illumine different things', as Hicks puts it. They are 'partial' in the sense of highlighting different aspects of the same real world process and not just in the straightforward sense that the theory of optics deals with only part of the physicist's universe. Nor are the different analytical traditions in economics – Hicks's plutology and catallactics make perfect examples – complementary in the sense that the wave and particle theories of light are. Each of the latter give precise representation for a well-defined class of phenomena. Although the economist has to make use of both plutology and catallactics and finds each tradition to have a comparative advantage for different classes of problems, neither one provides a precise description for any of the processes that are the subject of inquiry. Actual economic systems are of a higher order of *complexity* than are the models of economics.[19] Economics, so far, makes do with 'surrogate' models.

social system. There is a 'high-level presupposition', adopted by act of faith, here too – to wit, that economic activities are governed by their own 'internal logic' that allows their study to be usefully separated from that of teenage courtship patterns and other social interactions that, in principle, *might* complicate the economist's task beyond what he can manage.

The 'Maximizing Behavior postulate' has already been mentioned as an important link in the boundary defenses of economics. Jevons' so-called 'Law of Indifference' is another instructive example. It states that 'sellers will sell to the highest bidder and buyers buy from the source with the lowest offer-price'. Its standard use is as a 'harmless', technical postulate supporting the hypothesis of convergence to uniqueness of transactions-prices in a given market – a hypothesis needed, in turn, for 'supply-and-demand' analysis. But it also has a sociological interpretation, namely, that transactors interact in markets on the basis of 'most favorable price' and, in so doing, ignore relationships of status, kinship, caste, and so on. Nepotism is not a significant determinant of transactions-prices in the resulting theory, for example. So: sociology is kept out. Clearly, here too, we have an 'internalist' (as it were) theory that may work well for certain periods and societies but not for others.

One may suggest from this that a study of the boundary-maintaining mechanisms of a discipline should be capable of producing important clues to some of its high-level presuppositions (or hard-core propositions).

[18] 'Decline' and 'ascendancy' here because 'degenerating' and 'progressive' (in precise Lakatosian sense) would be inappropriate.

[19] Beginning students of economics often have a tendency to rebel against the more obvious and typical abstractions and simplifications of economic theory. Our textbooks, therefore, tend to include standardized sermons on the theme 'all useful theory is abstract', and illustrated, for example, by reference to the unwieldiness of relief maps built to natural

In economics, the *substance* and the *form* of theories are less tightly linked than in the physical sciences. In physics (or so the outsider supposes), practitioners would relatively seldom find reason to distinguish between the substance of a hypothesis and the formal statement of it.[20] There may, indeed, be only 'one way to put it' (accurately) and all other formulations are, at best, crude metaphors suitable only in expositions directed to a popular audience. To economists, however, the distinction is anything but a matter to be left to the rarified speculations of philosophers – it is a workaday problem. Our beliefs about the economic world are one thing; what we manage to 'catch' of these beliefs in formally structured representation is not altogether the same thing.

As a consequence, economists are forever concerned with the limitations of the languages they use to express what they know – or think they know – about their subject-matter.[21] The so-called 'index-number problem' will be the best-known example of a constantly used device that suppresses aspects of theoretical structure or loses empirical information that the economists, in either case, will know to be 'relevant' – but finds himself unable to handle. Another example has already been mentioned: the use of atemporal equilibrium constructions and the comparative static method for the analysis of questions pertaining to real-time 'dynamic' processes. Both illustrate a general and recurring issue, namely, how best to 'trade-off' analytical or empirical manageability against precision of conceptual representation or of empirical reference (to actually obtainable

scale and in complete detail. The fully acculturated economic student will gain confidence from recalling that Newton ignored the color of falling objects and got away with it.

It might be preferable to illustrate the relation that most economic models bear to their subject-matter by considering the use of models drawn from sciences dealing with systems of a relatively low order of complexity in fields grappling with systems of a qualitatively higher order of complexity. The use of mechanical models in anatomy and physiology is one such example – and it allows two points to be convincingly made: (i) the anatomist must handle the model with the same precision and 'rigor' as is done in mechanics, if it is to be of any use; (ii) even though that is not 'all there is' to the subject, refusing to utilize relevant models drawn for 'simpler' fields means ignorance, not 'wisdom'.

Even the anatomist's use of mechanics may be too flattering a comparison for general purpose dissemination. The more frequent use of models drawn from less complex systems is strictly analogical. Terminological vestiges in modern economics bear witness to the historical importance to the field's development of the practice – 'equilibrium' (like the political scientist's 'balance of power') is an example. Some early influential Keynesians favored hydraulic systems analogies in explaining the behavior of the simple 'expenditure-flows' Keynesian system. And so on.

[20] A philosophical issue still remains, of course. Cf., especially, N. R. Hanson [1958], chapter 5.

[21] These mathematical languages will in some important cases have been historically developed to serve some empirical science dealing with less complex systems. The calculus and classical mechanics (again) is the best example. The mathematically amateurish economist – of which there are quite a few – may be aware that the use of this language forces him to adopt some assumptions he would rather do without (for example, continuity and second-degree differentiability), but may not be alert to more subtle incongruities of 'form versus substance'. On this, cf. Karl Menger [1973].

data). The two last-mentioned objectives, moreover, are seldom entirely compatible. The one only too often has to be compromised in pursuit of the other. The most rigorous axiomatic models are frequently incapable of direct confrontation with data. Econometric models will have the measurements specified that are to yield the data for the values of every variable; in achieving that necessary objective, however, liberties often have to be taken with the strict logic of economic theory.[22]

The imperfect congruence between substantive 'theory' and formal 'models' means that the latter require *interpretation* and that this is not simply a task of defining variables and primitive terms. Two very noticeably different models may be found securely rooted in the same 'hard core', for simplification in pursuit of tractability will proceed by different paths depending on what is the main problem that the analyst seeks to bring into focus. Spurious disagreement is a nuisance but apt to be dissolved sooner or later; spurious agreement creates no 'collective dissonance' and is, therefore, a more serious matter. Two economic models may be similar, even identical,[23] in form, but be subject to substantively different interpretations. Interpretation of two very similar models in conformance with the intentions of their authors may, indeed, show them to derive from mutually inconsistent 'cosmological presuppositions' and, hence, to be products of different research programmes.

On the other hand, the imperfect correspondence between the models of pure theory and those that are the vehicles of quantitative empirical work means that decisive falsification or convincingly accumulating confirmation of economic theories are hard to come by. In economics, theoretical traditions survive side-by-side, as Hicks emphasized, because their methods of analysis provide complementary ways of structuring perceptions of complex economic reality. To this point one should add Joan Robinson's sobering counterpoint: 'In a subject where there is no agreed procedure for knocking out error, doctrines have a long life.'[24]

These problems of the substance of beliefs, the forms of their expression, and their confrontation with reality are, of course, not novel in kind. They have long been the stuff of epistemological inquiry. Nonetheless, the degree to which they force themselves on the average practitioner and

---

[22] The concerted drive for greater precision – 'quantification' was the motto – in economics may be dated back to the founding of the Econometric Society some 40 years ago. Its highly influential founders presumably envisaged mathematical economic analysis and statistical empirical measurement to develop hand-in-glove as in the physical sciences. In fact, mathematical economic theory and applied econometrics have developed as separate and distinct subfields of economics.

[23] The Walrasian and the Marshallian versions of the basic supply-and-demand model for an 'isolated market' are indistinguishable in the static form in which they are usually presented. Their divergent interpretations are discussed in my [1974*b*], a revised version of which will be included in *Maximization and Marshall* (forthcoming). A somewhat desperate attempt to squeeze the gist of the matter into a few pages can be found in Leijonhufvud [1974*a*].

[24] Joan Robinson [1963], p. 79.

shape the collective style of the pursuit of knowledge in economics will pose problems for the extension of natural science-based Growth of Knowledge theories to the field.

I.7

Lakatos makes empirical success with novel predictions or old anomalies the mark of the 'progressiveness' of a research programme. It may be fair to say that, in so doing, he is simply making explicit what most philosophical students of the natural sciences would take for granted. In economics, this pattern is much less prominent and certainly not exclusively predominant. Quantitative empirical work has a less direct bearing on the appraisal of theories. Genuinely novel predictions are, moreover, relatively rarely made; what the 'progressive' economist is usually engaged in is trying to incorporate more 'things that have been well-known for a long time' (or taken to be so) into a logically consistent structure. And ordinarily these 'things' are not quantified phenomena but qualitative 'patterns of behavior'. In economic parlance, a 'new theory' need not refer to a set of substantively novel hypotheses and conjectures; it is, in fact, more likely to refer to a 'new' mathematical language applied to 'old' subject matter. A very great proportion of what economists consider theoretical work – or work in so-called 'pure theory' – concerns the exploration of the potentialities of formal languages for ordering perceived economic realities.

As noted in Section I.1, Lakatos's MSRP is at once both normative and positive. At least in a first pass at the social sciences, it appears advisable to keep these two aspects of the 'progressivity' of research programmes distinct.

From the standpoint of positive Growth of Knowledge theory, aiming to explain the historical development of a discipline but not to appraise it, we might term a programme 'progressive' when it gives people in the field 'something new and worthwhile to do'. In judging the progressiveness in this sense of a programme, one might then view it as a historical sociologist of science would. A progressive programme should, for example, attract an increasing proportion of the members of a profession and especially of the best talent (most especially, perhaps, of the best young talent). Here, then, it is a fact that, in economics, professional interest and allegiance is, to a large degree, commanded by work in 'pure theory'. Such work may demonstrate, for instance, that an already familiar formal language can, by extension of well-known models, cope with phenomena hitherto given recognition only in *ad hoc*, unsystematic fashion. Or it may show that a 'new' language is similarly capable of consistently ordering a richer picture of perceived reality and, perhaps, infuse 'meaning' into economic behavior patterns previously neglected (as 'not making much sense') by economists.

From the standpoint of normative epistemology, the basic question is whether the actually observed behavior pattern of a disciplinary collective is 'progressive' in the sense of producing Growth of *validated* Knowledge. Empirical confirmation of novel predictions, I have just suggested, plays less of a role in making economists change the direction of their work than it does in Lakatos's account of 'progressiveness' in the natural sciences. Thus, we have what appears to be a clear-cut issue: Either we weaken Lakatos's conception of progressiveness so as to accommodate the actual behavior of economists or else we recognize that one (at least) of the social sciences will not lend itself to 'rational reconstruction' along Lakatosian lines.

The reasons for insisting that the two aspects of 'progressivity' be taken one at a time go beyond the point just made. The question of whether a strong epistemological rationale can be provided for the actual behavior-pattern of a disciplinary group is not necessarily best answered with a 'yes' or a 'no'. The criteria to which the group is seen to accord prestige may enable it to realize Growth of Knowledge in some directions but to miss out in others. They may slow the collective learning process down without halting it or making it veer-off across the 'demarcation' line into pretentious 'gobbledygook'. To an economist, at any rate, it seems natural to ask whether a scientific profession may not misallocate its endeavours without altogether wasting them in epistemically irrational pursuits.

Given the formal difficulties in the way of providing suitable representations for dynamic systems of a high order of complexity, the prestige and priority that economists accord work in 'pure theory' can hardly be totally 'irrational'. But it might be overdone. While many of those inside and outside the economics profession who habitually criticize 'mathematical game-playing', etc., may have little appreciation of the significance of the technical limitations of language that theorists seek to overcome, the chances are that the enterprise as a whole would nonetheless gain from a greater number of hardworking empirical positivists – or even 'naive falsificationists'.

I.8

Another problem (to the amateur, at least) relates to the issue just outlined. 'Hard cores' do not always spring fully armed from the brow of some venerated Thunderer. Surely, they usually take a considerable time to 'harden'. Yet, Lakatos tells us little about this 'hardening process'. We probably need a theoretical account of it and criteria for recognizing it (before it is completed), for the process whereby a hard core hardens is apt, I believe, to bear at least some superficial resemblances to the activities mentioned by Lakatos as characterizing a 'degenerating' research programme.[25]

[25] Note, again, that if we are to 'rationally reconstruct' the choices that scientists make between programmes we have to presuppose that they can recognize which is which.

In Section I.3 above, a distinction between 'presuppositions' and propositions of 'strictly hard-core' nature was suggested. A Lakatosian hard-core proposition is logically irrefutable and empirically untestable within the research programme in question. To adherents of the programme it is – it has become – a 'necessary condition for the intelligibility of the phenomena'.[26] A presupposition must be treated as indubitable as long as a given research programme is to be pursued. Without it, the programme 'would not make sense'.[27] Belief in it, we may still suppose, could be of a more 'reasonable' and 'hypothetical' character. That is by the way, however. Here, we want to stress that presuppositions 'underlie' the formal structure of theory, rather than being incorporated in it, and are in varying degrees 'informally' phrased. Consequently, while they have to be treated as 'indubitable', the strictly logical categories of 'irrefutability' or 'refutability' do not apply to them.[28]

Consider, then, the possibility that the maturation of a successful research programme may involve the gradual transformation of 'presuppositions' into 'hard-core propositions', as the term is (with some license) used here. One aspect of this process *may* be an unbroken string of empirical confirmations of hypotheses newly deduced with the help of the proposition in question. Another aspect, however, would *necessarily* be entailed – namely, considerable work on the 'refinement' of the formal language of representation. Common-sense definition of terms and an informal syntax will not produce statements having the character of 'mathematical necessity'.

Work on formal languages for the representation of phenomena is

[26] Cf. N. R. Hanson's discussion ([1958], chapter 5) of Newton's Laws as 'statements (that) are in some sense empirical, yet they seem often to resist the idea of disconfirmation: evidence against them is sometimes impossible to conceive'. Compare, Toulmin [1972], p. 70: 'For what would be the effect of abandoning the general axioms of Newton's dynamics entirely? To do so would not merely falsify a large number of statements about "forces", and their effects on the "momenta" of bodies...It would actually strip these terms of meaning, so that the statements in which they were employed would cease to arise, be operative, or even make sense.'
In my forthcoming *Maximization and Marshall*, I discuss the 'Maximizing Behavior Postulate' as an example in economics of a proposition that has (fairly recently) become a 'necessary condition for the intelligibility of the phenomena'.

[27] 'The substitution effect is always negative' is an example of a hard-core proposition (although not a primitive, but a derived one) in the sense that it cannot be negated without making nonsense of the formal structure of neoclassical theory. As an example of a presupposition, consider 'A market economy is a self-regulating (or "equilibrating") system.' *Some such phrase* would indicate a belief that one treats as indubitable for doing equilibrium analysis – an activity which otherwise would be merely an intellectual game. But its formulation could be varied; the terms appearing in the phrase do not have the 'hardness' and carry none of the 'inevitability' of statements taken from rigorous formal models.

[28] A presupposition such as 'the market economy is self-regulating' will tend to be 'untestable' in the common-sense meaning of the term, namely, no one can formulate and execute a test that will be collectively agreed upon to be decisive. It is not 'untestable' in the strictly 'hard-core' sense that would apply to Newton's Laws in classical mechanics, namely, that any conceivable experiment must use the hard-core concepts of that very theory to structure the observations to be utilized.

basically mathematical in character. A lot of effort is expended to assure that the theorems proposed will be 'necessarily true' once the language is only used 'correctly'. It is not surprising, then, that much of the work in pure economic theory is better described by Lakatos's 'Proofs and Refutations'[29] than by his later MSRP. 'Monster-barring' and the rest of the tactics that Lakatos named in such colorful fashion will be intriguingly familiar to those acquainted with the advanced economic theory literature.

The development of the language conventions, without which 'strictly irrefutable' hard-core propositions are impossible, pose a problem in applying Lakatos's theory (to economics, at least) in that the process will resemble that of degeneration. It is fairly clear that it will so appear to someone unsympathetic to the emerging research programme. What will this someone witness? That his criticisms and objections are increasingly met with the assertion of 'tautologies'. That anomalies are being 'accommodated' (through 'verbal legerdemain') and that certain hypotheses are gradually hedged around so as to remove all possibility of falsification. And, in some instances, of course, the enterprise seen to exhibit these repugnant symptoms *is* going nowhere in particular.

II

The 'Keynesian revolution' once again, then. It is a story that has been told in various ways to yield as many different messages. How the 'true' story should be told is, after forty years, still a 'live' question. If we could be certain of the answer to it, the agenda for research in macroeconomic theory would look much clearer than it now does. That is what gives the question its continuing importance. It is a matter of understanding our past trek, so as to know better the present position of the subject, and be able to chart a course for the future.[30] Versions of the story that do no more than tell a tale of brave, bygone days and a battle over issues now as 'dead' as the hero we may reject less as useless to us but as false. If the story does nothing to inform us about present-day problems in economic theory, it cannot be right.

The question of what the 'true' story of the Keynesian revolution might be only remains 'live', of course, because some of the original substantive issues have not been laid to rest. With our part of the woods full of sharpshooters gunning for them these past forty years, they would have been killed-off for sure, had we ever had them truly pinpointed in our sights. We may infer, therefore, that the natural habitat of these difficulties lies on that murky 'presuppositional' level where a clean shot is never to be

[29] Cf. Lakatos [1963].
[30] In recent years, a rising chorus of voices, equally as dissatisfied as distinguished, has urged economists to find a way out of the 'present position of the subject' with as much dispatch as can be mustered. For a sample of representative references, cf. the introduction to Clower [1975].

had. Could we but once truly trap them in a tight model, they would be done for. Sundry reports of successful captures notwithstanding, that has not been accomplished yet. 'Incongruities of form and substance' let them slip the net.

What did Keynes achieve – what was his contribution to economic theory? This question has been the favorite Snark of the hunt. The standard method has been to try to box the issues in by systematic comparisons of 'Keynesian' and 'classical' models; in so far as the quarry has eluded this pursuit, the presumption has been that more 'rigorous' and precise formulations of these models would do it.

> That's exactly the way I have always been told
> that the capture of Snarks should be tried!

The debate has coincided with the mathematization of pure economic theory. The bright ethos of that movement has cast a shadow of disreputability on the informalities of meta-language discourse. A certain abstemiousness from it has made real obstacles of 'translation difficulties' between 'paradigms' that might perhaps have been less debilitating. As a result, the purely theoretical aspect of the Keynesian debate became, in effect, a straight contest for hegemony between two theoretical languages.

> 'The question is,' said Alice, 'whether you *can* make words mean so many different things.'
> 'The question is,' said Humpty Dumpty, 'which is to be master – that's all.'

In this contest, the Keynesian language – starting with the handicaps of most 'revolutionary' tongues, and with its development entrusted to people who would rather save the world by action than by words – lost and lost badly.

An informal and improvised meta-language makes an uncomfortably blunt instrument of inquiry. But, perchance, 'presuppositional' Snarks must be bludgeoned by such means? The sketch that follows proceeds on that presumption.[31]

II.1

The first order of business should be to identify the research programmes that have had a role in the story. In important respects, the plots of various versions of the story differ simply as a function of the size of the cast of 'characters'. This matter had better be considered first, before an attempt is made to explain what it all has been about.

The simplest version puts but two actors on the stage – 'Keynesian economics' and an opposing programme, variously labelled 'classical' (by

---

[31] Below, I will have to state in crudely categorical form a number of points argued at greater length – and somewhat more 'reasonably' – elsewhere. Non-economist readers should be warned that this part of the paper does *not* represent a summary of 'generally accepted views' on Keynesian economics.

Keynes), 'neoclassical', or 'orthodox' economic theory, etc. Both programmes change and evolve as the story unfolds – appearing, for example, in the postwar acts in the guises of 'macrotheory' and 'microtheory' – but are here regarded as maintaining identities throughout that are readily recognizable even though the definition of their respective 'hard cores' might remain uncertain and in some dispute.

This 'Keynes and the Classics' version of the tale will bear telling in Kuhnian terms – up to a point.[32]

(i) By external, sociology of science criteria, it was without doubt a genuine Kuhnian revolution. It cannot be disputed: ask anyone who was there! The period had a high incidence of 'conversions', *Sturm und Drang* among the young, resistance from the old, etc.[33] Perhaps, it should be particularly emphasized that 'translation difficulties' were very much in evidence, since this particular theme of Kuhn's has found so little favor with critics.

(ii) Such 'external' professional behavior will necessarily have some strictly 'internal' counterpart. Economists do not migrate from their bases of assured competence unless the new pastures beckon with something worthwhile to do. A massive migration into 'Keynesian economics' did take place and the work done by the migrants within its fences was different from what they would otherwise have done or did before. And it would be quite ridiculous to suppose that some genuine Growth of Knowledge did not take place – and in novel, worthwhile directions.[34]

---

[32] I am indebted here to J. Ronnie Davis for whose paper 'Was There a Keynesian Revolution?', delivered at the 1973 Midwestern Economic Association Meetings, I was (*in absentia*) a discussant. Davis put his question in a strictly Kuhnian sense and argued a flatly negative answer. While I disagreed with him on a number of important points, I benefited from the interesting and provocative way in which he made his case.

Kuhn has been the subject of a bit of a fad in economics (as in other fields). The profession at large has become rather tired of facile employments of Kuhnian terminology (I was one of the earlier sinners), while those few of its members who have been intrigued enough with Kuhn to sample the subsequent philosophical discussion have become rather disenchanted with the evolution of Kuhn's position.

I ought perhaps to confess, therefore, that I remain an admirer of Kuhn's first edition. At one time, I found Kuhn (the historian) a great help in getting logical positivism into a more useful perspective – which was and remains enough! *Pace* Kuhn (the philosopher), I still have little sympathy with the criticisms, for example, of Masterman [1965]. Kuhn's original version comes off best if read as a work of historical induction. Twenty-odd descriptive statements to delineate the 'novel' class of empirical phenomena named 'paradigms' is then not too much. Read as a piece of philosophical model-building, twenty-odd definitions of a central primitive term for the deductive structure seems a bit much – and the difficulties will not end there. Thus, my attempt at assessing Kuhn's work has to end on a plaintive note: may one not read the work in the way that gives the best value – even if the author, *ex post*, won't cooperate?

[33] Cf. A. W. Coats [1969]; J. R. Davies [1973], and for an eloquent personal testimonial, P. A. Samuelson [1946].

[34] Note, however, that the macroeconomic work from the 1940s and early 1950s that has had the most lasting impact drew strength from two 'research programmes' that had developed quite independently of Keynesian theory, namely the work of Simon Kuznets (especially) under National Bureau of Economic Research auspices and what might

(iii) Next, we come to 'Kuhnian (or Frankian) losses'. The fact that they figure importantly in the story is a plus for Kuhn. But they play a largely *latent* role with consequences quite different from the typical Kuhnian scenario. The losses in prospect from an outright abandonment of 'orthodox' theory in favor of the Keynesian were of such magnitude as could not seriously be contemplated. For the central orthodox theory of value and resource allocation with its innumerable applications to important guns-or-butter issues the 'revolutionary' Keynesian doctrine provided no sufficiently coherent and well-developed substitute.

As a consequence, Keynesian economics could not decisively displace orthodox economics. Instead, both survived in what in retrospect – given the underlying 'presuppositional' discord between them – seems rather implausible comfort. Mutual tolerance was helped in part by institutional fence-building. From the early 1950s on, most teaching curricula split general economic theory right down the middle into separate, largely unrelated 'micro' and 'macro' segments.[35]

(iv) The next act of the drama will not fit the Kuhnian scenario at all. On the theoretical front, it deals largely with the 'Counterrevolution' (Clower) and 'Neoclassical Resurgence' (Eisner).[36] By the late fifties, Keynesianism had been defused by a revived 'neoclassicism' and gradually stagnated.[37] Significant empirical work, regarded by the profession at large as within the Keynesian frame, continued but on the basis of theoretical ideas derived from postwar 'neoclassicism'. The work by Modigliani, Brumberg and Ando on the consumption function and by Jorgensen on the investment function are examples. By the mid-sixties, moreover, macroeconomics was drawing most of its excitement from the challenge posed by another 'resurgence' of pre-Keynesian ideas – the 'monetarist' or 'new quantity' theory of Friedman, Schwartz, Cagan, Brunner and Melzer.

This, I take it, will not fit easily within the Kuhnian schema. Kuhn's revolutions displace the respective pre-existing orthodoxies permanently and definitively. In his natural science based sample, there are no stories of short-lived triumphs – of the Oxygene theory being stalemated, for example, by 'resurgent phlogistonism'. MSRP, on the other hand, does

perhaps be called the 'Econometric Society programme' (for which the leading center was the Cowles Commission, especially during Jacob Marschak's tenure as research director).

[35] This 'split' would have seemed odd to earlier generation economists – and to Keynes who had hoped that his *General Theory* would serve to heal the (rather differently defined) split between the theories of Money and of Value.

[36] Cf. Clower [1965], Eisner [1958].

[37] 'Degenerated' would be inappropriate here for the process was not marked by those accommodations to the new findings of an alternative and progressive programme that Lakatos stresses as symptoms of degeneration. There was not much forthcoming to which such accommodations would be required, for postwar neoclassicism no more addressed the main problems within the sphere of Keynesian macroeconomics than the latter did the traditional problems of microeconomics.

not present us with this problem. Lakatos emphatically admitted the possibility of reviving a programme temporarily eclipsed by the competition and the 'rationality' of keeping degenerating programmes alive with this prospect in view.

But this tale of two programmes will not make a satisfactory version of the Keynesian revolution story even in Lakatosian terms. The so-called 'neoclassical synthesis' – of which more below – whereby the supposedly older programme regained hegemony in theory from the Keynesians did not signify the hunting down and laying to rest of the presuppositional Snark. It was the adoption, rather, of a formula whereby one could – for a time – in decency forget about him and let him run loose. The version that ends here cannot be the whole story. For the Keynesian revolution is still unfinished. A more useful tale will have more than just two protagonists.

My 1968 book, *On Keynesian Economics and the Economics of Keynes*, was concerned with the problems and conundrums resulting from the collision of Keynesianism with the, by then stronger, 'neoclassical' programme. The then commonly taught 'image' of the Keynesian past failed to suggest directions out of the theoretical stagnation of the programme that by the mid-sixties was so clearly evident. My own search for clues in the history of the Keynesian debates led to the conclusion that this image was seriously over-simplified and in parts false. One theme of the book – dramatized by the title, perhaps, to a dysfunctional extent – became the distinction drawn between Keynes's theory and the subsequently developing, largely American, school of Keynesian economics.[38] The distinction is an important one to make, I contended, because it was this later version of Keynesianism that succumbed so readily to the 'neoclassical synthesis'.[39]

[38] The British Keynesians, centered at Keynes's old Cambridge headquarters, should properly be left out of this part of the story. While their rendering of Keynes may be more true to the original, the Cambridge school has for some considerable time figured more prominently as critics of the 'neoclassical' programme than as active contributors to the ongoing work in macroeconomics. As a consequence, the influence of this school has, in the later stages of the Keynesian debates, been relatively minor.

[39] This distinction I sought to drive home by exhausting, if not exhaustive, exegetical documentation referring to a 'list' of propositions that, while they had become commonplace in the later 'Keynesian' literature (and were with some frequency attributed to Keynes), were not in fact integral to the theory that Keynes advanced. (For a brief – and hard-drawn – version of this 'list', cf. my [1969].) Much of the critical attention that the book has received has concentrated on these matters with a resultant tendency to end up in argument about 'what Keynes really meant'. For my purposes, it was and remains important to insist on what 'Keynes did not say' (but which later Keynesians got in the habit of saying). In the case of a yet not fully 'hardened' programme, it makes a difference. The *General Theory* most certainly was not fully 'hardened'; it will not lend itself to a tightly formalized interpretation – any fully consistent axiomatic 'model' of the theory of that work is bound to leave something out or bring something in that was not there.

In significant respects, the *General Theory* was open-ended. Its significance today (if any) will lie, therefore, in 'what Keynes did *not* say...' What must be insisted on, in other words, is that the *General Theory* did not dictate the subsequent step-by-step development of 'Keynesian economics' into the particular stalemated stage in which, some 20 or 25

Though somewhat short of eternal, the 'triangle' of Keynes, 'the Keynesians', and the 'neoclassicists', entertained in my 1968 work, allowed for a richer and more realistic plot than can be made out of a see-saw context between Keynesianism and neoclassicism. But three protagonists are still not enough.

Elements of another needed distinction were pointed out in my book, but it may be that less than enough was made of the matter and that a more systematic appraisal is required. Pre-Keynesian economic theory must be clearly distinguished from the picture of it propagated by Keynes and some of the later Keynesians. The propagandistic distortions committed in the cause and course of the revolution were often severe. While the Keynesian version of 'classical theory' is not, of course, a research programme in a historical sense, this strawman must be allowed to play his role in the story. To refuse him recognition would be as playing Hamlet without the father's ghost. It remains influential to this day and will not be easily dislodged from the textbooks. When this historically distorted image of pre-Keynesian economics is used as the frame of reference for defining and explaining Keynes's contribution to theory – as has so often been done – one cannot hope for an understanding of the Keynesian revolution that would help us get a grasp on contemporary problems in theory.

The errors, omissions and misjudgments, that with the 'benefit' of hindsight I now see as bound to undermine the value to modern students of the doctrine-historical parts of the book, almost all stem from the undifferentiated notion of 'neoclassical economics' that pervades it.

Firstly, it is necessary clearly to distinguish pre-Keynesian 'orthodox' economics from the 'neoclassical' theory that has been predominant in the post-war period. The latter is more accurately referred to as 'neo-Walrasian' economic theory. Of all the 'schools' mentioned in this paper, the modern neo-Walrasian school may be the one with the best claim to being a research programme with a distinct hard core, protective belt and positive heuristic.[40] It is this programme that pulled off the 'counter-revolution'. But it was *not* the 'orthodoxy' against which the original revolution was directed. The pre-Keynesian 'neoclassicism' from which Keynes sought to break away was not neo-Walrasian.

Secondly, this 'neoclassical' economics of the 1930s was not a homogeneous doctrine.[41] A number of 'schools', dating from 'marginalist

years later, it found itself. Either there are 'alternative futures' to the one realized open to us in the *General Theory* – or the book is dead and of no possible help to anyone.

There will remain those who insist that textbook Keynesianism presents us with the 'real' Keynes skilfully embalmed by the faithful. Perhaps so – but have not the guts been removed from the mummy?

[40] Once more, I can only refer the reader to my forthcoming *Maximization and Marshall*.
[41] As usage has developed, the term 'neoclassical' has in fact been rendered all but totally useless for historical purposes.

revolution' days, were still distinctly recognizable despite cross-breeding and hybridization. Marshall's school dominated in Britain, the Austrian on the continent, with the Walrasian or Lausanne school everywhere a distant third. Among the then productive hybrids, one should mention the Stockholm school and the LSE school, with Austrian and Walrasian bloodlines most prominent in the former and Marshallian and Austrian in the latter. In most economics departments of repute, one must imagine, 'the' theory that students were taught would contain strains from all of these albeit mixed to local tastes.[42]

The analytical criticism and theoretical polemics in Keynes's *General Theory* were directed against the Marshallian school in which he had been trained and which at Cambridge – not so incidentally – had developed into about as good an example of British intellectual 'insularity' as one is likely to find. Keynes's particular target was in fact Marshall's successor at Cambridge, A. C. Pigou – although his 'classical doctrine' was hardly a fair representation even of Pigou's views. The very fact that Keynes advanced his new theory in opposition to the older Cambridge school means that he still shared many presuppositions as well as analytical method with the Marshallian school. This is of significance to an accurate rendering of the Keynesian revolution story, because the Marshallian school had begun to degenerate and was to be easily (and without climactic confrontation) swept aside by the neo-Walrasian programme which differed from it in ways that we are gradually coming to realize are important.

II.2

What then was it all about? What was – and remains – the substantive problem to which these controversies pertain?

My label for it is 'The Coordination of Economic Activities'.[43] It should be said at once, however, that this label refers to as nearly an 'internalist' conception of the problem as seems at all feasible. Thus con-

---

[42] It may be that we will eventually come in retrospect to regard two or more of these 'schools' as competing and essentially incompatible research programmes. That, however, is not yet clear for, until recently, most economists have remained quite content to lump them all together under the heading of 'neoclassical economics'. It could not have been clear to many economists back then. Economics in the interwar period did not have the technical equipment to bring deep-lying issues between 'schools' to sharp confrontation. The notion that the distinctive contributions of diverse schools would in time reach their confluence in one grand system would seem – and, one suspects, probably did seem – a most sensible attitude to adopt to most teachers.

Ever since the interwar period, the more purebred 'Austrians' have insisted on the distinctiveness of their tradition. Since, however, this (rather small) school has for a very considerable time been neither theoretically nor empirically progressive – its characteristic heuristic tending more to the 'prohibitive' than the 'positive' – its repeated challenges to the notional homogeneity of 'neoclassical doctrine' have gone unheeded by all but a few outsiders.

[43] Cf. Leijonhufvud [1973a], R. W. Clower [1975], and Clower and Leijonhufvud [1975], for a fuller statement of the argument sketched here.

ceived, the problem is to explain how, in an economic system, the activities that its numerous agents engage in, come to, are made to, or fail to 'mesh'. The coordination problem is particularly interesting when the system under study is one in which decision-making with regard to what activities to engage in or refrain from is decentralized to a high degree, i.e., 'market systems'. With regard to such economies, then, the central substantive problem of general macroeconomic theory is to determine the nature and limitations of the self-regulatory and self-organizing capabilities of market systems. In the 1930s, the issue used to be put as one of the 'automaticity' of the private sector.[44]

But in the case at hand, the alternative 'externalist' definition cannot simply be bypassed. From that standpoint, the problem was to contemporaries of Keynes – and remains in large measure to present-day economists – the Great Depression. How was that terrible, unparalleled disaster – from which the United States, the most 'capitalistic' of the systems affected, suffered the most severely – to be explained? What economic policies might be adequate to cope with it? The Depression started in 1929 with the collapse of the international monetary system. This was followed, in the United States, by an extraordinarily violent contraction of the banking system. Unemployment rose to unprecedented heights and remained at exceedingly high levels until the outbreak of the war.

For present purposes, two points will suffice about this 'external' reference of the theoretical work with which we are concerned. (i) The collapse of the international monetary system and the ensuing monetary contraction in the USA were historical events of the sort often referred to as 'unique'. They would not lend themselves readily to abstract, 'general' theorizing. The sheer magnitude as well as the ('monetary') nature of the *shocks* to the economic system that ushered in the Great Depression tended in fact to be lost sight of as the theoretical 'Keynes and the Classics' debate developed. The problem for general economic theory was that of the system's behavior in response to shocks. (ii) The duration and severity of unemployment at the time made it natural – indeed almost inevitable – that this last-mentioned problem should be defined by and for theorists by the question: Why does the 'modern, capitalist' system *fail* to absorb unemployment?

Is this the 'right question' to ask? As will become evident, I think not. The matter may be worth a digression, even though I am not able to make it of direct relevance to Lakatos's or Kuhn's theory. A philosophical problem would seem to be involved but, if so, it is a problem on which the

[44] It will be obvious to the reader that the problem can hardly even be stated so as to avoid entanglement in sundry political-ideological 'beliefs'. On complications arising from 'external' influences of this particular brand, this essay will have nothing to say, however.

Growth of Knowledge literature (to my less than comprehensive knowledge) has had little to say.

In the problem-area of the coordination of economic activities, it has always seemed to me, we have had a puzzling difficulty in keeping the basic question 'right'. It is as if it always tends to depreciate on our hands. Perhaps it is simply hard to maintain a requisite sense of wonder at things that happen every day and form part of our ordinary life more tangibly than they are part of our scientific life. The consumer wants milk in the morning. It is there on his doorstep, having arrived from a hundred miles away. The farmer milks his cow and has a consumer for it that he has never met a hundred miles away. How is this brought about and so on? How come shoes do not pile up unsold in New Mexico while people queue barefooted for shoes in Maine? In some parts of the world, such an event would not be all that unlikely. Consider a week's household purchases. To that 'basket', there will be 'value added' by individuals living and working on the other side of the globe who never knew of your existence. Again, how does it work? And so on.

Part of the problem with maintaining a sense of wonder about such trivial, everyday events may be that the easy, rather sloppy answer to such questions carries so much conviction exactly because of this daily acquaintance with the matter – but carries conviction, then, for no very good scientific reason.

The economist who finds it wondrous will ask: 'How is it possible – how is it even conceivable that decentralized economic activities can ever be reasonably coordinated when nobody, really, is trying to ensure that outcome?' That, I believe, is the 'right question'. If the economist does not find it curious, he is much more likely to ask a different question – one that sounds so much more promising from the standpoint of 'policy relevance', namely: 'How come the system sometimes fails to coordinate activities?' or 'How can there be persistent unemployment on a large scale?'

On what grounds can one argue that the former question is 'better' than the latter ones? My only answer comes by way of analogy. The philosophical problem adumbrated above is, in a sense, to decide whether the analogy is or is not apt in this case and whether for reasons of basic principle it does or does not have more general applicability.

In studying systems that have not been 'constructed' according to human 'rational design' (to use a Hayekian phrase) but are simply 'found' operating in nature or in society, it is tempting, the record shows, to start from the presumption that the system 'works' because Providence wills it so or it works for unstated reasons of 'natural law'. If the human body is the system under study, its 'natural state', on this presumption, is to be healthy. That being so, what is in need of explanation is: 'How can people ever fall ill?' The obvious 'policy-relevance' of this way of putting the question will reinforce the line of inquiry. One proceeds by 'listing' illnesses, and perhaps ranking them in order of the apparent desirability of finding a cure, and goes on to tackle them one by one. The trouble is, of course, that the various attempts to find cures for the illnesses on the list are most unlikely to form a coherent research programme (in the Lakatosian sense), that inquiry in certain directions may be halted when a cure deemed effective is found, and that the accumulation of treatments found capable of alleviating specific symptoms – 'aspirin for A, vitamins for B, psychoanalysis for C,' etc. – will not amount to a 'general theory' of how the body functions.

The ulterior motive behind the selection of this particular analogy will be obvious. The microbiological revolution, that in recent years has begun to transform medicine, came about when the presumption that 'health is only natural' was abandoned and the basic question changed: 'How is it possible that such an improbable arrangement of molecules as a cell maintains itself?' 'How is it even conceivable that it could?' The changed formulation of the question reflects an exchange of 'presuppositions' at a very basic level. To find the system under study in an 'organized' or 'coordinated' state is seen as unexpected and, consequently, in need of explanation. The *a priori* probability of some breakdown in organization, of a 'coordination failure', is on the other hand seen as so large as not to deserve priority in the search for explanations. Nonetheless – and this, of course, is the point – the pursuit of answers to the question of how life is, improbably, maintained has proved more productive of ideas, hypotheses and results relevant to the important 'failure' or 'illness' questions than did the old 'direct' approach. As answers to the 'new' and 'indirect' question begin to come in, it becomes apparent how tenuous life is in the case of the cell – how many things must 'go right' for it to be maintained – and, consequently, at how many points it is possible for the maintenance mechanisms to break down.

A modern economy is a highly improbable structure. Yet, by and large,[45] economists have not, apparently, regarded it as such and have not assigned a high priority to the coordination question. In particular, the Keynesian debate has not proceeded on such a 'presuppositional' basis.

The already mentioned 'external' factor of the persistent, large-scale unemployment of the depression decade explains this only in part. It is both true and trite, of course, to note the common-sensical sanity of the 'direct' approach in the face of a disastrous emergency. In the 1930s, the economist's attention *had to* be focused on what could be done immediately on the basis of available knowledge extended by the 'best' conjectures that might be mobilized. But an 'internal' logic to the epistemic

[45] One should except most of the 'Austrians' from this generalization and in particular F. A. Hayek whose now more than 30-year-old essays on this problem (collected in Hayek [1948]) are now at last receiving deserved attention.

situation must also be recognized if we are not to get too simplistic and one-sided an understanding of the origins of the Keynesian debate. The *General Theory*, one must remember, was 'chiefly addressed to my fellow economists' – which is to say, chiefly addressed to the 'internal situation' as Keynes saw it.

The inherited theory of the time – including in particular the Marshallian theory that was 'received doctrine' to Keynes – presupposed the 'automaticity' of the market system. The predominance of equilibrium analysis reveals the strength of the presupposition. Formal economic theory consisted almost altogether of static and comparative static models with mathematical solutions *only* for 'coordinated states' of the system, i.e., of models from which nothing specific could be deduced about uncoordinated states and what happens to them. On that problem, the pre-Keynesians had for the most part been satisfied to 'go along with' a sketchy and very informal 'story' as sufficient justification for their concentration on the equilibrium method.

One of the targets of Adam Smith's attack on the mercantilist doctrines of his day had been the 'presupposition' that 'unfettered' private enterprise was bound to be 'chaotic'. The mercantilist writers cannot be rated very favorably as contributors to the development of an economic science. Still, they posed, in effect, the 'right' question for Smith: 'How is it conceivable that the system will work coherently if you let economic agents do as they please?' To which Smith produced his 'Invisible Hand' analysis as an answer. That answer, it appears, was so satisfactory to succeeding generations of economists that for a long time little further work was done on the question.

The trouble with answers is that they tend to take the life out of questions.[46] A question remains interesting only as long as more than one answer seems possible. The satisfactory answer kills the alternative answers that earlier seemed possible. The question 'dies' with them. Repetition of the one answer becomes a matter of rote-learning – you do not really *understand* it any longer. Something of the sort happened with the coordination problem between Smith and Keynes. As a result, the 'internal' intellectual challenge to Keynes was to show how the system could 'fail'.

To the 'orthodox' presupposition that the economic system 'naturally' and 'automatically' works to coordinate activities, Keynes's theory thus came to be posed as a *denial*. To pre-Keynesian theories (of various 'schools') in which the system is presupposed *always* to tend 'smoothly' towards a restoration of a full coordination state, we get the alternative theory of a system that would *never* move near that state – except by pure chance or government intervention. The 'external' fact of the Great

[46] I am here paraphrasing the sociologist Dennis H. Wrong, whose [1961] has rapidly and justly become a classic.

Depression had so traumatically jolted the implicit faith in the 'orthodox' presupposition, that a theory advancing its polar contradiction found a prepared and ready audience among economists. Quite obviously, the message of the revolutionary doctrine at this presuppositional level was fraught with retrogressive potentialities for reassertions of mercantilist notions. British political economy has largely gone in that direction, taking British economic policy and Britain with it.

The dead hand of the past lies on these opposing presuppositions. Only minds caught in the *rigor mortis* of last century's ideologies could harbor the conviction that since one negates the other, the issue is to decide which one is 'true' and which 'false'. When two positions have become defined as diametrically opposed, an underlying basic agreement is implied, namely, a common 'understanding' of what the fundamental issue between them is. But if that issue is misconceived, neither camp will be in possession of the 'truth'. Rather each camp will possess some stock of perfectly genuine confirming 'evidence' and of incontrovertible arguments. A decision can never be reached.

If pre-Keynesian economic theories may be said to have lost an adequate appreciation of the question to which they carried forward a stock answer, the Keynesian negation of that answer did nothing to turn economic inquiry onto a more promising tack for the longer haul.

But the story cannot be ended with that assessment. Two loose ends are in evidence at this point.

First, economists have lived since the Keynesian revolution with two bodies of theory ('micro' and 'macro') based on incompatible presuppositions about what the real system under study is like. How could we possibly have done so? The two theories could not possibly be 'true' of the same external world. Yet, they have survived side-by-side for decades in reasonably peaceful co-existence and without a climactic confrontation. That a relationship of victor to vanquished, of progressive to degenerating programme has not developed is easily understandable.[47] As previously indicated, each of the two is singularly ill-adapted for coping with the phenomena that the other accords the first order of priority. But the actual 'truce', that allowed these two incompatible views of the world to be simultaneously entertained without acute intellectual discomfort by a couple of generations of economists, is so implausible on the face of it as to require explanation.

Second, there must be more to Keynes's contribution to economic theory than this turning of the tables on a basic presupposition of pre-Keynesian theory – or else our interest in it could be only antiquarian at

[47] 'Peaceful co-existence', of course, need not imply 'co-equal prosperity'. The two incompatible programmes could not very well prosper equally, if for no other reason than that the one seen to yield the 'best' crop of questions is bound to gain a near-monopoly on the recruitment of first-rate theoretical talent – as the neo-Walrasian programme has in fact had for a long period.

this date. And, in fact – or so I have industriously maintained – the theoretical reasons that he gave for why the market system would not work towards coordinating activities did introduce fundamental ideas of genuine novelty that belong (I believe) also in the structure of a general economic theory that abandons this ill-conceived battle of opposing presuppositions. These ideas – which I would lump together under the heading of 'effective demand failures'[48] – were swept under the rug of the so-called 'neoclassical synthesis' which embodies the terms of the afore-mentioned truce. They have, therefore, not been developed as yet to the point where the work of the originator becomes uninteresting and irrelevant to present-day researchers.

In addition to these two loose ends to the story, that will need to be followed up, the discussion of this section leaves us with the suggestion of a criterion for the appraisal of macroeconomic theories that, while it can be only broadly and informally stated, nonetheless will be of use. It is simply this. They should not be built around basic presuppositions that deny either of the following. (i) Market systems do possess self-regulating and self-organizing properties. If this mode of economic organization did not possess reasonably reliable mechanisms for the coordination of activities, they could never have evolved. Nor would we find, as we do, that certain broad features of market organization tend 'spontaneously' to assert (or reassert) themselves, practically speaking, wherever they are not actively suppressed or the conditions relevant to the security of property and contract anarchic. (ii) These self-regulating and self-organizing mechanisms of market economies will sometimes fail – and fail badly – in maintaining a socially tolerable degree of coordination of activities. If this were not so, the chances are that we would never have become aware of the coordination problem as one demanding scientific explanation but would still take the perfect 'health' – and, indeed, immortality – of the system as granted by Providence. (A benign or malign Providence, of course, depending upon your ideological standpoint.)

II.3

We turn then to the historical problem of the 'implausible truce'. The explanation, as I perceive it, is largely a matter of the incongruities of form and substance in economic theory that were harped on at such length in Part I above.

In form – what there was of it – Keynes's theory fitted the substance of his main problem badly in two respects. First, in directing his revolt most specifically against the Marshallian economics reigning in Cambridge, he sought to vanquish it with its own analytical weaponry. Among the main 'neoclassical schools' of the time, the Marshallian stands distinct from the rest by its conscientious guardianship of the 'plutological' analytical

---

[48] Cf. Leijonhufvud [1973b].

tradition.[49] Keynesian aggregative economics bears this plutological heritage. For the formal statement of the coordination problem, however, a 'catallactic' approach would have been more appropriate.[50] Both the Austrian and the Walrasian 'schools' were in the catallactic tradition – but with them, Keynes was not much concerned. Second, Keynes 'cast his theory in static, equilibrium form' whereas the coordination problem will ultimately require the development of methods of 'dynamic', 'disequilibrium' process analysis. One reason for casting the *General Theory* as an equilibrium 'model' – and, indeed, for insisting on it – may derive from a prior decision on his part to dramatize the presuppositional battle with 'orthodoxy' by presenting a model where large-scale unemployment is an equilibrium state of the system. (Many Keynesians insist to this day that therein lies the 'essence' of the Keynesian revolution.) But it seems more to the point to note that, whereas the choice of a catallactic in preference to a plutological formulation was open to him, the technical limitations of inherited modes of formal economic analysis left him no choice in this matter. Static, equilibrium modelling was the only technical form that we can reasonably say was available to him.

Had Keynes begun from the question: 'How is it conceivable that activities are ever reasonably coordinated?' these incongruities of form and substance would necessarily have presented rather immediate embarrassments. Setting out, instead, to answer the question: 'How has the system failed?' these problems were not that apparent either to him or to later followers and commentators. A model of a system that 'just does not work' can dispense with representation of sundry 'homeostats' that could not be omitted from a model of a system that could and often does work.

The Keynesian 'model' portrayed a system that could be in 'equilibrium' at *any* level of unemployment. Pre-Keynesian economists were not wont to deny evident facts of economic life so, naturally, orthodox theory would allow for the occurrence of prolonged periods of serious unemployment. But formal 'orthodox' models would not allow 'involuntary' unemployment as an equilibrium state. The primary task of the 'Keynes and the Classics' debate became that of analytically isolating the atypical assumption or assumptions of Keynes's theory that were responsible for its 'unemployment equilibrium' implications. In hindsight, one concludes that this red herring caught too much of the attention.

[49] Cf., especially, Shove [1942].

[50] It is entirely vain, of course, to 'wish' that Keynes would have chosen a catallactic formulation because of the superior analytical precision that this tradition affords in the statement of the 'purely theoretical' problems. The plutological tradition has the immense advantage, quite generally, that its conceptual categories have a fairly clear correspondence to National Income Account data, etc. It is empirically implementable in a way that catallactic theory has never been and consequently promises a practical 'engine of analysis' with which one can come to grips in rather direct manner with the economic policy issues of the day. Keynes, without doubt, would in any case have preferred the plutological approach on this basis.

The task of isolating the property of Keynes's theory that made the crucial difference was to be approached by systematic analytical comparison of a Keynesian model and a representative 'classical' model. Some 'hard' elements of a formal model could be clearly discerned in Keynes's exposition of his theory. But a complete, coherent, formal macromodel the *General Theory* did not 'nail down'. It had to be provided. Similarly, what was available in the way of inherited 'classical' models – non-monetary general equilibrium models, quantity theory models with the 'real' sector not represented, etc. – would not correspond sufficiently to Keynes's structure to make comparisons feasible. So a 'classical model' also had to be, if not made up out of whole cloth, then stitched together from inherited patches and pieces.

Things went askew over the course of the long discussion on three fronts. (i) Keynes's theory (I have maintained) was 'dynamic in substance, but static in form'. The constant feature of the debate was that it was conducted in terms of comparisons of static equilibrium models. Elements of Keynes's theoretical statement that were not to be captured by such representation drifted out of view. (ii) As the progressive neo-Walrasian programme gathered steam, and since the Marshallian tradition had stagnated already by the early 1930s, the model used to represent 'classical' economics eventually came to be a monetary neo-Walrasian one. This substitution was aided by the widespread notion that all neoclassical theories were 'basically the same' though the neo-Walrasian was better than the rest.[51] It meant that Keynes's model came to be reinterpreted as an 'aggregative, catallactic' structure rather than being seen as a late product of Marshallian plutology. (iii) The completion of Keynes's open-ended model could be done in various ways. As the debate proceeded, various writers took sundry liberties with Keynes's own statement. In most instances, there may have been or seemed to have been good reasons for the individual amendments to Keynes's theory stemming from better empirical data or from improved analysis. But in the event the accumulation of such substitutions of 'what Keynes ought to have said' for what he did say came to falsify the original gestalt conception.[52]

In a cruel job of reviewing, Keynes said of one of Hayek's early works that it was 'an extraordinary example of how, starting with a mistake, a remorseless logician can end up in Bedlam'. The 'Keynes and the Classics' debate ended up in the bedlam of the so-called 'neoclassical synthesis'. The last several steps to that conclusion were taken under the compulsion of virtual mathematical necessity. One has to trace back to the early slips between form and substance to find an escape from it.

Keynes was to play little part in the debate that ended in bedlam. But, ironically, he did 'set it up' so that, once the matter was turned over to

[51] This notion also permeates my own earlier work on the subject – to its detriment.
[52] Cf. Leijonhufvud [1968].

remorseless logicians, that is where his legacy to economics was bound to end up. Keynes sought to '*revolutionize*' the gestalt of the theory that he saw his 'fellow economists' as entertaining. He attempted no 'revolution' in inherited routines and methods of analysis. On the contrary, he went to great lengths to erect his novel structure of ideas using only the Marshallian tool-box (and a good dose of aggregation). But it may well be that no such feat is possible as *definitively* changing the 'pattern of beliefs' without also changing the routines people use for checking the logical consistency of simultaneously entertained beliefs. Keynes left the price-theoretical equilibrium analysis machinery in place. Released from his control, the old, proven logical machine – almost by itself, as it were – set about to clean up and restore order – *the Old* Established Order. The process leading up to the neoclassical synthesis featured the standard equilibrium constructions mindlessly eating away at the main Keynesian ideas until nothing was left but the trite and trivial propositions that if wages are (i) 'too high' for equilibrium, and (ii) 'rigid downwards', then unemployment will exist and persist. That end-product is the neoclassical synthesis in a nutshell.[53]

This 'synthesis', which concludes that Keynes's theory is that special case of 'classical' theory in which wages are constrained to be 'rigid', is patent nonsense any way you look at it. (i) From the 'external' standpoint, the Great Depression had the worst, most dramatic wage-deflation on the historical record. How could a theory whose 'critical feature' was the assumption that wages will not fall, no matter what, have any relevance to these external conditions? (ii) The first hypothesis that would come to *any* pre-Keynesian economist's mind, if asked to explain why the desired supply of labor (or any other good) was not being sold and why the situation persisted, would inevitably be that the ruling price must be in excess of the equilibrium price and that, for some reason, it would not come down. How could the use of that old standby in this instance constitute a 'revolutionary break' with inherited theory? (iii) To top it off, of course, Keynes definitely did *not* assume wages to be rigid and did not argue that the depression stemmed from insufficient flexibility of wages. On the contrary, he went to great lengths to bolster his insistent contention that a higher degree of wage-flexibility would not help get the system out of the large-scale unemployment state but, instead, make the situation worse.

The 'synthesis' gave an understandable answer to only one question, namely Humpty-Dumpty's: 'Who is to be master?' The neo-Walrasian programme came out the master with the Keynesian subordinated to the role of one of its 'special cases'.

The inherited conception of how markets function to coordinate activities, which provided the underlying informal support for all pre-Keynesian equilibrium theories, was based on the twin presuppositions:[54]

[53] ...and such an appropriate container too!   [54] Cf. Leijonhufvud [1968], pp. 26ff.

(i) that price-incentives effectively control the behavior of individual transactors; that transactors will respond to changes in relative prices by changing the quantities they desire to produce and consume in a qualitatively predictable manner;

(ii) that prices tend to move – and are 'free' to do so – in response to market excess demands or supplies and in such a manner as to induce transactors to alter their behavior in the directions required for all activities to 'mesh'.

These are necessary for the system envisaged by pre-Keynesian theory to work. Negate one or the other and the result is a theory of a system that cannot work. The 'synthesis' concluded that Keynes had thrown a spanner in the works of the 'classical' system by, as it were, 'fixing wages' so that they could not adjust to remove an excess supply of labor.

The novel theoretical idea in Keynes's work that was lost sight of in all of this was different. To appreciate it – and to appreciate how difficult it is to do it justice within the framework of equilibrium models – one has to envisage the possibility of coordination of 'desired' transactor activities in the system failing because communication between them fails to convey the needed information.

It is one of the great achievements of general equilibrium theory to have shown that the vector of equilibrium prices conveys, in principle, all the information that each transactor needs to know in order to be able to coordinate his activities with those of everybody else in the system. When starting from a disequilibrium state with prices diverging from their equilibrium values, transactor plans will be inconsistent and the necessity of adjusting will be forced on them. How can we be confident that the ensuing adjustment process converges on that equilibrium price vector which provides the requisite information? As it turns out, this should be possible (given certain subsidiary conditions) if the adjustments of market prices were effectively governed by the discrepancies, in the respective markets, between the sales and purchases that transactors would 'desire' to execute could they only be confident that they would be able to do so. But at disequilibrium prices not everyone will be able to sell or buy all that he might 'desire'.

The 'classical' conception of the market as a feedback-regulated servomechanism assumed that the 'error' in feedback that the mechanism sought to reduce to zero by iterative adjustments of prices would be the aggregative difference between these 'desired' demands and supplies. Keynes's 'Effective Demand Failure' theory challenged this assumption. The system will register, he argued, only those demand-signals that can be backed by ready purchasing-power. But transactors who in a disequilibrium state find themselves unable to realize their desired sales will not acquire the money with which to 'back' what would otherwise be their 'desired' demands. Consequently, the market excess demands that

97

effectively govern price-adjustments are not the 'appropriate' ones in such a situation.

II.4

The 'neoclassical synthesis' proposed a reconciliation of 'Keynesianism' and 'orthodoxy' on a purely formalistic plane. Substantively, each of the two world-views that were thus wrenched into the logical appearance of consistency was basically uncompromised by the adopted formula. Behind the formal screen, they stood poles apart. It is inconceivable that this deceptive 'papering-over' of the stark inconsistency of substantive beliefs could be indefinitely sustained. Yet, surprise at the extent that this modelling formula gained widespread acceptance, *despite* the incompatibility on a basic theoretical level, is possibly misplaced. It may be that it 'worked' in its time, rather, *because* it allowed the postponement of a confrontation that could not have been decided but that had tremendous latent potential for diverting energies away from the pursuit of 'normal science' within each 'paradigm'.

Any attempt to distil from the literature a really adequate characterization of the two 'cosmologies', noting (in fairness) the reservations appended to each by prominent and representative writers, etc., would cause the already distended frame of this paper to burst. Yet, it is necessary that some notion of the two be conveyed at this point. The crudity of the following metaphor may be objectionable but its use will have the advantage (in addition to brevity) that it is unlikely to be taken too seriously.

The simplest example of a self-regulating system is that of the hull of a ship. Let the 'even-keel' state of the hull correspond, metaphorically, to a 'fully coordinated' or general equilibrium state of the economic system.[55] Assume an external force impinging on the ship so as to displace it from the even-keel position. The stronger this 'disturbance' the larger the deviation from 'equilibrium' that it would, by itself, tend to bring about. Consider the strength (and direction) of the force exerted by the hull itself in the displaced position and how this force would vary as a function of the 'degree of list'.

Then, the 'ship' of classical or orthodox economic cosmology has the following properties. It always tends to move back towards an even keel from any displaced position. The force acting to bring it back, moreover, is proportional – or, perhaps, even better than that – to the magnitude of the displacement. This ship cannot conceivably capsize – when turned upside down in the water its inherent 'self-righteousness' would assert itself with maximum strength.

This caricatures the 'basic' orthodox presupposition. Less 'super-

[55] The ship may be on an even keel but on its way to an undesirable location. One must *not* entertain any presumption that the coordinated state of the economy would, if attained, be in any sense 'welfare optimal'.

classical', more sensible variations are available. Time-lagged adjustment behavior is accommodated, for example, by allowing momentum to enter into the account of the physical system metaphor – following a 'shock', the orthodox ship would go through a series of oscillations converging on the even-keel state. And so on. The basic presupposition is simply that the system will tend back to an even keel from any position, not that it will do so with maximum conceivable efficiency.

Thus, in broad economic terms, large-scale unemployment, for example, will not persist by itself. Unless the system is repeatedly exposed to adverse shocks 'involuntary unemployment' should tend to shrink and disappear. In terms of general equilibrium theory, the homeostatic force back towards an 'even keel' should be stronger the larger the displacement because, generally speaking, excess demands and supplies will be larger the farther prices in the respective markets diverge from their values in the general equilibrium 'solution' price vector; the adjustment velocities of prices depend on the magnitude of excess demands (supplies) with the adjustment of activity levels depending, in turn, on the behavior of prices.

The 'ship' of Keynesian cosmology is rather different – in fact, a tub 'unsafe in any weather'. Suppose we consider an external 'shock' (a decline in government expenditure, say) that by itself would suffice to give it a list of x degrees. Then one problem – distressing to those who have mankind travelling on this boat – is that (for reasons not to be clearly understood) it never sails with its cargo properly secured. When the ship is exposed to an external disturbance, therefore, the cargo shifts in the hold, and the ship goes to a list, not just of x degrees, but of mx degrees $(m > 1)$. This self-amplifying mechanism, that tends to increase the movement initiated by any given shock, is referred to as the 'multiplier'. (In clear contrast, all the feedback loops of our 'classical ship' operate always in a strictly deviation-counteracting manner.)

Furthermore, this ship will simply stick in any position of list that the above process would bring about, showing no 'inherent' tendency to right itself. Getting it into the reasonable neighborhood of an even keel will always – unless you are content to wait for the vagaries of wind and water to bring it about by chance – be a matter of 'doing something about it'. Having Central Bankers on the bridge 'lean against the wind' and such will accomplish nothing, moreover. What it takes is having your trusty Treasury stevedores down in the hold doing the honest, sweaty work of shifting the cargo from larboard to starboard and back again as conditions demand.

That will do. There is little point in trying by further elaboration to make what can be no more than a crude metaphor more palatable to the initiated. For some considerable time, economics has managed to accommodate the cohabitation of two such 'images' of the economic world. It is not a matter easily to be dismissed from mind by reassuring reflections on

99

'complementary' perceptual structurings of complex phenomena. For certain important problems, economists use models which presuppose that the economy is 'like a classical boat'. Other, equally important problems, are approached with the aid of constructions based on the presupposition that we sail in a Keynesian contraption. But the two classes of problems occur simultaneously in reality – and the actual external world could not be 'like' both ships at one and the same time.

It is not a trivial matter as two simple examples will suffice to show. (i) *Theoretical implications:* theories of the 'orthodox' variety will predict that an increase in the 'propensity to save' will raise the growth-rates of national income and wealth. It is something that governments might reasonably seek to encourage therefore. In the Keynesian view, on the other hand, an increase in the propensity to save will reduce the level of income, increase unemployment, and is also likely to have the 'paradoxical' result that the actually realized growth-rate of the wealth of nations falls. It seems, in fact, 'safer' for governments to discourage the private accumulation of wealth. Clearly, one or the other party must be capable of enormous mischief if put in a position, say, of guiding the policies of a developing nation bent on growth. (ii) *Empirical interpretations:* in comparison with the interwar period, Western economies have enjoyed high and relatively stable employment in the twenty-five years following World War II. In the Keynesian view, this improved employment performance is to be attributed to the much larger size of government sectors. More guns – more butter. In the absence of this expansion of state activity, Keynesians would infer, the postwar period would have had an employment record as dismal as that of the 1930s. In the more 'classical' view, in contrast, the interwar period now stands out as an 'abnormal' era sandwiched between the pre-World War I and post-World War II high employment periods. The high employment levels of recent decades reflects a return of the system to 'normal' functioning. In this view, the expansion of the state has come at the expense of correspondingly slower growth of the private sector. More guns – less butter. Thus, the same data have entirely different meanings depending on what type of 'ship' one believes one is observing.

A reconciliation on a substantive level is (naturally) feasible. What it eventually will be like cannot be forecast in very specific terms. Among the considerations that should play a role in shaping a 'substantive synthesis', the following two should, I think, belong. (i) As noted in Section II.2, the general theory debates focusing on the 'unemployment equilibrium' notion tended gradually to lose sight of the 'historical' matter of the magnitude and nature of the disturbances to which the system had been exposed. This matter should be brought back in. (ii) From all other fields in which self-regulating 'natural' systems and/or man-made mechanisms are studied, we know it to be the general case that the homeostatic capabilities of such systems are bounded. It is more than just likely that this is true also of economic systems.

In my [1973a], I proposed a 'cosmological working-hypothesis' (as it were) which in terms of the previous metaphor would come out somewhat as follows. Consider a hull-type such as might have evolved and survived over the centuries. Displacing this boat from the even-keel position further and further, we would first find the force acting at a displaced position to bring it back toward 'equilibrium' increasing in strength; at some point, however, it would reach its maximum and be found weakening for greater deviations from the even-keel state. Still further 'out' we could locate a critical state where the ship's deviation-counteracting tendency is zero and beyond which it would capsize. (Whether this last part of the metaphor can be given any sensible social system interpretation is perhaps questionable.)

In economic terms, what is being suggested may be summarily stated as follows. For the 'even-keel' state, substitute the economic system's general equilibrium motion defined as a path in gT-dimensional goods–time space. This is the motion the system would have to follow for all of its homeostats to 'report' zero error in feedback throughout; hence, it should be regarded as a purely notional reference-motion and not as a description of any actual motion. Given this theoretical reference-motion, we are able to speak of actual states of the system as 'displaced' from it to a greater or lesser extent. As before, we are concerned with the strength of the system's tendency to 'home in' towards the general equilibrium path from various such 'displaced' positions.

For states in the near neighborhood of the equilibrium path, basically the only tendencies at work will be those of the classical supply-and-demand mechanism (which will be deviation-counteracting). As the displacement being considered is gradually increased, these equilibrating forces would by themselves tend to grow in strength, but another element also starts to enter in as Keynesian 'effective demand failures' begin to affect the operation of various markets. At some point, the resulting net equilibrating tendencies reach a maximum and, beyond it, decline in strength as effective demand failures increasingly impair the system's capacity to adjust appropriately. For very sizeable displacements, the simple two-dimensional metaphor is a very halting one at best – as the system becomes increasingly *disorganized* its motion cannot be appraised in as simple a manner as that suggested by the notion of 'directed momentum' in relation to an equilibrium reference path. Some prices and activity levels may be moving in the direction of their notional general equilibrium values; others, however, will be moving further away. Some prices and activity levels that are 'wrong' may be unchanging, while those that are 'right' move, and so on. In a 'great depression' or 'great inflation', the system could wallow sluggishly through a succession of such states without, unaided, taking a decisive turn for the better for a long time. The consequences of prolonged, serious discoordination will show up in transformations of the social, legal and political framework of economic activity – at which point the economist's pretenses to 'tracking' the system through time with his theoretical constructions ought in all decency to be shed.

In simpler terms, consider a system that within certain bounds around the equilibrium path will 'home in' in the way presumed in pre-Keynesian economics. Outside this 'corridor' its behavior is more sluggish and well outside the forces emphasized in Keynesian theory predominate entirely.

The reasons for sketching a possible theoretical reconciliation having these broad features – naturally others might be contemplated – are (the reader will be glad to know) actually economic rather than nautical.

At a relatively simple level, where analytical manageability would seem within our present reach, the theory stresses the presence and functions of 'buffer-stocks' in the system. Transactors maintain both physical and financial 'buffers' – input and output inventories, spare capacity, liquid assets and less than fully utilized credit-lines, etc. – and do so exactly to prevent stochastically occurring disturbances from interrupting or disrupting the desired, 'orderly' flows of their production and consumption activities. Although the timing, specific nature and concrete causes of such disturbances cannot be foreseen, as long as they are not larger in magnitude and/or longer in duration than was anticipated in planning for the prudent provision of buffer-stocks, the system will absorb the shocks and adjust smoothly. When they are larger and more sustained than transactors had found it reasonable to guard against, buffer-stocks run out, and the Keynesian effective demand failures (exacerbated, probably, by contractions of credit, bankruptcies, etc.) then disrupt the 'normal' homeostatic adjustment mechanisms.

At a rather 'deeper' level, the basic conception relates less readily to accustomed modes of economic modelling. The day-to-day coordination of economic activities relies on the utilization of knowledge that overwhelmingly derives from the past experience of transactors. The information required for the task could not be created (or in the wake of an amnesia epidemic, recreated) overnight. New learning takes place gradually and at the margin of accumulated experience. As long as the system evolves gradually, what was 'normal' according to past experience continues to be a good guide to the present and transactors are able to update their conceptions of their economic environment in pace with its changes. An abrupt shock to the system of such magnitude as to require adaptation to a significantly different environment, wherein past experience is a bad guide to present behavior, is a different matter. Anyone who has moved to a foreign country and had to adapt to a very different structure of relative prices from the one he had been accustomed to will recall the time and effort required to create a new, 'rational' and relatively stable consumption pattern in a new milieu. That however is the rather simple task of one individual adapting to the pattern in which activities are already coordinated, as reflected in the prevailing (near-equilibrium) price structure, in a smoothly running system. The situation we are envisaging is one in which all transactors are simultaneously thrown into an analogous situation and where no one can have a very confident notion of what equilibrium prices will eventually emerge.

Collective adaptation to a drastically altered situation is likely to be slow for much of the new information that any given transactor acquires will pertain to the actions taken by others on the basis of no longer applicable precedents. And so on.

To sketch a theory that seems to offer the prospect of a substantive reconciliation is easy – only too easy, perhaps. But if the trouble with the previous formal 'synthesis' was that it did not make substantive sense, the trouble with proposals for a substantive 'synthesis' like this one is that we do not know very much at all about how to provide a reasonably disci-plined formal representation for systems behaving this way.

Mathematical general equilibrium theorists have at their command an impressive array of proven techniques for modelling systems that 'always work well'. Keynesian economists have experience with modelling systems that 'never work'. But, as yet, no one has the recipe for modelling systems that function pretty well most of the time but sometimes work very badly to coordinate economic activities. And the analytical devices and routines of neo-Walrasian general equilibrium theory and Keynesian theory will not 'mix'.

II.5

The last several years have seen a growing interest on the part of economic theorists in the problems of finding a more viable formal synthesis of neo-Walrasian and Keynesian economics. Work directed towards this task has come to be commonly labeled as concerned with 'the microfoundations of macroeconomic theory'. In the last couple of years, a few of the most widely respected senior theorists in the profession as well as many of its sharpest young mathematical economists have begun to take a hand. Despite a considerable number of interesting contributions, however, progress has been disappointingly slow.

The recent admirable survey of general equilibrium economics by Arrow and Hahn leads up to a concluding delineation of the remaining 'gap' between the two theories.[56] It is hard to know whether one should draw more encouragement or discouragement from this authoritative assessment of the state of the art. On the one hand, it is evident how much more clearly we are now able to define many of the obstacles in the way of a reunification of economic theory than was possible ten or fifteen years

[56] Arrow and Hahn [1972], chapters 13 and 14.

ago. On the other hand, the 'gap' is thereby also seen to yawn wider and the remaining tasks to loom more formidable than they looked – to relatively innocent eyes in any case – in the early sixties.[57] The most helpful contributions in the recent literature have, on balance, been more critical than constructive in nature. Critical assessments, conceptual clarifications, sharper definitions of problem aspects will, of course, mark a natural and required first stage of inquiry, preliminary to constructive solutions of problems of this type. But, in this instance, one may by now begin to wonder whether this 'first stage' is not threatening to become permanent – or as permanent as the patience of economists will allow before they walk away from the issues in disgust.

Are we yet again on the wrong track? It is almost always foolish to prejudge what may or may not be achieved by the dogged pursuit of a particular approach in a science. Still, it seems time to consider the possibility that we have withdrawn from the simple cul-de-sac of the 'neoclassical synthesis' only to enter a more intricate maze (in which more fun is to be had) that offers no through street either.

The 'microfoundations of macro' label attached to recent work on disequilibrium and monetary models in the neo-Walrasian vein is indicative of some presumptions (if not quite 'presuppositions') that may bear examination. First, it conflates the distinction between micro- and macro-theory with that between neo-Walrasian and 'Keynesian' theory.[58] Second, the phrase reflects a diagnosis of the state of the art and a view of the task at hand, namely, that the formally rigorous and so far progressive neo-Walrasian programme is in good intellectual health while the analytically mushy 'Keynesian' models need to be cleaned up in order to get that stagnant programme restarted on a more promising track. The notion of what is to be done is thus one of shoving the firm axiomatic neo-Walrasian microfoundations in under the ramshackle 'Keynesian' macro-superstructure which, once safely propped up on that basis, might then be reconstructed without risk to the life, limb and good repute (for formal competence) of those engaged in the task.

The actual work done in recent years has perhaps taught us a few things about those weaknesses of 'Keynesian' models that account for the lack of theoretical discipline imposed on their users and the ability of political economists to argue, with their help, for virtually any bundle of policies in almost any situation.[59] But, mainly, the results of this work have been of a character that should be rather unexpected to anyone who naively embraced the presumptions just outlined. For, in the main, the lessons

[57] The reader might be wise to read this as simply an autobiographical statement. My innocence on some of these matters will shine through much of my [1968] and [1969].

[58] Construing, here, 'Keynesian' as broadly as possible, for example, to include that brand of 'monetarism' which, according to Friedman, may be fitted into some version of the so-called 'IS-LM' modelling frame.

[59] Compare Clower and Leijonhufvud [1975], p. 182.

learned have been about the *limitations* of inherited neo-Walrasian theory – about what cannot be done with it as it now stands. And 'what cannot be done with it' includes, most specifically, of course, analysis of 'Keynesian' macro-processes.

Rather than identifying microtheory with neo-Walrasian models and macrotheory with 'Keynesian' ones, it might be better, I suggest, to emphasize a Lakatosian distinction between the two research programmes as the primary one and then to distinguish, secondarily, the micro- and macro-theoretical components of each. The result of putting it thus is to land us with two distinct questions in place of the previous one – 'What microfoundations for "Keynesian" macrotheory?' and 'What macro-superstructure on neo-Walrasian micro?' These questions force recognition of the following observations:

(i) There *were* some, albeit rudimentary, micro-underpinnings to Keynes's theory.[60] The elements of price theory utilized in the *General Theory* were not Walrasian, however, but Marshallian. Keynes's 'freehand sketch' of these price-theoretical aspects was not developed to the point of providing coherent microfoundations for macrotheory. With the abandonment of the already then degenerating Marshallian programme, very little work on their development has taken place since. Inadequate as these rudiments will appear when compared to the neo-Walrasian models that in the interim have seen 40 years of systematic development, they still do have the significant advantage to recommend them of being 'all of a piece' with Keynesian macrotheory. That one cannot claim for the results of the piecemeal substitutions of neo-Walrasian for Marshallian price-theoretical constructions that has since occurred.

This suggests that, in trying to assure *sui generis* microfoundations for Keynesian macro, the possibility might be explored of assembling them from building-blocks left lying about the abandoned intellectual site of the once so imposing Marshallian 'school'.[61] Whether this is worth pursuing or not is, perhaps, anyone's guess. It is quite clear from the start that the attempt would be a major undertaking with a most uncertain pay-off. For the Marshallian school presumably did not degenerate from sheer inattention 'without reason'. We do not have a very clear idea of what the reasons were. They would have to be dug out and diagnosed in order to judge whether the decline of Marshallian economics was avoidable.

(ii) There *are* some, not at all rudimentary, macro-superstructures erected on neo-Walrasian microfoundations. We find their prototype in

[60] The at one time fairly widespread view that price-theoretical *elementa* were absent from – and sometimes violated in – the *General Theory* was criticized as part of my attack on the 'neoclassical synthesis' in my [1968], [1969].

[61] The reasons for insisting (above, Section II:1) that pre-Keynesian 'neoclassical economics' was not a homogenous doctrine and that realization of the differences between the 'schools' of 40 years ago will be of relevance to present concerns finally come to light here.

Patinkin's classic achievement.[62] More recently, we have the products of the voluminous literature on 'neoclassical growth' models.

If, in the recent discussion, there has been a tendency to overlook Keynes's Marshallian micro-elements, the tendency with regard to this neo-Walrasian macro-literature – which, looming imposingly in plain view, cannot be overlooked – has been to disregard it. Since it does not address unemployment or other discoordination problems and gives no prescriptions for stabilization policy, the attitude towards it tends to be that 'it doesn't count'. Yet, there is nothing 'sketchy' or 'half-baked' about it. There is no need to issue plaintive calls for the development of neo-Walrasian macro-structures. We already have a full-fledged macro-theory within this programme.

Instead, the question here is whether 'this is all we are ever going to get' in the way of macrotheory out of the neo-Walrasian programme. May it be that Patinkin *et al.* have virtually exhausted the programme's potential in this important area and left only footnotes to be added?

My colleague, R. W. Clower, poses the matter this way:[63]

...the logical and empirical implications – and so also the conceptual limitations – of Neo-Walrasian theory were simply not clear to anyone until after the Neo-Walrasian Revolution had pretty well run its course. In the interim, it was only natural for economists generally to proceed on the presumption that general equilibrium theory had no inherent limitations. After all, even quite specialized economic models generally admit of a variety of alternative interpretations; that is to say, it is usually possible to add new variables and behavior relations without having completely to reconstruct the logical foundations of the original model. In mathematics, axiom systems that possess analogous properties are said to be *noncategorical*. That any even moderately 'general' economic model should be anything but *noncategorical*, therefore, would hardly occur naturally to any but a very perverse mind. That the elaborate Neo-Walrasian model set out in Hicks' *Value and Capital* might fail to satisfy this condition would have seemed correspondingly incredible to any sensible person at the outset of the Neo-Walrasian Revolution.[64]

The question Clower raises we may rephrase in Lakatosian terms: May it be that part of the neo-Walrasian programme's hard core must be relinquished in order to put Keynesian macrotheory on a consistent microbasis?

If the answer to this one is 'yes' – and even now it seems premature to assert that it must be 'yes' – the next question, and the crucial one, becomes: Which specific hard-core propositions of neo-Walrasian models

[62] Cf. Patinkin [1956].

[63] Cf. Clower [1975], p. 134.

[64] Clower's judgment that the neo-Walrasian revolution pretty well had to run its course before sensible persons could become aware of the programme's possible limitations may be compared with the – possibly overly 'defensive' – discussion of the preoccupation of theoretical economists with the exploration of formal languages, above Sections I:6 through I:8.

are responsible for setting the limits to their extension in the 'Keynesian' direction?[65]

On the first question, I tend, like Clower, to the belief that the neo-Walrasian hard core is limiting. With regard to the second, my suspicions focus (so far) on the Maximizing Behavior postulate in the particularly rigid form that it has come to take in neo-Walrasian economics, i.e. as a 'necessary condition for the intelligibility of behavior'.[66]

But, at the point where these questions are raised, this one-man's-view of the Keynesian revolution story has been brought up to date. It is a yet unfinished story. But the tale beyond the point just reached cannot be told without prejudging the answers to some questions that are still in the making.

[65] To avoid misunderstandings, some observations are in order. First, these questions are likely to seem of little consequence to most of those that have contributed to and/or are presently working within the neo-Walrasian programme. That programme has been one of 'pure formal exploration' to a degree that, in a natural science, would have made it a most curious anomaly in the history of science. Mathematical economists would be little discomfitted by a change in the basic ground-rules for further such explorations. To give up one or more of the formal 'hard-core' postulates of this programme need, generally speaking, occasion no traumatic revisions of cosmological beliefs. It has in fact long been apparent that some of the most accomplished and admired contributors to neo-Walrasian economics do not attach to its models the substantive belief that 'the world is like that'. In particular – and quite contrary to the allegations of the 'new Cambridge' economists (whom one must nonetheless credit with being out far ahead of the pack in arguing the fundamental irrelevance of neo-Walrasian general equilibrium theory to Keynesian economics) – the major contributors to this programme obviously have no ideologically based attachment to it whatsoever. Indeed, the 'typical' neo-Walrasian (loosely speaking) tends to be an 'interventionist' in matters of socio-economic policy; the 'Chicago school' (equally loosely speaking) known for its 'anti-interventionism' is notable also for its critical opposition to the neo-Walrasian mode of theorizing.

Second, much of what we have learned from neo-Walrasian literature – and it is a great deal – will carry over through a programme switch. These lessons of lasting value will not, in my view, be confined just to matters of techniques, 'tricks' of modelling and the like, important as these legacies of the period of neo-Walrasian hegemony are.

Third, genuine progress on an integrated micro–macro 'Keynesian' theory is undoubtedly much more likely to originate with mathematical economists known for masterful command of neo-Walrasian theory than to come from anywhere else.

[66] Neo-Walrasian closed system models have so far been inadequate – or, at best, grotesquely cumbersome – vehicles for representing the role of ignorance and the passage of time in human affairs. This has so far stood in the way of satisfactory modelling of the 'disequilibrium' motion of ongoing systems. Both problems are, it would appear, rooted in the hard-core heuristic routine of modelling the behavior of each individual agent so as to portray his every action as part of a comprehensively planned 'optimal' time-path.

Marshall's theory did not insist on representing all acts as part of an optimal plan. The behavior of individuals in his models is to be characterized rather as 'satisficing converging on maximizing'. A theory cast in such form provides escape from most of the embarrassing riddles of time and ignorance met with in current 'neoclassical' (growth) models.

These matters, however, can hardly be discussed adequately within brief compass. My *Maximization and Marshall* harps upon them at great length.

References

Arrow, K. and Hahn, F. H. [1972]: *General Competitive Analysis*.

Clower, R. W. [1965]: 'Keynesian Counterrevolution: A Theoretical Appraisal', in F. H. Hahn and F. P. R. Brechling (eds.): *The Theory of Interest Rates*.

Clower, R. W. [1975]: 'Reflections on the Keynesian Perplex', *Zeitschrift für Nationalökonomie*, **35**, pp. 126–45.

Clower, R. W. and Leijonhufvud, A. [1975]: 'The Coordination of Economic Activities: A Keynesian Perspective', *The American Economic Review*, **65**, pp. 182–8.

Coats, A. W. [1969]: 'Is There a "Structure of Scientific Revolutions" in Economics?' *Kyklos*, **22**, pp. 289–96.

Davies, J. R. [1973]: 'Was There a Keynesian Revolution?' delivered at the 1973 Midwestern Economic Association Meetings.

Eisner, R. [1958]: 'On Growth Models and the Neoclassical Resurgence', *Economic Journal*, **68**, pp. 707–21.

Friedman, M. [1970]: 'A Theoretical Framework for Monetary Analysis', *Journal of Political Economy*, **78**, pp. 193–238.

Friedman, M. [1971]: 'A Monetary Theory of Nominal Income', *Journal of Political Economy*, **79**, pp. 323–37.

Hanson, N. R. [1958]: *Patterns of Discovery*.

Hayek, F. A. [1948]: *Individualism and Economic Order*.

Keynes, J. M. [1936]: *The General Theory of Employment Interest and Money*.

Lakatos, I. [1963]: 'Proofs and Refutations', *The British Journal for the Philosophy of Science*, **14**, pp. 1–25, 120–39, 221–45, 297–342.

Latsis, S. J. [1972]: 'Situational Determinism in Economics', *The British Journal for the Philosophy of Science*, **23**, pp. 207–45.

Leijonhufvud, A. [1968]: *On Keynesian Economics and the Economics of Keynes*.

Leijonhufvud, A. [1969]: *Keynes and the Classics*.

Leijonhufvud, A. [1973a]: 'Effective Demand Failures', *Swedish Journal of Economics*, **75**, pp. 27–48.

Leijonhufvud, A. [1973b]: 'Life Among the Econ', *Western Economic Journal*, **11**, pp. 327–37.

Leijonhufvud, A. [1974a]: 'Keynes' Employment Function; Comment', *History of Political Economy*, **6**, pp. 164–70.

Leijonhufvud, A. [1974b]: 'The Varieties of Price Theory: What Microfoundations for Macro Theory?' Department of Economics, UCLA, Discussion Paper Number 44.

Leijonhufvud, A. [forthcoming]: *Maximization and Marshall*.

Masterman, M. [1965]: 'The Nature of a Paradigm', in I. Lakatos and A. Musgrave (eds.): *Criticism and the Growth of Knowledge*.

Menger, K. [1973]: 'Austrian Marginalism and Mathematical Economics', in J. R. Hicks and W. Weber (eds.): *Carl Menger and the Austrian School of Economics*.

Patinkin, D. [1956]: *Money, Interest, and Prices*.

Robinson, J. [1963]: *Economic Philosophy*.

Samuelson, P. A. [1946]: 'The General Theory', reprinted in *The Collected Scientific Papers of Paul A. Samuelson*, vol. 2, chapter 114.

Shove, G. E. [1942]: 'The Place of Marshall's "Principles" in the Development of Economic Theory', *Economic Journal*, **52**, pp. 294–329.

Toulmin, S. [1972]: 'The Collective Use and Evolution of Concepts', *Human Understanding*, vol. 1.

Wrong, D. H. [1961]: 'The Oversocialized Conception of Man in Modern Sociology', *American Sociological Review*, **26**, pp. 183–93.

Anomaly and the development of economics: the case of the Leontief paradox [1]

NEIL DE MARCHI
DUKE UNIVERSITY

There is a widespread belief that it is neither necessary nor becoming to a working scientist to attend too closely to methodology. In economics this belief at times finds expression in a curious disjunction between lip service paid to falsificationist ideals and an altogether different practice with respect to anomalies. In pragmatic terms there may be nothing inconsistent about this. For in the influential form of falsificationism propagated among economists by Milton Friedman, in which the most important mark of a good theory is the (relative) accuracy of its predictions, no guidance is given the researcher as to where he should turn when one or another of his hypotheses appears to have been contraverted.[2] Faced with a choice between specifying new propositions and acquiring the data and devising tests appropriate thereto and making adjustments to improve the fit of one already articulated, the economist will, by dint of his training, if for no other reason, choose the latter, less costly, alternative. This is a negative and somewhat specific line of defence, but it serves to highlight the fundamental problem that must be faced by a researcher of falsificationist bent, namely that he cannot judge the importance of an anomaly except in relation to a developed underlying research programme.

Awareness of such a programme does not, of course, guarantee that a scientist will make the right decisions about how to respond to anomalies, but it does mean that he has a rational basis for action where otherwise he would be dependent solely on his intuition.[3] The basis urged by Lakatos is that it is rational to adhere to an apparently refuted theory, so long as the research programme of which it forms a part is consistently predicting

---

[1] A number of improvements have been made to this paper as a result of comments by participants at the Nafplion Colloquium on Research Programmes in Physics and Economics, Nafplion, Greece, September 2–14, 1974. I am particularly indebted to Mark Blaug and Spiro Latsis for constructive suggestions.

[2] Compare Lakatos [1971], p. 99, 'the naive falsificationist's disconnected chains of conjectures and refutations'.

[3] Friedman has no advice to offer the scientist needing to assess the applicability and significance of some observation(s), nor any guidance for the scientist in search of a new, improved theory. The former problem involves a 'capacity to judge...that cannot be taught'. 'The construction of hypotheses is a creative act of inspiration, intuition, invention...The process must be discussed in psychological, not logical, categories...' Friedman [1953], pp. 25, 43.

novel facts (is 'progressive').[4] In the following pages an account is given of the development of a portion of modern trade theory (the Ohlin–Samuelson, or Ohlin–Lerner–Samuelson theory) employing the meta-historical criteria associated with Lakatos's methodology. Since only a single anomaly (the Leontief paradox) is to be discussed, general conclusions would be out of place. There is, however, an implication which carries us beyond whatever purely intrinsic interest may attach to this one case. A *convincing* historical reconstruction of a progressive problem shift in which an apparently crucial refutation fails to issue in the rejection of theory must cast doubt on the adequacy of the alternative falsificationist construction according to which it would be good scientific practice to dispense with the theory.[5]

I

The classical explanation of the basis of commodity trade, associated especially with the name of David Ricardo, proceeded in terms of assumed relative differences in labour productivity between nations. With the aid of the further assumption that relative commodity prices vary more or less in proportion to labour costs, these productivity differences were translated into differences in relative product prices. It could then be shown that mutual gain could result if trading partners each specialised in the production and free exportation of goods in which they possessed a comparative cost (or price) advantage.

Two prominent lacunae were present in this theory. First, no systematic explanation of international productivity differences was given. Second, no allowance was made for varying factor input-combinations in response to changes in factor prices.

More than a century passed before Bertil Ohlin, in the 1920s, supplied the necessary set of relations to fill both gaps. Ohlin took as his point of departure the labour theory of value, with its strict implication that labour–capital ratios are the same in all lines of production.[6] He substituted for this theory a modified version of Cassel's exposition of the general equilibrium theory of pricing, explicitly recognising the interaction of demand and supply in the form of four elements: wants and desires, the distribution of factor ownership (hence of incomes), the supply

[4] I adopt here the definition of 'novel fact' given by Elie Zahar: 'A fact will be considered novel with respect to a given hypothesis if it did not belong to the problem-situation which governed the construction of the hypothesis.' Zahar [1973], p. 103. Under this definition temporal novelty (a prediction, in the strict sense, of some new fact) is 'a sufficient but not a necessary condition for novelty'. *Ibid.* A known fact may be novel with respect to a given hypothesis or theory if it is accounted for by that theory *without* the theory's having been specifically designed with that end in view.

[5] It is perhaps arguable that Lakatos's advice to employ history as a test of methodologies only pushes the problem of criteria one stage further back.

[6] Ohlin [1967], pp. 20, 22.

of factors of production and the physical conditions of production.[7] If the physical conditions of production and the quality of each factor are assumed to be 'everywhere the same'; if, further, commodity prices equal costs of production; and if the proportions in which productive factors are combined are allowed to be functions of factor prices (closing one gap in the classical theory), then equal relative factor prices in each of two regions implies the same factor proportions in an industry in both regions, the same costs of production in each for the same commodity and common relative commodity prices as between the two regions. In other words, no comparative advantage would then exist. The other conditions holding, common relative factor prices may be the result of exactly offsetting differences in factor supplies on the one hand and demand conditions on the other. But if factor endowments differ significantly between the regions then, in Ohlin's view, it would be 'practically inconceivable' for demand conditions to vary in an opposite manner to the extent necessary for equality of relative factor prices to obtain. Ohlin, indeed, deemed differences in factor supplies 'probably as a rule more important than differences in demand'. And he was led to conclude that 'in a loose sense, therefore, differences in equipment of factors of production will be the cause [of differences in relative commodity prices, thence] of trade'.[8]

At the heart of Ohlin's theory was an implied, but unproven, one-to-one relation between relative commodity outputs and factor endowments.[9] The existence of such a relation, plus normal neoclassical assumptions about differentiability, implies that 'continuous variation of factor endowments would yield continuous (rather than arbitrary) variation in production relations', thereby closing the remaining gap in the classical theory.[10] Moreover, given such a relation, it can be shown that a capital abundant country will tend to specialise in the production of, and will export, commodities using relatively large amounts of capital. The general form of this proposition has become known as the Heckscher–Ohlin theorem on the pattern of trade.[11]

Research might have proceeded from this point in either of two obvious directions: (i) attempts to specify precisely the sufficient, then the necessary conditions for the Heckscher–Ohlin theorem to hold; (ii) attempts to discover whether the theorem is true to observed trade flows. Neither of these direct routes was in fact followed. Analysts turned instead to a separate proposition, also outlined in Ohlin's work, to the effect that trade

[7] Ohlin [1967], pp. 8, 23n, Appendix I.
[8] Ohlin [1967], pp. 10, 63.
[9] See, for example, Jones [1956–7] in Bhagwati [1969a], and Minabe [1966], especially pp. 1196–8.
[10] Chipman [1966], p. 18.
[11] Heckscher's contribution to the development of the theorem is deliberately ignored here since Ohlin ([1967], p. 306) records that 'Heckscher was rather averse to coordinating the factor proportion analysis with the Walràs–Cassel theory', whereas it is precisely this conjunction that concerns us.

in goods, on the pattern predicted by the Heckscher–Ohlin theorem, will tend to equalise factor scarcities and hence factor prices between nations.[12]

This inference issued naturally out of Ohlin's 'mutual interdependence' theory of pricing, which for the first time integrated factor markets into trade theory. It drew the attention of Paul Samuelson, who quickly came to see in it one possible chain of causation that one might choose to isolate to give substance to the notion of general equilibrium in a world of competitive exchange. Within any isolated region, if constant returns to scale prevail, minimum unit cost will depend only on factor prices, not on the level of output. Assuming perfect mobility of factors and each factor actually used in every industry, a single price for each factor will obtain equal to the value of its marginal product. So long as every commodity is produced in some amount, competitive product market assumptions guarantee that the price of each will equal its cost of production. Then, with a knowledge of production functions, it follows trivially that there will be a one-to-one relation between commodity and factor prices. If the region is now considered to be part of a free-trade world, each commodity will have a common price in all regions, in the absence of transport costs. It follows that if the same commodity is produced everywhere by the same technique and all commodities continue to be produced after the opening up of trade, absolute factor prices will also be equalised.

Provided that the one-to-one relation between commodity and factor prices is invertible (a critical condition of which is that each commodity remains intensive in the use of a factor at all factor prices) one can argue either from given factor prices to equilibrium commodity prices, as a Ricardian might do, or from commodity prices, given, for example, by international markets, back to factor prices. Both the classical and Ohlin versions of an explanation of trade may thus be viewed as adaptations of a common general equilibrium framework.[13]

With the articulation of this framework by Samuelson in the early 1950s, the Ohlin approach acquired a significance unconnected with its accuracy as a description of real world trade flows. This is not to say that the Heckscher–Ohlin theorem itself could be dropped and all attention given to the structural characteristics of an exchange model which retained at best a tenuous historical connection with Ohlin's work. For it was implicit in Samuelson's models, and would be made quite explicit by subsequent researchers, that the assumptions sufficient to yield factor-price equalisation also suffice (when supplemented by the condition that common consumption patterns prevail) to yield the Heckscher–Ohlin theorem. Nonetheless a shift of emphasis was involved. What Samuelson did was graft Ohlin's trade theory and the problems connected with its

[12] Ohlin [1967], pp. 24–6.
[13] Samuelson [1953–4]. Summary expositions are to be found in Chipman [1966], pp. 20–1 and Bhagwati [1969b], pp. 40–1.

rigorous articulation and generalisation onto the mainline research tradition concerned with the conditions governing the existence, uniqueness and stability of general competitive equilibrium.

This is the necessary background to a discussion of the Leontief paradox, to which we now turn.

II

In 1953 – the same year that Samuelson attempted the rigorous generalisation of Ohlin's 'interdependence' theory – Wassily Leontief published the results of an application of his input–output analysis to USA trade. His main finding was that if USA exports and imports were each to be reduced by an equal amount (all commodities being cut proportionally) and the imports replaced so far as possible by additional domestic production of the same products, factor requirements for the additional output would be biased in the direction of capital, whereas more labour than capital would be released by the reduction in output of export industries. USA exports, in other words, appeared to be relatively labour-intensive and her imports capital-intensive. Invoking the theory that a country's exports will embody more of its relatively abundant (hence cheaper) factor, Leontief drew the inference that, contrary to common belief, the USA is a labour- rather than a capital-abundant nation. Being unwilling, however, to accept this conclusion, he argued that USA workers are more effective than those abroad, and when labour requirements are appropriately scaled up to incorporate this fact the paradoxical finding will be found to reverse itself.

Leontief's technique required that scale factors be ignored, and it assumed that the same technique of production would prevail internationally for each commodity considered separately. Demand conditions (differences in consumption patterns) were assumed not to offset differences in factor endowment; and impediments to free trade were neglected.[14] In all these respects Leontief's was a true test of the simple version of the Heckscher–Ohlin theorem.

III

The Leontief test, though not perfectly controlled, is probably about as clear an example of a 'crucial experiment' as one is likely to encounter in economics. How did economists react? At first sight, much as Thomas Kuhn suggests in his discussion of predictive failure in physical science. Once an area of theory has been fully mathematicised, Kuhn argues, the emergence of quantitative anomaly signals not only *that* something has

---

[14] Leontief [1953], in Bhagwati [1969a]; Leontief [1956]. Chipman [1966], pp. 44–57 gives the best available critical exposition.

gone wrong, but tells the members of the scientific community 'where to look for a new qualitative phenomenon'. Kuhn elaborates on this by commenting elsewhere that it is frequently the case that elements of the successful resolution of anomalies have been 'as least partially anticipated during a period when there was no crisis...[though] in the absence of crisis those anticipations ha[ve] been ignored'.[15]

One way to judge the extent to which scientists have been brought up short in their work by the sudden appearance of serious anomaly is to examine the patterns of citations in publications circumscribing their research area. Kuhn's remarks would lead us to expect that serious breakdown in existing theory would be followed by a marked shift in the pattern, towards citation of sources both more numerous and older than the standard ones, changes reflected in, for example, a decline in the degree of concentration of citations and a lengthened half-life of the literature of the research area. Further, one may look at the ratio of actual to possible citations within the group of publications representing exploration of the pool of likely or earlier anticipated explanations of the difficulty that has arisen. If it is found that this ratio is even greater than that for a coherent and narrowly-defined sub-area of research (such as, in our case, is constituted by work on factor-price equalisation), this might be interpreted as indirect support for Kuhn's suggestion that the search for an explanation is not random. These expectations are confirmed by measures derived from a bibliography and citation index of the literature in the Ohlin–Samuelson tradition of trade theory comprising some 171 articles and covering the period 1933–68.[16] Nonetheless, it is doubtful whether this signifies a standard (falsificationist) response to the Leontief paradox, both because the measures themselves are extremely crude and not unambiguous and because – more importantly – closer inspection of the writings of those involved simply does not support that notion.

At least a four-way classification of responses seems necessary. First, there is a sizeable group, some of whose members have criticised Leontief's method (for example, his exclusion of natural resources and of human capital, and of non-competitive imports) or his data (for example, 1947 – the year of his input–output table – was atypical). A much larger subset of this group has set about finding an explanation of the paradox, chiefly in terms of failures of one or another of the assumptions made in the simple version of the Heckscher–Ohlin theorem tested. Thus it has been repeatedly asserted in various ways that neither factors nor techniques are everywhere the same; that demand conditions may have operated perversely to produce the strange result; that commodities do not neces-

---

[15] Kuhn [1961], p. 180; Kuhn [1970], pp. 74–5.

[16] A more detailed account is given in an unpublished paper I presented at the first conference of the History of Economics Society, Chicago, May 1973, under the title, 'History of Economics as the Development of Research Areas: An Application of Citation Data.'

sarily remain intensive in one factor at all relevant factor prices (factor-intensity reversal); and so on. In some instances evidence has been offered in support of these contentions, but for the most part they represent purely speculative and *ex post* rationalisations.[17]

A second group of theorists was spurred by Leontief's work to try to produce rigorous demonstrations of the conditions under which the Heckscher–Ohlin theorem would hold – something Samuelson had undertaken only for the factor-price equalisation theorem.[18]

These two groups, and the fourth one, to be considered presently, dominate the empirical measures of response referred to above. But from the point of view informing the present historical account they are not the most important. That distinction belongs to the third group, led by Samuelson though over a fifteen year period embracing a succession of prominent theorists, who chose to all but ignore the Leontief paradox. This behaviour was entirely consistent with the research programme pursued by Samuelson in three important papers of 1948, 1949 and 1953.

(i) In the earlier two papers Samuelson attempted to demonstrate factor-price equalisation in a world of two countries, two commodities and two factors.[19] It is interesting to note that this was not the first such attempt. Quite unbeknown to Samuelson, Abba Lerner, as a student at LSE in the early 1930s, had produced a perfectly satisfactory proof under comparable assumptions. Lerner's work derived nothing from Ohlin's *Interregional and International Trade*,[20] which he had not read; rather it formed part of a series of analytical exercises designed to show the nature of production and exchange equilibrium, making use of the then new and extraordinarily powerful geometrical devices of transformation and indifference curves.[21] This is a perfect instance of parallel ('multiple') discovery, and the fact that Lerner apparently owed nothing to Ohlin strengthens the point made above concerning the relative unimportance within the Ohlin–Samuelson programme of the factual accuracy of the Heckscher–Ohlin theorem. Whether or not the factor proportions model turned out to be an accurate way of accounting for real world trade flows, it was a potentially fruitful point of entry into the general network of

---

[17] A convenient summary of the relevant studies is in Chipman [1966], pp. 52–5.

[18] See especially Robinson [1956a] and [1956b], Jones [1956–7] and Lancaster [1957], the latter two in Bhagwati [1969a].

[19] Samuelson [1948], [1949]. The work was in fact begun somewhat earlier; see Stolper and Samuelson [1941].

[20] Ohlin [1933].

[21] Lerner [1932], [1933], both reprinted in Lerner [1953]. Professor Lerner has assured me in conversation that his work was pursued in ignorance of Ohlin's theory. It seems likely that the immediate stimulii behind Lerner's work were an early presentation by Haberler of the doctrine of comparative cost in opportunity cost terms and a lecture delivered by Jacob Viner at LSE in 1931, in which he made use of the notions of opportunity cost and of consumer preferences in the form of transformation and indifference curves, to illustrate trade equilibrium. See Haberler [1930], Viner [1955], p. 521 note 8, and Robbins [1971], p. 132.

interdependent relations operating to determine competitive prices. As Lerner himself noted at the end of his essays on the geometrical representation of cost and demand conditions in international trade, 'the constructions...apply to any kind of trade, between individuals, towns, regions, countries and continents as well as between social classes or between people at different points of time; and...it is only an historical accident of the development of Economic Theory that all these problems are called "International Trade"'.[22]

Both Samuelson and Lerner recognised that factor-intensity reversal could prevent factor-price equalisation, and Samuelson explicitly acknowledged the importance to that result of the condition that the factor intensities of the two commodities differ significantly by comparison with the factor endowments of the two trading partners.[23]

(ii) In 1953 Samuelson tackled the more difficult task of demonstrating the uniqueness of the relation between (given) commodity prices and the corresponding factor prices in a world of many goods and factors. He repeated the point that factor endowments should not differ too greatly, lest production of some commodities cease altogether in certain regions, thereby weakening the connection between prices and costs of production.[24] He did not, however, show that there does exist some factor endowment for which incomplete specialisation in production is compatible with competitive equilibrium.

(iii) This gap was filled by Kuhn in 1959.[25]

(iv) Samuelson's 1953 proof that factor prices are uniquely determined from goods prices, turned out on further scrutiny to be inadequate. Corrected theorems have been presented by Nikaido and Gale, and by Samuelson himself, these advances depending in part on developments in pure mathematics. The problem turns out to be equivalent to finding the conditions for the uniqueness of general equilibrium prices in the case where demand for goods is perfectly elastic.[26] And a major finding has been that a sufficient condition to establish the uniqueness of the relation between commodity and factor prices is the same as that derived by earlier theorists (for example, Hicks) for the stability of the general equilibrium pricing process.[27]

A considerable amount of auxiliary theoretical research has by now been conducted, incorporating complications into the basic factor proportions approach by relaxing the assumptions of Samuelson's early

[22] Lerner [1953], p. 122.
[23] Samuelson [1948], pp. 175 note 1, 178–9 and [1949], p. 188 note 1; Lerner [1952], in Lerner [1953], pp. 78–80.
[24] Samuelson [1953–4], p. 12.
[25] Kuhn [1959]. See Chipman [1966], pp. 25–9 for an exposition.
[26] Arrow and Hahn [1972], p. 14.
[27] Chipman [1966], pp. 29–30; Gale and Nikaido [1965]; Samuelson [1966], vol. 2, p. 908; Arrow and Hahn [1972], chapters 9 and 12.

models. Thus allowance has been made for 'neutral' (scalar) national differences in production functions and factor productivities, for untraded goods, for trade in intermediate goods and for changes in factor supplies; capital has received explicit recognition as a factor, its migration across national boundaries has been allowed for and the equalisation of interest rates has been investigated; and technical progress has been treated.[28]

This coherent line of theoretical enquiry can be traced back to Ohlin's initial vision that the 'trade question' is essentially a matter of determining the location of production or of flows of goods in a world of separate but related markets.[29] Ohlin also expressed a design principle ('positive heuristic') for elaborating this conception. He envisaged a sequence of models, each designed to illuminate some important aspect or aspects of international economic relations and connected through the 'mutual interdependence' theory of pricing. The factor proportions model was to be but the first in the sequence, being modified in the direction of realism by the successive consideration of taxes, tariffs and transport costs, economies of scale, consumer preferences, different conditions of production as between countries, variable factor supply and mobility and imperfections in competition.[30] In the matter of proscription ('negative heuristic') Ohlin in effect urged researchers to avoid models which do not incorporate a unified pricing principle.[31] Thus he objected to the classical model of comparative costs on the ground that it was a 'conglomerate' of cost of production and real or labour cost notions of pricing which did not lend itself as naturally as did a unified (money) cost pricing model to the incorporation of other costs (for example, taxes, transport costs). Furthermore, in standard expositions, capital and labour and the different qualities of labour exist and are combined in given proportions, rendering the theory unfit to handle issues such as the impact of changes in demand and factor prices. Nor in its labour–cost aspect was it capable of being developed in the direction of realism to accommodate the case where no productive factors or commodities were common between

[28] See Chipman [1966], pp. 41–4; Bhagwati [1969b], pp. 48–55; Kemp [1969], chapters 6 and 7.

[29] Ohlin [1967], pp. ix, 2, 305–6, 307.

[30] Ohlin [1967], Appendix II, 'Reflections on Contemporary International Trade Theories', added in 1966 to the revised version of Ohlin [1933], outlines in summary fashion the mode of treatment which Ohlin deemed appropriate. It corresponds exactly, though reflecting, as one might expect, a heightened degree of methodological self-consciousness, to the way the argument was developed in the original treatise.

[31] Lakatos defines 'positive heuristic' as 'a partially articulated set of suggestions or hints on how to develop the "refutable variants" of the research programme...'. It is at the same time a 'strategy both to predict (produce) and to digest [anomalies]'. The 'negative heuristic', by contrast, comprises a set of prohibitions. It defines the 'hard core' of a programme and directs that research be devoted *not* to undermining this 'hard core', which is deemed irrefutable, but to inventing, articulating, and testing models built around this core. Lakatos [1968], pp. 167–8, 168–9, 170–1, 173. Ohlin in effect designated the mutual interdependence theory of pricing 'hard core' and simply eschewed working with theories at odds with this principle.

trading partners. And so on.[32] Samuelson's work, and that of those who followed his lead, was an effort to display the conditions for and structure of general equilibrium prices in a generalised factor proportions model, and represents virtually another programme, of theoretical research, superimposed on Ohlin's programme at stage 1 of the latter.

Now neither Ohlin nor Samuelson was under any illusion about the realism of the factor proportions model. Samuelson explored its simple version in the conviction that it '*does convey insight* into the forces shaping world trade' and pressed his investigation of a generalised, though still avowedly 'idealised, statical, and competitive' version, for what it revealed about 'the nature of pricing' and 'also for the light it casts on so many of the often-confused issues of [general] economic theory'.[33] Both were aware that this starting model, even in its fullest theoretical development, was bound to be replaced in the effort to secure closer approximation to reality. But this fact, and possession of a clear positive heuristic, together render irrelevant the refutation of the factor proportions model implied in Leontief's findings. As Lakatos has maintained in a more general context: 'The positive heuristic sets out a programme which lists a chain of ever more complicated *models* simulating reality: the scientist's attention is riveted on building his model following instructions which are laid down in the positive part of his programme. He ignores the *actual* counter-examples, the available "*data*".'[34]

The notion of an Ohlin–Samuelson research programme enables us to rationalise the reaction – or absence of it – of certain economic theorists to the Leontief paradox. It would be nice to be able to add that no perverseness or ignoble tenaciousness was involved; in other words, that

[32] Ohlin [1967], pp. 8, note 2; 15, note 7; 303–4; 308–9. A detailed set of objections to the classical approach is to be found in Ohlin [1933], Appendix III. In the case last mentioned above, as Ohlin noted, neither the classical nor the factor proportions model is applicable, though the mutual interdependence theory of pricing was still superior in his view, since it could incorporate more naturally the relevant influences ('new demand conditions and the reactions of factor supply'). *Ibid.*, p. 304. This bears out the point stressed immediately below that the factor proportions model was never in Ohlin's estimate more than a strategic simplification, useful 'as a general introduction to illuminate the character of trade in some essential respects'. It was to be assessed not in isolation but as the first of a naturally cohering sequence of models, that is, as part of a whole programme. *Ibid.*, pp. 307, 309. J. R. Hicks has urged that if we do not know or cannot observe 'whether the "same" factor, in different countries, is really the same factor or not' then in this respect the comparative cost model (expressed in terms of opportunity cost) is the more suitable tool. For the latter at least compares *products actually traded* (hence observable). Hicks [1959], p. 266. Ohlin would presumably be the first to agree, while still maintaining that if *neither* factors nor commodities are the same, one's only recourse is to the mutual interdependence approach to pricing. To repeat, it is on the basis of this 'hard core' and its derivative sequence of models that Ohlin's approach must be judged, not the factor proportions model as such.

[33] Samuelson [1948], pp. 180–3; [1949], pp. 195–6; [1951–2], p. 121; [1953–4], p. 14; [1960] in [1966], vol. 2, p. 910. Cf. Ohlin [1967], p. 309, and his candid comments in Harrod and Hague [1963], pp. 398–9.

[34] Lakatos [1968], pp. 171, 173.

the programme was a good one, worth retaining in the face of this counter-example. That would be the case if it could be shown that the programme involved a progressive theoretical problem shift (predicted novel 'facts') without being inferior in an empirical sense to the pro-scribed alternative – the classical – account of the pattern of trade.[35]

IV

Theoretical progress within the Ohlin–Samuelson programme has already been indicated. On the empirical side two developments of note have occurred. One of these is a finding derived from a succession of tests, that in general Leontief's results are reversed by expanding the number of factors to include natural resources and human skills.[36] The second, in-volving a comparison of a range of goods internationally, identifies elasti-cities of substitution by industry, and implies that, since different elastici-ties are observed as between industries factor-intensity reversal is likely to occur in the production of the same good in different countries.[37] At first sight this finding seems to nullify the first one, since factor-intensity reversal undermines both the factor-price equalisation and the Heckscher–Ohlin theorems. However, in the case of the latter result, an apparently destructive initial research report has been turned into a corroborating instance, and the two sets of studies taken together tend in fact to strengthen the empirical claims of the factor proportions approach to trade theory.

The finding, by Minhas, that factor-intensity reversal is likely within the relevant range of factor prices, made use of a constant elasticity of substitution production function. Among numerous technical objections that have been applied to Minhas's work, it has been argued by one critic that use of the CES production function in conjunction with data for many commodities but only two factors renders factor-intensity reversal 'absolutely impossible'.[38] At the same time, further empirical work strongly suggests that even Minhas's original data, when fully utilised, point to the confirmation, not refutation, of the assumption that a com-modity remains intensive in the use of one factor at all factor prices.[39]

[35] The concept of problem shift is introduced by Lakatos in the following context: 'if theories are falsified all the time, they are problematic all the time, and therefore we may speak of. . .*problem-shifts*.' A theoretically progressive problem shift would be represented by a sequence of theories each of which had greater content ('explained' more) than its predecessor. Lakatos [1968], p. 164. Presumably, then, we may speak of theoretical novel facts, in the sense of novelty outlined in footnote 4 above. At the same time, it should be stressed that for Lakatos the ultimate goal is not theoretical but empirical progress, or verified excess (novel) content.

[36] Surveys are contained in Bhagwati [1969b] addendum, pp. 107–8, Morrall [1972], chapter 1.

[37] Minhas [1962], reprinted in Bhagwati [1969a], also Minhas [1963]. Critical dis-cussions of this research are to be found in Chipman [1966], pp. 57–70 and Bhagwati [1969b], addendum, pp. 100–7. See also Samuelson [1960], in Samuelson [1966], vol. 2, p. 918.   [38] Chipman [1966], p. 70; cf. pp. 32–3, 34.

[39] Bhagwati [1969b], addendum, pp. 100–1, summarising Leontief [1964].

Finally, tests controlling for natural resources and human skills suggest that factor-intensity reversal is empirically insignificant.[40]

In reconstructing a piece of history using the methodology of research programmes one is on the lookout for predictions of novel facts, and it is tempting to interpret as such both the finding about the effect of incorporating natural resources and human skills, and the apparent overturning of the early evidence that suggests factor-intensity reversal was empirically significant. For as early as 1948 Samuelson recognised the probable importance of natural resources and of 'know-how' in accounting for the location of production and patterns of specialisation.[41] And in 1951 – a decade prior to the Minhas research report – he recorded his 'impression that the phenomenon of goods that interchange their roles of being more labour intensive is much less important empirically than it is interesting theoretically'.[42] Nonetheless, while the (demonstrated) complementarity of capital and natural resources can account for the Leontief paradox, this explanation is not consistent with a model in which factor-price equalisation is achieved. To adopt this explanation thus involves explicitly allowing for transport costs or abandoning one or another of the assumptions of the simple version of the Heckscher–Ohlin theorem.[43] As to factor-intensity reversal, it could scarcely be argued that Samuelson's early judgment that the phenomenon would prove empirically unimportant was more than an intuitively well-informed guess. The intuition of 'good' scientists is undoubtedly important to the progress of science, but even they can be mistaken and the worth of a research programme cannot be allowed to depend critically on this fact. On the other hand, it seems fair to regard the resolution of the paradox via the addition of 'human' to physical capital as a natural development within the Ohlin programme. Allowing for skill differences presents no such fundamental problem within the interdependence theory of pricing as it does for the adherent of the strict labour theory of value, and Ohlin himself, within his own 'simplified' version of the factor proportions approach, distinguished between unskilled, skilled and technical labour.[44] Similarly, the discovery of parallelism in the conditions for uniqueness and stability of competitive equilibrium appears to be genuinely novel, in the sense that it is a natural outgrowth of the factor proportions approach though it did not belong to the problem situation which governed the original formulation of that model. (As far as Samuelson's role in this discovery is concerned, it may well have been a hunch of his to work his early proof of uniqueness by studying the properties of the Jacobian matrix of goods prices expressed in

[40] Morrall [1972], pp. 7–9. Not all the evidence, however, is in that direction: see Hodd [1967], Naya [1967].
[41] Samuelson [1948], pp. 181–3.
[42] Samuelson [1951–2], pp. 121–2.
[43] Baldwin [1971], pp. 129, 142.
[44] Ohlin [1967], p. 51. Cf. his comments in Harrod and Hague [1963], p. 398.

terms of factor prices, but the parallelism was implicit in, though not determinative of, the character of the exchange model he specified and was in this sense predictable.)

Returning for a moment to our two noteworthy empirical developments, they contain one additional implication which should be mentioned, since it bears on the question whether the factor proportions explanation of trade is scoring better or worse relative to the classical account. Prior to the publication of Leontief's anomalous results the most careful test of comparative advantage that had been conducted tended to support the classical theory.[45] With one notable exception, modified repetitions of this test during the subsequent decade confirmed this result, so that by the mid-sixties a typical judgment was that 'the classical theory ...based on differences in productivity levels emerges as an important determinant of trade patterns'.[46] But the same evidence that suggests the absence on any large scale of factor-intensity reversals implies that technological differences between countries must be 'neutral' (neither capital- nor labour-saving in general). And as one commentator explains, this simply 'rules out a large class of differing technology explanations of trade patterns'.[47]

One further point is worth making before we turn to the fourth main type of response to the Leontief paradox. Some economists have been bothered about the factor proportions approach for the dual reasons that the critical notion of the factor-intensity of production has no obvious meaning when there are more than two factors involved, and because it is increasingly less likely that the restrictions on conditions of production necessary to ensure factor-price equalisation will be realised as the number of factors and goods is assumed to increase. This has caused some theorists, notably Ivor Pearce, to stand apart from the Ohlin–Samuelson programme.[48] The important thing to note here is simply that the reason existed, and was recognised, prior to and quite independently of the Leontief test.

V

A fourth and final group of economists has taken Leontief's finding as an occasion to develop an alternative to the factor proportions approach. Ironically, one starting point is the same – Ohlin's *Interregional and International Trade* – though an equally important source of inspiration is

[45] MacDougall [1951–2].

[46] Ingo Walter [1968], p. 136. Cf. Caves [1960], p. 281, Caves and Jones [1973], p. 204. For a useful survey of the tests and an account of his own – unsuccessful – attempt to verify the key hypotheses in the Ricardian theory of comparative advantage see Bhagwati [1969b], pp. 7–22.

[47] Morrall [1972], p. 10.

[48] See Chipman [1966], p. 30, but more especially James and Pearce [1951–2] and Pearce [1959].

John H. Williams's criticisms of the classical theory.[49] Raymond Vernon and a group of mainly business-school economists with interests in marketing have taken the major qualifications discussed by Ohlin and compiled a loosely integrated set of propositions (sometimes graced with the name product cycle model) to account for the flow of manufactured goods in a world characterised by tariff impediments to trade, imperfect flows of information and economies of scale, in which both commodities and the processes by which they are produced change over time, and in which goods are purchased in proportions dependent not only on relative prices but also on income levels.

In general terms, the product cycle (and related) models stress that product innovation, or at least the first commercial production of a new good, requires a large supply of technical expertise and the presence of high-income consumers. In the early stages of production neither the product nor the process is standardised and the location of production is much influenced by familiarity with the market and the existence of efficient communications so that market information can be translated rapidly into product changes. Also at first, the product is likely to require relatively large inputs of skilled labour, and this fact, plus related technological and scale barriers may give the home producer a temporary production and export monopoly; though as incomes rise and the product and its production process become standardised, it may become profitable for the home producer to establish subsidiaries abroad (for example, to take advantage of cheaper local labour or ensure responsiveness to local preferences).[50] This chain of hypotheses can be extended much further, but enough has been said to give the flavour of the reasoning typically employed. In a concrete application of this approach, it has been argued that the USA is more likely than other nations to initiate production of 'sophisticated' (high-income) consumer goods and that the additional considerations mentioned above mean that her exports of manufactured goods at any point in time will tend to be concentrated in those that are new and therefore skill-intensive. Leontief's findings are thus entirely in line with the expectations generated by this new approach.[51]

This 'neo-technology' account of trade in manufactured goods sheds light on the pattern of international capital movement (especially in the context of the behaviour of the multinational corporation) and supplies a reason why trade may continue to grow where there are partners of relatively similar tastes and income levels.[52] Its findings, however, while sometimes novel in the strict sense that they could not have been predicted

[49] Williams [1929].

[50] See especially Vernon [1966] and the introductory essay by Louis T. Wells in Wells [1972].   [51] Wells [1969], in Wells [1972].

[52] Cf. Hufbauer in Vernon [1970], p. 197. Hufbauer designates the new account the 'neo-technology' approach.

by the factor proportions approach, do not belong to any overarching theoretical structure: in Lakatos's terminology they are *ad hoc*$_3$.[53] Samuelson's research was unashamedly the explication of 'a very idealised, statical, competitive' world.[54] A research programme based on non-static and non-competitive assumptions has been deemed desirable by probably a majority of economists in all times and places, and could conceivably be built, but it does not yet exist.

VI

The conclusions suggested by this account are straightforward and must indeed seem obvious to anyone familiar with Lakatos's work.

The response of the Samuelson group to Leontief's findings is necessarily problematic to a falsificationist like Milton Friedman. Here was 'evidence...about as direct, dramatic, and convincing as any that could be provided by controlled experiments', yet as unaccountably as economists remain skeptical about the adequacy of correlated changes in the quantity of money and of prices as an account of inflation, a group of leading theorists failed to reject the apparently refuted factor proportions theory of trade.[55] A plausible explanation, I hope I have shown, can be given in terms of the Ohlin–Samuelson research programme.

The description given by Lakatos fits that programme surprisingly well. We can discern both positive hints for the development of a coherent sequence of models and a negative heuristic proscribing attempts to base the sequence on any but the 'mutual interdependence' theory of pricing. There is a belt of auxiliary hypotheses, the empirical content of some of which has been corroborated (this is true to some extent, for example, of the no factor-intensity reversal assumption in the basic model), though the empirical meaning of some remains obscure (What is a factor? What is the meaning of strong factor-intensity in a multifactor world?). And there has been a modest harvest of novel facts (for example, that factor endowments are a sufficient explanation of comparative advantage; that whereas the international movement of factors would destroy the basis for trade in a classical model, in the Ohlin–Samuelson approach factor-price equalisation under trade implies that there will be no incentive for factor migration to proceed so far as to eliminate differences in factor endowments and therefore trade; that similar conditions suffice for there to be a unique relation between goods and factor prices as for stability to prevail in competitive exchange models). The fruitfulness of the programme, however, has lain less in its generation of such major unexpected findings

---

[53] This is openly acknowledged by researchers in the area: see Wells [1972], pp. 5, 26 and Hufbauer in Vernon [1970], pp. 195–7. A theory is said to be *ad hoc*$_3$ if it involves a modification of some preceding theory in a way out of keeping with the positive heuristic of a programme. See Zahar [1973], p. 101.

[54] Samuelson [1953–4], p. 14.   [55] Friedman [1953], p. 11.

than in the stream of technical puzzles that it has fed the theoretical researcher. The real difficulties in this programme have been, as Lakatos predicts, mathematical rather than empirical (chiefly the search for conditions governing uniqueness).[56] These characteristics stem from the special nature of the problem shift – really the best word to describe it – that took place when Samuelson began to explore the theoretical implications of the factor proportions model guided by the belief that 'international trade...constitutes an analytical special case of general economic theory'.[57] This coupling was crucial; without it research in the Ohlin tradition would have comprised research informed only in a general way by his positive heuristic and more immediately by his qualifications and disclaimers about the classical *and* factor proportions approaches, and might well have proceeded in a piecemeal fashion, exemplified by the 'neo-technology' accounts of trade.[58] The Leontief paradox was important to an economist such as Charles Kindleberger with a strong concern about the immediate relevance of theory. Kindleberger could conclude that 'what he [Leontief] proves is not that the USA is capital-scarce and labour-abundant, but that the Heckscher–Ohlin theorem is wrong'.[59] At the same time we may argue that under the wider theoretical perspective adopted by Samuelson it was entirely proper that Leontief's finding did *not* determine the direction of research.

It does not follow from all this that the Samuelson programme is a paradigm of virtuous economic research. Much of it, indeed, represents what some would deem an excessive preoccupation with formal structure. But that is beside the point. The programme serves to illustrate for economics two more general propositions, and it is on that basis that it has been pressed into service here. The first of these propositions is that good reasons may be adduced, in place of mere inertia or perverseness, why scientists fail to abandon a theory in the face of strong evidence against it. The methodology of research programmes is one way – not necessarily the only one – to get at some of these reasons in particular instances.[60] The

---

[56] Lakatos [1970], pp. 136–7.

[57] Samuelson [1945], in Samuelson [1966], vol. 2, p. 802.

[58] Ohlin himself was so eager to run ahead and incorporate various additional elements of reality into his basic factor proportions model that he did not stop to show exactly how this could be done in accordance with the mutual interdependence pricing principle. A good deal of painstaking, often apparently barren, theoretical work has had to be devoted to sorting out how and to what extent general competitive equilibrium analysis will serve to realise Ohlin's goals. Those who have espoused the 'neo-technology' approach display an impatience with this work and therein lies their affinity with Ohlin.

[59] Kindleberger [1962], p. 75.

[60] Much the same conclusion in this respect would have emerged had the chosen emphasis been the problems surrounding the empirical evidence for factor-intensity reversal and against the Heckscher–Ohlin theorem, an emphasis with which economists in general might feel themselves more at home. Compare Feyerabend [1970], and Caves [1960], p. 282. Caves alludes to 'the swamp of uncertainty wherein Leontief and his critics clash by night'. This speaks volumes for the difficulties of testing in economics.

second proposition, closely related to the first, is that the prescription that scientists should reject apparently refuted theories is at best incomplete advice, while if it is to be read also as an account of how scientists do in fact behave, it is inaccurate and on its own terms therefore lacks warrant.

References

Arrow, K. J. and Hahn, F. H. [1972]: *General Competitive Analysis*.
Baldwin, R. E. [1971]: 'Determinants of the Commodity Structure of U.S. Trade', *The American Economic Review*, **61**, pp. 126–46.
Bhagwati, J. (ed.) [1969*a*]: *International Trade*.
Bhagwati, J. [1969*b*]: 'The Pure Theory of International Trade: A Survey', reprint of 1964 paper, with later addendum, *Trade, Tariffs and Growth: Essays in International Economics*, pp. 3–118.
Caves, R. E. [1960]: *Trade and Economic Structure*.
Caves, R. E. and Jones, R. W. [1973]: *World Trade and Payments*.
Chipman, J. S. [1966]: 'A Survey of the Theory of International Trade: Part 3, The Modern Theory', *Econometrica*, **34**, pp. 18–76.
Feyerabend, P. K. [1970]: 'Problems of Empiricism, Part II', in R. G. Colodny (ed.): *The Nature and Function of Scientific Theories*, pp. 275–353.
Friedman, M. [1953]: 'The Methodology of Positive Economics', in *Essays in Positive Economics*, pp. 3–43.
Gale, D. and Nikaido, H. [1965]: 'The Jacobian Matrix and Global Univalence of Mappings', *Mathematische Annalen*, **159**, pp. 81–93.
Haberler, G. [1930]: 'Die Theorie der komparativen Kosten und ihre Auswertung für die Begründung des Freihandels', *Weltwirtschaftliches Archiv*, **32**, pp. 349–70.
Harrod, R. and Hague, D. [1963]: *International Trade Theory in a Developing World*, Proceedings of a Conference held by the International Economic Association, ed. Harrod, assisted by Hague.
Hicks, J. R. [1959]: 'The Factor Price Equalization Theorem', supplementary note C, *Essays in World Economics*, pp. 260–9.
Hodd, M. [1967]: 'An Empirical Investigation of the Heckscher–Ohlin Theory', *Economica* N. S., **34**, pp. 20–9.
Hufbauer, G. C. [1970]: 'The Impact of National Characteristics and Technology on the Commodity Composition of Trade in Manufactured Goods', in R. Vernon (ed.): *The Technology Factor in International Trade*, pp. 145–231.
James, S. F. and Pearce, I. F. [1951–2]: 'The Factor Price Equalisation Myth', *Review of Economic Studies*, **19**, pp. 111–20.
Jones, R. W. [1956–7]: 'Factor Proportions and the Heckscher–Ohlin Theorem', *Review of Economic Studies*, **24**, pp. 1–10, reprinted in Bhagwati [1969*a*], pp. 77–92.
Kemp, M. C. [1969]: *The Pure Theory of International Trade and Investment*.
Kindleberger, C. P. [1962]: *Foreign Trade and the National Economy*.
Kuhn, H. W. [1959]: 'Factor Endowments and Factor Prices: Mathematical Appendix', *Economica* N. S., **26**, pp. 142–4.
Kuhn, T. S. [1961]: 'The Function of Measurement in Modern Physical Science', *Isis*, **52**, pp. 161–93.
Kuhn, T. S. [1970]: *The Structure of Scientific Revolutions*, 2nd edn, enlarged.
Lakatos, I. [1968]: 'Criticism and the Methodology of Scientific Research Programmes', *Proceedings of the Aristotelian Society*, **69**, pp. 149–86.
Lakatos, I. [1970]: 'Falsification and the Methodology of Scientific Research Programmes', in I. Lakatos and A. Musgrave (eds.): *Criticism and the Growth of Knowledge*, pp. 91–195.

Lakatos, I. [1971]: 'History of Science and Its Rational Reconstructions', in R. C. Buck and R. S. Cohen (eds.): *Boston Studies in the Philosophy of Science*, vol. 8, pp. 91–136.

Lancaster, K. [1957]: The Heckscher–Ohlin Trade Model: A Geometric Treatment. *Economica* N. S., **24**, 19–39, reprinted in Bhagwati [1969a], pp. 49–74.

Leontief, W. W. [1953]: 'Domestic Production and Foreign Trade: The American Capital Position Re-examined', *Proceedings of the American Philosophical Society*, **97**, reprinted in Bhagwati [1969a], pp. 93–139.

Leontief, W. W. [1956]: 'Factor Proportions and the Structure of American Trade: Further Theoretical and Empirical Analysis', *Review of Economics and Statistics*, **38**, 386–407.

Leontief, W. W. [1964]: 'An International Comparison of Factor Costs and Factor Use', *The American Economic Review*, **54**, 335–45.

Lerner, A. P. [1932]: 'The Diagrammatical Representation of Cost Conditions in International Trade', *Economica*, **12**, 346–56, reprinted in Lerner [1953], pp. 85–100.

Lerner, A. P. [1933]: 'Factor Prices and International Trade', *Economica* N.S., **19**, pp. 1–15, reprinted in Lerner [1953], pp. 67–84.

Lerner, A. P. [1934]: 'The Diagrammatical Representation of Demand Conditions in International Trade', *Economica* N.S., **1**, pp. 319–34, reprinted in Lerner [1953], pp. 101–22.

Lerner, A. P. [1953]: *Essays in Economic Analysis*.

MacDougall, G. D. A. [1951/1952]: 'British and American Exports: A Study Suggested by the Theory of Comparative Costs', *Economic Journal*, **61**, pp. 697–724 (Part I), **62**, pp. 487–521 (Part II).

Minabe, N. [1966]: 'The Heckscher–Ohlin Theorem, The Leontief Paradox, and Patterns of Economic Growth', *The American Economic Review*, **56**, pp. 1193–211.

Minhas, B. S. [1962]: 'The Homohypallagic Production Function, Factor-Intensity Reversals and the Heckscher–Ohlin Theorem', *Journal of Political Economy*, **70**, pp. 138–56, reprinted in Bhagwati [1969a], pp. 140–68.

Minhas, B. S. [1963]: *An International Comparison of Factor Costs and Factor Use*.

Morrall, J. F. III [1972]: *Human Capital, Technology, and the Role of the United States in International Trade*.

Naya, S. [1967]: 'Natural Resources, Factor Mix, and Factor Reversal in International Trade', *The American Economic Review* (Proceedings), **57**, pp. 561–70.

Ohlin, B. [1933]: *Interregional and International Trade*.

Ohlin, B. [1967]: *Interregional and International Trade*, revised edition, with the author's 'reflections on contemporary international trade theories'.

Pearce, I. F. [1959]: 'A Further Note on Factor-Commodity Price Relationships', *Economic Journal*, **69**, pp. 725–32.

Robbins, L. C. [1971]: *Autobiography of an Economist*.

Robinson, R. [1956a]: 'Factor Proportions and Comparative Advantage: Part I', *Quarterly Journal of Economics*, **70**, pp. 169–92.

Robinson, R. [1956b]: 'Factor Proportions and Comparative Advantage: Part II', *Quarterly Journal of Economics*, **70**, pp. 246–63.

Samuelson, P. A. [1945]: 'Review of Jacob L. Mosak, *General Equilibrium Theory in International Trade*', *The American Economic Review*, **35**, pp. 943–5, reprinted in Samuelson [1966], pp. 802–4.

Samuelson, P. A. [1948]: 'International Trade and the Equalisation of Factor Prices', *Economic Journal*, **58**, 163–84, reprinted in Samuelson [1966], pp. 847–68.

Samuelson, P. A. [1949]: 'International Factor-Price Equalisation Once Again,' *Economic Journal*, **59**, 181–97, reprinted in Samuelson [1966], pp. 869–85.

Samuelson, P. A. [1951–2]: 'A Comment of Factor-Price Equalisation', *Review of Economic Studies*, **19**, 121–2, reprinted in Samuelson [1966], pp. 886–7.

Samuelson, P. A. [1953–4]: 'Prices of Factors of Goods in General Equilibrium', *Review of Economics Studies*, **21**, pp. 1–20, reprinted in Samuelson [1966], pp. 888–907 (with 1965 postscript, *Ibid.* p. 908).

Samuelson, P. A. [1960]: 'Equalization by Trade of the Interest Rate along with the Real Wage', mimeo, 1960, printed in Samuelson [1966], pp. 909–24.

Samuelson, P. A. [1966]: *The Collected Scientific Papers of Paul A. Samuelson*, ed. J. E. Stiglitz, 2 vols.

Stolper, W. F. and Samuelson, P. A. [1941]: 'Protection and Real Wages', *Review of Economic Studies*, **9**, 58–73, reprinted in Bhagwati [1969a], pp. 245–68.

Vernon, R. [1966]: 'International Investment and International Trade in the Product Cycle', *Quarterly Journal of Economics*, **80**, 190–207.

Vernon, R. (ed.) [1970]: *The Technology Factor in International Trade.*

Viner, J. [1955]: *Studies in the Theory of International Trade.*

Walter, I. [1968]: *International Economics: Theory and Policy.*

Wells, L. T., Jr. [1969]: 'Test of a Product Cycle Model of International Trade: U.S. Exports of Consumer Durables', *Quarterly Journal of Economics*, **83**, pp. 152–62, reprinted in Wells (ed.): *The Product Life Cycle and International Trade*, 1972, pp. 55–79.

Wells, L. T., Jr. [1972]: 'International Trade: The Product Cycle Approach', Introduction to Wells (ed.): *The Product Life Cycle and International Trade*, pp. 3–33.

Williams, J. H. [1929]: 'The Theory of International Trade Reconsidered', *Economic Journal*, **39**, 195–209, reprinted in American Economic Association: *Readings in the Theory of International Trade*, 1950, pp. 253–71.

Zahar, E. [1973]: 'Why did Einstein's Programme Supersede Lorentz's?' (I), *The British Journal for the Philosophy of Science*, **24**, pp. 95–123.

From substantive to procedural rationality[1]

HERBERT A. SIMON
CARNEGIE-MELLON UNIVERSITY

1 Substantive rationality
2 Procedural rationality
  (a) Study of cognitive processes
  (b) Computational efficiency
  (c) Computation: risky decisions
  (d) Man's computational efficiency
3 Economics' concern with procedural rationality
  (a) The real world of business and public policy
  (b) Operations research
  (c) Imperfect competition
  (d) Expectations and uncertainty
4 The empirical study of decision-making
5 Conclusion

In his paper on 'Situational Determinism in Economics',[2] Spiro J. Latsis has described two competitive research programs dealing with the theory of the firm, one of which he calls 'situational determinism', the other, 'economic behavioralism'. A basic contrast between these two programs is that the latter does, but the former does not, require as an essential component a psychological theory of rational choice. Both situational determinism and economic behavioralism postulate behavior that is, in a certain sense, rational, but the meaning of the term 'rational' is quite different for the two programs.

The conflict between situational determinism and economic behavioralism has been most often discussed from the vantage point of the discipline of economics, and as though the discrepant views of rationality associated with the two programs were both indigenous to economics. In point of fact, situational determinism is indigenous to economics, but economic behavioralism is largely an import from psychology, brought into economics to handle certain problems that appeared not to be treated satisfactorily by the situational approach. Thus, the concept of rationality employed in the program of economic behavioralism is not merely an

---

[1] An earlier version of this paper was presented in the Autumn of 1973 at the University of Groningen, The Netherlands, on the occasion of the twenty-fifth anniversary of the faculty of economics there. The Nafplion Colloquium provided me with a welcome opportunity to revise it and make more explicit its relation to the competition among research programs in economics that is discussed in the Colloquium papers of Messrs Coats, Hutchison and Latsis.
[2] Latsis [1972].

adaptation of the concept previously used by economists following the program of situational determinism. It is a distinct concept that has its own independent origins within psychology. I shall use the phrase 'substantive rationality' to refer to the concept of rationality that grew up within economics, and 'procedural rationality' to refer to the concept that developed within psychology.

A person unfamiliar with the histories and contemporary research pre-occupations of economics and cognitive psychology might imagine that there were close relations between them – a constant flow of theoretical concepts and empirical findings from the one to the other and back. Mr Coats, in his chapter in this volume, describes a whole series of earlier attempts, mostly unsuccessful, to bring the findings of psychology to bear upon economic theory. At the present time there is still little communica-tion between the two fields. In the United States, at least, there seem to be no doctoral programs in economics that require their students to master the psychological literature of rationality, and no psychology programs that insist that their students become acquainted with economic theories of rationality. (I would be gratified to learn that such programs exist, but if they do, they are inconspicuous in the extreme.) This state of mutual ignorance becomes understandable when we recognize that the two fields of economics and psychology are interested in answering rather different sets of research questions, and that each has adopted a view of rationality that is more or less appropriate to its own research concerns. As these concerns change, of course, so must the underlying concepts and the research programs that imbed them.

In this paper, I will undertake, first, to explain the two terms 'sub-stantive rationality' and 'procedural rationality' – the differences between them as well as their relations. I shall then try to document the growing interest, during the past twenty-five years, of economists in procedural rationality and in the associated program of economic behavioralism. Finally, I will set forth some reasons for thinking that procedural rationality will become an even more central concern of economics over the next twenty-five years. These changes, past and pre-dicted, are a response to changes in the central research questions with which economics is occupied. The new research questions bring new empirical phenomena into the focus of attention, and the explanation of the new phenomena calls, in turn, for an understanding of the processes that underlie human rationality.

1. *Substantive rationality*

Behavior is substantively rational when it is appropriate to the achieve-ment of given goals within the limits imposed by given conditions and constraints.[3] Notice that, by this definition, the rationality of behavior

---

[3] Cf. the entry under 'rationality' in Gould & Kolb [1964], pp. 573–4.

depends upon the actor in only a single respect – his goals. Given these goals, the rational behavior is determined entirely by the characteristics of the environment in which it takes place.

Suppose, for example, that the problem is to minimize the cost of a nutritionally adequate diet, where nutritional adequacy is defined in terms of lower bounds on intakes of certain proteins, vitamins, and minerals, and upper and lower bounds on calories, and where the unit prices and compositions of the obtainable foods are specified. This diet problem can be (and has been) formulated as a straightforward linear-programming problem, and the correct solution found by applying the simplex algorithm or some other computational procedure. Given the goal of minimizing cost and the definition of 'nutritionally adequate', there are no two ways about it – there is only one substantively rational solution.

Classical economic analysis rests on two fundamental assumptions. The first assumption is that the economic actor has a particular goal, for example, utility maximization or profit maximization. The second assumption is that the economic actor is substantively rational. Given these two assumptions, and given a description of a particular economic environment, economic analysis (descriptive or normative) could usually be carried out using such standard tools as the differential calculus, linear programming, or dynamic programming.

Thus, the assumptions of utility or profit maximization, on the one hand, and the assumption of substantive rationality, on the other, freed economics from any dependence upon psychology. As long as these assumptions went unchallenged, there was no reason why an economist should acquaint himself with the psychological literature on human cognitive processes or human choice. There was absolutely no point at which the findings of psychological research could be injected into the process of economic analysis. The irrelevance of psychology to economics was complete.

2. Procedural rationality

Behavior is procedurally rational when it is the outcome of appropriate deliberation. Its procedural rationality depends on the process that generated it. When psychologists use the term 'rational', it is usually procedural rationality they have in mind. William James, for example, in his *Principles of Psychology*,[4] uses 'rationality' as synonymous with 'the peculiar thinking process called reasoning'. Conversely, behavior tends to be described as 'irrational' in psychology when it represents impulsive response to affective mechanisms without an adequate intervention of thought.

Perhaps because 'rationality' resembles 'rationalism' too closely, and because psychology's primary concern is with process rather than out-come, psychologists tend to use phrases like 'cognitive processes' and

[4] James [1890], chapter 22.

'intellective processes' when they write about rationality in behavior. This shift in terminology may have contributed further to the mutual isolation of the concepts of substantive and procedural rationality.

(a) The study of cognitive processes

The process of rational calculation is only interesting when it is non-trivial – that is, when the substantively rational response to a situation is not instantly obvious. If you put a quarter and a dime before a subject and tell him that he may have either one, but not both, it is easy to predict which he will choose, but not easy to learn anything about his cognitive processes. Hence, procedural rationality is usually studied in problem situations – situations in which the subject must gather information of various kinds and process it in different ways in order to arrive at a reasonable course of action, a solution to the problem.

Historically, there have been three main categories of psychological research on cognitive processes: learning, problem solving, and concept attainment. Learning research is concerned with the ways in which information is extracted from one problem situation and stored in such a way as to facilitate the solving of similar problems subsequently. Problem-solving research (in this narrower sense) focuses especially upon the complementary roles of trial-and-error procedures and insight in reaching problem solutions. Concept attainment research is concerned with the ways in which rules or generalizations are extracted from a sequence of situations and used to predict subsequent situations. Only in recent years, particularly since the Second World War, has there been much unification of theory emerging from these three broad lines of research.

(b) Computational efficiency

Let us return for a moment to the optimal diet problem which we used to illustrate the concept of substantive rationality. From a procedural standpoint, our interest would lie not in the problem solution – the prescribed diet itself – but in the method used to discover it. At first blush, this appears to be more a problem in computational mathematics than in psychology. But that appearance is deceptive.

What is the task of computational mathematics? It is to discover the relative efficiencies of different computational processes for solving problems of various kinds. Underlying any question of computational efficiency is a set of assumptions about the capabilities of the computing system. For an omniscient being, there are no questions of computational efficiency, because the consequences of any tautology are known as soon as the premises are stated; and computation is simply the spinning out of such consequences.[5]

---

[5] This statement is a little over-simple in ignoring the distinction between induction and deduction, but greater precision is not needed for our purposes.

Nowadays, when we are concerned with computational efficiency, we are concerned with the computing time or effort that would be required to solve a problem by a system, basically serial in operation, requiring certain irreducible times to perform an addition, a multiplication, and a few other primitive operations. To compare the simplex method with some other method for solving linear programming problems, we seek to determine how much total computing time each method would need.

The search for computational efficiency is a search for procedural rationality, and computational mathematics is a normative theory of such rationality. In this normative theory, there is no point in prescribing a particular substantively rational solution if there exists no procedure for finding that solution with an acceptable amount of computing effort. So, for example, although there exist optimal (substantively rational) solutions for combinatorial problems of the travelling-salesman type, and although these solutions can be discovered by a finite enumeration of alternatives, actual computation of the optimum is infeasible for problems of any size and complexity. The combinatorial explosion of such problems simply outraces the capacities of computers, present and prospective.

Hence, a theory of rationality for problems like the travelling-salesman problem is not a theory of best solutions – of substantive rationality – but a theory of efficient computational procedures to find good solutions – a theory of procedural rationality. Notice that this change in viewpoint involves not only a shift from the substantive to the procedural, but a shift also from concern for optimal solutions to a concern for good solutions. I shall discuss this point later.

(c) Computation: risky decisions

But now it is time to return to psychology and its concern with computational efficiency. Man, viewed as a thinker, is a system for processing information. What are his procedures for rational choice?

One method of testing a theory of human rational choice is to study choice behavior in relatively simple and well-structured laboratory situations where the theory makes specific predictions about how subjects will behave. This method has been used by a number of investigators – including W. Edwards, G. Pitts, A. Rapaport, and A. Tversky – to test whether human decisions in the face of uncertainty and risk can be explained by the normative concepts of statistical decision theory. This question is particularly interesting because these norms are closely allied, both historically and logically, to the notions of substantive rationality that have prevailed in economics, and make no concessions to computational difficulties – they never choose the computable second-best over the non-computable best.

Time does not permit me to review the extensive literature that this line

133

of inquiry has produced. A recent review by Rapaport[6] covers experimental tests of SEU (subjective expected utility) maximization, of Bayesian strategies for sequential decisions, and of other models of rational choice under uncertainty. I think the evidence can be fairly summarized by the statements (i) that it is possible to construct gambles sufficiently simple and transparent that most subjects will respond to them in a manner consistent with SEU theory; but (ii) the smallest departures from this simplicity and transparency produce behavior in many or most subjects that *cannot* be explained by SEU or Bayesian models. I will illustrate this statement by just three examples, which I hope are not atypical.

The first is the phenomenon of event matching.[7] Suppose that you present a subject with a random sequence of X's and 0's, of which 70 per cent are X's and 30 per cent 0's. You ask the subject to predict the next symbol, rewarding him for the number of correct predictions. 'Obviously' the rational behavior is always to predict X. This is what subjects almost never do.[8] Instead, they act as though the sequence were patterned, not random, and guess by trying to extrapolate the pattern. This kind of guessing will lead X to be guessed in proportion to the frequency with which it occurs in the sequence. As a result, the sequence of guesses has about the same statistical properties as the original sequence, but the prediction accuracy is lower than if X had been predicted each time (58 per cent instead of 70 per cent).

In a recent study by Kahneman and Tversky,[9] a quite different phenomenon showed up. The rational procedure for combining new information with old is to apply Bayes's theorem. If a set of probabilities has been assigned to the possible outcomes of an uncertain event, and then new evidence is presented, Bayes's theorem provides an algorithm for revising the prior probabilities to take the new evidence into account. One obvious consequence of Bayes's theorem is that the more extensive and reliable the new evidence, the greater should be its influence on the new probabilities. Another consequence is that the new probabilities should not depend on the new evidence only, but upon the prior probabilities as well. In the experiments conducted by Kahneman and Tversky, the estimates of subjects were independent of the reliability of the new evidence, and did not appear to be influenced by the prior probabilities at all.

On the other hand, Ward Edwards[10] has reviewed a large body of experimental evidence describing quite conservative behavior. In these experiments, subjects did not revise prior probability estimates nearly as

[6] Rapaport and Wallsten [1972].

[7] Feldman [1963].

[8] The sole exceptions of which I am aware were two well-known and expert game theorists who served as subjects in this experiment at the RAND Corporation many years ago!

[9] Kahneman and Tversky [1973].

[10] Edwards [1968].

much as would be called for by Bayes's theorem. It appears, then that humans can either over-respond to new evidence or ignore it, depending upon the precise experimental circumstances. If these differences in behavior manifest themselves even in laboratory situations so simple that it would be possible for subjects to carry out the actual Bayes calculations, we should be prepared to find variety at least as great when people are required to face the complexities of the real world.

(d) Man's computational efficiency

If these laboratory demonstrations of human failure to follow the canons of substantive rationality in choice under uncertainty caused any surprise to economists (and I do not know that they did), they certainly did not to experimental psychologists familiar with human information processing capabilities.

Like a modern digital computer's, Man's equipment for thinking is basically serial in organization. That is to say, one step in thought follows another, and solving a problem requires the execution of a large number of steps in sequence. The speed of his elementary processes, especially arithmetic processes, is much slower, of course, than those of a computer, but there is much reason to think that the basic repertoire of processes in the two systems is quite similar.[11] Man and computer can both recognize symbols (patterns), store symbols, copy symbols, compare symbols for identity, and output symbols. These processes seem to be the fundamental components of thinking as they are of computation.

For most problems that Man encounters in the real world, no procedure that he can carry out with his information processing equipment will enable him to discover the optimal solution, even when the notion of 'optimum' is well defined. There is no logical reason why this need be so; it is simply a rather obvious empirical fact about the world we live in – a fact about the relation between the enormous complexity of that world and the modest information-processing capabilities with which Man is endowed. One reason why computers have been so important to Man is that they enlarge a little bit the realm within which his computational powers can match the complexity of the problems. But as the example of the travelling-salesman problem shows, even with the help of the computer, Man soon finds himself outside the area of computable substantive rationality.

The problem space associated with the game of chess is very much smaller than the space associated with the game of life. Yet substantive rationality has so far proved unachievable, both for Man and computer,

---

[11] In my comparison of computer and Man, I am leaving out of account the greater sophistication of Man's input and output system, and the parallel processing capabilities of his senses and his limbs. I will be primarily concerned here with thinking, secondarily with perceiving, and not at all with sensing or acting.

even in chess. Chess books are full of norms for rational play, but except for catalogues of opening moves, these are procedural rules: how to detect the significant features of a position, what computations to make on these features, how to select plausible moves for dynamic search, and so on.

The psychology of chess-playing now has a considerable literature. A pioneer in this research was Professor Adriaan de Groot, of the University of Amsterdam, whose book, *Het Denken van den Schaker*, has stimulated much work on this subject both in Amsterdam, and in our own laboratory at Carnegie-Mellon.[12] These studies have told us a great deal about the thought processes of an expert chessplayer. First, they have shown how he compensates for his limited computational capacity by searching very selectively through the immense tree of move possibilities, seldom considering as many as 100 branches before making a move. Second, they have shown how he stores in long-term memory a large collection of common patterns of pieces, together with procedures for exploiting the relations that appear in these patterns. The expert chessplayer's heuristics for selective search and his encyclopedic knowledge of significant patterns are at the core of his procedural rationality in selecting a chess move. Third, the studies have shown how a player forms and modifies his aspirations for a position, so that he can decide when a particular move is 'good enough' (satisfices), and can end his search.

Chess is not an isolated example. There is now a large body of data describing human behavior in other problem situations of comparable complexity. All of the data point in the same direction, and provide essentially the same descriptions of the procedures men use to deal with situations where they are not able to compute an optimum. In all these situations, they use selective heuristics and means–end analysis to explore a small number of promising alternatives. They draw heavily upon past experience to detect the important features of the situation before them, features which are associated in memory with possibly relevant actions. They depend upon aspiration-like mechanisms to terminate search when a satisfactory alternative has been found.

To a moderate extent, this description of choice has been tested outside the laboratory, in even more complex 'real-life' situations; and where it has been tested, has held up well. I will only mention as examples Clarkson's well-known microscopic study of the choices of an investment trust officer,[13] and Peer Soelberg's study of the job search and job choice of graduating management students.[14] I cannot supply you with a large number of more recent examples, possibly because they do not exist, or possibly because my own research has taken me away from the area of field studies in recent years.

[12] Newell and Simon [1972]; Chase and Simon [1973a].
[13] Clarkson [1963].
[14] Soelberg [1967].

Contrast this picture of thought processes with the notion of rationality in the classical theory of the firm in its simplest form. The theory assumes that there is given, in addition to the goal of profit maximization, a demand schedule and a cost curve. The theory then consists of a characterization of the substantively rational production decision: for example, that the production quantity is set at the level where marginal cost, calculated from the cost curve, equals marginal revenue, calculated from the demand schedule. The question of whether data are obtainable for estimating these quantities or the demand and cost functions on which they are based is outside the purview of the theory. If the actual demand and cost curves are given, the actual calculation of the optimum is trivial. This portion of economic theory certainly has nothing to do with procedural rationality.

3. *Economics' concern with procedural rationality*

In my introductory remarks, I said that while economics has traditionally concerned itself with substantive rationality, there has been a noticeable trend, since the Second World War, toward concern also with procedural rationality. This trend has been brought about by a number of more or less independent developments.

(*a*) *The real world of business and public policy*

The first of these developments, which predated the war to some extent, was increasing contact of academic economists with real-world business environments. An early and important product was the 1939 Hall–Hitch paper 'Price Theory and Business Behavior',[15] which advanced the heretical proposition that prices are often determined by applying a fixed mark-up to average direct cost rather than by equating them with marginal cost.

I am not concerned here to determine whether Hitch and Hall, or others who have made similar observations, were right or wrong. My point is that first-hand contact with business operations leads to observation of the procedures that are used in reaching decisions, and not simply the final outcomes. Independently of whether the decision processes have any importance for the questions to which classical economics has addressed itself, the phenomena of problem solving and decision-making cannot help but excite the interest of anyone with intellectual curiosity who encounters them. They represent a fascinating and important domain of human behavior, which any scientist will wish to describe and explain.

In the United States, in the decade immediately after the Second World War, a number of large corporations invited small groups of academic economists to spend periods of a month or more as 'interns' and observers

---

[15] Hall and Hitch [1939].

in their corporate offices. Many young economists had their first opportunity, in this way, to try their hands at applying the tools of economic theory to the decisions of a factory department, or a regional sales office.

They found that businessmen did not need to be advised to 'set marginal cost equal to marginal revenue'. Substantive norms of profit maximization helped real decisions only to the extent that appropriate problem-solving procedures could be devised to implement them. What businessmen needed – from anyone who could supply it – was help in inventing and constructing such procedures, including the means for generating the necessary data. How could the marginal productivity of R & D expenditures be measured? Or of advertising expenditures? And if they could not be, what would be reasonable procedures for fixing these quantities? These – and not abstract questions of profit maximization in a simplified model of the firm – were the questions businessmen wrestled with in their decisions.

Matters were no different with the economists who were increasingly called upon by governments to advise on national fiscal and monetary policy, or on economic development plans. We have the notable example in The Netherlands of Tinbergen's schemes for target planning[16] – a pioneering example of 'satisficing', if I may speak anachronistically. In the face of difficult problems of formulating models, designing appropriate and implementable instruments of measurement, taking account of multidimensional criteria and side conditions, questions of optimization generally faded into the background. The rationality of planning and development models was predominately a procedural rationality.

(b) Operations research

With the end of the war also, businessmen and government departments began to exhibit an interest in the tools of operations research that had been developed for military application during the war. At the same time, operations analysts began to cast about for peacetime problems to which their skills might be applicable. Since the rapid burgeoning of operations research and management science in industry, and the even more rapid development of powerful analytic tools during the first decade after the war is familiar to all of you, it does not need recounting.

The coincidence of the introduction of the digital computer at the same time undoubtedly accelerated these developments. In fact, it is quite unclear whether operations research would have made any considerable impact on practical affairs if the desk calculator had been its only tool.

Operations research and management science did not alter the economic theory of substantive rationality in any fundamental way. With linear programming and activity analysis it did provide a way of handling the old problems and their solutions without the differential calculus, and the

[16] Tinbergen [1952].

classical theorems of marginalism were soon restated in terms of the new formalism.[17]

What was genuinely new for economics in operations research was the concern for procedural rationality – finding efficient procedures for computing actual solutions to concrete decision problems. Let me expand on the specific example with which I am most intimately familiar: decision rules for inventory and work-force smoothing.[18] Here the problem was to devise a decision rule for determining periodically the production level at which a factory should operate. Since the decision for one period was linked to the decisions for the following periods by the inventories carried over, the problem fell in the domain of dynamic programming.

The nub of the problem was to devise a dynamic programming scheme that could actually be carried out using only data that could be obtained in the actual situation. Dynamic programming, in its general formulations, is notoriously extravagant of computational resources. A general algorithm for solving dynamic programming problems would be a non-solution to the real-world decision problem.

The scheme we offered was an algorithm, requiring only a small amount of computing effort, for solving a very special class of dynamic programming problems. The algorithm required the costs to be represented by a quadratic function. This did not mean that we thought real-world cost functions were quadratic; it meant that we thought that many cost functions could be reasonably approximated by a quadratic, and that the deviations from the actual function would not lead to seriously non-optimal decisions. This assumption must, of course, be justified in each individual case, before an application can safely be made. Not only did the quadratic function provide good computational efficiency, but it also greatly reduced the data requirements, because it could be proved that, with this function, only the expected values of predicted variables, and not their higher moments, affected the optimal decision.[19]

This is only part of what was involved in devising a procedurally rational method for making these inventory and production decisions. The problems had also to be solved of translating an aggregate 'production level' into specific production schedules for individual products. I will not, however, go into these other aspects of the matter.

Observe of our solution that we constructed a quite classical model for profit maximization, but we did not have the illusion that the model reflected accurately all the details of the real-world situation. All that was

[17] Dorfman, Samuelson and Solow [1958].

[18] Holt, Modigliani, Muth and Simon [1960].

[19] It is interesting that this same dynamic programming procedure for quadratic cost functions was invented independently and simultaneously by Henri Theil of the Rotterdam School of Economics. See Theil [1958]. The Rotterdam group was also concerned with concrete applications – in this case to national economic planning in The Netherlands – and hence gave a high priority to the demands of procedural rationality in the solutions it developed.

expected of the solution was that the *optimal* decision in the world of the model be a *good* decision in the real world. There was no claim that the solution was substantively optimal, but rather that formal optimization in the dynamic programming model was an effective procedural technique for making acceptable decisions (i.e., decisions better than those that would be made without this formal apparatus).

Some operations research methods take the other horn of this dilemma: they retain more of the real-world detail in the model, but then give up, for reasons of computational feasibility, the goal of searching for an optimum, and seek a satisfactory solution instead.[20]

Thus, the demands of computability led to two kinds of deviation from classical optimization: simplification of the model to make computation of an 'optimum' feasible, or, alternatively, searching for satisfactory, rather than optimal choices. I am inclined to regard both of these solutions as instances of satisficing behavior rather than optimization. To be sure, we can *formally* view these as optimizing procedures by introducing, for example, a cost of computation and a marginal return from computation, and using these quantities to compute the optimal stopping-point for the computation. But the important difference between the new procedures and the classical ones remain. The problem has been shifted from one of characterizing the substantively optimal solution to one of devising practicable computation procedures for making reasonable choices.

(c) Imperfect competition

More than a century ago, Cournot identified a problem that has become the permanent and ineradicable scandal of economic theory. He observed that where a market is supplied by only a few producers, the notion of profit-maximization is ill-defined. The choice that would be substantively rational for each actor depends on the choices made by the other actors; none can choose without making assumptions about how others will choose.

Cournot proposed a particular solution for the problem, which amounted to an assumption about the *procedure* each actor would follow: each would observe the quantities being produced by his competitors, and would assume these quantities to be fixed in his own calculations. The Cournot solution has often been challenged, and many alternative solutions have been proposed – conjectural variations, the kinky demand curve, market leadership, and others. All of them rest on postulates about the decision process, in particular, about the information each decision-maker will take into account, and the assumptions he will make about the reactions of the others to his behavior.

[20] I have already mentioned the pioneering work of Jan Tinbergen in The Netherlands, who employed national planning models that aimed at target values of key variables instead of an optimum.

I have referred to the theory of imperfect competition as a 'scandal' because it has been treated as such in economics, and because it is generally conceded that no defensible formulation of the theory stays within the framework of profit maximization and substantive rationality. Game theory, initially hailed as a possible way out, provided only a rigorous demonstration of how fundamental the difficulties really are.

If perfect competition were the rule in the markets of our modern economy, and imperfect competition and oligopoly rare exceptions, the scandal might be ignored. Every family, after all, has some distant relative it would prefer to forget. But imperfect competition is not a 'distant relative', it is the characteristic form of market structure in a large part of the industries in our economy.

In the literature on oligopoly and imperfect competition one can trace a gradual movement toward more and more explicit concern with the processes used to reach decisions, even to the point – unusual in most other areas of economics – of trying to obtain empirical data about these processes. There remains, however, a lingering reluctance to acknowledge the impossibility of discovering at last 'The Rule' of substantively rational behavior for the oligopolist. Only when the hope of that discovery has been finally extinguished will it be admitted that understanding imperfect competition means understanding procedural rationality.[21]

This change in viewpoint will have large effects on many areas of economic research. There has been a great burgeoning, for example, of 'neoclassical' theories of investment – theories that undertake to deduce the rates of investment of business firms from the assumptions of profit-maximization and substantive rationality. Central to such theories is the concept of 'desired capital' – that is, the volume of capital that would maximize profits. Jorgenson, for example, typically derives 'desired capital' by an argument that assumes a fixed price for the firm's products and a production function of the Cobb–Douglas type, all in the absence of uncertainty.[22] Under these assumptions, he shows that the optimal level of capital is proportional to output.

Since the data which Jorgenson and others use to test these theories of investment derive mostly from oligopolistic industries, their definitions of rationality are infected with precisely the difficulties we have been discussing. Can we speak of the capital desired by General Motors or the American Can Company without considering their expectations for size and share of market or the interactions of these expectations with price

---

[21] My colleagues Richard Cyert and Morris de Groot have recently developed some interesting dynamic decision rules for oligopolists, which illustrate further the wide range of alternative formulations of what 'rationality' means in this situation. See Cyert and de Groot [1973].

[22] Jorgenson [1963]. For a thorough critique of Jorgenson's approach, see Kornai [1971]. Kornai's book also develops other arguments about the nature of economic rationality that are much in the spirit of this essay.

policies and with the responses of competitors?[23] Under conditions of imperfect competition, one can perhaps speak of the procedural rationality of an investment strategy, but surely not of its substantive rationality. At most, the statistical studies of investment behavior show that some business firms relate their investments to output; they do not show that such behavior is predictable from an objective theory of profit maximization. (And if that is what is being demonstrated, what is the advantage of doing it by means of elaborate statistical studies of public data, rather than by making inquiries or observations of the actual decision processes in the firms themselves?)

(d) Expectations and uncertainty

Making guesses about the behavior of a competitor in an oligopolistic industry is simply a special case of forming expectations in order to make decisions under uncertainty. As economics has moved from statics to dynamics – to business cycle theory, growth theory, dynamic investment theory, theory of innovation and technological change – it has become more and more explicit in its treatment of uncertainty.

Uncertainty, however, exists not in the outside world, but in the eye and mind of the beholder. We need not enter into philosophical arguments as to whether quantum-mechanical uncertainty lies at the very core of nature, for we are not concerned with events at the level of the atom. We are concerned with how men behave rationally in a world where they are often unable to predict the relevant future with accuracy. In such a world, their ignorance of the future prevents them from behaving in a substantively rational manner; they can only adopt a rational choice procedure, including a rational procedure for forecasting or otherwise adapting to the future.

In a well-known paper, my former colleague, John F. Muth,[24] proposed to objectify the treatment of uncertainty in economics by removing it from the decision-maker to nature. His hypothesis is 'that expectations of firms (or, more generally, the subjective probability distribution of outcomes) tend to be distributed, for the same information set, about the prediction of the theory (or the "objective" probability distributions of outcomes)'. In application this hypothesis involves setting the expected value (in the statistical sense) of a future economic variable equal to its predicted value.

Muth's proposal is ingenious and important. Let us see exactly what it means. Suppose that a producer has an accurate knowledge of the consumer demand function and the aggregate supply function of producers in his industry. Then he can estimate the equilibrium price – the price at which the quantities that producers will be induced to offer will just

---

[23] Cyert, Feigenbaum and March [1959].
[24] Muth [1961].

balance demand. Muth proposes essentially that each producer takes this equilibrium price as his price forecast. If random shocks with zero expected value are now introduced into the supply equation, and if producers continue to act on price forecasts made in the manner just described, then the forecast price will equal the expected value of the actual price.

Notice that the substantively rational behavior for the producer would be to produce the quantity that would be optimal for the price that is *actually* realized. The assumption of Muth's model that the random shocks are completely unpredictable makes this impossible. The producer then settles for a procedure that under the assumptions of the model will give him an unbiased prediction of the price. Nor, as Muth himself notes, will this procedure be optimal, even under uncertainty, unless the loss function is quadratic.

Uncertainty plays the same innocuous role in the optimal linear production smoothing rule I described earlier,[25] which is closely related to Muth's analysis. Here the explicit assumption of a quadratic cost function makes it possible to prove that only the expected values and not the higher moments of predicted variables are relevant to decision. This does not mean that action based on unbiased estimates is substantively rational, independently of the variances of those estimates. On the contrary, performance can always be improved if estimation errors can be reduced.

Even if it turns out to be empirically true that the forecasts of business firms and other economic actors are unbiased forecasts of future events, this finding will have modest implications for the nature of human rationality. Unbiased estimation can be a component of all sorts of rational and irrational behavior rules.

In an earlier section I commented on the psychological evidence as to human choice in the face of uncertainty. Only in the very simplest situations does behavior conform reasonably closely to the predictions of classical models of rationality. But even this evidence exaggerates the significance of those classical models for human affairs; for all of the experiments are limited to situations where the alternatives of choice are fixed in advance, and where information is available only from precisely specified sources.

Once we become interested in the procedures – the rational processes – that economic actors use to cope with uncertainty, we must broaden our horizons further. Uncertainty not only calls forth forecasting procedures; it also calls forth a whole range of actions to reduce uncertainty, or at least to make outcomes less dependent upon it. These actions are of at least four kinds:

(i) intelligence actions to improve the data on which forecasts are based, to obtain new data, and to improve the forecasting models;

[25] See footnote 19 *supra*.

143

(ii) actions to buffer the effects of forecast errors: holding inventories, insuring, and hedging, for example;

(iii) actions to reduce the sensitivity of outcomes to the behavior of competitors: steps to increase product and market differentiation, for example;

(iv) actions to enlarge the range of alternatives whenever the perceived alternatives involve high risk.

A theory of rational choice in the face of uncertainty will have to encompass not only the topic of forecasting, but these other topics as well. Moreover, it will have to say something about the circumstances under which people will (or should) pursue one or the other of these lines of action.

Confronting a list of contingencies of this sort fills many economists with malaise. How can a unique answer be found to the problem of choice if all of these considerations enter it? How much more attractive is classical economics, in allowing strong conclusions to be drawn from a few *a priori* assumptions, with little need for empirical observation!

Alas, we must take the world as it is. As economics becomes more concerned with procedural rationality, it will necessarily have to borrow from psychology or build for itself a far more complete theory of human cognitive processes than it has had in the past. Even if our interest lies in normative rather than descriptive economics, we will need such a theory. There are still many areas of decision – particularly those that are ill-structured – where human cognitive processes are more effective than the best available optimization techniques or artificial intelligence methods. Every Class A chessplayer plays a far better game than any existing chess-playing computer program. A great deal can still be learned about effective decision procedures by studying how humans make choices.

The human mind is programmable: it can acquire an enormous variety of different skills, behavior patterns, problem-solving repertoires, and perceptual habits. Which of these it will acquire in any particular case is a function of what it has been taught and what it has experienced. We can expect substantive rationality only in situations that are sufficiently simple as to be transparent to this mind. In all other situations, we must expect that the mind will use such imperfect information as it has, will simplify and represent the situation as it can, and will make such calculations as are within its powers. We cannot expect to predict what it will do in such situations unless we know what information it has, what forms of representation it prefers, and what algorithms are available to it.

There seems to be no escape. If economics is to deal with uncertainty, it will have to understand how human beings in fact behave in the face of uncertainty, and by what limits of information and computability they are bound.

4. *The empirical study of decision-making*

Since my own recent research has removed me from the study of decision-making in organization settings, I am not in a position to comment on the current state of our empirical knowledge of organizational decision-making. In trying to understand procedural rationality as it relates to economics, we do not have to limit ourselves, however, to organizational studies. I have already commented upon the understanding we have gained, during the past 20 years, of human problem-solving processes – mostly by study in the laboratory, using puzzle-like tasks. Most of these studies have used naive subjects performing tasks with which they had little or no previous experience. In one case, however – the research on chess-playing – an intensive investigation has been made of highly skilled, professional performance, and a body of theory constructed to explain that performance.

Chess may seem a rather esoteric domain, but perhaps business is no less esoteric to those who do not practice it. There is no reason to believe that the basic human faculties that a chess professional of 20 years' experience brings to bear upon his decisions are fundamentally different from the faculties used by an experienced professional businessman. In fact, to the extent that comparable studies of business decision-making have been carried out, they give us positive reasons to believe in the basic similarity of those faculties.

On the basis of the research on chess-players, what appears to distinguish expert from novice is not only that the former has a great quantity and variety of information, but that his perceptual experience enables him to detect familiar patterns in the situations that confront him, and by recognizing these patterns, to retrieve speedily a considerable amount of relevant information from long-term memory.[26] It is this perceptual experience that permits the chess-master to play, and usually win, many simultaneous games against weaker opponents, taking only a few seconds for each move. It is very likely similar perceptual experience about the world of business that enables the executive to react 'intuitively', without much awareness of his own cognitive processes, to business situations as they arise.

There is no reason to suppose that the theory of cognitive processes that will emerge from the empirical study of the chessmaster's or businessman's decision processes will be 'neat' or 'elegant', in the sense that the Laws of Motion or the axioms of classical utility theory are neat and elegant. If we are to draw an analogy with the natural sciences, we might expect the theory of procedural rationality to resemble molecular biology, with its rich taxonomy of mechanisms, more closely than either classical mechanics

[26] de Groot [1965]; Chase and Simon [1973*b*].

or classical economics. But as I suggested earlier, an empirical science cannot remake the world to its fancy: it can only describe and explain the world as it is.

A major source of complication in theories of professional decision-making is the dependence of decisions upon large quantities of stored information and previously learned decision procedures. This is true not only at an individual psychological level, but also at a social and historical level. The play of two chess-players differs as a result of differences in what they know about chess: no less do the decisions of two businessmen differ as a result of differences in what they know about business. Moreover, Bobby Fischer, in 1972, played chess differently from Paul Morphy, in 1861. Much of that latter difference was the result of the knowledge of the game that had cumulated over the century through the collective experience of the whole society of professional chess-players.

Economics, like chess, is inevitably culture-bound and history-bound. A business firm equipped with the tools of operations research does not make the same decisions as it did before it possessed those tools. The substantial secular decline over recent years of inventories held by American firms is probably due in considerable part to this enhancement of rationality by new theory and new computational tools.

Economics is one of the sciences of the artificial.[27] It is a description and explanation of human institutions, whose theory is no more likely to remain invariant over time than the theory of bridge design. Decision processes, like all other aspects of economic institutions, exist inside human heads. They are subject to change with every change in what human beings know, and with every change in their means of calculation. For this reason the attempt to predict and prescribe human economic behavior by deductive inference from a small set of unchallengeable premises must fail and has failed.

Economics will progress as we deepen our understanding of human thought processes; and economics will change as human individuals and human societies use progressively sharpened tools of thought in making their decisions and designing their institutions. A body of theory for procedural rationality is consistent with a world in which human beings continue to think and continue to invent; a theory of substantive rationality is not.

5. Conclusion

In this paper I have contrasted the concept of substantive rationality, which has dominated classical economics and provided it with its program of structural determinism, with the concept of procedural rationality, which has prevailed in psychology. I have described also some of the

[27] Simon [1969].

concerns of economics that have forced that discipline to begin to concern itself with procedural rationality – with the actual processes of cognition, and with the limits on the human organism that give those processes their peculiar character.

One can conceive of at least two alternative scenarios for the continuation into the future of this gradual change in the program of economics. One involves the direct 'psychologizing' of economics, the explicit adoption of the program of economic behavioralism.[28] The second scenario pictures economists as borrowing the notions of optimal search and computational efficiency from operations research and statistical decision theory, and introducing a wider and wider range of computational considerations into the models of rationality. Since these computational constraints can be viewed (at least formally) as located in the external world rather than in the mind of the decision-maker, they give the appearance of avoiding the need for psychologizing. Of course that need is in fact only postponed, not avoided permanently. It is illusory to describe a decision as 'situationally determined' when a part of the situation that determines it is the mind of the decision-maker. Choosing between alternative models of the situation then calls for determining empirically the processes used by the person or organization making the decisions. Hence, our second scenario leads as inevitably, if not as directly, as does the first to economic behavioralism.

The shift from theories of substantive rationality to theories of procedural rationality requires a basic shift in scientific style, from an emphasis on deductive reasoning within a tight system of axioms to an emphasis on detailed empirical exploration of complex algorithms of thought. Undoubtedly the uncongeniality of the latter style to economists has slowed the transition, and accounts in part for the very limited success of economic behavioralism in the past. For this reason, the second scenario appears more promising than the first, and, indeed, appears to be unfolding visibly at the present time.

In other chapters in this volume, Messrs Coats and Latsis have described the largely successful resistance of economics to earlier attempts at injecting behavioral premises into its body of theory. The present situation is different from the earlier ones because economics is now focusing on new research questions whose answers require explicit attention to procedural rationality. As economics becomes more and more involved in the study of uncertainty, more and more concerned with the complex actuality of business decision-making, the shift in program will become inevitable. Wider and wider areas of economics will replace the over-simplified assumptions of the situationally constrained omniscient decision-maker

[28] This path has already been followed for some distance, for example, in Part IV of my own *Models of Man* [1957], in Cyert and March [1963] and in Katona's *Psychological Analysis of Economic Behaviour* [1951].

with a realistic (and psychological) characterization of the limits on Man's rationality, and the consequences of those limits for his economic behavior.

References

Chase, W. G. and Simon, H. A. [1973a]: 'Skill in Chess', *American Scientist*, **61**, pp. 394–403.

Chase, W. G. and Simon, H. A. [1973b]: 'Perception in Chess', *Cognitive Psychology*, **4**, pp. 55–81.

Clarkson, G. P. E. [1963]: 'A Model of the Trust Investment Process' in E. A. Feigenbaum and J. Feldman (eds.): *Computers and Thought*, pp. 347–71.

Cyert, R. M., Feigenbaum, E. A. and March, J. G. [1959]: 'Models in a Behavioural Theory of the Firm', *Behavioral Science*, **4**, pp. 81–95.

Cyert, R. M. and March, J. G. [1963]: *Behavioral Theory of the Firm*.

Cyert, R. M. and de Groot, M. H. [1973]: 'An Analysis of Cooperation and Learning in a Duopoly Context', *American Economic Review*, **63**, pp. 24–37.

Dorfman, R., Samuelson, P. A. and Solow, R. M. [1958]: *Linear Programming and Economic Analysis*.

Edwards, W. [1968]: 'Conservatism in Human Information Processing', in B. Kleinmuntz (ed.): *Formal Representation of Human Judgment*, pp. 17–52.

Feldman, J. [1963]: 'Simulation of Behaviour in the Binary Choice Experiment' in E. A. Feigenbaum and J. Feldman (eds.): *Computers and Thought*, pp. 329–46.

Gould, J. and Kolb, W. L. (eds.) [1964]: *The Dictionary of the Social Sciences*.

Groot, A. D. de [1965]: *Thought and Choice in Chess*.

Hall, R. L. and Hitch, C. H. [1939]: 'Price Theory and Business Behaviour', *Oxford Economic Papers*, **2**, pp. 12–45.

Holt, H. G., Modigliani, F., Muth, J. F. and Simon, H. A. [1960]: *Planning Production, Inventories and Work Force*.

James, W. [1890]: *Principles of Psychology*.

Jorgenson, D. W. [1963]: 'Capital Theory and Investment Behavior', *American Economic Review Proceedings*, **53**, pp. 247–59.

Kahneman, D. and Tversky, A. [1973]: 'On the Psychology of Prediction', *Psychological Review*, **80**, pp. 237–51.

Katona, G. [1951]: *Psychological Analysis of Economic Behavior*.

Kornai, J. [1971]: *Anti-Equilibrium*.

Latsis, S. J. [1972]: 'Situational Determinism in Economics', *The British Journal for the Philosophy of Science*, **23**, pp. 207–45.

Muth, J. F. [1961]: 'Rational Expectations and the Theory of Price Movements, *Econometrica*, **29**, pp. 315–35.

Newell, A. and Simon, H. A. [1972]: *Human Problem Solving*.

Rapaport, A. and Wallsten, T. S. [1972]: 'Individual Decision Behavior', *Annual Review of Psychology*, **23**, pp. 131–76.

Simon, H. A. [1957]: *Models of Man*.

Simon, H. A. [1969]: *The Sciences of the Artificial*.

Soelberg, P. [1967]: 'A Study of Decision Making: Job Choice'. Unpublished PhD dissertation, Carnegie-Mellon University.

Theil, H. [1958]: *Economic Forecasts and Policy*.

Tinbergen, J. [1952]: *On the Theory of Economic Policy*.

Kuhn versus Lakatos *or* Paradigms versus research programmes in the history of economics

MARK BLAUG
UNIVERSITY OF LONDON INSTITUTE OF EDUCATION
AND
LONDON SCHOOL OF ECONOMICS

1 From Popper to Kuhn to Lakatos
2 Scientific revolutions in economics
3 The theory of the firm as a case in point
4 Do economists practise what they preach?
5 Conclusions

In the 1950s and 1960s economists learned their methodology from Popper.[1] Not that many of them read Popper. Instead, they read Friedman and perhaps a few of them realised that Friedman is simply Popper-with-a-twist applied to economics. To be sure, Friedman was criticised, but the 'Essay on the Methodology of Positive Economics' nevertheless survived to become the one article on methodology that virtually every economist has read at some stage in his career. The idea that unrealistic 'assumptions' are nothing to worry about provided the theory deduced from them culminates in falsifiable predictions carried conviction to economists long inclined by habit and tradition to take a purely instrumentalist view of their subject.

All that is almost ancient history, however. The new wave is not Popper's 'falsifiability' but Kuhn's 'paradigms'. Again it is unlikely that many economists have read *The Structure of Scientific Revolutions*,[2] but that is neither here nor there. Nevertheless, appeal to paradigmatic reasoning has quickly become a regular feature of controversies in economics and 'paradigm' is now the by-word of every historian of economic thought.[3] Recently, however, some commentators have expressed misgivings about Kuhnian methodology applied to economics, throwing doubt in particular on the view that 'scientific revolutions' characterise the history of economic thought.[4] With these doubts I heartily concur. I will argue that the term 'paradigm' ought to be banished from economic literature, unless surrounded by inverted commas. Suitably qualified, however, the term

---

[1] An earlier version of this paper was presented at the History of Economic Thought Society Conference in London, September 1974. I wish to express my thanks to A. W. Coats, N. de Marchi, J. Hicks, S. J. Latsis, D. P. O'Brien, R. Towse and D. Winch for comments on this earlier draft and to the participants in the London Conference for a helpful discussion of its contents.

[2] Kuhn [1962], 1st edn.

[3] Similarly, sociologists have seized avidly on the Kuhnian apparatus: see e.g. Ryan [1970], pp. 233–6, Martins [1972], and the collection of essays in Whitley [1974].

[4] See Coats [1969], Bronfenbrenner [1971] and Kunin and Weaver [1971].

retains a function in the historical exposition of economic doctrines as a reminder of the fallacy of trying to appraise particular theories without invoking the wider, metaphysical framework in which they are embedded. This notion that theories come to us, not one at a time, but linked together in a more or less integrated network of ideas, is however better conveyed by Lakatos's 'methodology of scientific research programmes' (MSRP). The main aim of my paper is indeed to explore Lakatos's ideas in application to the history of economics.[5]

The task is not an easy one. Lakatos is a difficult author to pin down. His tendency to make vital points in footnotes, to proliferate labels for different intellectual positions, and to refer back and forth to his own writings – as if it were impossible to understand any part of them without understanding the whole – stand in the way of ready comprehension. In a series of papers, largely published between 1968 and 1971, Lakatos developed and extended Popper's philosophy of science into a critical tool of historical research, virtually resolving a long-standing puzzle about the relationship between positive history of science and normative methodology for scientists. The puzzle is this. To believe that it is possible to write a history of science *wie es eigentlich gewesen ist* without in any way revealing our concept of sound scientific practice, or how 'good' science differs from 'bad', is to commit the 'inductive fallacy' in the field of intellectual history; by telling the story of past developments one way rather than another, we necessarily disclose our view of the nature of scientific explanation. On the other hand, to preach the virtues of *the* scientific method, while utterly ignoring the question of whether scientists now or in the past have actually practised that method, seems arbitrary and metaphysical. We are thus caught in a vicious circle, implying the impossibility both of a value-free, descriptive historiography of science and an ahistorical, prescriptive methodology of science.[6] From this vicious circle there is, I believe, no real escape, but what Lakatos has done is to hold out the hope that the circle may be eventually converted into a virtuous one.

Enough said by way of introduction. Let us look briefly at Popper and Kuhn, before putting Lakatos's MSRP to work in a field such as economics.

[5] I dedicate this paper to the memory of Imre Lakatos, Professor of Logic and the Philosophy of Science at the London School of Economics, who died suddenly at the age of 51 on 2 February 1974. We discussed an early draft of this paper a number of times in the winter of 1973 and, for the last time, the day before his death. He promised me a rebuttal, which now alas I will never read.

[6] One of Lakatos's fundamental papers (Lakatos [1971], p. 91) opens with a paraphrase of one of Kant's dictums, which perfectly expresses the dilemma in question: 'Philosophy of science without history of science is empty: history of science without philosophy of science is blind.'

1. *From Popper to Kuhn to Lakatos*

Popper's principal problem in *The Logic of Scientific Discovery*[7] was to find a purely logical demarcation rule for distinguishing science from non-science. He repudiated the Vienna Circle's principle of verifiability and replaced it by the principle of falsifiability as the universal, *a priori* test of a genuinely scientific hypothesis. The shift of emphasis from verification to falsification is not as innocent as appears at first glance, involving as it does a fundamental asymmetry between proof and disproof. From this modest starting point, Popper has gradually evolved over the years a powerful anti-inductionist view of science as an endless dialectical sequence of 'conjectures and refutations'.[8]

A hasty reading of *The Logic of Scientific Discovery* suggests the view that a single refutation is sufficient to overthrow a scientific theory; in other words, it convicts Popper of what Lakatos has called 'naive falsificationism'.[9] But a moment's reflection reminds us that many physical and virtually all social phenomena are stochastic in nature, in which case an adverse result implies the improbability of the hypothesis being true, not the certainty that it is false. To discard a theory after a single failure to pass a statistical test would, therefore, amount to intellectual nihilism. Patently, nothing less than a whole series of refutations is likely to discourage the adherents of a probabilistic theory. A careful reading of Popper's work, however, reveals that he was perfectly aware of the so-called 'principle of tenacity' – the tendency of scientists to evade falsification of their theories by the introduction of suitable *ad hoc* auxiliary hypotheses – and he even recognised the functional value of such dogmatic stratagems in certain circumstances.[10] Popper, in other words, is a 'sophisticated falsificationist', not a 'naive' one.[11]

In general, however, Popper deplores the tendency to immunise theories against criticism and instead advocates a bold commitment to falsifiable predictions, coupled with a willingness and indeed eagerness to abandon theories that have failed to survive efforts to refute them. His methodology

[7] Logik der Forschung [1935], English edn [1965].

[8] Not to mention his formulation of a political philosophy, generated by the same conception. For a splendid, if somewhat hagiographic, introduction to the wide sweep of Popper's work, see Magee [1973].

[9] Lakatos and Musgrave [1970], pp. 116, 181; Lakatos [1971], pp. 109–14.

[10] For example: 'In point of fact, no conclusive disproof of a theory can ever be produced; for it is always possible to say that the experimental results are not reliable, or that the discrepancies which are asserted to exist between the experimental results and the theory are only apparent and that they will disappear with the advance of our understanding (Popper [1965], p. 50; see also pp. 42, 82–3, 108); in the same spirit, see Popper [1962], vol. 2, pp. 217–20; Popper [1972], p. 30; and Popper in Schilpp [1974], vol. 1, p. 82.

[11] Economists will recognise immediately that Lipsey really was a 'naive falsificationist' in the first edition of his *Introduction to Positive Economics* and only adopted 'sophisticated falsificationism' in the second edition of the book: see Lipsey [1966], pp. xx, 16–17.

is thus plainly a normative one, prescribing sound practice in science, possibly but not necessarily in the light of the best science of the past; it is an 'aggressive' rather than a 'defensive' methodology because it cannot be refuted by showing that most, and indeed even all, scientists have failed to obey its precepts.[12]

In Kuhn's *Structure of Scientific Revolutions*, the emphasis shifts from normative methodology to positive history: the 'principle of tenacity', which for Popper presents something of an exception to best-practice science, becomes the central issue in Kuhn's explanation of scientific behaviour. 'Normal science', or problem-solving activity in the context of an accepted theoretical framework, is said to be the rule, and 'revolutionary science', or the overthrow of one 'paradigm' by another in consequence of repeated refutations and mounting anomalies, the exception in the history of science. It is tempting to say that in Popper science is always in a state of 'permanent revolution', the history of science being the history of continuous 'conjectures and refutations'; in Kuhn, the history of science is marked by long periods of steady refinement, interrupted on occasions by *discontinuous* jumps from one ruling 'paradigm' to another with no bridge for communicating between them.[13]

To judge a dispute such as this, we must begin by defining terms. In the first edition of his book, Kuhn frequently employed the term 'paradigm' in a dictionary sense to stand for certain exemplary instances of scientific achievement in the past. But he also employed the term in quite a different sense to denote both the choice of problems and the set of techniques for analysing them, in places going so far as to give 'paradigm' a still wider meaning as a general metaphysical *Weltanschauung*: the last sense of the term is, in fact, what most readers take away from the book. The second edition of *The Structure of Scientific Revolutions* admitted to terminological imprecision in the earlier version,[14] and suggested that the term 'paradigm' be replaced by 'disciplinary matrix': '"disciplinary" because it refers to the common possession of the practitioners of a particular discipline; "matrix" because it is composed of ordered elements of various sorts, each requiring further specification'.[15] But whatever language is employed, the focus of his argument remained that of 'the entire constellation of beliefs, values, techniques and so on shared by the members

---

[12] I owe the vital distinction between 'aggressive methodologies' and 'defensive methodologies' to Latsis [1974]. Popper does make references to the history of science and clearly Einstein is his model of a great scientist. Nevertheless, he is always insistent on the metaphysical and hence irrefutable basis of the falsifiability principle (see, for example, Schilpp [1974], vol. 2, pp. 1036–7).

[13] Kuhn [1970]. See the revealing criticism of Popper by Kuhn and the equally revealing criticism of Kuhn by Popper (Lakatos and Musgrave [1970], pp. 14–15, 19, 52–5).

[14] Masterman (Lakatos and Musgrave [1970], pp. 60–5) has in fact identified 21 different definitions of the term 'paradigm' in Kuhn's [1962] book.

[15] Kuhn [1970], p. 182.

of a given community', and he went on to say that if he were to write his book again, he would start with a discussion of the professionalisation of science before examining the shared 'paradigms' or 'disciplinary matrices' of scientists.[16]

These are not fatal concessions for the simple reason that the distinctive feature of Kuhn's methodology is not the concept of paradigms that everyone has seized on, but rather that of 'scientific revolutions' as sharp breaks in the development of science, and particularly the notion of a pervasive failure of communications during periods of 'revolutionary crises'. Let us remind ourselves of the building-bricks of Kuhn's argument: the practitioners of 'normal science', although widely scattered, form an 'invisible college' in the sense that they are in agreement both on the 'puzzles' that require solution and on the general form that the solution will take; moreover, only the judgement of colleagues is regarded as relevant in defining problems and solutions, in consequence of which 'normal science' is a self-sustaining, cumulative process of puzzle-solving within the context of a common, analytical framework; the breakdown of 'normal science' is heralded by a proliferation of theories and the appearance of methodological controversy; the new framework offers a decisive solution to hitherto neglected 'puzzles' and this solution turns out in retrospect to have long been recognised but previously ignored; the old and new generations talk past each other as 'puzzles' in the old framework become 'counter-examples' in the new; conversion to the new approach takes on the nature of a religious experience, involving a 'gestalt-switch'; and the new framework conquers in a few decades to become in turn the 'normal science' of the next generation.

The reader who is acquainted with the history of science thinks immediately of the Copernican revolution, the Newtonian revolution, or the Einstein–Planck revolution. The so-called 'Copernican revolution', however, took 150 years to complete and was argued out every step of the way; even the Newtonian revolution took more than a generation to win acceptance throughout the scientific circles of Europe, during which time the Cartesians, Leibnizians and Newtonians engaged in bitter disputes over every aspect of the new theory; likewise, the switch in the twentieth century from classical to relativistic and quantum physics involved neither mutual incomprehension nor quasi-religious conversions, at least if the scientists directly involved in the 'crisis of modern physics' are to be believed.[17] It is hardly necessary, however, to argue these points because

---

[16] Kuhn [1970], p. 173.

[17] Toulmin [1972], pp. 103–5. Of all the many critiques that Kuhn's book has received (Lakatos and Musgrave [1970]) and references cited by Kunin and Weaver [1971], none is more devastating than that of Toulmin ([1972], pp. 98–117), who traces the history of Kuhn's methodology from its first announcement in 1961 to its final version in 1970. For an extraordinarily sympathetic but equally critical reading of Kuhn, see Suppe [1974], pp. 135–51.

in the second edition of his book Kuhn candidly admits that his earlier description of 'scientific revolutions' suffered from rhetorical exaggeration: 'paradigm-changes during "scientific revolutions" do not imply absolute discontinuities in scientific debate, that is a choice between competing but totally incommensurate theories; mutual incomprehension between scientists during a period of intellectual crisis is only a matter of degree; and the only point of calling paradigm-changes "revolutions" is to underline the fact that the arguments that are advanced to support a new paradigm always contain ideological elements that go beyond logical or mathematical proof'.[18] As if this were not enough, he goes on to complain that his theory of 'scientific revolutions' was misunderstood as referring solely to major revolutions, such as the Copernican, Newtonian, Darwinian, or Einsteinian; he now insists that the scheme was just as much directed at minor changes in particular scientific fields, which might not seem to be revolutionary at all to those outside 'a single community [of scientists], consisting perhaps of fewer than twenty-five people directly involved in it'.[19]

In short, in this later version of Kuhn, any period of scientific development is marked by a large number of overlapping and interpenetrating 'paradigms'; some of these may be incommensurable but certainly not all of them are; 'paradigms' do not replace each other immediately and, in any case, new 'paradigms' do not spring up full-borne but instead emerge as victorious in a long process of intellectual competition. It is evident that these concessions considerably dilute the apparently dramatic import of Kuhn's original message and in this final version the argument is difficult to distinguish from the average historian's account of the history of science. What remains, I suppose, is the emphasis on the role of values in scientific judgements, particularly in respect of the choice between competing approaches to science, together with a vaguely formulated but deeply held suspicion of cognitive factors like epistemological rationality, rather than sociological factors like authority, hierarchy, and reference-groups, as determinants of scientific behaviour. What Kuhn has really done is to conflate prescription and description, deducing his methodology from history, rather than to criticise history with the aid of a methodology. Kuhn does his best, of course, to defend himself against the charge of relativism and to explain 'the sense in which I am a convinced believer in scientific progress',[20] but the defence is not altogether convincing. Actually, a wholly convincing defence would reduce his account of 'scientific revolutions' to a nonsense.

[18] Kuhn [1970], pp. 199–200. This is almost obvious because if two 'paradigms' were truly incommensurable they could be held simultaneously, in which case there would be no need for a 'scientific revolution': the strong incommensurability-thesis is logically self-contradictory (Achinstein [1968], pp. 91–106). What Kuhn must have meant is 'incommensurability to some degree' and the new version is simply a belated attempt to specify the degree in question.

[19] Kuhn [1970], pp. 180–1.   [20] Kuhn [1970], pp. 205–7.

Which brings us to Lakatos.[21] As I read him, Lakatos is as much appalled by Kuhn's lapses into relativism as he is by Popper's ahistorical if not antihistorical standpoint.[22] The result is a compromise between the 'aggressive methodology' of Popper and the 'defensive methodology' of Kuhn, which however stays within the Popperian camp;[23] Lakatos is 'softer' on science than Popper but a great deal 'harder' than Kuhn and he is more inclined to criticise bad science with the aid of good methodology than to temper methodological speculations by an appeal to scientific practice. For Lakatos, as for Popper, 'methodology' has nothing to do with laying down standard procedures for tackling scientific problems; it is concerned with the 'logic of appraisal', that is, the normative problem of providing criteria of scientific progress. Where Lakatos differs from Popper is that this 'logic of appraisal' is then employed at one and the same time as a historical theory which purports to retrodict the development of science. As a normative methodology of science, it is empirically irrefutable because it is a definition. But as a historical theory, implying that scientists in the past did in fact behave in accordance with the methodology of falsifiability, it is perfectly refutable. If history fits the normative methodology, we have reasons additional to logical ones for subscribing to fallibilism. If it fails to do so, we are furnished with possible reasons for abandoning our methodology. No doubt, Hume's Guillotine tells us that we cannot logically deduce 'ought from is' or 'is from ought'. We can, however, influence 'ought' by 'is' and *vice versa*: moral judgements may be altered by the presentation of facts and facts are theory-laden so that a change of values may alter our perception of the facts. But all these problems lie in the future. The first task is to re-examine the history of science with the aid of an explicit, falsificationist methodology, to see if indeed there is any conflict to resolve.

Lakatos begins by denying that isolated individual theories are the appropriate units of appraisal; what ought to be appraised are clusters of interconnected theories or 'scientific research programmes' (SRP). Duhem and Poincaré had argued long ago that no individual scientific hypothesis is conclusively verifiable or falsifiable, because we always test

[21] My sketch of recent developments in the philosophy of science omits discussion of such influential writers as Feyerabend, Hanson, Polanyi and Toulmin, who have each in their own way challenged the traditional positivist account of the structure of scientific theories. But see Suppe [1974], whose masterful essay of book-length covers all the names mentioned above. Lakatos, however, is deliberately omitted in Suppe's account (Suppe [1974], p. 166n).

[22] See the characteristic reaction of Popper to Kuhn: 'to me the idea of turning for enlightenment concerning the aims of science, and its possible progress, to sociology or to psychology (or...to the history of science) is surprising and disappointing' (Lakatos and Musgrave [1970], p. 57).

[23] Bloor [1971], p. 104 seems wide off the mark in characterising Lakatos's work as 'a massive act of revision, amounting to a betrayal of the essentials of the Popperian approach, and a wholesale absorption of some of the most characteristic Kuhnian positions'.

the particular hypothesis in conjunction with auxiliary statements and, therefore, can never be sure whether we have confirmed or refuted the hypothesis itself. Since any hypothesis, if supplemented with suitable auxiliary assumptions, can be maintained in the face of contrary evidence, its acceptance is merely conventional. Popper met this 'conventionalist' argument by distinguishing between '*ad hoc*' and '*non ad hoc*' auxiliary assumptions: it is perfectly permissible to rescue a falsified theory by means of a change in one of its auxiliary assumptions, if such a change increases the empirical content of the theory by augmenting the number of its observational consequences; it is only changes which fail to do this which Popper dismissed as '*ad hoc*'.[24] Lakatos generalises this Popperian argument by distinguishing between 'progressive and degenerating problem shifts'. A particular research strategy or SRP is said to be '*theoretically* progressive' if the successive formulations of the programme contain 'excess empirical content' over its predecessor, 'that is,...predicts some novel, hitherto unexpected fact'; it is '*empirically* progressive if this excess empirical content is corroborated'.[25] Contrariwise, if the programme is characterised by the endless addition of *ad hoc* adjustments that merely accommodate whatever new facts become available, it is labelled 'degenerating'.

These are relative, not absolute distinctions. Moreover, they are applicable not at a given point in time, but over a period of time. The forward-looking character of a research strategy, as distinct from a theory, defies instant appraisal.[26] For Lakatos, therefore, an SRP is not 'scientific' once and for all; it may cease to be scientific as time passes, slipping from the status of being 'progressive' to that of being 'degenerating' (astrology is an example), but the reverse may also happen (parapsychology?). We thus have a demarcation rule between science and non-science which is itself historical, involving the evolution of ideas over time as one of its necessary elements.

The argument is now extended by dividing the components of an SRP into rigid and flexible parts. 'The history of science', Lakatos observes, 'is the history of research programmes rather than of theories' and 'all scientific research programmes may be characterized by their "hard core", surrounded by a protective belt of auxiliary hypotheses which has to bear the brunt of tests.' The 'hard core' is irrefutable by 'the methodological

[24] Although Popper's distinction succeeds in refuting 'conventionalism', it tends to erode the fundamental asymmetry between verification and falsification which is the linchpin of his philosophy of science: see Grünbaum [1973], pp. 569–629, 848–9. Archibald [1967] illustrates the problem of distinguishing *ad hoc* auxiliary assumptions in testing the Keynesian theory of income determination.

[25] Lakatos and Musgrave [1970], p. 118.

[26] If the term 'scientific research programmes' strikes some readers as vague, it must be remembered that the term 'theory' is just as vague. It is in fact difficult to define 'theory' precisely, even when the term is employed in a narrow sense: see Achinstein [1968], chapter 4.

decision of its protagonists' – shades of Kuhn's 'paradigm'! – and it contains, besides purely metaphysical beliefs, a 'positive heuristic', consisting of 'a partially articulated set of suggestions or hints on how to change, develop the "refutable variants" of the research-programme, how to modify, sophisticate, the "refutable" protective belt'.[27] The 'protective belt', however, contains the flexible parts of an SRP and it is here that the 'hard core' is combined with auxiliary assumptions to form the specific testable theories with which the SRP earns its scientific reputation.

If the concept of SRP is faintly reminiscent of Kuhn's 'paradigms', the fact is that Lakatos's picture of scientific activity is much richer than that of Kuhn's. Furthermore, it begins to provide insight as to why 'paradigms' are ever replaced, which is one of the central weaknesses of Kuhn's work. 'Can there be any objective (as opposed to socio-psychological) reason to reject a programme, that is, to eliminate its hard core and its programme for constructing protective belts?' Lakatos asks. His answer, in outline, is that 'such an objective reason is provided by a rival research programme which explains the previous success of its rival and supersedes it by a further display of heuristic power'.[28] He illustrates the argument by analysing Newton's gravitational theory – 'probably the most successful research programme ever' – and then traces the tendency of physicists after 1905 to join the camp of relativity theory, which subsumed Newton's theory as a special case.[29] The claim is that this move from one SRP to another was 'objective', because most scientists acted as if they believed in the normative MSRP. Lakatos goes on to advance the startling claim that all history of science can be similarly described; he defines any attempt to do so as 'internal history'.[30] 'External history', by contrast, is not just all the normal pressures of the social and political environment that we usually associate with the word 'external', but any failure of

[27] Lakatos and Musgrave [1970], pp. 132–5. Lakatos's 'hard core' expresses an idea similar to that conveyed by Schumpeter's notion of 'Vision' – 'the preanalytic cognitive act that supplies the raw material for the analytic effort (Schumpeter [1954], pp. 41–3) – or Gouldner's 'world hypotheses', which figure heavily in his explanation of why sociologists adopt certain theories and reject others (Gouldner [1971], chapter 2). Marx's theory of 'ideology' may be read as a particular theory about the nature of the 'hard core'; Marx was quite right in believing that 'ideology' plays a role in scientific theorising but he was quite wrong in thinking that the class-character of ideology was decisive for the acceptance or rejection of scientific theories.

[28] Lakatos and Musgrave [1970], p. 155; also Lakatos [1971], pp. 104–5.

[29] However, he is not committed to the belief that every progressive SRP will be more general than the degenerate SRP which it replaces. There may well be a Kuhnian 'loss of content' in the process of passing from one SRP to another, although typically the overlap between rival programmes will be larger than either the content-loss or content-gain.

[30] Lakatos [1971], pp. 91–2. This is what Suppe ([1974], pp. 53–6) has called the 'thesis of development by reduction', namely, that scientific progress comes largely, and even exclusively, by the succession of more comprehensive theories which include earlier theories as special cases. The thesis, even in its weaker version, has been hotly debated by philosophers of science for many years.

scientists to act according to MSRP, as, for example, preferring a degenerating SRP to a progressive SRP, on the grounds that the former is more 'elegant' than the latter possibly accompanied by the denial that it is in fact degenerating.[31] The claim that all history of science can be depicted as 'internal' may of course be difficult to sustain in the light of historical evidence but Lakatos recommends that we give priority to 'internal history' before resorting to 'external history'. Alternatively, what we can do is 'to relate the internal history *in the text*, and indicate in the footnotes how actual history "misbehaved" in the light of its rational reconstruction',[32] advice which he himself followed in his famous Platonic dialogue on the history of Euler's 'Conjecture on Polyhedra'.[33]

In reply to Lakatos, Kuhn minimised the differences between them: 'Though his terminology is different, his analytic apparatus is as close to mine as need be: hard core, work in the protective belt, and degenerating phase are close parallels for my paradigms, normal science, and crisis.'[34] He insisted, however, that 'what Lakatos conceives as history is not history at all but philosophy fabricating examples. Done in that way, history could not in principle have the slightest effect on the prior philosophical position which exclusively shaped it.'[35] This seems to ignore Lakatos's deliberate attempt to keep history as such separate from 'philosophy fabricating examples' and provides no resolution of the dilemma which surrounds the historiography of science: either we infer our scientific methodology from the history of science, which commits the fallacy of induction, or we preach our methodology and rewrite history accordingly, which smacks of 'false consciousness'.[36]

Lakatos, replying to Kuhn, tries to score a logical victory for his own approach to the historiography of science by claiming that it is perfectly capable of postdicting novel historical facts, unexpected in the light of the extant approaches of historians of science. In that sense, the 'methodology of historiographical research programmes' may be vindicated by MSRP itself: it will prove 'progressive' if and only if it leads to the discovery of novel historical facts.[37] The proof of the pudding is therefore in the eating. It remains to be seen whether the history of a science, whether natural or

---

[31] Lakatos holds that one cannot rationally criticise a scientist who sticks to a degenerating programme, if, recognising it is degenerating, he is determined to resuscitate it. This is somewhat contradictory. Feyerabend ([1975], pp. 185–6) seizes on this weakness and others in a penetrating but sympathetic critique of Lakatos from the standpoint of epistemological anarchism (*ibid.*, pp. 181–220).

[32] Lakatos [1971], p. 107.

[33] Lakatos [1963–4].

[34] Lakatos and Musgrave [1970], p. 256.

[35] Lakatos and Musgrave [1970], p. 240.

[36] The dilemma in question is widely recognised by philosophers of science, as well as historians of science: see, for example, Lakatos and Musgrave [1970], pp. 46, 50, 198, 233, 236–8; Achinstein in Suppe [1974], pp. 350–61; and Hesse's essay in Teich and Young [1973].

[37] Lakatos [1971], pp. 116–20.

social, is more fruitfully conceived, not as steady progress punctured every few hundred years by a scientific revolution, but as a succession of progressive research programmes constantly superseding each other with theories of ever-increasing empirical content.[38]

2. *Scientific revolutions in economics*

Both Kuhn and Lakatos jeer at modern psychology and sociology as pre-paradigmatic, proto-sciences and although economics seems to be exempted from the charge, Lakatos seems to think that even economists have never seriously committed themselves to the principle of falsifiability: 'The reluctance of economists and other social scientists to accept Popper's methodology may have been partly due to the destructive effect of naive falsificationism on budding research programmes'.[39] It is perfectly true that a dogmatic application of Popper to economics would leave virtually nothing standing but it is a historical travesty to assert that economists have been hostile to Popper's methodology at least in its more sophisticated versions. What is the central message of Friedman's 'as-if' methodology if not commitment to the idea of testable predictions? And indeed the pronouncements of nineteenth-century economists on methodology, summed up in John Neville Keynes's magisterial treatise on *The Scope and Method of Political Economy*[40] are squarely in the same tradition even if the language is that of verification rather than falsification plus or minus a naive Baconian appeal to 'realistic' assumptions. The real question is whether the 'principle of tenacity' does not figure much more heavily in the history of economics than in the history of, say, physics.[41] Analytical elegance, economy of theoretical means, and generality obtained by ever more 'heroic' assumptions have always meant more to economists than relevance and predictability. They have in fact rarely practised the methodology to which they have explicitly subscribed and that, it seems to me, is one of the neglected keys to the history of economics. The

[38] Contrast Kuhn [1957] and Lakatos and Zahar [1976] on the so-called Copernican revolution. See also Zahar [1973] and Feyerabend [1974] on the Einsteinian revolution and Urbach [1974] on the IQ debate. Several other case studies applying Lakatos's MSRP to the history of physics, chemistry, and economics, presented at the Nafplion Colloquium on Research Programmes in Physics and Economics, September 1974, will be published in 1976. For the only published application to economics, see Latsis [1972], discussed below.

[39] Lakatos and Musgrave [1970], p. 179n.

[40] Keynes [1955] (1st edn [1891]).

[41] 'It may be said without qualification', Keynes wrote in *Scope and Method*, 'that political economy, whether having recourse to the deductive method or not, must begin with observation and end with observation...the economist has recourse to observation in order to illustrate, test, and confirm his deductive inferences' (Keynes [1955], pp. 227, 232). But it is characteristic that most of chapters 6 and 7, from which these sentences are drawn, is about the difficulties of verifying deductive inferences by empirical observations; we are never told when we may reject an economic theory in the light of the evidence and indeed whether any economic theory was ever so rejected.

159

philosophy of science of economists, ever since the days of Senior and Mill, is aptly described as 'innocuous falsificationism'.[42]

Let us begin by reviewing the attempts to apply Kuhn's methodology to economics. What are the ruling 'paradigms' in the history of economic thought? According to Gordon, 'Smith's postulate of the maximizing individual in a relatively free market...is our basic paradigm'; 'economics has never had a major revolution; its basic maximizing model has never been replaced...it is, I think, remarkable when compared to the physical sciences that an economist's fundamental way of viewing the world has remained unchanged since the eighteenth century'.[43] Likewise, Coats asserts that economics has been 'dominated throughout its history by a single paradigm – the theory of economic equilibrium via the market mechanism' but, unlike Gordon, Coats singles out the so-called Keynesian revolution as a paradigm-change, a Kuhnian 'scientific revolution', and subsequently he has claimed almost as much for the so-called 'marginal revolution' of the 1870s.[44] Benjamin Ward, a firm believer in Kuhn's methodology, also dubs the Keynesian revolution a Kuhnian one and, furthermore, he claims that the recent post-war period has witnessed 'formalist revolution', involving the growing prestige of mathematical economics and econometrics, which leaves him wondering why such a radical change should have made so little substantive difference to the nature of economics.[45] Lastly, Bronfenbrenner, after defining a 'paradigm' as 'a mode or framework of thought and language', goes on to cite Keynesian macroeconomics, the emergence of radical political economy, the recent revival of the quantity theory of money, and the substitution of the Hicksian LS-LM cross for the Marshallian demand-and-supply cross as cases in point, which falls into the trap set by Kuhn himself.[46] Bronfenbrenner identifies three revolutions in the history of economic thought: 'a laissez-faire revolution', dating from Hume's *Political Discourses*;[47] the 'marginal revolution' of the 1870s as a 'second possible revolution'; and the Keynesian revolution of 1936.

If we had not previously recognised the inherent ambiguities in Kuhn's concepts, this brief review would suffice to make the point. Be that as it may, it appears that if economics provides any examples at all of Kuhnian 'scientific revolutions', the favourite example seems to be the Keynesian revolution, which at any rate has all the superficial appearance of a paradigm-change. It is perfectly obvious, however, that the age-old paradigm of 'economic equilibrium via the market mechanism', which Keynes is supposed to have supplanted, is actually a network of interconnected sub-paradigms; in short, it is best regarded as a Lakatosian

[42] I owe this happy phrase to an unpublished paper by A. Coddington.
[43] Gordon [1965], pp. 123, 124.
[44] Coats [1969], pp. 292, 293; Black, Coats and Goodwin [1970], p. 38; but see p. 337.
[45] Ward [1972], pp. 34–48.
[46] Bronfenbrenner [1971], pp. 137–8.   [47] Hume [1752].

SRP. It is made up, first of all, of the principle of constrained maximisation, 'Smith's postulate of the maximizing individual in a relatively free market', or what Friedman calls for short the 'maximization-of-returns hypothesis'. The principle of maximising behaviour subject to constraints is then joined to the notion of general equilibrium in self-regulating competitive markets to produce the method of comparative statics, which is the economist's principal device for generating qualitative predictions of the signs rather than the magnitudes of his critical variables. The 'hard core' or metaphysical part of this programme consists of weak versions of what is otherwise known as the 'assumptions' of competitive theory, namely, rational economic calculations, constant tastes, independence of decision-making, perfect knowledge, perfect certainty, perfect mobility of factors, et cetera. If they are not stated weakly, they become refutable by casual inspection and cannot, therefore, be held as true *a priori*. The 'positive heuristic' of the programme consists of such practical advice as: (i) divide markets into buyers and sellers, or producers and consumers; (ii) specify the market structure; (iii) create 'ideal type' definitions of the behavioural assumptions so as to get sharp results; (iv) set out the relevant *ceteris paribus* conditions; (v) translate the situation into an extreme prolem and examine first- and second-order conditions; et cetera. It is evident that the marginalists after 1870 adopted the 'hard core' of classical political economy but they altered its 'positive heuristic' and provided it with a different 'protective belt'.

Keynes went still further in tampering with the 'hard core' that had been handed down since the time of Adam Smith. First of all, Keynes departed from the principle of 'methodological individualism', that is, of reducing all economic phenomena to manifestations of individual behaviour. Some of his basic constructs, like the propensity to consume, were simply plucked out of the air. To be sure, he felt impelled by tradition to speak of a 'fundamental psychological law' but the fact is that the consumption function in Keynes is not derived from individual maximising behaviour; it is instead a bold inference based on the known, or at that time suspected, relationship between aggregate consumer expenditure and national income. On the other hand, the marginal efficiency of capital and the liquidity-preference theory of the demand for money is clearly if not rigorously derived from the maximising activity of atomistic economic agents. Similarly, and despite what Leijonhufvud would have us believe, Keynes leaned heavily on the concepts of general equilibrium, perfect competition, and comparative statics, making an exception only for the labour market, which he seems to have regarded as being inherently imperfect and hence always in a state, not so much of disequilibrium as of equilibrium of a special kind.[48]

[48] The best single piece of evidence for this statement is Keynes's reaction to Hicks's famous paper on 'Mr Keynes and the Classics'. 'I found it very interesting', he wrote to

The really novel aspects of Keynes, however, are, first of all, the tendency to work with aggregates and indeed to reduce the entire economy to three interrelated markets for goods, bonds and labour; secondly, to concentrate on the short period and to confine analysis of the long period, which had been the principal analytical focus of his predecessors, to asides about the likelihood of secular stagnation; and, thirdly, to throw the entire weight of adjustments to changing economic conditions on output rather than prices. Equilibrium for the economy as a whole now involved 'underemployment equilibrium' and the introduction of this conjunction, an apparent contradiction in terms, involved a profound change in the 'hard core' of nineteenth-century economics, which undoubtedly included the faith that competitive forces drive an economy towards a steady-state of full employment. Furthermore, the classical and neoclassical 'hard core' had always contained the idea of rational economic calculation involving the existence of certainty-equivalents for each uncertain future outcome of current decisions. Keynes introduced pervasive uncertainty and the possibility of destabilising expectations, not just in the 'protective belt' but in the 'hard core' of his programme. The Keynesian 'hard core', therefore, really is a new 'hard core' in economics. The Keynesian 'protective belt' likewise bristled with new auxiliary hypotheses: the consumption function, the multiplier, the concept of autonomous expenditures, and speculative demand for money, contributing to stickiness in long-term interest rates. It is arguable, however, whether there was anything new in the marginal efficiency of capital and the saving-investment equality. Keynesian theory also had a strong 'positive heuristic' of its own, pointing the way to national income accounting and statistical estimation of both the consumption function and the period-multiplier. There is hardly any doubt, therefore, that Keynesian economics marked the appearance of a new SRP in the history of economics.

Furthermore, the Keynesian research programme not only contained 'novel facts' but it also made novel predictions about familiar facts: it was a 'progressive research programme' in the sense of Lakatos. Its principal novel prediction was the chronic tendency of competitive market economies to generate unemployment. Now, the fact that there was unemployment in the 1930s was not itself in dispute. Orthodox economists had no difficulty in explaining the persistence of unemployment. The government budget in both the United States and Britain was in surplus during most years in the 1930s. It did not need Keynes to tell economists that this was deflationary. It was also well known that monetary policy between 1929 and 1932 was more often tight than easy; at any rate, neither the United States nor Britain pursued a consistent expansionary monetary policy.

Hicks, 'and really have next to nothing to say by way of criticism.' Since Hicks's LS-LM diagram ignores the labour market, the reaction is hardly surprising. On Leijonhufvud's reading of Keynes, see Blaug [1974a] and the references cited there.

Furthermore, the breakdown of the international gold standard aggravated the crisis. There was, in other words, no lack of explanations for the failure of the slump to turn into a boom, but the point is that these explanations were all 'ad hoc', leaving intact the full-employment-equilibrium implications of standard theory. The tendency of economists to join the rank of the Keynesians in increasing numbers after 1936 was therefore perfectly rational; it was a switch from a 'degenerating' to a 'progressive' research programme, which had little to do with contentious issues of public policy.

This assertion is likely to arouse consternation because we all have been taken in, to a greater or lesser extent, by the mythology which has come to surround the Keynesian revolution. According to the Walt Disney version of interwar economics, the neoclassical contemporaries of Keynes are supposed to have believed that wage cutting, balanced budgets and an easy-money policy would soon cure the Great Depression. It comes as a great surprise to learn from Stein[49] and Davis[50] that no American economist between 1929 and 1936 advocated a policy of wage cutting; the leaders of the American profession strongly supported a programme of public works and specifically attacked the shibboleth of a balanced budget. A long list of names, including Slichter, Taussig, Schultz, Yntema, Simons, Gayer, Knight, Viner, Douglas and J. M. Clark, concentrated mainly at the universities of Chicago and Columbia, but with allies in other universities, research foundations, government and banking circles, declared themselves in print well before 1936 in favour of policies that we would today call 'Keynesian'. Similarly, in England, as Hutchison has shown,[51] names such as Pigou, Layton, Stamp, Harrod, Gaitskell, Meade, E. A. G. and J. Robinson came out publicly in favour of compensatory public spending. If there were any anti-Keynesians on questions of policy it was Cannan, Robbins and possibly Hawtrey, but definitely not Pigou, the bogey man of the General Theory.[52] This, by the way, explains the reactions of most American and British reviewers of the General Theory: they questioned the new theoretical concepts, but dismissed the policy conclusions of the book as 'old hat'.

A fair way of summarising the evidence is to say that most economists, at least in the English-speaking countries, were united in respect of practical measures for dealing with the depression but utterly disunited in respect of the theory that lay behind these policy conclusions. What orthodoxy there was in theoretical matters extended only so far as microeconomics. Pre-Keynesian macroeconomics in the spirit of the quantity

[49] Stein [1969].   [50] Davis [1971].   [51] Hutchison [1968].
[52] I ignore the Stockholm school which developed, independently of any clearly discernible influence from Keynes, most of the concepts and insights of Keynesian macroeconomics before the publication either of *The General Theory* [1936] or *The Means of Prosperity* [1933]: see Uhr [1973]. For Ohlin's recollections of the impact of Keynes on the Stockholm theorists, see Ohlin [1974], pp. 892–4.

theory of money presented an incoherent mêlée of ideas culled from Fisher, Wicksell, Robertson, Keynes of the *Treatise*, and continental writers on the trade cycle. In a sense then the Keynesian theory succeeded because it produced the policy conclusions most economists wanted to advocate anyway, but it produced these as logical inferences from a tightly-knit theory and not as endless epicycles on a full-employment model of the economy.[53]

It would seem that certain puzzles about the Keynesian revolution dissolve when it is viewed through Lakatosian spectacles. The attempt to give a Kuhnian account of the Keynesian revolution, on the other hand, creates the image of a whole generation of economists, dumbfounded by the persistence of the Great Depression, unwilling to entertain the obvious remedies of expansionary fiscal and monetary policy, unable to find even a language with which to communicate with the Keynesians, and, finally, in despair, abandoning their old beliefs in an instant conversion to the new paradigm. These fabrications are unnecessary if instead we see the Keynesian revolution as the replacement of a 'degenerating' research programme by a 'progressive' one with 'excess empirical content'. More-over, viewed in this perspective, we gain a new insight into the post-war history of Keynesian economics, a history of steady 'degeneration' as the Keynesian prediction of chronic unemployment begins to lose its plausi-bility. In the 1950s, the contradiction between cross-section and time-series evidence of the savings-income ratio, the former yielding a declining and the latter a constant average propensity to save, spawned a series of revisions in the Keynesian research programme from Duesenberry's rela-tive income hypothesis, to Friedman's permanent income hypothesis, to Modigliani's life-cycle theory of saving. Simultaneously, Harrod and Domar converted static Keynesian analysis into a primitive theory of growth, a development which discarded principal elements in the Keynesian 'protective belt' and more or less the whole of the 'hard core' of the original Keynesian programme. Friedman's monetarist counter-revolution went a good deal further and for a few years in the late 1960s it almost looked as if Keynes had been decisively repudiated. The efforts of Patinkin, Clower and Leijonhufvud to give a disequilibrium interpretation of Keynesian economics, and thus to integrate Keynesian theory into a more general neoclassical framework with still greater 'excess empirical content', would seem to constitute a 'progressive' research programme, superseding both static pre-Keynesian microeconomics and static Key-

---

[53] Keynes himself put it in a nut-shell. Writing to Kahn in 1937 with reference to D. H. Robertson and Pigou, he observed: 'when it comes to practice, there is really extremely little between us. Why do they insist on maintaining theories from which their own practical conclusions cannot possibly follow? It is a sort of Society for the Preserva-tion of Ancient Monuments' (Keynes [1973], p. 259). A hint of the same argument is found in the *General Theory*: a footnote in the first chapter refers to Robbins as the one contemporary economist to maintain 'a consistent scheme of thought, his practical recommendations belonging to the same system as his theory'.

nesian macroeconomics. Keynes's *General Theory* is now a special case and this is scientific progress in economics, perfectly analogous to the absorption of Newton as a special case in the general theory of relativity.

It is possible to give a similar 'internalist' account of the so-called 'marginal revolution' as further demonstration of the applicability of MSRP to economics. The difficulties in the standard notion that marginalism was a new 'paradigm' in economics were thoroughly thrashed out at the Bellagio Conference[54] and it is only necessary to add that the innovations of Menger, Jevons and Walras are more suitably described, not as a new SRP, but as a 'progressive problem-shift' in the older research programme of classical political economy. As frequently happens in such cases, there was 'loss of content' as well as gain. What was lost, such as theories of population growth and capital accumulation, had become by the 1860s an incoherent body of ideas, virtually empty of empirical implications. The reaction against the classical school was more a reaction against Ricardo than against Adam Smith. The Ricardian system was itself a 'progressive problem-shift' in the Smithian research programme, motivated by the experiences of the Napoleonic wars and designed to predict the 'novel fact' of the rising price of corn, leading in turn to rising rents per acre and a declining rate of profit. The 'hard core' of Ricardo is indistinguishable from that of Adam Smith but the 'positive heuristic' contains elements which would have certainly surprised Adam Smith, and this explains the difficulties that many commentators have experienced in identifying disciples of Ricardo who were not also disciples of Adam Smith.[55]

I once argued that the distinctive feature of the Ricardian system was, not the labour theory of value, not Say's Law, not even the inverse relation between wages and profits, but 'the proposition that the yield of wheat per acre of land governs the general rate of return on invested capital as well as the secular changes in the distributive shares'.[56] The notion that Ricardo is at one and the same time the heir of Adam Smith and his principal critic can be conveyed succinctly in the language of MSRP. All the leading British classical economists up to Jevons and even up to Sidgwick subscribed to the basic Ricardian link between the productivity of agriculture and the rate of capital accumulation, and it is in this sense that we can speak of a dominant Ricardian influence on British economic thought throughout the half-century that spanned Waterloo to the Paris Commune. There are unmistakable signs after 1848 of 'degeneration' in the Ricardian research programme, marked by the proliferation of '*ad hoc*' assumptions to protect the theory against the evidence that repeal of

---

[54] Black, Coats and Goodwin [1970].

[55] See, for example, O'Brien [1970] who shows that even John Ramsay McCulloch, Ricardo's leading disciple, never succeeded in resolving the conflict in his mind between Smith and Ricardo.

[56] Blaug [1958], p. 3.

the Corn Laws of 1846 had failed to bring about the effects predicted by Ricardo.[57] On the other hand, the Ricardian research programme was by no means dead by 1850 or even 1860. Cairnes's work on the Australian gold discoveries and Jevon's study of *The Coal Question*[58] showed that there was still unrealised potential in the Ricardian system. Nevertheless, Mill's 'recantation' of the wages fund theory in 1859 expressed a widely-felt sense of malaise, typical of those who find themselves working within a steadily degenerating SRP.

The trouble with this line of argument is that Ricardo did not exert a preponderant influence on Continental economic thought. There is absolutely no evidence of any widely held sense of increasing discomfort in France or Germany around 1870 with classical economic doctrine, conceived broadly on the lines of Adam Smith rather than of Ricardo. What was missing in the British tradition, it was felt, was the utility theory of value, which had roots on the Continent going back to Condillac, Galiani and even Aristotle. What we see in Menger and even more in Walras, therefore, is the attempt to concentrate attention on the problem of price determination at the expense of what Baumol has called the 'magnificent dynamics' in Smith, Ricardo and Mill, in the course of which due emphasis was given to the neglected demand side. This could be seen, and indeed was seen, as an improvement rather than an outright rejection of Adam Smith. There was no room in this schema for the specifically Ricardian elements, except in afterthoughts about long-run tendencies. In the Continental perspective, that is, the whole of the Ricardian episode in British classical political economy was regarded as something of a detour from the research programme laid down by Adam Smith. In other words, whatever we say about Jevons and the British scene, there was no 'marginal revolution' on the Continent: there was a 'problem shift', possibly even a 'progressive problem shift', if predictions about 'the price of an egg' may be regarded as more testable than predictions about the effects of giving free rein to the workings of 'the invisible hand'.

Clearly, economists after 1870, or rather 1890, reassessed the nature of the facts that economics ought to be concerned with. It is conceivable that this 'gestalt-switch' can only be explained in terms of 'external history'. If so, and particularly if we lack any independent corroboration for this historical explanation we have a refutation of MSRP as a metahistorical

---

[57] Blaug [1968], pp. 227–8. In an illuminating paper on Ricardo's and John Stuart Mill's treatment of the relationship between theory and facts, de Marchi [1970] argues that Mill did not, as I have alleged, evade refutations of Ricardo's predictions by retreating into an unspecified *ceteris paribus* clause; he was simply careless with facts and declined to reject an attractive theory merely because it predicted poorly. The issue between us is one of subtle distinctions and, as I am going to argue later on, these distinctions still plague modern economics. Suffice it to say that a defensive attitude to the Ricardian system is increasingly felt in successive editions of the *Principles* and even more in the writings of Cairnes and Fawcett (Blaug [1958], pp. 213–20).

[58] Jevons [1865].

research programme. I have been arguing, however, that an 'internalist' account makes it unnecessary to resort to 'external factors'. It would be premature, however, to arrive at that conclusion on the basis of my crude sketch of historical developments. Only a series of detailed case studies of the spread of marginalism on the Continent after 1870 could settle that question.[59] What I want to insist here is simply that MSRP gives us a powerful handle for attacking these problems.

3. The theory of the firm as a case in point

It is tempting to bring the story forward and to ask whether MSRP is capable of shedding light on the apparent 'degeneration' of the Marshallian research programme in the first two decades of the twentieth century, culminating in the debate on 'empty economic boxes' and the emergence of the theory of monopolistic or imperfect competition; or the less controversial 'degeneration' of the Austrian theory of capital after Wicksell's failure to resolve certain outstanding anomalies in the concept of an 'average period of production'; or the startling failure of the Walrasian programme to make much progress until Hicks's *Value and Capital* and Samuelson's *Foundations* provided it with a new 'positive heuristic';[60] and so forth and so forth. But I will resist these temptations[61] and turn instead to an examination of Latsis's indictment of the traditional theory of the firm, the first attempt in the literature to provide a case study of MSRP in economics.

Latsis argues convincingly that theories of perfect and imperfect competition may be considered together as forming part of the same neoclassical research programme in business behaviour with one identifiable 'hard core', one 'protective belt', and one 'positive heuristic'. The 'hard core' is made up of '(1) profit-maximisation, (2) perfect knowledge, (3) independence of decisions, and (4) perfect markets'.[62] The 'protective belt' includes several auxiliary assumptions: '(1) product homogeneity, (2) large numbers, and (3) free entry and exit'. The 'positive heuristic' consists of 'the analysis of equilibrium conditions as well as comparative statics'.[63] This research programme is labelled 'situational determinism'

---

[59] Black, Coats and Goodwin [1970] provide a few of such case studies which seem to me to strengthen the internalist thesis.

[60] Hicks [1939], Samuelson [1948].

[61] I will also resist the temptation to apply MSRP to Marxian economics, which began badly to 'degenerate' in the first decade of this century when the German Marxist failed to respond creatively to Bernstein's revisionism, and which has continued to 'degenerate' ever since, the unmistakable signs of which are endless regurgitation of the same materials, the continual substitution of appeals to authority for analysis and a persistently negative attitude to empirical research.

[62] This formulation strikes me as being too strong to constitute the irrefutable metaphysic of the neoclassical research programme, which only shows that two Lakatosians need not agree on how to apply MSRP to a particular case in question.

[63] Latsis [1972], pp. 209, 212.

because 'under the conditions characterising perfect competition the decision-maker's discretion in choosing among alternative courses of action is reduced simply to whether or not to remain in business'.[64] This seems to ignore the fact that, apart from remaining in business, the competitive firm also has to decide what output to produce. But the nub of the argument is that the firm either produces the profit-maximising level of output or no output at all: 'I shall call situations where the obvious course of action (for a wide range of conceptions of rational behaviour) is determined uniquely by objective conditions (cost, demand, technology, numbers, etc.), "*single exit*" or "straightjacket" situations'.[65]

In other words, once an independent decision-maker with a well-ordered utility map in a perfect competitive market is given perfect information about the situation he faces, there is nothing left for him to do according to neoclassical theory but to produce a unique level of output, or else to go out of business. There is no 'decision process', no 'information search', no rules for dealing with ignorance and uncertainty in the theory: the problem of choice among alternative lines of action is so reduced that the assumption of profit maximisation automatically singles out one best course of action. The motivational assumptions of 'orthodox theory', Latsis concludes, could be 'weakened from profit maximisation to bankruptcy avoidance', without affecting its predictions.[66]

But what are these predictions? The 'positive heuristic' of the research programme is directed at such questions as '(1) Why do commodities exchange at given prices?; (2) What are the effects of changes in parameters (say demand) on the variables of our model once adjustment has taken place?'[67] But Latsis spends little time considering the specific predictions of neoclassical theory under given circumstances. For example, a standard prediction of the traditional theory of the firm is that a change in the corporate income tax, being a change in a proportionate tax on business income, does not affect the level of output of a competitive firm in the short run because it does not alter the level of output at which profits are maximised; for that reason, the theory predicts that the tax will not be shifted. There is a considerable literature which tends to refute that prediction[68] and this is relevant, although not necessarily clinching, evidence against traditional theory and, by the way, in favour of the sales-maximisation hypothesis. Latsis largely ignores these and other refutations. At various points he does refer to evidence indicating that highly competitive industries sometimes fail to behave in the way predicted by

[64] Latsis [1972], p. 209. The phrase 'situational determinism' is derived from Popper's *Open Society* where the method of economic theory is described as 'analysis of the situation, the situational logic' (cited in Latsis [1972], p. 224).
[65] Latsis [1972], p. 211.
[66] Latsis [1972], p. 223.
[67] Latsis [1972], pp. 212–13.
[68] Ward [1972], p. 18.

the theory[69] but for the most part he takes it for granted that traditional theory has a poor predictive record.[70]

He has little difficulty in showing that the habitual appeal to conditions of perfect competition as an 'ideal type' fails to specify the limits of applicability of the traditional theory of profit-maximisation, so that even the behaviour of oligopolists has come to be analysed with the same tools. But such 'immanent criticism' tells us nothing about 'the degree of corroboration' of a theory. For that we need a report on the past performance of the theory in terms of the severity of the tests it has faced and the extent to which it has passed or failed these tests.[71] Latsis provides no such report. In part, this is because his central argument is that all the programme's successive versions have failed to generate empirical results. But the fact of the matter is that they were thought to do so. For example, the Chamberlin tangency-solution was supposed to predict excess capacity in the case of many sellers with differentiated products. Similarly, theories of joint profit-maximisation under conditions of oligopoly were supposed to predict price rigidities. We cannot avoid asking, therefore, whether these predictions are borne out by the evidence.

Thus, it is difficult to escape the conclusion that Latsis's characterisation of the neoclassical theory of the firm as 'degenerating'[72] is actually based on an examination of the theory's assumptions rather than its testable implications. This conclusion is strengthened by considering his discussion of 'economic behaviouralism' in the writings of Simon, Cyert

[69] Latsis [1972], pp. 219–20.

[70] In the same way, Friedman simply takes it for granted that traditional theory has a splendid predictive record: 'An even more important body of evidence for the maximization-of-returns hypothesis is experience from countless applications of the hypothesis to specific problems and the repeated failure of its implications to be contradicted. This evidence is extremely hard to document; it is scattered in numerous memorandums, articles and monographs concerned primarily with specific concrete problems rather than with submitting the hypothesis to test. Yet the continued use and acceptance of the hypothesis over a long period, and the failure of any coherent, self-consistent alternative to be developed and widely accepted, is strong indirect testimony to its worth' (Friedman [1953], p. 23). This is without doubt the most controversial passage of an otherwise persuasive essay because it is unaccompanied by even a single instance of these 'countless applications'. No doubt, when the price of strawberries rises during a dry summer, when an oil crisis is accompanied by a sharp rise in the price of oil, when share prices tumble after a deflationary budget, we may take comfort in the fact that the implications of the maximisation-of-return hypothesis have once again failed to be refuted. However, given the multiplicity of hypotheses that could account for the same phenomena, we can never be sure that the repeated failure to produce refutations is not a sign of the reluctance of economists to develop and test unorthodox hypotheses. It would be far more convincing to be told what economic events are excluded by the maximisation-of-returns hypothesis, or better still, what events, if they occurred, would impel us to abandon the hypothesis.

[71] In Popper's words: 'By the degree of corroboration of a theory I mean a concise report evaluating the state (at a certain time t) of the critical discussion of a theory, with respect to the way it solves its problems; its degree of testability; the severity of the tests it has undergone; and the way it has stood up to these tests. Corroboration (or degree of corroboration) is thus an evaluating *report of past performance*' (Popper [1972], p. 18).

[72] Latsis [1972], p. 234.

and March, Williamson and Baumol as a rival research programme in business behaviour. He usefully distinguishes 'behaviouralism' from 'organisationalism', the former emphasising learning and 'slack' in a fluid and only partially known environment, the latter emphasising the survival needs of organisations; 'behaviouralism' is applicable to a single decision-maker but 'organisationalism' denies that there are such animals and insists that the objectives of decision-makers should not be postulated *a priori* but ascertained *a posteriori* by observation of decision-making in the real world. Traditional theory turns the decision-maker into a cypher, whereas both behavioural and organisational theories focus attention on the nature and characteristics of the decision-making agent or agents; they do so by repudiating all 'hard core' concepts of optimisation, rejecting even the notion of general analytical solutions applicable to all business firms facing the same market situation.

It would be premature, Latsis argues, to attempt an appraisal of 'behaviouralism' as a budding research programme. The approach may have potential for problems to which the traditional theory is unsuited but 'neoclassical theory gives some simple answers to questions which we cannot even start asking in terms of behaviouralism (namely, in the domain of market structure and behaviour)'.[73] Likewise, behaviouralism has not 'successfully predicted any unexpected novel fact' and 'as a research programme, it is much less rich and much less coherent than its neoclassical opponent'.[74] But lest this imply the superiority of traditional theory, Latsis hastens to add that these are uncommensurable research programmes: 'the two approaches are, in my view, importantly different and mutually exclusive over an extensive area'.[75] In other words, the neoclassical research programme is condemned as 'degenerating' although it has no rival in its own domain and, furthermore, the condemnation is based on the logic of single-exit determinism and not on its record of repeated refutations. In the final analysis, therefore, Latsis denies the normative 'hard core' of MSRP: neoclassical theory is primarily rejected because it is theoretically sterile and only secondarily because it fails to be empirically corroborated. There is nothing wrong with such a criticism but it is less than might have been expected from an application of MSRP to economics.

There is a further point. One of the promising features of Lakatos's

[73] Latsis [1972], p. 233.

[74] Latsis [1972], p. 234.

[75] Latsis [1972], p. 233. Loasby [1971] reaches the same conclusions, using Kuhn's methodology; like Latsis, he views profit maximisation as irrefutable because it is not a hypothesis but a 'paradigm'. In reply to Latsis, Machlup [1974] has seized eagerly on the admission of incommensurability between behaviouralism and marginalism, claiming that 'a research programme designed to result in theories that explain and predict the actions of particular firms can never compete with the simplicity and generality of the marginalist theory, which, being based on the constructs of a fictitious profit-maximiser, cannot have the ambition to explain the behaviour of actual firms in the real world'.

methodology is the insistence that we literally cannot appraise single theories: we test theories but we appraise research programmes. The neoclassical research programme is much more than a theory of the firm; it is also a theory of the determination of wage rates and interest rates and it includes, and some would say it starts with, a theory of consumer behaviour. If the neoclassical research programme in the economics of industry is to be written off as 'degenerating', the rot should show up in the theory of factor pricing and in the theory of demand. One can sympathise with an author who declines to review the whole of microeconomics in order to assess its 'degree of corroboration' but that is no excuse for not mentioning the entire research programme. It is certainly impossible to understand the tenacious defence of marginalism in the field of business behaviour without recognition of the fact that what is at stake is the whole of price theory.[76] Here, as elsewhere, Latsis seems to me to do less than justice to Lakatos's methodology.

4. *Do economists practise what they preach?*

Having said that much, it only remains for me to do what I criticise Latsis for not doing, namely to appraise the whole of neoclassical economics with the aid of Lakatos's methodology. But I am not equal to that task. What I will do is to voice some misgivings about the applicability of any philosophy of science grounded in the history of the physical sciences to a social science like economics. I express these misgivings tentatively. If they are widely shared, so much the worse for the prospect of writing an entirely 'internalist' history of economic thought.

I begin by quoting Machlup, who in his long career has returned repeatedly to problems of the methodology of economics:

When the economist's prediction is *conditional*, that is based upon specified conditions, but where it is not possible to check the fulfilment of all the conditions stipulated, the underlying theory cannot be disconfirmed whatever the outcome observed. Nor is it possible to disconfirm a theory where the prediction is made with a stated *probability* value of less than 100 per cent; for if an event is predicted with, say, 70 per cent probability, any kind of outcome is consistent with the prediction. Only if the same 'case' were to occur hundreds of times could we verify the stated probability by the frequency of 'hits' and 'misses'. This does not mean complete frustration of all attempts to verify our economic theory. But it does mean that the tests of most of our theories will be more nearly of the character of *illustrations* than of verifications of the kind possible in relation with

[76] As Krupp has so aptly observed: 'The degree of confirmation of an entire theory is highly intertwined with value judgements which reflect, among other things, the selection of its constituent hypotheses. It is not coincidental, therefore, that the advocates of the theories of competitive price will simultaneously defend diminishing returns to scale, a low measure of economic concentration, the demand-pull explanation of inflation, a high consumption function, the effectiveness of monetary policies on full employment, the insignificance of externalities, and the general pervasiveness of substitution rather than complementarity as a basic relation of the economic system' (Krupp [1966], p. 51).

repeatable controlled experiments or with recurring fully-identified situations. And this implies that our tests cannot be convincing enough to compel acceptance, even when a majority of reasonable men in the field should be prepared to accept them as conclusive, and to approve the theory so tested as 'not disconfirmed'.[77]

This passage may be read as a criticism of 'naive falsificationism' but it may also be read as a plea for still more 'sophisticated falsificationism'. It is precisely because tests of economic theories are 'more nearly of the character of illustrations than of verifications' (I would prefer to say 'falsifications') that we need as many 'illustrations' as possible. But that implies that we concentrate our intellectual resources on the task of producing well-specified falsifiable predictions; in other words, we give less priority to such standard criteria of appraisal as simplicity, elegance and generality, and more priority to such criteria as predictability and empirical fruitfulness. It is my impression, however, that most modern economists would order their priorities precisely the other way round.

Ward's recent book asks *What's Wrong With Economics?* and his answer in brief is that economics is basically a normative policy science travelling in the false disguise of a positive one. Insofar as it is a positive science however, he agrees that 'the desire systematically to confront the theory with fact has not been a notable feature of the discipline', although that, he contends, 'is not the central difficulty with modern economics'.[78] What I want to argue, by way of contrast, is that the central weakness of modern economics is in fact the reluctance to produce theories which yield unambiguously refutable implications.

When, in the long process of refining and extending the neoclassical research programme over the last hundred years, have we ever worried about 'excess empirical content', much less 'corroborated excess empirical content'? Consider, for example, the preoccupation since 1945 of some of the best brains in modern economics with problems of growth theory, when even practitioners of the art admit that modern growth theory is all about 'shadows of real problems, dressed up in such a way that by pure logic we can find solutions for them'.[79] But that example is too easy. Take rather that part of the neoclassical research programme which comes closest in matching the rigour and elegance of quantum physics, the modern theory of consumer behaviour, based on axiomatic utility theory, to which a long line of economists from Fisher, Pareto, Slutsky and Johnson to Hicks, Allen, Samuelson and Houthakker have devoted their most intense efforts. There is little sign that these prodigious labours have had a substantive impact on household budget studies or on the literature dealing with statistical demand curves. Or to switch fields, consider the endless arguments in textbooks on labour economics about the assumptions that underlie the misnamed 'marginal productivity theory of wages'

[77] Machlup [1955], p. 19. In the same spirit, see Grunberg and Boulding in Krupp [1966].   [78] Ward [1972], p. 173.   [79] Hicks [1965], p. 183.

at the expense of space devoted to considering what the theory actually predicts and how well it has fared. If this is not misplaced emphasis, what is? We all recognise that misplaced emphasis at least implicitly, which is why Lipsey's textbook was so well received when it first appeared: to this day, its relative emphasis on empirical testing stands out among the current textbooks on elementary economics.

But surely economists engage massively in empirical research? Certainly they do, but much empirical work in economics is like 'playing tennis with the net down': instead of attempting to refute testable predictions, economists spend much of their time showing that the real world bears out their predictions, thus replacing falsification, which is difficult, with confirmation, which is easy. A single example must suffice. Ever since Solow's celebrated article of 1957, estimation of aggregate Cobb–Douglas production functions for purposes of measuring the sources of economic growth and drawing inferences about the nature of technical progress has become a wide-spread practice in economic research. Ostensibly, such work tests the prediction that production functions in the aggregate obey the condition of constant-returns-to-scale and that individual markets, despite trade unions and despite monopolies, impute prices to factors in accordance with the theory of perfect competition. It took more than a decade before Fisher[80] showed conclusively that it is perfectly possible to obtain a good fit of an aggregate Cobb–Douglas production function even if the underlying pricing mechanism is anything but competitive. But long before that, several econometricians had argued convincingly that the concept of aggregate production functions, as distinct from micro-production functions, lacks a firm theoretical foundation.[81] If the advice was ignored, it was because most economists are delighted with 'puzzle-solving' activity of an empirical kind even if it is virtually tantamount to 'measurement without theory'. Marshall used to say that 'explanation is prediction written backwards'. Many economists forget that 'prediction' is not necessarily 'explanation written forwards'.[82] It is only too easy to engage in empirical works that fail utterly to discriminate between competing explanations and which consist largely of mindless 'instrumentalism'.

Those who explicitly revolt against orthodoxy are often infected by the same disease. So-called Cambridge controversies in the theory of capital, which actually are controversies about the theory of functional income distribution, have raged on for twenty years without so much as a reference to anything but 'stylised facts', such as the constancy of the capital–output ratio and the constancy of labour's relative share, which turn out on examination not to be facts at all. The fundamental issue at stake between

---

[80] Fisher [1971].

[81] For a fuller discussion, see Blaug [1974].

[82] What I am denying is the well-known 'thesis of the structural symmetry of explanation and prediction': see Hempel [1965], pp. 367–76 and Grünbaum [1973], chapter 9.

173

Cambridge UK and Cambridge US, we are told by no less an authority on the debate than Joan Robinson, is not so much the famous problem of how to measure capital but rather the question of whether saving determines investment instead of investment determining saving.[83] That issue depends in turn on the question of whether the world is better described by full employment or by underemployment equilibrium. Inasmuch as the entire debate is carried out in the context of steady-state growth theory, and as everyone agrees that steady-state growth is never even approximated in real economics, there is no reason whatever for refusing to operate with both models, depending on the problem at hand. Neither models have any predictive power and Cambridge controversies, therefore, are incapable of being resolved by empirical research. This has not, however, prevented either side from battling over the issues with redoubled fury. Protagonists in both camps have described the controversy as a war of 'paradigms' but in fact the two 'paradigms' intersect and indeed overlap almost entirely.

Even the radical political economists in the United States have spent most of their efforts on 'telling a new story': the same old facts are given a different interpretation around the 'paradigm' of power-conflict in contrast to the 'paradigm' of utility-maximisation in mainstream economics.[84] What little empirical work has appeared in the *Review of Radical Political Economy* on race and sex discrimination, the financial returns to education and patterns of social mobility in the United States has lacked discriminating, well-articulated hypotheses that could distinguish between orthodox and radical predictions.[85] But the movement does at least have the excuse of explicitly announcing their preference for social and political relevance over simplicity, generality and falsifiability as characteristics of 'good' theory.[86]

Neoclassical economists do not have the same excuse. They preach the importance of submitting theories to empirical tests but their practice suggests that what they have in mind is merely 'innocuous falsificationism'. Of all the great modern economists who have advocated a falsificationist methodology – Harrod, Koopmans, Friedman, Samuelson, Baumol and Boulding – Friedman is almost the only one whose analysis and research exemplifies his own precepts. His work on Marshallian demand curves, on the expected-utility hypothesis, on flexible exchange rates and particularly on the permanent income hypothesis is marked by a constant search for refutable predictions. The *Theory of the Consumption*

[83] For references and details, see Blaug [1974b].
[84] See Worland [1972].   [85] See Bronfenbrenner [1970].
[86] Franklin and Resnik ([1974], pp. 73–4) provide a typical methodological pronouncement: 'From a radical perspective, in which analysis is closely linked to advocacy of fundamental changes in the social order, an abstract model or category is not simply an aesthetic [sic] device. It is purposely designed to assist in the changes advocated, or in describing the nature of the barriers that must be broken down if the advocated changes are to occur.'

Function[87] is surely one of the most masterly treatments of the relationship between theory and data in the whole of the economic literature. But even Friedman produced his 'theoretical framework for monetary analysis' long after making dramatic claims of direct empirical evidence in favour of the quantity theory of money.[88] As a monetarist, even Friedman has failed to live up to his own methodology.[89]

I have left to the last the issue of welfare economics, where of course no questions of testable implications can arise. Here the Lakatos methodology is helpless because there is nothing in the physical sciences that corresponds to theories which deduce the nature of a social optimum from certain fundamental value judgements. Economists have talked a great deal of nonsense about 'value-free' welfare economics on the curious argument that the standard value judgements that underlie the concept of a Pareto optimum – every individual is the best judge of his own welfare; social welfare is defined only in terms of the welfare of individuals; and the welfare of individuals may not be compared – command wide assent and this concensus somehow renders them 'objective'. They have also swallowed whole the untenable thesis that 'normative' as distinct from 'methodological' value judgements are not subject to rational discourse and have thus denied themselves a fruitful area of analysis.[90] But these issues apart, the intimate relationship between normative and positive economics has been a potent source of 'ad hocery' in economics, the effort to retain theories at all costs by the addition of assumptions that lack testable implications.

No doubt, welfare economics and positive economics are separable in principle. However, practical policy recommendations typically violate the logical separability of the two. Decision-makers demand as much advice on their objectives as on the means to achieve these objectives and

[87]   Friedman [1957].   [88] Friedman [1970].

[89] The case of Friedman also illustrates the fact that agreement on falsificationism among modern economists disguises a significant spectrum of attitudes in respect of the type of test that is deemed appropriate in different circumstances. As Briefs [1961] argues, in an unduly neglected book, economists have always disagreed about the role of statistical significance tests versus that of historical analysis as alternative methods of refuting economic hypotheses; even supporters of statistical testing differ about the admissability of single-equation regressions in contrast to simultaneous equation estimates, depending in turn on whether the individual writer favours partial or general equilibrium analysis. Friedman's writings exemplify all three methods.

[90] For the beginnings of such an analysis, see Sen [1970], pp. 58–64. The positive suggestions for reconstructing economics in Ward [1972] are along similar lines. It is worth noting that the failure to distinguish 'methodological' and 'normative' value judgements has been productive of much misunderstanding surrounding the value-fact dichotomy in social inquiry. Methodological judgements involve criteria for judging the validity of a theory, such as levels of statistical significance, selection of data and assessment of its reliability, adherence to the canons of formal logic, et cetera, which are indispensable in scientific work. Normative judgements, on the other hand, refer to ethical judgements about the desirability of certain kinds of behaviour and certain social outcomes. It is the latter which are said to be capable of being eliminated in positive science. See Nagel [1961], pp. 485–502 for almost the last word on this endlessly debated topic.

the supply of advice naturally responds accordingly. Besides, as Samuelson said in the *Foundations*: 'At least from the time of the physiocrats and Adam Smith, there has never been absent from the main body of economic literature the feeling that in some sense perfect competition represented an optimal situation.' The modern Invisible Hand theorem provides a rigorous demonstration of that feeling: every long-run perfectly competitive equilibrium yields an optimal allocation of resources and every optimal allocation of resources is a long-run perfectly competitive equilibrium. Of course, this leaves out the 'justice' of the associated distribution of personal income; furthermore, 'optimal allocation' is strictly defined with reference to the three basic value judgements of Paretian welfare economics. Nevertheless, every economist feels in his bones that the Invisible Hand theorem is almost as relevant to socialism as to capitalism, coming close indeed to a universal justification for the role of market mechanisms in any economy. It is hardly surprising, therefore, that economists fight tooth and nail when faced with an empirical refutation of a positive theory involving the assumption of perfect competition. For what is threatened is not just that particular theory but the entire conception of 'efficiency' which gives *raison d'etre* to the subject of economics. No wonder then that the 'principle of tenacity' – the fear of an intellectual vacuum – looms so large in the history of economics.

The upshot of this long harangue is to suggest that MSRP may not fit the history of economics: economists may cling to 'degenerating' research programmes in the presence of rival 'progressive' research programmes while denying that the 'degenerating' programme is in need of resuscitation because they are suspicious of hard data, inclined to assign low priority to the discovery of novel facts, accustomed by long habit to deny the feedback of evidence on theory, or simply because they are deeply attached to the welfare implications of their theories. If this should prove to be the case after a detailed examination of twentieth century economics with the aid of MSRP, it may tell us something more fundamental about the difference between natural and social science than the old saws about the unchanging universe of physics and the continually changing universe of economics.

5. *Conclusions*

Lakatos's metahistorical research programme has a 'hard core' of its own: scientists are rational and accept or reject ideas for good intellectual reasons, the only problem being to determine what they are. The programme also has a 'protective belt' which contains such propositions as: scientists attach importance to the ability of theories to survive tests but they do not discard theories after a single failure; scientists appraise programmes, not theories; scientists appraise programmes historically as they evolve over time and continually revise their appraisals; lastly, scientists appraise programmes in competition with rivals and will retain a programme at any cost if no alternatives are available. The 'positive heuristic' of the metahistorical research programme is equally obvious: collect theories into research programmes; spell out the 'hard core', 'the protective belt' and 'the positive heuristic' of the respective programmes; examine the efforts that have been made to test theories and trace the manner in which falsifications are dealt with in the programme; set out the anomalies that are recognised by practitioners of a programme and, if possible, the anomalies that have come to be forgotten; trace the standards by which the adherents of a research programme judge their predecessors and by which they hope to be judged by their followers, that is, analyse their methodological pronouncements; and, finally, highlight the novel facts which are discovered in the course of a programme. The object of the exercise is to show that most scientists join research programmes that have 'excess empirical content' and desert 'research programmes' that lack this characteristic. This is 'internal history' and every other reason for joining one camp rather than another is 'external'. It was Lakatos's claim that the 'rational reconstruction' of the history of science conceived in these terms would in fact need few footnotes referring to 'external history'.

Can the history of economics be written in this fashion? It is perfectly true that most externalist accounts of scientific progress are very persuasive – they are selected to be so. When certain theories become the ruling scientific ideas of their times for 'good' internalist reasons, there are frequently also ideological reasons that make the theory palatable to vested interests and appealing to the man-in-the-street. These can be invoked subsequently to argue that the theory was in fact accepted for external reasons (consider Malthus's theory of population, or Darwin's theory of natural selection). But such externalist explanations, while not wrong, are nevertheless redundant if we have regard to professional rather than popular opinion. To be convincing, the externalist thesis in the history of ideas must produce instances of (i) internally consistent, well corroborated, fruitful and powerful scientific ideas which were rejected at specific dates in the history of a science because of specific external factors, or (ii) incoherent, poorly corroborated, weak scientific ideas which were in fact accepted for specific external reasons. I can think of no unambiguous examples of either (i) or (ii) in the history of economics and therefore conclude that a Lakatosian 'rational reconstruction' would suffice to explain virtually all past successes and failures of economic research programmes.

M. BLAUG

References

Achinstein, P. [1968]: *Concepts of Science.*
Archibald, G. C. [1967]: 'Refutation or Comparison?', *British Journal for the Philosophy of Science*, **17**.
Black, R. D. C., Coats, A. W. and Goodwin, C. D. W. [1970]: *The Marginal Revolution in Economics. Interpretation and Evaluation.*
Blaug, M. [1958]: *Ricardian Economics.*
Blaug, M. [1968]: *Economic Theory in Retrospect*, 2nd edn.
Blaug, M. [1974a]: 'Comments on C. J. Bliss, "Reappraisal of Keynesian Economics"', in M. Parkin (ed.): *Current Economic Problems. The Proceedings of the Association of University Teachers of Economics Conference*, 1974.
Blaug, M. [1974b]: *The Cambridge Revolution. Success or Failure?*
Bloor, D. [1971]: 'Two Paradigms for Scientific Knowledge', *Science Studies*, **1**.
Briefs, H. W. [1961]: *Three Views of Method in Economics.*
Bronfenbrenner, M. [1970]: 'Radical Economics in America: A 1970 Survey', *Journal of Economic Literature*, **8**.
Bronfenbrenner, M. [1971]: 'The "Structure of Revolutions" in Economic Thought', *History of Political Economy*, **3**, pp. 136–51.
Coats, A. W. [1969]: 'Is There a "Structure of Scientific Revolutions" in Economics?', *Kyklos*, **22**, pp. 289–96.
Davis, J. R. [1971]: *The New Economics and the Old Economists.*
De Marchi, N. B. [1970]: 'The Empirical Content and Longevity of Ricardian Economics', *Economica*, **37**, pp. 257–76.
Feyerabend, P. K. [1974]: 'Zahar on Einstein', *The British Journal for the Philosophy of Science*, **25**, pp. 25–8.
Feyerabend, P. K. [1975]: *Against Method. Outline of an Anarchistic Theory of Knowledge.*
Fisher, F. M. [1971]: 'Aggregate Production Functions and the Explanation of Wages: A Simulation Experiment', *Review of Economics and Statistics*, **53**, pp. 305–25.
Franklin, R. J. and Resnik, S. [1974]: *The Political Economy of Racism.*
Friedman, M. [1953]: *Essays in Positive Economics.*
Friedman, M. [1957]: *Theory of the Consumption Function.*
Friedman, M. [1970]: 'A Theoretical Framework for Monetary Analysis', *Journal of Political Economy*, **78**, pp. 193–238.
Gordon, D. F. [1965]: 'The Role of the History of Economic Thought In the Understanding of Modern Economic Theory', *The American Economic Review*, **55**, pp. 119–27.
Gouldner, A. W. [1971]: *The Coming Crisis of Western Sociology.*
Grünbaum, A. [1973]: 'Philosophical Problems of Space and Time', in R. S. Cohen and M. Wartofsky (eds.): *Boston Studies in the Philosophy of Science.*
Hempel, C. G. [1965]: *Aspects of Scientific Explanation.*
Hicks, J. R. [1939]: *Value and Capital.*
Hicks, J. R. [1965]: *Capital and Growth.*
Hume, D. [1752]: *Political Discourses.*
Hutchison, T. W. [1968]: *Economics and Economic Policy in Britain, 1946–1966.*
Jevons, W. S. [1865]: *The Coal Question.*
Keynes, J. M. [1933]: *The Means of Prosperity.*
Keynes, J. M. [1936]: *The General Theory.*
Keynes, J. M. [1973]: *The Collected Writings of John Maynard Keynes*, XIV, *The General Theory and After*, Part II.

Keynes, J. N. [1955]: *The Scope and Method of Political Economy*, 4th edn.

Krupp, S. R. (ed.) [1966]: *The Structure of Economic Science. Essays on Methodology*.

Kuhn, T. S. [1957]: *The Copernican Revolution*.

Kuhn, T. S. [1970]: *The Structure of Scientfic Revolutions*, 2nd edn (1st edn 1962).

Kunin, L. and Weaver, F. S. [1971]: 'On the Structure of Scientific Revolutions in Economics', *History of Political Economy*, **3**.

Lakatos, I. [1963–4]: 'Proofs and Refutations', *The British Journal for the Philosophy of Science*, **14**, pp. 1–25, 120–39, 221–43, 296–342.

Lakatos, I. [1971]: 'History of Science and Its Rational Reconstructions', in R. C. Buck and R. S. Cohen (eds.): *Boston Studies in the Philosophy of Science*, vol. 8, pp. 91–136.

Lakatos, I. and Musgrave, A. (eds.) [1970]: *Criticism and the Growth of Knowledge*.

Lakatos, I. and Zahar, E. [1976]: 'Why Did Copernicus's Programme Supersede Ptolemy's?', in R. Westman (ed.): *The Copernican Achievement*.

Latsis, S. J. [1972]: 'Situational Determinism in Economics', *The British Journal for the Philosophy of Science*, **23**, pp. 207–45.

Latsis, S. J. [1974]: 'Situational Determinism in Economics', unpublished PhD dissertation, University of London.

Lipsey, R. G. [1966]: *An Introduction to Positive Economics*, 2nd edn.

Loasby, B. J. [1971]: 'Hypothesis and Paradigm in the Theory of the Firm', *Economic Journal*, **81**, pp. 863–85.

Machlup, F. [1955]: 'The Problem of Verification in Economics', *Southern Economic Journal*, **22**, pp. 271–84.

Machlup, F. [1974]: 'Situational Determinism in Economics', *The British Journal for the Philosophy of Science*, **25**, pp. 271–84.

Magee, B. [1973]: *Popper*.

Martins, H. [1972]: 'The Kuhnian Revolution and Its Implications for Sociology', in A. H. Hanson, T. Nossiter and S. Rokkau (eds.): *Imagination and Precision in Political Analysis*.

Nagel, E. [1961]: *The Structure of Science*.

O'Brien, D. P. [1970]: *J. R. McCulloch. A Study in Classical Economics*.

Ohlin, B. [1974]: 'On the Slow Development of the "Total Demand" Idea in Economic Theory: Reflections in Connection with Dr. Oppenheimer's Note', *Journal of Economic Literature*, **12**, pp. 888–96.

Popper, K. R. [1962]: *The Open Society and Its Enemies*, 4th edn.

Popper, K. R. [1965]: *The Logic of Scientific Discovery*.

Popper, K. R. [1972]: *Objective Knowledge. An Evolutionary Approach*.

Ryan, A. [1970]: *The Philosophy of the Social Sciences*.

Samuelson, P. A. [1948]: *Foundations*.

Schilpp, P. A. (ed.) [1974]: *The Philosophy of Karl Popper*, 2 vols., Library of Living Philosophers, vol. 24.

Schumpeter, J. A. [1954]: *History of Economic Analysis*.

Sen, A. K. [1970]: *Collective Choice and Social Welfare*.

Stein, H. [1969]: *The Fiscal Revolution in America*.

Suppe, F. [1974]: *The Structure of Scientific Theories*.

Teich, M. and Young, R. (eds.) [1973]: *Changing Perspectives in the History of Science*.

Toulmin, S. [1972]: *Human Understanding*.

Uhr, C. G. [1973]: 'The Emergence of the "New Economics" in Sweden: A Review of a Study by Otto Steiger', *History of Political Economy*, **5**, pp. 243–60.

Urbach, P. [1974]: 'Progress and Degeneration in the "IQ Debate" (I), (II)', *The British Journal for the Philosophy of Science*, **25**, pp. 99–135, 235–59.

Ward, B. [1972]: *What's Wrong With Economics?*

Whitley, R. [1974]: *Social Processes and Scientific Development.*
Worland, S. T. [1972]: 'Radical Political Economy As A "Scientific Revolution"', *Southern Economic Journal*, **34**, pp. 274–84.
Zahar, E. [1973]: 'Why Did Einstein's Programme Supersede Lorentz's?' *The British Journal for the Philosophy of Science*, **24**, pp. 95–123, 223–62.

On the history and philosophy of science and economics[1]

T. W. HUTCHISON

UNIVERSITY OF BIRMINGHAM

I

Methodological questions in economics have often been discussed in terms that are too abstract and too exclusively normative. Slim volumes or essays about the 'scope and method' or the 'nature and significance' of the subject, seem often to have been concerned mainly with ideal epistemological models which are almost as remote from the actuality of what economists do, as economic models of smoothly and ideally self-equilibrating processes are remote from the processes of the real economic world.[2] Intellectual norms are prescribed, and, it seems to be implied, are actually upheld, which are certainly not in fact followed, and perhaps could not practicably *be* followed, by economists.[3] Moreover, generalisations,

[1] This paper developed out of the discussions at the Nafplion Colloquium of September 1974 on Research Programmes in Physics and Economics. I am very grateful to the organisers and especially to Dr Spiro Latsis.

[2] As the author, long ago, of one of these slim volumes, I would not want to suggest that abstract, largely normative essays are necessarily useless, or worse. But returns to general abstract methodological arguments are apt to diminish rather sharply for those whose interests are primarily centred on their own particular subject. Regarding the views expressed in that earlier essay – *The Significance and Basic Postulates of Economic Theory* [1938] and [1960] – I would still support for economics the criteria of testability and falsifiability. On the other hand, the optimistic 'naturalism' of this earlier essay seems now indefensible: that is its suggestions that the 'social sciences' could and would develop in the same manner as physics and the natural sciences. This is certainly not now to assert that economists and 'social scientists' should not *try* to follow natural scientific methods, and the 'mature' sciences, *as far as they can, while respecting the nature of their material*. In fact economics has achieved *some* degree of success along these lines. But it should not be imagined or suggested that they can 'succeed' – and, above all, not be pretended that they have 'succeeded' – in anything approaching the same manner and extent as physics and other natural sciences. Whether these differences between economics and physics are regarded as a matter of degree or a matter of principle does not seem to be very important as long as their full significance is understood. However, it seems highly misleading to insist on certain general similarities between the natural and social sciences (although such general similarities certainly exist) and to assert that the differences are only ones 'of degree', *without* making it clear how important in practice these differences are.

[3] For example, regarding 'disagreement about facts' Oskar Lange wrote: '*Such disagreement can always be removed by further observation* and study of the empirical material. Frequently, however, the empirical data necessary to resolve the disagreement are unavailable. In such cases the issue remains unsettled. The conclusion that the issue cannot be settled with the data available has interpersonal validity. *Agreement is reached to withold judgment*' (Lange [1945–6], p. 748, my italics). The notion of real-world economists, on any considerable scale, actually reaching agreement to 'withold judgment', because adequate empirical data to resolve disagreements are unavailable, is, unfortunately, as

181

normative or positive, are inevitably highly abstract, or stylised, when they relate to 'science' and 'scientific method' in general, or to 'the social sciences' generally, or even to economics as a whole, which comprises theories and arguments of very varying epistemological types and calibres.

It could, therefore, constitute a most welcome and significant example, as far as economics is concerned, that in their different ways, in the work of both Kuhn and Lakatos, the history of science, and its analysis or philosophy, have been brought together for mutual illumination. Certainly there is the danger here of normative–positive confusion, insofar as the philosopher of science may be seeking to prescribe what scientists ought to have done or decided (or be doing or deciding) while the historian is attempting rather to set out what they actually *did* do or decide.[4] Certainly one feels bound to record the impression that what economists actually do and decide (and have done and decided) is not, and has not been, invariably what, according to tenable methodological or scientific criteria, they *ought* to have done or decided. Nevertheless, though this danger of normative–positive confusion needs close attention, there does not seem to be any inevitable, fundamental difficulty, ruling out from the start, useful, mutual illumination between the philosophy and the history of economics.

It may well seem, however, that a larger relative component of *recent* or *contemporary* history might be more suitable than the relatively heavy concentration on the history of physics from the sixteenth to the early twentieth centuries – which is what 'the history of science' seems to a large extent, though not exclusively, to consist of. Certainly a relatively greater concentration on the recent and contemporary history of sciences might seem to be justified, if the estimate is accepted that about ninety per cent or more of the scientists (including presumably physicists and economists) who have ever lived, are alive today.[5]

fantastic as is a model of real-world firms and households generally returning smoothly and rapidly to some ideal equilibrium position.

[4] Cf. Paul Feyerabend: 'Whenever I read Kuhn, I am troubled by the following question: are we here presented with *methodological prescriptions* which tell the scientist how to proceed: or are we given a description, void of any evaluative element, of those activities which are generally called "scientific"?' Kuhn's answer does not seem entirely satisfactory when he maintains that he is concerned with both description and prescription *at once*, because 'scientists should behave essentially as they do if their concern is to improve scientific knowledge.' Whatever may be claimed on behalf of physicists, it seems doubtful whether *economists* have always behaved exactly as they would if their concern is, or had been, to 'improve economic knowledge'. On the other hand, criticising Lakatos, Kuhn writes: 'What Lakatos conceives as history is not history at all, but philosophy fabricating examples.' (Feyerabend [1970], p. 198; Kuhn [1970], p. 237.) Also see Lakatos [1970], p. 143.

[5] The history of recent or contemporary policy proposals and doctrines seems particularly significant in economics as revealing the kind of claims regarding effective economic knowledge entertained by economists. However, this is not to be recommended as an area in which a forthright account of the fruits of his research will be likely to promote the professional popularity of the researcher.

But we come now to what seems a more serious danger, which is that of drawing methodological lessons, or conclusions, about the development of a wide range of sciences, from a version of the history of science in general which is concentrated too exclusively on a particular kind of success story, that of the development of physics, and similar subjects, from the sixteenth century onwards. In fact, a possibly serious danger which might emanate from the 'history of science', as it seems widely to be pursued, is that of a kind of oversimplified *historicism* of science leading to excessive and misleading generalisations about how sciences *must* develop. There seems to be a danger of forgetting that, as Kuhn puts it, 'the sciences are not, in fact, all of a piece';[6] or that as Ravetz has emphasised: 'The world of science is a very variegated one...and the "methods" of science are a very heterogeneous collection of things.'[7]

The 'history of science', in fact, is not actually made up of the history of a single, epistemologically homogeneous activity, because, basically, the nature of the *materials* which different sciences deal with is significantly different. Of course, it is time and again asserted that these differences are only differences of degree, and not of kind or principle. But an insistence on this way of putting it can be seriously misleading when the differences are as wide and consequential as they are. As has been well said: 'The single most important discovery of social science in these last decades is that social science does not yield the kind of knowledge of society – and the kind of power over society – that natural science possesses vis-à-vis the natural world.'[8]

To some extent, philosophers of science have been recognising differences between sciences simply by distinguishing between what they call 'mature' and 'immature' sciences. This pair of adjectives, as we shall see, has been used by Kuhn, Lakatos, and Ravetz, among others, and suggests, rather obviously, the kind of historicism of science which is open to complaint.

If one calls a science 'immature' one seems to be suggesting that *either* in due course it will, more or less inevitably, by some natural process of 'maturation' become like physics – the supremely 'mature' science – *or*, if this does not happen, or does not seem to be happening, there must be something wrong: the subject is being mishandled, and the wrong can be set right by following certain philosophical or methodological prescriptions. It seems even to be suggested that possibly there are inevitable 'stages of development' – to introduce a favourite historicist concept – which must and will be passed through in the development of sciences, as in the development of economies.[9]

---

[6] Kuhn [1968], p. 76.
[7] Ravetz [1971], pp. 173 and 410.   [8] Kristol [1964].
[9] A somewhat similar suggestion in terms of the mildly historicist concept of 'underdevelopment' (rather than 'immaturity') has been made by Professor Phelps Brown, as the conclusion of his Presidential address to the Royal Economic Society entitled, 'The

Similarly, it is sometimes suggested in a plausibly optimistic manner by economists and social scientists, that their subjects got started later and got left behind by the natural sciences, with the implication that they will, in due course, catch up. But the question has to be posed as to *why* economics and the social sciences somehow started late, or got left behind, if it was not for reasons in the nature of the basic material which may preclude any eventual 'catching up' with physics, or anything like it.

Suggestions of a kind of historicism of science, and of 'laws', or stages, of development, fail to take account of fundamental differences in material: notably, for example, that the material of physics possesses constancies and an absence of significant historical change and development, which the material of economics does *not* possess. If the material which economics deals with was to come to resemble, sufficiently significantly, the material which physics deals with, then the science of economics might come in due course to resemble the science of physics in 'maturity' and 'development'. Meanwhile, the often-quoted dictum of Aristotle remains relevant: 'Our discussion will be adequate if it has as much clearness as the subject-matter admits of.'[10]

We would add that not only 'clearness' but what is reached in the way of conclusions, 'theories', predictions and 'laws' (if any) must depend on what 'the subject matter' of different sciences 'admits of'.

It is certainly not argued here that there are no relevant and valuable methodological lessons, parallels and examples, which may be drawn for economics from the history of physics and chemistry. There certainly are such. But there are, also, easily assumed but fundamentally misleading parallels which may be drawn, including a questionable and perhaps unjustified presumption that economics will eventually one day, come to a 'maturity' resembling that of physics today.[11]

Underdevelopment of Economics'. Professor Phelps Brown concludes that economics 'has hardly yet reached its 17th Century. I believe we shall make better progress when we realise how far we still have to go' (Phelps Brown [1972], p. 10). It is not that one should question the healthy and realistic message that economics is in a very different epistemological position from that of physics. What should be questioned is the implication that economics is progressing along the same kind of road as physics, towards the same kind of goal or destination, to be reached in due course, though at the moment two or three hundred years away. Professor Phelps Brown cites in support Professor Morgenstern's conclusion that 'the principal condition for the advancement of economics is still to improve the empirical background...Our knowledge of the relevant facts of economics is incomparably smaller than that commanded in physics when the mathematisation of the subject was achieved...backed by several millenia of systematic scientific, astronomical observation...Nothing of this sort has occurred in economic science.' But it should be emphasised, by way of a significant major addition to this argument, that the millenia of systematic astronomical observation were of *mainly constant phenomena*, in contrast with most economic observation. This point strengthens still further Professor Phelps Brown's condemnation of the neglect of history by economists. (Morgenstern [1965], pp. 12–29; von Neumann and Morgenstern [1955], paragraphs 1, 2 and 4.)

[10] Aristotle, *Nicomachaean Ethics*, chapter 3 (quoted by Ravetz [1971], p. 158n).

[11] See the article by M. J. Roberts [1974] 'Social science has accomplished less than it might because social scientists have inappropriately tried to imitate certain characteristics

We shall now explore what some leading philosophers of science have recently had to say about economics as a science. We shall take note of one or two brief but significant suggestions, notably by Lakatos and Ravetz, regarding sciences at different stages of 'maturity' or 'immaturity'. We shall also review certain arguments of Sir Karl Popper, T. S. Kuhn, J. R. Ravetz and Imre Lakatos. It may be remarked at this point, that some economists and their methodological PROs, seem to have argued confidently over the merits or demerits, so far as economics is concerned, of the methodological analyses and prescriptions of Popper, Kuhn, and Lakatos, without taking into account that the analyses and prescriptions of these distinguished philosophers of science have been derived and distilled, very largely, or almost exclusively, from the history and philosophy of physics or similar subjects. Thus the suggestion is conveyed (which is, of course, likely to be highly popular with some economists) of a kind of epistemological parity between economics and physics, which will render the methodological analysis, prescriptions, strategy or tactics, derived from the one science, entirely appropriate, almost without qualification or reservation, to the other science.

As regards philosophers of science, they seem, in recent decades, to have been rather reticent regarding the particular, peculiar, methodological position of economics. However, they may be found discussing very sharp contrasts between physics, on the one hand – in the history and method of which they have been primarily interested – and certain other social, or 'human' sciences, or subjects, on the other hand. But economics is usually left out of these comparisons and its epistemological position is left somewhat obscure. Alternatively, it seems to be rather too readily assumed that by cultivating the history and philosophy of physics the road is being cleared, paved, and lit up along which, in due course, economics can and will advance to the 'maturity' of physics, even if, perhaps, those economists who apparently have professed that it is already far advanced towards that objective may be a little premature.

II

Let us start with Sir Karl Popper. Sir Karl has told us in his autobiography: 'The social sciences never had for me the same attraction as the theoretical natural sciences.'[12]

of natural science, especially physics. Social scientists have not understood that the nature of the particular phenomena they study has implications both for how they should proceed and what they can hope to find out...This view implies giving up the notion that there is some close analogy in the social sciences to basic research in the physical sciences. With complex heterogeneous objects that have many characteristics, we can hope to discern only limited regularities...This makes the typical task of social science less glamorous, less general, and more expensive than it has generally been considered'. (Roberts [1974], pp. 47 and 162.)

[12] Popper [1974], p. 96.

In *The Open Society*, and *The Poverty of Historicism*, Popper writes of 'the somewhat unsatisfactory state of some of the social sciences'. He maintains that 'much of our "social science" belongs to the Middle Ages'[13] (which, apparently, Sir Karl intended as a pejorative judgment). In fact, according to Sir Karl: 'The social sciences do not as yet seem to have found their Galileo...There is very little in the social sciences that resembles the objective and ideal quest for truth which we meet in physics'.[14]

Moreover, as Sir Karl has subsequently insisted: 'Compared with physics, sociology and psychology are riddled with fashion and with uncontrolled dogmas... The natural sciences are largely free from verbal discussion, while verbalism was, and still is, rampant, in many forms in the social sciences.'[15]

We would hold, for our part, that though economics may not be exactly 'riddled' with fashion and uncontrolled dogmas, and though 'verbalism' may not be precisely 'rampant' in the subject, nevertheless these phenomena are not exactly conspicuous by their absence from economics. However, Sir Karl's strictures on the social sciences generally are not applied to economic theory, which, he seems to suggest, occupies a quite exceptional position. In fact, in *The Poverty of Historicism* Sir Karl remarks: 'The success of mathematical economics shows that one social science at least has gone through its Newtonian revolution.'[16]

Certainly one might find similar claims suggested by mathematical economists. But the mathematical 'revolution' in economics has been one mainly (or almost entirely) of *form, with very little or no, empirical, testable, predictive content involved*. In accepting as 'Newtonian' a purely, or almost purely, formal, or notational, 'revolution', Sir Karl seems to have allowed himself to be taken in by over-optimistic propaganda. Not only has nothing genuinely describable as 'a Newtonian revolution' taken place in economics, it is reasonable to suggest that it is not probable that anything of the sort is going to occur in the foreseeable future. Anyhow, if economic theory, mathematically formulated, constitutes such a shining, unique exception and contrast, compared with the 'medieval', pre-Galilean condition of the social sciences generally, then, surely such an outstanding post-Newtonian salient would deserve the closest analysis and appraisal *from philosophers of science*, instead of the neglect it has recently, in the main, received.

In *The Poverty of Historicism* Sir Karl held to a predominantly, not exclusively, 'naturalistic' line regarding the social sciences, that is, he argued in favour of applying in the social sciences the criteria and methods of the natural sciences. One might well have derived from Sir Karl's treatment much confidence that if such monstrous errors as 'historicism',

[13] Popper [1945], vol. 1, p. 2 and vol. 2, p. 9.
[14] Popper [1957], pp. 1 and 16.
[15] Popper [1970], p. 57; Popper [1974], p. 14.
[16] Popper [1957], p. 60n.

'essentialism', 'verbalism', etc., could be exposed and eliminated, then the social sciences could and would develop and 'mature' along the lines on which physics had developed and 'matured'. Certainly, one cannot but acknowledge the force and cogency of most of Sir Karl's pro-naturalist arguments, and few concessions need or should be made to the older anti-naturalist attitudes which he so convincingly criticised. Certainly also, it is desirable to *attempt* the advancement of economics and the social sciences along 'naturalistic' lines *to the utmost, but limited, extent, to which such advance is feasible or possible*. But what it is just as essential to emphasise is not only that the advance along these lines, though not negligible, has been so far comparatively limited, but that there are no good grounds for supposing that any *very* great advances of the kind and extent made in physics in the last three or four centuries, are *very* likely to ensue in economics. Meanwhile, misleading comparisons between economics and physics and the methods, tactics and criteria appropriate to the two sciences, neglect vital differences in the nature of the basic materials with which they are engaged. It is ultimately because of the differences in basic materials that 'historicism', 'essentialism', 'verbalism', 'fashion', 'uncontrollable dogmas', and all the other methodological monstrosities discerned by Sir Karl in the social sciences, are so *much* more difficult, or *almost* impossible, to root out, and will not give way very far to methodological prescriptions however trenchant, although significant improvements in this respect are not impossible to achieve if critical standards are constantly upheld, however unpopular this may be.

Sir Karl's over-optimism regarding the post-Newtonian character of economic theory seems to be illustrated by his claim that sociological or economic laws or hypotheses exist, 'which are analogous to the laws or hypotheses of the natural sciences'.

As Sir Karl shows:

Every natural law can be expressed by asserting that *such and such a thing cannot happen*; that is to say, by a sentence in the form of the proverb: 'You can't carry water in a sieve.'[17]

Sir Karl then claims to cite parallel examples of such laws or hypotheses in economics:

'You cannot introduce agricultural tariffs and at the same time reduce the cost of living.' – 'You cannot in an industrial society, organise consumers' pressure groups as effectively as you can organise certain producers' pressure groups.' – 'You cannot have a centrally planned society with a price system that fulfils the main functions of competitive prices.' – 'You cannot have full employment without inflation.'

[17] Popper [1945], pp. 61–2. I have commented before on this argument of Popper's regarding economic 'laws', when discussing prediction in economics: see Hutchison [1964], p. 95.

These generalisations, listed by Sir Karl, are certainly not useless. They represent the kind of rough-and-ready material, in the form of patterns, trends, or tendencies, which economists have to work with if they do not – as some do – take refuge in 'rigorous' fantasies and unrealities. But these generalisations do not really begin to compare with their counterparts in physics in terms of reasonably precise, testable and well-tested, empirical and predictive content. Behind the informal, proverbial, physical generalisation about the impossibility of carrying water in a sieve, there stand the kind of well-tested laws, with precise, measurable, and easily tested initial conditions, which one relies on when travelling by aeroplane or crossing a bridge. *Virtually no laws of this quality, or of anything approaching this quality, stand behind Sir Karl's collection of economic generalisations,* which, indeed, simply confirm that:

A typical law in the physical sciences is stated precisely, usually in mathematical terms, and is quite free of ambiguity. It has been tested repeatedly and has withstood the tests. The usual law in the social sciences, on the other hand, is ordinarily couched in Big Words and a great deal of ambiguity.[18]

Admittedly in Sir Karl's economic generalisations he does not descend to 'Big Words', but he does not avoid 'a great deal of ambiguity'. Anyhow, later on in *The Poverty of Historicism* Sir Karl agrees that:

It cannot be doubted that *there are some fundamental difficulties here.* In physics, for example, the parameters of our equations can, in principle, be reduced to a small number of natural constants – a reduction which has been successfully carried out in many important cases. This is not so in economics; here the parameters are themselves in the most important cases quickly changing variables. This clearly reduces the significance, interpretability *and testability* of our measurements.[19]

Unfortunately, Sir Karl broke off at this point without commenting on the significance of these 'fundamental difficulties' for his claims regarding sociological and economic laws, 'analogous to the laws or hypotheses of the natural sciences', and for that 'Newtonian revolution' in economic theory which he had claimed to discern. But if the parameters in economic

---

[18] Kemeny [1959], p. 244. The following conclusion of Barrington Moore may also be noted: 'Social science, after some two hundred years, has not yet discovered any universal propositions comparable in scope or intellectual significance to those in the natural sciences...Classical economics managed to erect at one time a comprehensive and elegant theory to organise its subject matter in a scientific manner. Somehow the facts have changed since the formulation of the theory...We do not yet have any laws in social science comparable to those in the natural sciences.' (Barrington Moore [1958], pp. 127–8.) However, economists, both orthodox and Marxist, from Ricardo to Robbins, *until quite recently*, have had no compunction about proclaiming Economic Laws (often with capital letters) in a most impressive manner. This insistence upon strict laws in the economic cosmos may have had healthy intentions, and briefly some healthy effects in countering the Utopian delusions of politicians and public. But it was bound to be found out. Nevertheless it remains very desirable to insist that there seem to be genuine prohibitive laws restricting the economic world, though they are too complex and shifting for us to be able to formulate them at all precisely at any particular moment.

[19] Popper [1957], p. 143, my italics.

theories, or quasi-theories, are 'in the most important cases quickly changing variables', and there are no reliable laws but only historical trends or patterns on which to base predictions, then the question arises as to the relevance and suitability *for economics* of the strongly anti-inductive emphasis in Popper's methodology. Such methodological principles may have been most serviceable in physics, from the history of which they have been derived. But they may be too exclusivist for a subject with a fundamental historical aspect, like economics. The relevance of methodological principles must depend on the nature of the material with which a particular subject has to deal. It is not good advice to condemn induction if the nature of the material restricts the genuine scope for the hypothetico-deductive method. And the material with which economics has to deal shows certain crucial differences from the material with which physics has to deal, which it is dangerously misleading to neglect. As Professor M. J. Roberts has argued:

As a first step, social scientists must recognise that all science is not physics. Physics has obtained equations that apply to all electrons because all electrons are in the relevant sense alike. When phenomena are heterogeneous, generality can only be obtained at the price of content. One is forced to say less and less about each case in order to include all possible cases. Such abstract non-phenomena-oriented theorizing in the social sciences, most emphatically cannot be justified by analogy to basic research in natural science since the latter, unlike the former, is concerned with explicating real empirical events.[20]

However, it is essential to distinguish between Sir Karl's rather over-optimistic, incidental comments on economic theory, which may well have fostered a certain complacency among economists, and his general prescriptions in terms of a vitally valuable, and salutary, critical 'falsificationism'. We shall return later to the contrasting effects on economists of Sir Karl's teachings.

III

Let us now turn very briefly to T. S. Kuhn's writings, in which there is little or nothing specifically about economics, but which employ the concept of 'mature' and 'immature' sciences (also used, as we shall see, by Ravetz and Lakatos). 'Immature' sciences, or 'proto-sciences' as Kuhn calls them, are those 'in which practice does generate testable conclusions but which nonetheless resemble philosophy and the arts rather than the established sciences in their developmental patterns...The proto-sciences like the arts and philosophy, lack some element which, in the mature sciences permits the more obvious forms of progress. It is not, however, anything that a methodological prescription can provide.'[21]

[20] Roberts [1974], p. 58.
[21] Kuhn [1970], p. 244.

Kuhn includes 'many of the social sciences today', alongside the arts and philosophy, among the 'proto-sciences', as contrasted with the 'established' or 'mature' sciences.

In view of the way in which Kuhn's earlier views and concepts were unjustifiably exploited and misrepresented – by some economists among others – it may be worth underlining the fairly hard criteria which he sets out for scientific 'maturity'. These criteria include the following: '*First* is Sir Karl's demarcation criterion without which no field is potentially a science...*Second*...predictive success must be consistently achieved... *Third*, predictive techniques must have roots in a theory...'.[22]

The uncertain position of economics could be indicated by citing the quite contradictory views that leading economists have expressed, and are expressing, on just such issues as these three (to which, incidentally, my own answer would be marginally positive, but severely hedged and qualified).

It is to be noted that Kuhn agrees regarding Popper's falsificationist prescriptions: 'Even in the developed sciences, there is an essential role for Sir Karl's methodology. It is the strategy appropriate to those occasions when something goes wrong with normal science.'[23]

It may be suggested that in the 'underdeveloped' science of economics (as the President of the Royal Economic Society has recently called it) or in 'immature' sciences generally, there nearly always is, or has been – from any not thoroughly complacent and uncritical point of view – 'something going wrong'. In other words there hardly ever is or has been an even *relatively* adequately based 'normality' in such subjects, comparable with 'normality' in physics. So whether or not one accepts Kuhn's concept of 'normality' for a 'developed' or 'mature' science, such as physics – which is a condition when, according to Kuhn, Sir Karl's strategy or prescriptions would be inappropriate – *a fortiori*, in Kuhn's view, there is *always* a role for these trenchant Popperian prescriptions in economics and the social sciences – contrary to what is maintained by economists and sociologists who have purveyed a false impression of Kuhn's views in order to controvert Popper's.

IV

Let us turn next to a contribution which, though it may not seem to present a fairly balanced appraisal of the state of economics, certainly deserves much more attention from economists, or philosophers of the subject, than it has so far received. This contribution is contained in J. R. Ravetz's impressive work on *Scientific Knowledge and its Social Problems*. Mr Ravetz provides a much fuller, more explicit and more severe appraisal of where economics belongs in the spectrum of the sciences, than Popper,

[22] Kuhn [1970], p. 245.   [23] Kuhn [1970], p. 247.

Kuhn, or Lakatos. Using, like Kuhn, and as we shall see, Lakatos, the terminology of 'mature' and 'immature' subjects, Ravetz places economics firmly among what he calls, in a chapter of that title, 'Immature and Ineffective Fields of Enquiry'. According to Ravetz:

At the present time, the disciplines that present the most obvious evidence of ineffectiveness or at least immaturity, are those which attempt to study human behaviour in the style of the mathematical-experimental sciences...The situation becomes worse when an immature or ineffective field is enlisted in the work of resolution of some practical problem.[24]

Somehow Ravetz seems to have missed Sir Karl's 'Newtonian revolution' in mathematical economics. He goes on, with reference to economics:

In spite of the vacuity or irrelevance of most of its theory, and the patent unreliability of its statistical information, it ranks as the queen of the sciences in the formation of national policy.[25]

Mr Ravetz perceives very clearly where the root of the difficulty lies:

The condition of ineffectiveness is not an accidental deficiency in some component of the materials of a field, but is a systematic weakness in those materials.[26]

We would emphasise next, a distinction which Ravetz draws, which is somewhat similar to one made by Kuhn, and also, as we shall see, by Lakatos. This is, that in subjects of different levels of 'maturity' or 'immaturity', methodological criteria or 'criteria of adequacy' have to be enforced with different degrees of stringency. Ravetz maintains that in a field which has 'achieved maturity', with a 'set of appropriate and stable criteria of adequacy', such methodological criteria 'become part of the basic unselfconscious craft knowledge of the fields...In these conditions the very existence of criteria of adequacy can be overlooked'.[27]

In other words, in thoroughly 'mature' fields, what we shall find Lakatos describing as 'Polanyite autonomy' may be accepted or tolerated as appropriate. On the other hand, as Ravetz insists, 'in less mature fields',

[24] Ravetz [1971], p. 366.
[25] Ravetz [1971], p. 396. A similar conclusion is propounded by Professor S. Andreski in his trenchant essay 'Social Sciences as Sorcery', (Andreski [1974], pp. 149–51): 'The sophisticated mathematical models, which one finds in books on economics, might mislead an unwary reader into believing that he is facing something equivalent to the theories of physics...It is important to bear in mind that even in the branch which has opportunities for measurement unrivalled in the other social sciences, an infatuation with numbers and formulae can lead to empirical irrelevance and fraudulent postures of expertise. The most pernicious manifestations of the last-named tendency (abetted by the natural proclivity of every occupation to extol its wares) have been the claims of numerous economists to act as arbiters on matters of planning, on the assumption (whose efficacy depends on its being tacitly made rather than explicitly recognized) that the factors which can be measured must serve as the basis for decision...The assumption in question has often led economists to aid and abet the depredations of a soul-destroying and world-polluting commercialism, by silencing the defenders of aesthetic and humane values with the trumpets of one-sided statistics.'
[26] Ravetz [1971], p. 369.
[27] Ravetz [1971], p. 159.

criteria of adequacy or methodological standards 'cannot be taken for granted'.

Mr Ravetz points out the problems in terms of funds and prestige of admitting or recognising 'immaturity' in a subject:

The present social institutions of science, and of learning in general, impose such constraints that the growth and even the survival of an immature field would be endangered by the simple honesty of public announcement of its condition. For these institutions were developed around mature or rapidly maturing fields in the nineteenth century...If the representatives of a discipline announce that they do not fit in with such a system, they can be simply excluded from it, to the benefit of their competitors for the perennially limited resources. The field would be relegated to amateur status, and thereby pushed over to the very margin of the world of learning; it would be deprived of funds and prestige.[28]

But appearances can be deceptive:

An immature field, in chaos internally, experiences the additional strains of hypertrophy; its leaders and practitioners are exposed to the temptations of being accepted as consultants and experts for the rapid solution of urgent practical problems. The field can soon become identical in outward appearance to an established physical technology, but in reality be a gigantic confidence-game... To thread one's way through these pitfalls, making a genuine contribution both to scientific knowledge and to the welfare of society, requires a combination of knowledge and understanding in so many different areas of experience, that its only correct title is wisdom.[29]

[28] Ravetz [1971], p. 378. Marc J. Roberts has made a similar point: 'The failure of economists to make clear how little they know or can hope to know is understandable. Society seems to be most generous to and respectful of the "real sciences". Material well-being, power, status, and the scientist's ability to "fulfill his moral obligations" by influencing policy – all these depend on the acceptance by the wider society of his expertise. And when politics become involved, the chances increase that more will be promised than can be delivered, especially by the political actors in whose retinue social scientists are enlisted...The pressures on contemporary social scientific guilds have prevented a full and frank assessment of this situation. Accomplishments have often been oversold.' (Roberts [1974], pp. 58 and 61.)

[29] Ravetz [1971], p. 400. The following is from a review of a leading textbook of econometrics: 'Anyone reading this book could be excused if he were left with the impression that at last Economics has become a Science. For here are set out first the underlying mathematical techniques, then the mathematical structure of the various econometric models, the techniques of estimation of the parameter values and the properties of the estimators obtainable. Problems are duly provided at appropriate points in the text, and there are half a dozen or more tables of down-to-earth statistics which form the basis of many further tables illustrating techniques of estimation. *One almost has to pinch oneself to keep in mind that it is highly dubious whether the structure of the determination of the variables in the real world approximates the structure of the theoretical models for which this impressive apparatus of thought is designed to provide parameter estimates.* However, it would be as churlish to blame an author expounding econometrics for the fact that the real world can seldom be fruitfully studied by econometric methods, as it would be to criticise a monarch for taking part in pageantry which has no immediate practical utility'. (Champernowne [1972], pp. 222–3, my italics.)

I would only comment that it seems to me that it would probably be *much more* 'churlish' to blame the monarch than the econometrician. Anyhow, the comparison is quite far-reaching: decisions have to get taken in a world of ignorance and uncertainty. It may be desirable socially that there should be a certain confidence in the decisions and the

Mr Ravetz concludes:

Since immature and ineffective fields are due to be involved in public affairs to an increasing extent as our social problems become ever more complex, an awareness of their limitations is necessary if their application is to produce more good than harm.[30]

Perhaps Mr Ravetz is excessively censorious and gloomy regarding economics and its potential contribution. In particular, the heavily value-loaded words 'immature', 'ineffective' and 'weakness', are unnecessary and inappropriate. The state of economics and the nature of its material are simply *different* from that of physics. But this kind of critical severity may be much less dangerous than the excessive optimism and pretentiousness which is so much more common among economists. *The dangers which Mr Ravetz stresses should not be underestimated.* Surely he is right in maintaining that to inculcate an awareness of the limitations of the subject is today *a* major, and perhaps *the* major, task of the philosopher of economics, rather than the suggestion of misleading and over-optimistic parallels between economics and physics. The limitations of economic knowledge and its 'ineffectiveness' are not to any *very* large extent the fault of economists. There is no simple methodological remedy or formula for 'maturity' and 'effectiveness'. A re-allocation of economists' efforts, or a reshaping of their education and training, might be both illuminating and marginally beneficial in terms of less unsuccessful policy-making, but could hardly provide solutions satisfying the excessive expectations which have grown up regarding government policies. However, failure to grasp limitations and a failure to try to bring them home to politicians and public, could certainly constitute a *very* serious fault, as still more so, the fostering of excessive expectations.

V

Imre Lakatos also – like Kuhn and Ravetz – employed the distinction between 'mature sciences' and what he called 'immature and indeed dubious disciplines'. (Incidentally it might be useful to pinpoint *exactly* what it is in this context that is 'dubious' and why). Lakatos also referred to 'the underdeveloped social sciences', and to 'a process of degeneration' occurring in 'some of the main schools of modern sociology, psychology and social psychology'.[31]

But the only explicit reference to economics to be found in his writings claimed that: 'The reluctance of economists and other social scientists to

decision-makers, however profound and inevitable their ignorance. The magic of monarchy and traditional deference having faded as sources of reassurance, the 'professional' mysteries of mathematical model-building and 'expertise' take their place. (I am indebted for the quotation to Professor D. P. O'Brien's distinguished inaugural lecture, *Whither Economics?* [1974].)   [30] Ravetz [1971], p. 401.

[31] Lakatos [1970], p. 93; Lakatos [1971], pp. 122 and 123.

accept Popper's methodology may have been partly due to the destructive effects of naive falsificationism on budding research programmes.'[32]

We shall return later to the alleged 'reluctance' of economists 'to accept Popper's methodology' (which reluctance became indeed considerable, but far from total, and may have been based on widely differing and contrasting grounds). Anyhow, presumably the reluctance of economists or of anyone else to accept what is 'naive' and (unduly) 'destructive', *must* be justified. One may well agree that it provides, in some ways, a more enlightening historical perspective to look at 'research programmes' rather than particular theories or propositions. But 'research programmes' in economics have such *very* long lives. In fact, exactly what are these 'budding research programmes' which were so 'naively' and unjustifiably threatened? It might be said that 'orthodox' economics, in the 200 years since Adam Smith, has consisted largely of a single 'research programme' of building and qualifying self-adjusting models. In monetary and 'macro'-economics the rival 'research programmes' of the quantity theory of money and of the income, 'aggregate demand', or 'Keynesian' theories, could be said to have been 'budding' for over 200 years. The orthodox 'research programme', or theory, of the firm has surely been 'budding' since Cournot wrote nearly 140 years ago. The general equilibrium 'research programme' has only been budding for just a century: or could Lakatos have been referring to the comparatively recent 'research programmes' of growth-modelling? Or that of the radical 'chiconomics' of the Cambridge capital analysis and the Sraffa models? It is impossible to say, since Lakatos gave no examples. In fact it seems difficult to escape the suspicion that Lakatos's 'naively' and unfairly threatened, 'budding research programmes' in economics are as insubstantial, or even mythical, as Sir Karl's 'Newtonian revolution'. Taking a critical look at the history of political economy and economics one simply fails to find timorous, cautious economists hastily retreating and abandoning their 'budding research programmes' to the first crude and 'cruel' attacks of 'naive' and undiscriminating falsificationists. Quite the reverse – and dangerously and even reprehensibly so. The history of the subject is, in fact, full of exaggerated theoretical claims put forward in order to sell particular professed policies of one political stripe or another; and these claims have often been tenaciously and dogmatically maintained with the aid of every kind of conventionalist strategem for decades, and indeed half-centuries on end, regardless of evidence or the lack of it. There may possibly be *some* justification for such tenacity. But there is even more justification for sustaining criticism, on falsificationist principles, especially so long as these century-old (but still 'budding')

---

[32] Lakatos [1970], p. 179n. Two years earlier Lakatos had insisted in *much stronger terms* that 'the reluctance of economists...*was primarily*' (not '*may have been partly*') due etc. (Lakatos [1968], p. 183).

programmes are being unjustifiably employed for the selling of questionable policies.

Perhaps Lakatos's remarks about 'budding research programmes' in economics should be interpreted in terms of his prescription that 'to give a stern "refutable interpretation" to a fledgling version of a programme is dangerous methodological cruelty'.[33]

Lakatos may have considered that the precepts of gentleness and patience, which he had argued for in the case of theoretical physics, were equally and automatically appropriate in the case of economic theory, in spite of the basic difference in the material, and consequently in the history and processes of 'research programmes', in the two subjects. For Lakatos had developed his arguments against Popper's more severe, 'falsificationist' prescriptions as inappropriately destructive, *from the case of physics*, and had distilled his own more 'flexible' brand of 'falsificationism' from the history of physics. We are not attempting to criticise Lakatos's prescriptions on their home ground of theoretical physics. The question is how suitable and relevant these arguments are in the case of theoretical economics.

We should now consider the distinguished pioneer attempt by Dr Latsis to apply the prescriptions of Lakatos to the criticism and appraisal of the theory of the firm. The critical approach of Dr Latsis seemed to evolve somewhat as between his first article of 1972 and his Nafplion paper (1974). We would only call attention to what may be a detail in this evolution, but one which seems to be quite significant with regard to the applicability of the methodological prescriptions of Lakatos to economics. In his earlier article Dr Latsis discussed Professor Machlup's defence of the orthodox theory of the firm and Machlup's criticism of destructive 'falsificationism'. Dr Latsis described these criticisms by Professor Machlup as 'an almost complete anticipation of Lakatos's similar criticism'.[34]

In his later paper Dr Latsis, after describing Machlup (and Friedman) as 'conventionalists', maintains that they wanted 'the neoclassical research programme' or orthodox theory of the firm 'to come out as satisfactory when judged by *general* methodological standards; at least it should not be impatiently rejected at the behest of Utopian norms'.[35]

According to Dr Latsis, Professor Machlup 'repeatedly argues that counter-intuitive and apparently refuted assumptions may nevertheless be valuable for explanation and prediction in neoclassical microeconomics'.[36]

No attempt here is being made to deny all value to 'neoclassical

[33] Lakatos [1970], p. 151.
[34] Latsis [1972], p. 237. Actually Professor Machlup's criticism, discussed by Dr Latsis, is a criticism of this writer. It might be assumed that Professor Lakatos himself did not disagree with Dr Latsis's description.
[35] *This volume*, p. 10.
[36] *This volume*, p. 10.

microeconomics'. But I observe that Dr Latsis then goes on to find, regarding Professor Machlup's criticism, that it is based on an 'interpretation of the neoclassical theory of the firm, which 'generates built-in defence mechanisms enabling the reconciliation of almost any recalcitrant evidence with the theory'.

Moreover, Professor Machlup's interpretations of the assumptions of the 'theory' 'tell us nothing about the limits of applicability of the perfectly competitive model; they only tell us that the perfectly competitive model is only applicable when it can be applied'.

Dr Latsis goes on to maintain:

Since Machlup and other neoclassical economists are either reluctant or unsuccessful in spelling out in advance the specific circumstances in which their models are applicable, any adverse evidence whatsoever can be attributed to 'special circumstances'.

Dr Latsis concludes regarding 'conventionalism':

Conventionalist methodology is, as we have indicated, peculiarly suited to account for the appraisals of economists. Direct empirical confrontation of the theory's postulates with lower level statements is excluded. Empirical anomalies, i.e. clashes between the theory's consequences and experiential statements, are accommodated by means of a battery of conventionalist stratagems. Finally, those empirical successes, if any, which the theory secures are hailed as triumphs and used as arguments for putting up with its intuitive implausibility and its empirical deficiencies.[37]

This is an admirably perceptive, precise, and penetrating criticism (and quite as 'destructive' as any bloodthirsty 'falsificationist' would want to be). It should only be added that in its treatment of 'conventionalism', and the stratagems thereof, it seems to be entirely and centrally Popperian. Also especially welcome is Dr Latsis' conclusion regarding the key problem of sorting out 'the genuine (or justified), defense manoeuvres from the *ad hoc* ones':

Falsificationism may be very useful here. For instead of attempting to knock out theoretical systems by furnishing empirical counter-examples we may employ falsificationist criteria to rule out defensive manoeuvres that are unacceptable.[38]

One is simply left wondering about the almost completely Lakatosian nature of the *criticism* of falsificationism put forward by Professor Machlup, if Machlup's methodological criteria allowed or encouraged the extensive use of the conventionalist tactics so pungently criticised by Dr Latsis.

One cannot show that the testability principle of Popper should be replaced in economics by the prescriptions of Lakatos, by proceeding to deal justly and destructively, by means of Popperian criteria, with the historical examples one selects. Not much significance can arise *for economics* in the revisions of Popper by Lakatos, if all, or virtually all, economic programmes are either vulnerable – or approved – *both* according to Popper's principles, *and* according to those of Lakatos. To justify

[37] *This volume*, pp. 11 and 14   [38] *This volume*, p. 9.

the replacement of Popper's prescriptions by those of Lakatos in economics one must set out in precise terms, from the history of economics, an example of a 'budding research programme', which went on subsequently to a fruitful or illuminating career, and which would have been allowed through uncriticised by the more discriminating Lakatos prescriptions, but which would have been unjustly and prematurely attacked by Popper's testability criterion. At the same time it should be shown that the more flexible prescriptions would not, in practice, in economics, be reduced to 'anything goes'. Such a demonstration does not seem yet to have been performed and would seem inherently rather difficult to perform.

We come now to an acutely interesting point suggested by Lakatos, although he only just touches upon it without specifically mentioning economics. This is his brief intimation that methodological prescriptions may need to be enforced more explicitly or less explicitly according to the degree of 'immaturity' or 'maturity' of the subject.

According to Lakatos: 'While Polanyite academic autonomy should be defended for departments of theoretical physics, it must not be tolerated say, in institutes of computerised social astrology, science planning or social imagistics.'

In fact, Lakatos goes on to enquire: 'Is it not then *hubris* to try to impose some *a priori* philosophy of science on the most advanced sciences?'[39]

Lakatos seems to suggest here that while a kind of methodological autonomy should be tolerated for *some* subjects, or sciences, like theoretical physics, on which it would be '*hubris*' to seek to impose methodological precepts, there are other subjects whose claims to autonomy 'must *not* be tolerated', and whose procedures it is by no means *hubris* to criticise from outside. Lakatos does not explicitly place economics in respect of this distinction of his. He mentions such intellectual phenomena as 'computerised social astrology' and 'social imagistics' as coming clearly on the wrong side of the tracks, as presumably would 'computerised *economic* astrology', which can certainly be said to exist.[40]

The question, therefore, arises as to how far the claims of such subjects to 'Polanyite autonomy' should be accepted. Perhaps Lakatos's Royal Society for the Prevention of Cruelty to Budding Research Programmes should prosecute any naively destructive critic of the procedures of such subjects? Should, it might be asked, critics of the 'Marxist' research programme, which, in various forms (such as the Stalinist 'research programme', much praised by some famous economists) has been now 'budding' for over a century (and the criticism of which was the original starting-point of Popper's falsificationist prescriptions) *also* be prosecuted

[39] Lakatos [1971], pp. 121 and 133.
[40] Hutchison [1968], pp. 213–16.

for cruelty to 'budding research programmes'? Just when would a prosecution for 'cruelty' be in order and when not?

Indeed there may well be many economists (with their tame methodologist PROs) who would be eager to claim, by a kind of Polanyite UDI, the 'mature', 'developed', or 'advanced', condition, which would entitle them, according to Lakatos, to what he called 'Polanyite autonomy' – like theoretical physicists – on whom it would be *hubris* to seek to impose the critical standards of 'some *a priori* philosophy of science', and whose budding research programmes it would be culpable cruelty to criticise on falsificationist lines.

Lakatos's own 'criteria of adequacy', or his methodological prescriptions, have been described from differing viewpoints as completely, or irrationally, lax by both Feyerabend and Kuhn. Professor Feyerabend has even maintained: 'Scientific method, as softened up by Lakatos, is but an ornament which makes us forget that a position of "anything goes" has in fact been adopted.'[41]

It may be emphasised that (i) no view is being expressed here as to whether Professor Feyerabend's description of Lakatos's precepts is accurate or not; nor (ii) is it being argued that, in any case, a methodological doctrine of 'anything goes' might not be tolerable or appropriate *for theoretical physics and similar subjects*, from the history and philosophy of which this prescription has been derived. What is asserted here is that *it would be far more difficult to prevent Lakatos's prescriptions being reduced to 'anything goes' or to something practically indistinguishable, in economics*, even though it might not be intended or admitted that such total permissiveness should result. It seems that the essential distinctions, or tools, of Lakatos may be too finely calibrated for handling adequately the softer and more inchoate intellectual material of which economic 'research programmes' consist. The Lakatos prescriptions may not, in economics, provide sufficiently clear-cut scientific choices or decisions. Moreover, testing in economics, as compared with physics, tends to be so much more ambiguous, uncertain, and inconclusive in its results, partly because the phenomena being tested are liable to historical change.

Lakatos himself expressed alarm at the permissive 'irrationalism' which he considered, rightly or wrongly, would be, and had been, encouraged by Kuhn's earlier views: 'If *even in science* there is no way of judging a theory but by assessing the number, faith and vocal energy of its supporters, then *this must be even more so in the social sciences*: truth lies

---

[41] Feyerabend [1970], p. 229. Professor Alan Musgrave has expressed, in an unpublished paper, his agreement with Professor Feyerabend 'that "anything goes" is the position which Lakatos has finally adopted...As it stands, therefore, his methodology gives *carte blanche* to any group who wants to erect their pet notion into a dogma'. Professor Musgrave emphasises the close parallels and similarities between the methodological criteria of Kuhn and Lakatos. (See Musgrave [1973], p. 400, and Professor Musgrave's unpublished revision of this paper which I am most grateful for having been shown).

in power. Thus Kuhn's position would vindicate, no doubt, unintention-
ally, the basic political *credo* of contemporary religious maniacs ("student
revolutionaries").'[42]

Needless to say, Kuhn flung the charge of encouraging 'irrationalism'
back at Lakatos, and certainly a doctrine of 'anything goes' would open
the gates for the exponents of 'truth is power'. It is not necessary here to
try to assess whether it was Kuhn or Lakatos who was bringing the more
unjustified charge against the other. But attention should be called to
*Lakatos's explicit distinction between 'science' on the one hand, and 'the social
sciences' on the other hand.* Lakatos seems to be arguing – with much validity
– that different degrees of stringency in applying or enforcing methodological prescriptions may be necessary for '*the social sciences*' (including
economics), as contrasted with 'science' proper. For a formula or strategy
which might be adequate in theoretical physics, where today the danger
from the exponents of 'truth lies in power' is hardly acute, might be
disastrously inadequate in the social sciences, in which rule by 'number, faith and vocal energy' (or by sheer physical violence as on some
'university' campuses) is a prospect or possibility not lightly to be dismissed.

It is obvious that the difficulties of testing, or falsifying, are generally
incomparably greater in economics than in physics. In the social sciences
the ratio of conjectures to refutations – the plethora of conjectures and the
paucity of refutations – is significantly higher. Theories and 'programmes'
in economics and the social sciences tend to have extremely long lives,
surviving often in a stagnant or semi-moribund condition. They hardly
need any anxious protection against 'cruelty' or 'impatience', many of
them resisting the worst their critics can do for decades, or even centuries, on end. In fact, in the social sciences and economics, intellectual
over-population is a chronic condition. So also are wildly over-confident
claims, pretensions, and applications, from the more exuberant 'classicals'
to our 'growth' experts of a century and a half later; and so also may now
be the threats of the violent propagandists of the idea that 'truth lies in
power'. It must be weighed up how far the doctrine of 'truth lies in
power' might not be fostered and facilitated by the vetoing of attempts to
seek falsifiable formulations, even with regard to the most dubious among
the excess population of unrefuted conjectures.[43]

[42] Lakatos [1970], p. 93 (my italics). As an example of this kind of exploitation of
Kuhn's views (unintended by Kuhn himself) by a well-known 'radical' economist, we
might cite the statement of Dr Rose Dugdale: 'Kuhn has cast serious doubts upon this
paragon of the virtues of objectivity – the natural sciences. After all it is not at all clear
that science advances as Popper would have us believe, from hypothesis to falsifying
evidence and so the replacement of the hypothesis by a better theory.' (Dugdale [1972],
p. 166.)

[43] Regarding the 'falsification' principle, Professor Musgrave emphasises its anti-
dogmatic significance: 'To regard a theory as falsified is, in other words, to be aware of a
problem:...Should falsified theories be rejected? Well, if "rejected" means "rejected

199

VI

In conclusion we may turn briefly to Lakatos's suggestion about the reluctance of economists to accept Popper's methodological criteria and prescriptions. As noted earlier, one must distinguish between the vitally important issues of Popper's general methodological principles, and his highly over-optimistic, but more-or-less incidental, comments, regarding a 'Newtonian revolution' in economic theory, and the comparability of economic laws with those of physics. Such comments as these latter are bound to be highly popular with 'theoretical' economists and their influence could probably be shown to have been quite important in the fifties and early sixties.[44] But as regards Sir Karl's general methodological principles, there is some justification for Lakatos's claim that economists have been reluctant to accept them. Of course at one time Popper's name was often invoked and a good deal of fair-weather lip-service was paid to the principles of empirical testability and falsifiability. But when it was discovered that to press home such prescriptions or criteria might be disconcertingly destructive from the point of view of 'professional' status or particular cherished dogmas, Popper's name became rather unfashionable with economists and their methodological spokesmen.

For the kind of 'methodology' which many economists want and value is one that boosts up their prestige – vital for raising funds – as 'Scientists' with a capital 'S', while being flexibly permissive, barring no holds, or even letting 'anything go', when it comes to throwing one's weight around in the political arena as a professional 'expert' on behalf of one's particular favourite policies.[45] Alfred Marshall said that economists

as being false" then the answer is obviously "Yes". But if rejected means "rejected as not being the best available theory" then the answer is equally obviously "No, not necessarily".' Professor Musgrave also objects to 'the needless paradoxes...created by arguing that since theories which have been empirically falsified are not "rejected" or "eliminated" or "scrapped", they cannot really have been falsified at all'. In fact, 'it is the peculiarities of the scientific context which will in large part determine how an apparent refutation will be handled'. (See Musgrave [1973], p. 403.)

[44] For example, in the discussion of 'scientific prediction' in Lipsey [1963], pp. 13–14. Also see Lipsey [1966], 2nd edition and Lipsey [1971], 3rd edition.

[45] As Professor H. G. Johnson has put it (Johnson [1972], p. 91): 'In a competition between scholars and political propagandists, the scholar is likely to lose', or, in other words, 'nice guys finish last'. The 'scholar' may be taken to be someone who accepts some kind of intellectual discipline rather than 'anything goes'; and where he is a 'loser' or 'finishes last' *is not in respect of the objectives of his discipline, scholarship, or 'science', but in terms of political influence and power* – which is what some economic 'experts' are primarily or exclusively after. They therefore tend to follow the principles (without perhaps professing them so openly) of that robust party-politician, the late Sir Gerald Nabarro MP: 'I am a propagandist. When one is propagating views and ideals, one does not determine too closely what is fact and what is supposition. They are all mixed up together.' However, Sir Gerald did not claim any 'professional' scholarly or 'scientific' status. Neither did he try to invoke the rather feeble, pseudo-philosophical, excuse, much indulged in by 'Marxists' in recent years, that since it is impossible or very difficult or restrictive to keep

ought to be suspicious of, and critically inclined towards, all policies popular with politicians and the public.[46] Similarly, philosophers of science and methodological critics should be suspicious of methodological claims and prescriptions which are popular with economists.

However, although Lakatos's generalisation regarding economists' 'reluctance' to accept Popper's methodological prescriptions is not without justification, it should, on the other side, be recognised that they have exercised at least *some* significant impact on economics in recent decades. It is not *quite* so easy today, as it was before Popper's prescriptions began to gain ground, to dismiss entirely the principle of testability or refutability in spite of the difficulties of its application in practice. It has been a major item on the credit side (countering a certain amount on the other side) in the development of econometrics, that it has, up to a point, brought a wider recognition of the principle of testability. As Professor Samuelson has said:

In connection with the exaggerated claims that used to be made in economics for the power of deduction and *a priori* reasoning – by classical writers, by Carl Menger, by the 1932 Lionel Robbins (first edition of *The Nature and Significance of Economic Science*), by disciples of Frank Knight, by Ludwig von Mises – I tremble for the reputation of my subject. Fortunately we have left that behind us.[47]

Though rather severe on one or two of those mentioned, this judgment is substantially justifiable. It must be, to a considerable extent, ascribed to the influence of Popper's prescriptions that we have left *some* of that behind. In fact, Popper's prescriptions and criteria, in spite of his main interests being focussed on theoretical physics, had their origin and starting-point in the epistemological problems of 'social science', or, more specifically, were devised to counter the claims to omniscience and irrefutability of a degenerate 'Marxism'.[48] From this original source of theirs,

absolutely, perfectly separate all the time, 'what is fact' from 'what is supposition' therefore there is no obligation to attempt to do so, and so any kind of crude Marxist political propaganda is legitimized.

[46] Pigou [1925], p. 306.

[47] Samuelson [1964], p. 736. It may now be largely forgotten how long, powerful, and confident, the a priorist tradition in economics was, coming down from Senior and Cairnes to Wieser and Mises, and maintaining that far from facing greater difficulties, *the economist started with great advantages compared with the natural scientist*: 'The economist starts with a knowledge of ultimate causes. He is already, at the outset of his enterprise, in the position which the physicist only attains after ages of laborious research' (Cairnes). Moreover: 'We can observe natural phenomena only from outside, but ourselves from within... What a huge advantage for the natural scientist if the organic and inorganic world clearly informed him of its laws, and why should we neglect such assistance?' (Wieser). No wonder economists have been confident in their policy pronouncements. (Hutchison [1938], pp. 131ff.)

[48] 'The most characteristic element in this situation seemed to me the incessant stream of confirmations, of observations which "verified" the theories in question, and this point was constantly emphasized by their adherents. A Marxist could not open a newspaper without finding on every page confirming evidence for his interpretation of history; not only in the news, but also in its presentation – which revealed the class bias of the paper –

Popper's doctrines derive a certain relevance to the problems of the social sciences not shared by doctrines or precriptions which have been predominantly derived and distilled from the history and problems of theoretical physics.

But in spite of a tendency to some kinds of improvement, new and old forms of the kind of intellectual malpractices which Popper's prescriptions were designed to combat are still widespread in economics: 'verbalism', 'conventionalist' and 'immunizing' stratagems, and the erosion of testable formulations and testing. It has long been taken for granted by many economists, and their methodologist PROs, that no criticisms of the 'assumptions' underlying models, which would require their testing or testability, need to be heeded. As far as 'assumptions' are concerned, that virtually 'anything goes' is a pretty well-established practice: they may simply be 'plucked from the air', as Professor Phelps Brown has put it. Similarly, among some economists, prediction, also, may now be rejected as a test of theories. Moreover, the blurring of the empirical with the purely conceptual, or definitional, seems to continue almost unabated, at least until quite recently. It was not some pedantic methodologist, but the Economic Adviser to HMG, who complained of 'what I regard as a besetting sin among economists; that of enunciating purely definitional relationships when they purport to be making statements about reality'.[49]

A variant of this kind of 'besetting sin' is prominent in the form of ambiguous, but obviously oversimplified, and insistently dogmatic propositions about what 'determines', or 'governs', saving and investment, or wages etc. (a kind of ambiguous dogmatism cultivated by 'Keynesians'); or, on the other hand, oversimplified propositions about the 'cause' of inflation (favoured by 'monetarists').[50] Much of the steam in the monetarist–Keynesian debate would fade away without this kind of dogmatic ambiguity, which could best be dealt with by a precise application of the falsifiability principle.

Certainly Popper's youthful difficulties with the constant confirmations of their theories discovered every day in the newspapers by 'Marxists', might be compared with Professor Patinkin's recent bewilderment over the almost unfailing stream of confirmations of their theories achieved by the leading rival schools of monetary theory:

and especially of course in what the paper did *not* say?' (Popper [1963], p. 35.) See, on the other hand, Popper's denial that his interpretation of the methods of science was 'influenced by any knowledge of the methods of the social sciences'. (Popper [1957], p. 137.)

[49] Roberthall [1959], p. 651.

[50] It may be noted that Professor Milton Friedman is duly cautious about causation: 'I myself try to avoid the use of the word "cause"...it is a tricky and unsatisfactory word.' (Friedman [1974], p. 101.) But a few pages away Professor Laidler is insisting: 'What we do argue is that *the cause* of inflation really is very simple: it is monetary expansion.' (Laidler [1974], p. 64.)

What generates in me a great deal of skepticism about the state of our discipline is the high positive correlation between the policy views of a researcher (or, what is worse, of his thesis director), and his empirical findings. I will begin to believe in economics as a science when out of Yale there comes an empirical Ph.D. thesis demonstrating the supremacy of monetary policy in some historical episode – and out of Chicago, one demonstrating the supremacy of fiscal policy.[51]

We would emphasise, in conclusion, that no one has insisted or explained more clearly than Sir Karl that any methodological prescriptions for scientific decisions and investments must inevitably be based on certain ethical or political choices. The philosopher of science, no more than the economist, can lay down, for the kind of decision-makers or 'investors' with whom he is concerned, any general formula, with any significant degree of content and applicability, for absolutely and objectively 'rational' conduct in real-world conditions of uncertainty and ignorance. The attempt might be made to analyse the investment decisions, or the 'portfolio' of theories, the 'rational' scientist should take or hold, but no very practically informative formula would emerge. All that can be set out are 'reasonable' principles, or maxims, for scientific decision-making and investments, which will not yield any uniquely correct answers and will inevitably need interpretation and judgement for their practical application. The principle of falsifiability is linked with what Popper calls 'fallibilism' as the epistemological basis for a free, pluralist society.[52] Watering down, disarming, or stifling this critical principle, by leaving the green light switched on permanently, signalling 'anything goes' for every kind of complacent, pretentious and noxious dogmatism would constitute a grand new 'trahison des clercs'.[53]

[51] Patinkin [1972], p. 142. But at least Yale and Chicago recognise the desirability or obligation of trying to produce some kind of empirical evidence. This is, at any rate far in advance of other 'schools' which have dogmatised for decades, in 'high priori' terms, about the effects or non-effects of fiscal and monetary policy without ever having produced any empirical evidence – verificatory or falsificatory – other than the most casual.

[52] 'Our often unconscious views on the theory of knowledge and its central problems ("What can we know?" "How certain is our knowledge?"), are decisive for our attitude towards ourselves and towards politics'. (Popper [1974], p. 91.)

[53] Nobody has attacked more eloquently and discerningly than Professor Paul Feyerabend on the one hand the dangerous pretensions of contemporary science, and on the other hand the appalling intellectual pollution of our times. His attacks have a great deal of significance and even a fortiori strong relevance, regarding 'social science'. Feyerabend complains of science having 'become too powerful, too pushy, and too dangerous to be left on its own'. Meanwhile 'illiterate and incompetent books flood the market, empty verbiage full of strange and esoteric terms claim to express profound insights, "experts" without brains, without character, and without even a modicum of intellectual, stylistic emotional temperament tell us about our "condition" and the means of improving it'. (Feyerabend [1975], pp. 216–17.) It seems all the more strange that Professor Feyerabend should be trying to remove and destroy such critical weapons as are available against both these dangerous and appalling phenomena (i.e. the weapons of 'falsificationism').

References

Andreski, S. [1974]: *Social Sciences as Sorcery*.
Aristotle: *Nicomachaean Ethics*. Translated by W. D. Ross (1915).
Barrington Moore [1958]: *Political Power and Social Theory*.
Cairnes, J. E. [1857]: *The Character and Logical Method of Political Economy* (2nd edn 1875).
Champernowne, D. G. [1972]: Review of H. Theil's *Principles of Econometrics* in *Economic Journal*, **82**, pp. 222–3.
Dugdale, R. [1972]: 'Economic Theory in Class Society', in T. Pateman (ed.): *Counter-course*, p. 166.
Feyerabend, P. K. [1970]: 'Consolations for the Specialist' in I. Lakatos and A. E. Musgrave (eds.): *Criticism and the Growth of Knowledge*.
Feyerabend, P. K. [1975]: *Against Method*.
Friedman, M. [1974]: *Inflation: Causes, Consequences, Cures*, IEA.
Hutchison, T. W. [1938]: *The Significance and Basic Postulates of Economic Theory*, 2nd edn 1960.
Hutchison, T. W. [1964]: *'Positive' Economics and Policy Objectives*.
Hutchison, T. W. [1968]: *Economists and Economic Policy in Britain 1946–1966*.
Johnson, H. G. [1972]: Letter to *Encounter*, **38**, p. 91.
Kemeny, J. G. [1959]: *A Philosopher Looks at Science*.
Kuhn, T. S. [1968]: *Encyclopaedia of the Social Sciences*, vol. 14.
Kuhn, T. S. [1970]: 'Reflections on my Critics', I. Lakatos and A. Musgrave (eds.): *Criticism and the Growth of Knowledge*.
Kristol, I. [1964]: *The Observer*, 4 October.
Laidler, D. [1974]: *Inflation: Causes, Consequences, Cures*, IEA.
Lakatos, I. [1968]: 'Criticism and the Methodology of Scientific Research Programmes', *Proceedings of the Aristotelian Society*, **69**, pp. 149–86.
Lakatos, I. [1970]: 'Falsification and the Methodology of Scientific Research Programmes', in I. Lakatos and A. Musgrave (eds.): *Criticism and the Growth of Knowledge*, pp. 91–195.
Lakatos, I. [1971]: 'History of Science and its Rational Reconstructions', in R. C. Buck and R. S. Cohen (eds.): *Boston Studies in the Philosophy of Science*, vol. 8, pp. 91–136.
Lange, O. [1945–6]: The Scope and Method of Economic Science, *Review of Economic Studies*, **13**, pp. 19–32. References are to the reprint in H. Feigl and M. Brodbeck (eds.): *Readings in the Philosophy of Science*.
Latsis, S. J. [1972]: 'Situational Determinism in Economics', *The British Journal for the Philosophy of Science*, **23**, pp. 207–45.
Lipsey, R. G. [1963]: *An Introduction to Positive Economics*.
Lipsey, R. G. [1966]: *An Introduction to Positive Economics*, 2nd edn.
Lipsey, R. G. [1971]: *An Introduction to Positive Economics*, 3rd edn.
Morgenstern, O. [1965]: *Limits to the Uses of Mathematics in Economics*, Mathematics and Social Sciences Monograph.
Musgrave, A. [1973]: 'Falsification and its Critics', in P. Suppes *et al.* (eds.): *Logic Methodology and Philosophy of Science* IV, pp. 45, 48, 393–406.
Neumann, J. von and Morgenstern, O. [1955]: *The Theory of Games and Economic Behaviour*, 3rd edn.
O'Brien, D. P. [1974]: *Whither Economics?* Inaugural Lecture at Durham University.
Patinkin, D. [1972]: Keynesian Monetary Theory and the Cambridge School, *Banca Nazionale del Lavoro Quarterly Review*, June 1972, p. 142.

Phelps Brown, E. H. [1972]: 'The Under-Development of Economics', *Encounter*, **82**, p. 10.

Pigou, A. C. [1925]: *Memorials of A. Marshall*.

Popper, K. R. [1945]: *The Open Society and its Enemies*. References are to the 2nd edn, 1962.

Popper, K. R. [1957]: *The Poverty of Historicism*.

Popper, K. R. [1963]: *Conjectures and Refutations*.

Popper, K. R. [1970]: 'Normal Science and its Dangers', in I. Lakatos and A. Musgrave (eds.): *Criticism and Growth of Knowledge*.

Popper, K. R. [1974]: 'Autobiography', in P. A. Schilpp (ed.): *The Philosophy of Karl Popper*.

Ravetz, J. [1971]: *Scientific Knowledge and its Social Problems*.

Roberthall, Lord [1959]: 'Reflections on the Practical Application of Economics', *Economic Journal*, **69**, p. 651.

Roberts, M. J. [1974]: 'On the Nature and Condition of Social Science', *Daedalus*, Summer 1974, pp. 10n, 20, 29.

Samuelson, P. A. [1964]: 'Theory and Realism: a Reply', *The American Economic Review*, September 1964, p. 736.

'Revolutions' in economics

SIR JOHN HICKS
OXFORD

The study of scientific 'revolutions', in which one system of thought (or 'research programme') has given place to another, has been shown, in several of the preceding essays, to be a powerful tool in the methodology of natural science. Economics also has had its 'revolutions'; it is fruitful to study them in much the same manner. I think however that when one looks at them comparatively, one finds that their significance is very largely different.

This is a matter of importance, for economics itself. Economics is more like art or philosophy than science, in the use that it can make of its own history. The history of science is a fascinating subject; it is important (as has been shown) for the philosophy of science; but it is not important to the working scientist in the way that the history of economics is important to the working economist. When the natural scientist has come to the frontier of knowledge, and is ready for new exploration, he is unlikely to have much to gain from a contemplation of the path by which his predecessors have come to the place where he now stands. Old ideas are worked out; old controversies are dead and buried. The Ptolemaic system may live on in literature, or it may form the framework of a mathematical exercise; it has no direct interest to the modern astronomer.

Our position in economics is different; we cannot escape in the same way from our own past. We may pretend to escape; but the past crowds in on us all the same. To 'neoclassical' succeeds 'neomercantilist'; Keynes and his contempoaries echo Ricardo and Malthus; Marx and Marshall are still alive. Some of us are inclined to be ashamed of this traditionalism, but when it is properly understood it is no cause for embarrassment; it is a consequence of what we are doing, or trying to do.

The facts which we study are not permanent, or repeatable, like the facts of the natural sciences; they change incessantly, and change without repetition. Considered as individual events, they are often events of great interest. Every business has a history of its own, every consumer a history of his own; any of these histories may have its own drama when we come close to it. But, as a general rule, it is not our business as economists to come close. We are trying to detect general patterns amid the mass of absorbing detail; shapes that repeat among the details that do not repeat.

207

We can only do this if we select something less than the detail which is presented to us. In order to analyse, we must simplify and cut down.

Further, in practice, we must simplify quickly. Our special concern is with the facts of the present world; but before we can study the present, it is already past. In order that we should be able to say useful things about what is happening, before it is too late, we must select, even select quite violently. We must concentrate our attention, and hope that we have concentrated it in the right place. We must work, if we are to work effectively, in some sort of blinkers.

Our theories, regarded as tools of analysis, are blinkers in this sense. Or it may be politer to say that they are rays of light, which illuminate a part of the target, leaving the rest in the dark. As we use them, we avert our eyes from things that may be relevant, in order that we should see more clearly what we do see. It is entirely proper that we should do this, since otherwise we should see very little. But it is obvious that a theory which is to perform this function satifactorily must be well chosen; otherwise it will illumine the wrong things. Further, since it is a changing world that we are studying, a theory which illumines the right things now may illumine the wrong things another time.[1] This may happen because of changes in the world (the things neglected may have grown relatively to the things considered) or because of changes in our sources of information (the sorts of facts that are readily accessible to us may have changed) or because of changes in ourselves (the things in which we are interested may have changed). There is, there can be, no economic theory which will do for us everything we want all the time.

Accordingly, while we are right to allow ourselves to become wrapped up in those theories which are useful now, we are unwise if we allow ourselves to forget that the time may come when we shall need something different. We may then be right to reject our present theories, not because they are wrong, but because they have become inappropriate. Things which we formerly left unnoticed (more or less deliberately unnoticed) may rise up and become essential; we shall have to bring them in, even if that means averting our attention from things we thought important before. That is the *special* reason why economics is prone to revolutions – revolutions which appear, while they are occurring, to be steps in advance, though from a different point of view they may take on quite another character.

The revolutions may be large or small. Big revolutions are (fortunately) rare. The Keynesian revolution is the obvious example of a big revolution; there are not more than two or three others which might conceivably be compared to it. It is possible that big revolutions are more likely to take their origins outside the ranks of academic economists in the narrow

[1] As an example of this, see the discussion of the evolution of market theory in my [1965] chapter 5.

sense (Keynes was only a part-time academic economist). For big revolutions can only occur when something rather far away from the previous concentration of attention comes to the forefront, so that its recognition compels a major readjustment. Small revolutions, that are revolutions in my sense nonetheless, can more easily be made by academics. Working in 'blinkers' is uncongenial to the academic mind; it is difficult to teach the concentration without keeping an eye on what is around it. So it comes naturally to us to be on the watch for ways of bringing into attention things which have been only just left out; we have a bias in favour of inclusiveness and generality, even at the cost of ineffectiveness. We do keep that sort of watch fairly well.

There are however two ways in which we may keep our watch. One is by generalisation, by constructing 'more general' theories, theories which put more things into their places, even if we can do less with them when we have put them there.[2] This is a perfectly respectable activity; but what I am here concerned to point out is that it is not the only way in which we can do that particular business. The same function can be performed by the history of economics in another way. If we seek to discover how it was, and why it was, that concentrations of attention have changed, and theories (effective theories) have changed with them, we find ourselves 'standing back' just as we do when we pursue the generalisation method; we get something of the same gain, and it may be that we run less risk of losing our appreciation of 'effectiveness' as we get it. But I have no need to champion one of these ways of broadening our minds against the other. There is plenty of room for both.[3]

The first of the 'revolutions' which I shall be considering is that which led to the establishment of 'classical' economics – the system of thought which was taken over by Adam Smith from the Physiocrats in France. If one asks what it is that distinguishes those great (and highly 'effective') economists from their relatively ineffective predecessors, the answer is surely to be found in the vision of the economic process which they possessed, a vision which made it possible for them to think economic problems through, not in separate bits, but together. This vision was not a vague sense of everything being inter-related; it had content that is capable of being identified and described.

There is an exact indication of that content in the full title of Adam Smith's book – *An Inquiry into the Nature and Cause of the Wealth of Nations.* If we take that title, not as a mere label in the modern manner, but as a description which means what it says, its meaning is apparent: wealth is production; the wealth of a nation is what we now call the national

---

[2] Keynes's theory is of course not a general theory in this sense; it is a superbly effective theory, which gains power by what it leaves out.

[3] I have emphasised another set of reasons why we should study the history of economics – its function as a means of communication – in the paper on 'Capital Controversies' [1974].

product.[4] Adam Smith is to tell us what the social product of a nation is; what is meant by its being large or small; what is meant by its growing. That is 'nature'. Then he is to tell us why the social product is large or small, and why it grows. That is 'causes'.

Much of what we say, and much of what Smith said, on these matters seems uncontroversial. The social product is large when the quantities of the factors of production that are used to make it are large, and when those large quantities are used with high efficiency. The social product grows by growth in the factors of production, by increase in the numbers and in the efficiency of labour, and by the accumulation of capital. And it grows by improvements in the efficiency with which capital is applied to labour; that is, by improvements in the efficiency with which the factors of production are combined. These statements sound obvious but when we take them to be obvious, we are not taking them literally, as (I believe) Smith did, or was at the least beginning to do.

There is of course no question that the flow of wealth is production; things are produced, and it is in these products that the flow or wealth consists. But the things that are produced are heterogeneous; it is not obvious that we can take them together and reduce them to a common 'stuff'. What is implied in the classical approach is that for essential purposes we can take them together. We can represent them by a flow of wealth, which is so far homogeneous that it can be greater or less. It was the study of this flow of wealth which the classics called *political economy*.[5]

How did Smith and his successors come to think in this way? By analogy, surely, with the experience of business. The products of a business may be heterogeneous, but they are reduced to a common measure by being valued in terms of money. It is in money terms that we can tell whether the turnover of one business is greater than that of another; cannot we do the same for nations? Adam Smith always found it easy, indeed too easy, to jump from the firm to the whole economy; it is not surprising that he found the analogy compelling. That, at the least, is the way he must have begun.

He soon found, however, that the money measure could not be used

[4] Smith [1776]. We are nowadays so accustomed to thinking of wealth as capital wealth that it may not be easy to realise that in Smith wealth is normally taken in a 'flow' sense. Even in the first sentence of his book there is a snag which worries the modern reader. 'The annual labour of every nation is the fund which originally supplies it with all the necessities and conveniences of life which it annually consumes.' The repeated *annual* emphasises *flow*; but what about *fund*? I suggest that we get nearest to Smith's meaning if we interpret *fund* to mean *revolving fund*. This would square with what he says later (in vol. 2) about capital. The *flow* interpretation of the sentence, which is meant to set course for the whole work, and must therefore be coherent with the title, would then become clear.

[5] *Political economy* is identified by Smith with 'the nature and causes of the wealth of nations' (Smith [1776], vol. 2, p. 177). For the subject as defined by Smith's title, it was, I would maintain, a most appropriate name. It is not appropriate for a great part of what we now call economics, so one can understand why it was abandoned.

without precaution. It was necessary to distinguish between market values (which might not be significant as a means of valuation) and 'natural' or normal values which should be; and it was necessary to find a 'standard of value' so as to be able to correct for changes in the value of money. Thus, already in Smith, *political economy* is based upon a theory of value. It is of the first importance to emphasise that the primary purpose of that theory of value is not to explain prices, that is to say, to explain the working of markets; its primary purpose is to identify the values which are needed for the *weighing* of the social product, the reduction of the heterogeneous commodities which compose it to a common measure.

This, admittedly, is not very clear in Smith; it is much clearer in Ricardo. It was as a means of reducing heterogeneous commodities to a common measure that Ricardo used his labour theory of value. But it is not simply that device which marks the originality of Ricardo. The transition from Smith to Ricardo was itself a minor 'revolution'; but it did not come about, in the scientific manner, because of the need to take account of new facts, revealed by experiment or observation, facts which however had been *there* all the time. It did come about as a result of the need to accommodate new facts, but they were genuinely new facts, facts which had come into existence in the course of history – new *events*. Ricardo's rent theory, and the growth theory which followed from it, were reactions to the problems of his own time – the problems of feeding a growing population, forced upon attention, first by the Napoleonic blockade, and then in terms of reconstruction after the War. Ricardian economics is a remarkable intellectual achievement; but it could not have taken the form it did, except under the pressure of particular events.

As time went on, the land problem became less acute; thus though Ricardo's theory remained, for it had no intellectual rival, it became less and less *relevant*. So the time came when economics was ready for another 'revolution'. In fact there were two revolutions, at about the same time; one made by Marx, the other by Jevons, Walras and Menger.[6] As a result of these two revolutions, economics was divided; economists proceeded, for many years, on quite separate tracks. How do we describe these revolutions, and how do we explain them?

In relation to the classical political economy, the distinguishing feature of the work of Marx is its distributism. Classical economics had been a theory of production and distribution, but production came first. *The Wealth of Nations*, as indicated, is a book about production ('nature' and 'causes'); though Adam Smith says much, incidentally, about distribution, what he says is unsystematic. It is true that if one judges Ricardo by that famous passage in the preface to his *Principles*, he is stressing distribution, against what he held to be its neglect by Adam Smith. 'To determine the laws which regulate this distribution is the principal problem of

[6] Marx [1867], Jevons [1871], Menger [1871], Walras [1874].

Political Economy.' (That, of course, is the way Marx took Ricardo; it explains why Marx, and Marxists, have always had some affection for Ricardo.) Nevertheless, in spite of this passage, the general tendency of Ricardo's work is to treat distribution as secondary. He was interested in distribution because of the importance which he attached to the effects of distribution on production, not because he had much interest in distribution *per se*. It is only in the third of the major classics, in John Stuart Mill's *Principles*,[7] that there is much attention to distribution for its own sake. By that change of emphasis Mill opened the way to Marx.

The half-way house which we find in Mill explains a good deal. At the date when Mill was writing, the fact of the Industrial Revolution was unmistakeable; a great increase in productive power had already occurred. But it had not brought with it the social gains which 'friends of humanity' (Ricardo's phrase) had expected from it. Thus already, to Mill, increase in production had come to seem to be of less importance than improvement in distribution. Further increase in production did not much matter; so the achievement of a distributive or 'socialist' society seemed near at hand. That was where the classical vision, in Mill, appeared to have led; and from that point Marx could fairly easily take over.

The other revolution is not so easy to describe, or to explain. The economists who led it are commonly called 'marginalists'; but that is a bad term, for it misses the essence of what was involved. The 'margin' is no more than an expression of the mathematical rule for a maximum (or minimum); any sort of economics is marginalist when it is concerned with maximising.[8] (Ricardo himself could be quite marginalist at times.) The essential novelty in the work of these economists was that instead of basing their economics on production and distribution, they based it on exchange. I therefore propose to make use of a term which was sometimes used, at the time in question, to mean the theory of exchange; it was called catallactics.[9] So I shall re-name the so-called marginalists as catallactists.

There is of course no doubt that exchange is a basic feature of economic life, at least in a 'free', or what Marx would have called a 'capitalist' economy. By none of the classical economists would that have been denied. But while the classics looked at the economic system primarily from the production angle, the catallactists looked at it primarily from the side of exchange. It was possible, they found, to construct a 'vision' of economic life out of the theory of exchange, as the classics had done out of the social product. It was quite a different vision.

[7] Mill [1848].

[8] I am of course aware that there are problems of maximising which cannot be developed in terms of marginal *equations*.

[9] See for instance Edgeworth [1881], p. 30. The term has been used, more recently, in the book by von Mises [1949].

How do we explain the rise of catallactics? It can, I think, be explained in more than one way. Some will want to explain it as a reaction against socialism – hardly, at first, against Marx who must have been practically unknown to the first catallactists, but against the more general socialist tendencies which were already 'in the air'. One can make a case for that. It can be claimed that political economy is always in some sense socialist, catallactics individualist; though one cannot make that fit the history unless one distinguishes between means and ends. The Old Political Economists were socialists (or at least 'social') in the ends they set up; but they were individualist in practice, because they held that individualism was the way to the achievement of their social ends. As long as that was tenable, the conflict between ends was not acute. Whether one's objective was the 'welfare' of society or the freedom of the individual, the path to be followed was the same. Those to whom the one mattered more and those to whom the other mattered more could march under the same banner; they did not need to emphasise their differences. But as faith in the 'hidden-hand' declined, as the 'socialists' became socialist, the die-hard individualist was bound to cut adrift. He perceived, as he had to perceive before, that his objectives differed from those of his former allies. He was bound to insist upon his rejection of purely social ends, and to make a fuss about his rejection of them.

I admit that this is one strand which can be recognised in the work of the more politically minded catallactists. It appears in Pareto, at some stages of his work, and in an extreme form in some members of the Austrian school, especially Ludwig von Mises.[10] It is certainly one way in which the catallactic approach can be used; there are living writers, in America and elsewhere, who continue to use it in this manner. The exchange economy is a free economy; so to those who put freedom at the head of their values, it is bound to have a particular attraction. For it seems to show that a world is workable in which we are all allowed to go own ways, our different ways, with a minimum of interference from other people.[11]

There is this individualist strand, especially in later work, but it will hardly do as an explanation of the 'revolution'. One can find it in Pareto, and perhaps even in Wicksell,[12] but in the work of the first generation (Jevons, say, or Menger) where is it? The most that could be argued in their case is that they were responding to a challenge. The socialists had made it impossible for the exchange economy to be taken for granted;

---

[10] See in particular von Mises' book *Die Gemeinwirtschaft* [1922] which was translated into English under the title *Socialism* [1959].

[11] '*Ce n'est pas qu'elle gouverne bien, mais elle gouverne peu*' as someone in Anatole France says of the Third Republic. The British classical economists would never have said that of *their* state.

[12] It is in his book on public finance (*Finanztheoretische Untersuchungen*) [1896] that Wicksell carries his individualism to the most extreme lengths.

whether one was for it, or against it, the time had come when it needed to be better understood. There may be something in that; but even that does not have to be the main answer.

I have insisted that the Old Political Economy, like other 'powerful' economic theories, was a concentration of attention. It gained strength by its omissions, by the things it put on one side. Some of the things it put on one side were rather obvious. Thus throughout the century in which it was dominant, there had been numerous writers who had refused to put on the Smithian 'blinkers'; they had been unwilling to think in the way in which that system of thought required them to think. But they had been unable to develop any system of thought with comparable potency. That is just what it was that Walras and Menger did.[13]

I would therefore maintain that the principal reason for the triumph of catallactics – in its day it was quite a triumph – was nothing to do with socialism or individualism; nor did it even have much to do with the changes that were then occurring in the 'real world'. The construction of a powerful economic theory, based on exchange, instead of production and distribution, had always been a possibility. The novelty in the work of the great catallactists is just that they achieved it.

The appeal of catallactics lay in its intellectual quality, much more than in its individualism. The first catallactists were poor mathematicians, but they were thinking mathematically; and the mathematics that is implied in their theories has proved to be capable of enormous development. Already, before that happened, there was enough of intellectual interest to set its mark on the minds of many economists (who were now it should be noticed, to a large extent academic economists). Though 'marginal utility' had its difficulties (difficulties of which we in our time have become increasingly aware) it was becoming easier to think of 'individuals' having given wants, or given utility functions, than to swallow the homogeneous 'wealth' of the Old Political Economy. It was easier to think of the economic system as a system of interrelated markets (Walras) or as an adjustment of means to ends (Menger) than to keep up the fiction of the social product any longer.[14]

[13] The Lausanne and the Austrian versions of catallactics are by no means identical, and it is possible that Jevon's version, if he had completed it, would have constituted a third variety. But it is noticeable that as time has gone on, these versions, at first distinct, have grown together. Later catallactists, such as Wicksell and Schumpeter and many more modern writers, have drawn upon Menger and upon Walras in equal measure. So the distinction between them is not one which we shall need to emphasise for our present purpose.

[14] A superb example of the way in which commitment to a catallactic outlook can blind one to the importance of the alternative is to be found in Schumpeter's *History of Economic Analysis* [1954]. There are countless ways in which Schumpeter deepens one's understanding of what economists – ourselves and our predecessors – have been doing. But it is impossible not to notice that he always judges economists by their contribution to theory in the catallactic sense. It is the great catallactists (Jevons, Walras and Menger, together with their forerunners such as Turgot and Say) who receive particular praise; while some

I have devoted this much space to the 'marginal revolution' (or 'catallactist revolution') because it seems to me to be the best example in economics of something which fits the Lakatos scheme.[15] It provided a new way of taking up the economic problem; not just a new theory, but a new approach which was capable of much development. It was not (I have tried to show) in the main a reaction to contemporary events. The possibility of a utility theory had been there all the time; what the catallactists showed was that something could be done with it.

I pass on to what happened afterwards, in this century. That, from the point of view I am here adopting, was not just the Keynesian revolution; there was another thing too. You may be thinking that what I have called catallactics should be given a more familiar name – microeconomics; it is true that what I have called the catallactist revolution can be regarded as the rise of microeconomics. But if I used that term I might find myself saying that Keynesianism was macroeconomics; and that is not right. There are two kinds of modern macroeconomics. One is Keynesian; the other is quite different.

If we must have a founder for this other kind of macroeconomics, it must be Pigou. Pigou of the *Economics of Welfare*;[16] or perhaps of *Wealth and Welfare*.[17] Long before the (relevant) work of Keynes! But what I mean by the other kind of macroeconomics is not welfare economics in the modern sense; for what happened in the new welfare economics (in which I myself played my part) was that welfare economics was captured by the catallactists and it has never got quite free. If one looks at the whole of Pigou's book, not just at its (now) misleading title, one sees that it is a revival of the classical political economy. It is a book on production and distribution, in the classical manner. The definition of the real social product; how it can be increased; and how it is divided up. There is a line of descent, from Pigou, through my own *Theory of Wages*[18] to a great deal of modern growth theory (which, if one looks at it critically, is quite un-Keynesian). I think, for instance, of much of the work of Professor Solow. It is surely, in Lakatos's sense a 'research programme'; it has been capable of much development, and it is by no means extinct.

If we are to think clearly about it, we must give it a name. I tried, at one time, to keep the classical name, and to call it political economy. But that does not do. I am now inclined to match catallactics, and to call what I am now talking about plutology. (I know that the only writer who has previously used that term was a catallactist! But he was not of great importance; his ghost will doubtless forgive us.) Plutology is good Greek for theory of wealth.

Classical politicial economy, then, is the old plutology; that which

---

who would usually be regarded as greater names (Smith, Ricardo, Marshall) are treated somewhat grudgingly. Why does he write them down? Because they belong on the political economy side.

[15] See Lakatos [1970].
[17] Pigou [1912].
[16] Pigou [1920].
[18] Hicks [1932].

descends from Pigou is the new. Why has it come up, and why has it flourished? Surely the reason for its success is the availability of the statistical material on which it can feed. We now have vast quantities of statistical material, on the macro-level; much more abundant (at least apparently) than the empirical material for microeconomics. The old plutologists did not have this material; that is why their work appears so abstract. They did not have the statistics to give it flesh and blood.

Why do we have these statistics, which they did not? It is not the case, as might be supposed from natural science analogies, that the lack of statistics, of this kind, was shown up by the classical theories; and that gave an incentive to collect them. There was something of this, but it was not the main thing. The statistics are a by-product of a great historical change, the great extension of the powers of the State which has occurred in this century. That, in its turn, is partly to be ascribed to political changes; but it is also, very importantly, a consequence of the cheapening of the costs of administration, which has made it possible for modern governments to collect information on a vastly greater scale than was previously practicable. One must always remember, when reading the older economists, that they were desperately short of facts. Nowadays we are swamped by floods of facts, or what appear to be facts, welling, all the time, out of the machines.

I turn, finally, to Keynes. Keynesianism also, as it has developed, has had to accommodate the flood of facts; but it is clear that it did not start in that way. The 'social accounting Keynesianism' which is now in all the textbooks (and in the articles of journalists) was quite a late development; it is not really present even in the *General Theory*. If one looks at that book in terms of what led up to it (not in terms of what happened afterwards), one sees where it comes out. Where it belongs, when it is so considered, is not in the field of general (or 'real') economics – to which nearly all I have hitherto been saying refers. Where it belongs is in monetary economics; and since monetary statistics have long been abundant (much more abundant than most other statistics until the present century) monetary economics has always been topical; it has always had a close relation to the circumstances of the time in which it has been written; it has had to change as they have changed.

As I have stated elsewhere (at more length) it is my own view that if the Keynes story is to be told properly (in its historical context) it should begin before Keynes. It begins with Hawtrey: *Currency and Credit*.[19] It must begin there, for there is a large part of Keynes's *Treatise*[20] which is a reply to Hawtrey. A reply, on the matters where Keynes and Hawtrey differed; these are important, but they can only be seen in proper proportion once we have realised that on the most basic matter they were on the same side. Neither of them held that the economic system is automatically

[19] Hawtrey [1919].   [20] Keynes [1930].

self-righting. The 'instability of capitalism' is nowadays commonly held to be a characteristically Keynesian doctrine; but it is already there – in Hawtrey. It has never been better stated than in the first chapter of Hawtrey's book, the chapter that is called 'Credit without Money'. In Hawtrey as in Keynes, the system has to be stabilised, by policy and by some instrument of policy. It was over the instrument of policy that they differed.

As the difference began, it looked rather small. Both agreed that the instrument was a rate of interest; but Hawtrey looked to the short rate, Keynes to the long. At this point I would accept that Keynes was more up to date. It was a change in the structure of the industrial system which Keynes perceived, and one on which Hawtrey was much less clear, making fixed capital investment of greater importance than it had been in the past, which impelled Keynes to make his first departure from the Hawtrey system. Another example, you will notice, of a theoretical development echoing a historical process.

But then Keynes discovered that his long rate was not only less directly susceptible to banking control than Hawtrey's short, but that it was very likely to be found that just when it was wanted it could not move enough. So he moved away from monetary methods to the 'fiscal' methods which have later been so largely associated with his name. That is a process that is taking place *inside* the *General Theory*.[21] The structure of the book dates from the time when the long rate was pre-eminent; but as the work develops he cuts the ground under his own feet. Thus it was, that what began as monetary theory became 'fiscalism'.

It was nevertheless the particular circumstances of the 1930s which had this effect; it was because of his desire (his very proper desire) to apply his theory to the particular conditions of the time in which he was living that he moved in this way. At other times he might have reacted differently; one can even be fairly sure, from a general knowledge of his work, that he would have reacted differently. So it does no honour to Keynes to go on applying his theory, without drastic amendment, to the very different circumstances of the time in which we are now living. The Keynes theory has 'dated', just as the Hawtrey theory 'dated'. That does not mean that we must go back to the Hawtrey theory, or to still older theories, as many contemporaries would like to do. We must still push on. One can yet recognise that there may be something dramatically appropriate – nice for the historian, though not for those who have to live through it – if it should turn up, as now seems to be likely, that it is on the field of primary commodities (which Hawtrey emphasised, but Keynes, at least in the *General Theory*, so much under-emphasised) that the Age of Keynes will have met its nemesis.

I have covered a wide field – I had to! Let me sum up by returning

21 Keynes [1936].

to what I said at the beginning. What we want, in economics, are theories which will be useful, practically useful. That means that they must be selective. But all selection is dangerous. So there is plenty of room for criticism, and for the filling in of gaps, building some sort of bridge between one selective theory and another. There is plenty of room for academic work, doing that sort of a job. Much of it, I am well aware, works in its own 'blinkers', seeing the mote that is in one's brother's eye but not the beam that is in one's own. That, I am afraid, is the nature of the case. Still, one could learn a little humility.

There is also, one must not forget, the application to history – not to the history of thought, with which I have here been concerned, but to economic history in the other sense. It is not only for application to the present that we need economics; we need it also for the interpretation of the past. If what I have said is true, this is a most delicate matter. We should not analyse (say) nineteenth-century history in terms of nineteenth-century theories; for our knowledge of the facts of that time is different from that of contemporaries, and the questions we ask are different from those that contemporaries asked. Yet we have to be careful in the application of modern theories, which arise out of modern experience. Neither is necessarily right.

References

Edgeworth, F. Y. [1881]: *Mathematical Psychics.*
Hawtrey, R. [1919]: *Currency and Credit.*
Hicks, J. R. [1932]: *The Theory of Wages.*
Hicks, J. R. [1965]: *Capital and Growth.*
Hicks, J. R. [1974]: 'Capital Controversies: Ancient and Modern', *The American Economic Review*, **64**, pp. 307–16.
Jevons, W. S. [1871]: *The Theory of Political Economy.*
Keynes, J. M. [1930]: *A Treatise on Money.*
Keynes, J. M. [1936]: *The General Theory of Employment, Interest and Money.*
Lakatos, I. [1970]: 'Methodology of Scientific Research Programmes', in I. Lakatos and A. Musgrave (eds.): *Criticism and the Growth of Knowledge.*
Marx, K. [1867]: *Das Kapital.*
Menger, C. [1871]: *Principles of Economics.*
Mill, J. S. [1848]: *Principles of Political Economy, With Some of Their Applications to Social Philosophy.*
Mises, L. von [1922]: *Die Gemeinwirtschaft.*
Mises, L. von [1949]: *Human Action.*
Mises, L. von [1959]: *Socialism: An Economic and Sociological Analysis.*
Pigou, A. C. [1912]: *Wealth and Welfare.*
Pigou, A. C. [1920]: *Economics of Welfare.*
Schumpeter, J. A. [1954]: *History of Economic Analysis.*
Smith, A. [1776]: *The Wealth of Nations* (Cannan edition).
Walras, L. [1874]: *Principes d'une théorie mathématique de l'échange.*
Wicksell, K. [1896]: *Finanztheoretische Untersuchungen nebst Darstellung und Kritik des Stenerwesus Schwedens.*

Index

Achenstein, P. (1968), *178*, 154n, 156n; (1974), 158n, 179
activity analysis, 138
ad hoc: defined, 123n; auxiliary assumptions, 156, 165, 175; defense manoevres 196; explanations of the slump, 163; theories, 123
aggregation, Keynes's use of, 96, 162, 194
Allen, R. G. D., 52, 172
America *see* United States
Amsterdam, 136
Anderson, B. M. (1911), *61*, 48n
Andreski, S. (1974), *204*, 191n
Angelmar, R. *see* Zaltman, G.
anomalies: problem of, 109–10; Kuhn on, 114; in the positive heuristic of research programmes, 177; in conventionalist methodology, 196; *see also* Leontief paradox
appraisal: demarcated from advice, 3; criteria of, 10, 93, 172; irrational, 30n; appropriate units of, 155–6, 171, 176–7; and behaviouralism, 170; in conventional methodology, 14–15, 196; and Keynesian effective demand failures, 101; in Lakatosian MSRP, viii, 2, 15–16, 78; *also mentioned*, 20, 186, 190
apriorism, 1, 2, 3–7, 201
Archibald, G. C., 28
   (1961), *39*, 8n, 29n; (1967), *178*, 156n
Aristotle, 166, 184
Arrow, K. J. and Hahn, F. H. (1972), *125*, 103, 116n
assumptions: 'anything goes' attitude to, 202; in classical economics, 144, 159; controversy over, 10; in demand theory, 49, 53–4; in Heckscher–Ohlin theorem, 114; in neo-classical theory, 195–6; in operations research, 139; in perfect competition theory, 23, 161, 168; in imperfect, 140; in Popper, 149; and uncertainty, 147
auxiliary assumptions (hypotheses): *ad hoc* and *non ad hoc*, 156; in Keynesian programme, 162, 164; in MSRP, 15, 157; in neoclassical programme, 167; in Ohlin–Samuelson, 123; and principle of tenacity, 151, 175

Austrian school of economics, 68, 87, 90n 213; theory of capital, 167
automatic self-righting, 88, 91, 93, 97, 98, 100–1, 216–17; *see also* Invisible Hand
Ayres, C. B. (1958), *61*, 47n

Bain, J. S., 33–4, 38n, 39
   (1949), *39*, 35n; (1956), *39*, 66; (1967), *39*, 30
   see also Sylos-Bain model
Baldwin, Robert E. (1971), *125*, 120n
Barrington Moore (1958), *204*, 188n
Bauer, P. T. (1945), *39*, 28n
Baumol, W. J., 166, 170, 174
Bayes theorem, 134–5
behaviouralism, economic: Knight on, 51–2; as a theory of the firm, 129, 169–70; as a research programme, 147, 169–70
Bellaggio Conference, 165
Bentham, Jeremy, 47n
Bernstein, E., 167n
Bertrand, J. (1883), *39*, 31n; Bertrand–Edgeworth model, 32n
   see also Cournot–Bertrand model
Bhagwati, J. (1969*a*), *125*, 111n, 113n, 115n, 119n; (1969*b*), *125*, 112n, 117n, 119n, 121n
Bishop, Robert (1964), *39*, 30
Black, R. D. C. (1970), *61*, 47n
Black, R. D. C., Coats, A. W. and Goodwin, C. D. W. (1970), *61*, 45n, 160n, 165n, 167n
Blaug, Mark, vii, 43n, 109n
   Nafplion Colloquium paper, 149–80
   (1958), 178, 165n, 166n; (1968), *178*, 55n, 56n, 166n; (1974*a*), *178*, 162n, 173n; (1974*b*), *178*, 174n
Bloor, D. (1971), *178*, 155n
Boucke, F. (1922), *61*, 50n
Boulding, K. E., 172n, 174
Brems, H. (1963), *39*, 34
Briefs, W. W. (1961), *178*, 175n
Britain: monetary policy in, 162–3; British classical economists, 165–6, 213n; Keynesians, 85n; political economy, 92; schools of economists, 87

* Italic page numbers denote reference list.

Bronfenbrenner, M., 160
(1970), *178*, 174n; (1971), *178*, 149n, 160n
budding research programmes, 44, 159, 170, 194–5, 197–8
buffer stocks, 102
business: and chess, 145–6, 147; behaviour, research programmes in, 170; *see also* firm, theory of

Cairnes, J. E., 166, 201n
Cambridge, U.K.: school of economics, 68, 85n, 87, 93; 'new Cambridge economists', 107n; capital theory controversies, 173–4; capital analysis, 194
Cambridge, U.S., capital theory controversies, 173–4
Cannan, Edwin, 163
capital: as a factor, 117; and labour, 117; international movement of, 117, 122; desired, 141–2; accumulation, 165; theory, controversy in, 173–4; analysis, 194
Carnegie-Mellon University, 136
Cassel, Gustav, 110
catallactics, 47, 75, 94, 95; or marginalism, 212–15
causalism, 5–6; causation, 202n
Caves, Richard E. (1960), *125*, 121n, 124n
Caves, R. E. and Jones, R. W. (1973), *125*, 121n
Chamberlin, E. H.: monopolistic competition theory, 25n, 26–30, 32–3; tangency-solution, 169
(1933), *39*, 26–7; (1957), *39*, 33n; (1966), *39*, 33n
Chamberlin-Chicago controversy, 30
Champernowne, D. G. (1972), *204*, 192n
Chase, W. G. and Simon, H. A. (1973*a*), *148*, 136n; (1973*b*), *148*, 145n
chess, 135–6, 144, 145–6
Chicago University, 68, 107n, 163, 203; Chamberlin controversy with, 30
Chipman, John S. (1966), *125*, 111n, 112n, 115n, 116n, 117n, 119n, 121n
choice, 133–5, 140, 142–4, 147, 168, 198, 203; in science, 154
Clapham, J. E., 'empty boxes', *39*, 26n, 167
Clark, J. B. (1901), *39*, 33
Clark, J. M., 163
(1921), *61*, 50n; (1936), *61*, 48; (1946), *61*, 48n
Clarkson, G. P. E. (1963), *148*, 136
classical economics: assumptions, 131, 137, 139, 143; a degenerating programme, 59; hard cores, 162; and Keynesian economics, 82–4, 86–7, 95–101, 161; and marginalists, 161, 165–6; and

Marxism, 211–12; models, 95; oligopoly theory, 31; optimisation, 140; psychology, independence of, 57–8; a revolution against physiocrats, 209–11; substantive rationality, dominated by, 145–6; theory and fact in, 188, 216; trade theory, 110–12, 117, 119, 121–2, 123–4; *see also* Marshall, A.; orthodox economics; Ricardo, D.; Smith, Adam
Clower, R. W., 107, 164
(1965), *108*, 84n; (1975), *108*, 81n, 87n, 106
Clower, R. W. and Leijonhufvud, A. (1975), *108*, 87n, 104n
Coats, A. W., vii, 129n, 130, 147, 149n, 160
Nafplion Colloquium paper, 43–64
(1953), *61*, 43n, 45n; (1954), *61*, 47n; (1969), *108*, 83n, 149n, 160n; (1970), *61*, 61n; (1971), *62*, 55n; (1974,) *62*, 43n; *see also* Black, Coats and Goodwin
Cobb–Douglas production function, 141, 173
Coddington, A., 160n
Columbia University, 163
cognitive processes, 132, 144, 145, 147, 154
Collingwood, R. G., 72n
comparative cost, 110–11, 115n, 117, 121, 123
competition: atomistic, 27; imperfect, 26–7, 68, 140–2; monopolistic, 17, 23–6, 27, 28, 141, 167, 178, 196; potential, 33; and research programmes, 123. Competitive equilibrium, 112, 116, 120, 124n, 176; price theories, 171n
computation, 132–7; computational efficiency, 132–3, 139–40, 147; of man, 135–7; digital computer, 138
Condillac, E. B. de, 166
constant returns-to-scale, 173
Continental economic thought, 166
conventionalism, 2, 9–14n, 195; methodology of, 196
Cooley (1913), *62*, 48n
coordination of economic activities, 87–93, 94, 96–7, 102–3
Copeland, M. A. (1931), *62*, 49n
Copernicus, 68; Copernican revolution, 153, 154, 159n
cost: controversy, 26n; quadratic cost functions, 139, 143; schedule, 24, 27, 28, 37, 137
Cournot, A. A.: profit-maximisation, 13; infinitesimal calculus, 23n; imperfect competition, 26n, 140; duopoly, 32, 35, 36
(1838), *39*, 13, 23n, 31n

Cournot-Bertrand model, 31
Cowles Commission, 84n
Cyert, Richard, 141n
Cyert, R., Feigenbaum, E. A. and March,
    J. G. (1959), *148*, 142n
    and de Groot, M. H. (1973), *148*, 141n
    and March, J. G. (1963), *148*, 142n,
    147n, 169–70

Darwin, Charles, 177
Davenport, Herbert (1894), *62*, 46n;
    (1908), *62*, 46n; (1913), *62*, 46n, 47n
Davis, J.E. (1971), *178*, 163; (1973), *108*, 83n
decision-making, 12, 17, 24, 38, 58, 147,
    175; empirical study of, 145–6; in
    market systems, 88; in multiple-exit
    situations, 21; single-exit, 33; in oligo-
    poly, 31, 141; optimal and good
    decisions, 140; in perfect competition,
    25–6, 167–8; imperfect, 140–1; in real
    business, 137–8, 139; research pro-
    gramme for, 22; in uncertainty, 142–4,
    192n, 203. Decision schema, 6;
    statistical decision theory, 133
de Groot, Adriaan, 136, 141n
    (1965), *148*, 136, 145n; *see also* Cyert, R.
demand: analysis, 52; curves, 27, 137;
    effective demand failures, 93, 97, 101–
    2; supply-and-demand mechanism,
    101, 110, 160; theory, 45, 48n, 49, 53,
    56, 57–8
De Marchi, N. B., vii, 149n
    Nafplion Colloquium paper, 109–27
    (1970), *178*, 166n; (1973), *178*, 114n
Demsetz, H., 28, 29
    (1964), *40*, 29n
depression, 101–2; the Great, 88, 90, 91–2,
    96, 163, 164
Descartes, 153
Deutsch, K. W. (1958), *62*, 59n
Deutsch, M. and Krauss, R. M. (1960), *40*,
    39n
Dewey, D. (1958), *40*, 29n; (1969), *40*, 33n
Dewey, John, 48
Dickinson, Z. C. (1922), *62*, 51n, 53n, 57n;
    (1924), *62*, 58n
disciplinary matrix, 152–3
Dodd, S. C., 55n
Dolbear, F. T. *see* Tobin, J.
Domar, 164
Dorfman, R., Samuelson, P.A. and Solow,
    R. M. (1958), *148*, 139n
Douglas, Paul, 163
dualism *see* methodology
Duesenberry, J. S., 164
Dugdale, Dr Rose (1972), *204*, 199n
Duhem, P., 155–6
duopoly, 31–3
dynamics: in Smith, Ricardo and Mill,

166; dynamic programming, 15–16,
    139, 140; systems, 79; theories, 50,
    142, 166; and static processes, 76; in
    Keynes, 94, 95

Econometric Society, 77n, 84n
econometrics, 160, 192n, 201; models, 77
economic man, 12, 48, 53
economics: economic analysis and policy,
    94; and business, 137–8; and chess,
    145–6; controversies, 69, 149; a crucial
    experiment in, 113; history of, 177,
    182, 194, 207, 209, 218; and politics,
    138, 191, 192n, 193, 200–1, 203; a
    case of scientific progress in, 165;
    scope of, 50, 51–2, 57, 74n, 146;
    schools of, 68, 86–7, 105n; and natural
    sciences, 43–4, 60–1, 76, 107n, 145,
    160, 216; Growth of Knowledge,
    theories in, 67–8, 72, 78–9; external
    factors in, 73; value judgements in,
    175; fundamental differences between,
    184, 207; economics as an immature
    or undeveloped science, 190–3
and physics, 59, 75, 182n, 191n; principle
    of tenacity in, 159; differences be-
    tween, 181n, 183n, 184, 193; Popper
    on, 186–9, 201–2; Lakatos's prescrip-
    tions and, 195, 197, 198–9
and psychology: controversy in America,
    44–9, 51–2, 54, 130; revived interest
    in economic psychology, 55, 57–8; and
    maximising postulate, 67, 131; econo-
    mic behaviouralism, 129, 147–8; and
    principles of rationality, 130–1, 133,
    135, 144, 146–8; Lakatos on, 159
and other social sciences, 55, 159, 185, 186
see also under particular schools of economics
Edgeworth, F. Y. (1881), *218*, 212n
Edwards, Ward, 133–4
    (1968), *148*, 134
efficiency, 176
Einstein, A., 73, 152n; Einstein–Planck
    revolution, 153, 154, 159n
Eisner, R. (1958), *108*, 84n
Ekelund, R. B., Jr, Furubotn, E. W. and
    Gramm, W. P. (1972), *62*, 53n, 58n
equilibrium: compared with 'balance of
    power', 76n; in Chamberlin's theorem,
    29–30, 33; in Keynesian model, 94–7,
    162–3; in limit-price theory, 37; mar-
    ginalist conception of, 48; *via* market
    mechanism, 160–1; models of, 18, 167;
    in monetarist theory, 71; in perfect
    competition, 24, 25, 176; and in
    monopolistic, 27, 167. General equili-
    brium, 95, 97–103, 106, 110–13, 116,
    118, 124n, 161, 175n; underemploy-
    ment, 94, 162, 174

Euler, L. 'Conjecture on Polyhedra', 158
excess capacity theorem, 29, 30n, 169
excess empirical content, 172, 177
exchange: economy, 213; model, 112, 121, 123; theory of, *see* catallactics; values, 47, 54
expectations and uncertainty, 142–4, 147
external and internal factors: in the history of economics, 73–4, 171, 177; of science, 157–8; in the Keynesian revolution, 83, 88, 90–2, 96; in the marginalist revolution, 165, 166–7; 'externalist rubbish', 60, 67

factor-intensity, 121; reversal, 115, 116, 119–21, 123, 124n
factor-price equalisation theory, 112, 114, 115–16, 119–21, 123
factor-proportions model, 111n, 115–21, 123, 124
falsifiability: Hutchison on, vii, 181n; degrees of, 8; principle of, Popper's, 149, 151, 152n, 159, 202; Vienna Circle's, 151; methodology of, 155; and fallibilism, 155, 203; falsifiable predictions, 172; formulas, 199
falsification: considered as a methodology for economics, 1, 2, 7–9, 15; *ad hoc* theories banned by, 2, 196; and anomalies, 109–10, 114, 123; assumptions and, 10; contrasted with confirmation, 173; in Friedman, 109, 123, 174, 175n; in Growth of Knowledge theories, 69; innocuous, 160, 174; Lakatos's version, 195; in metahistorical research programme, 177; naive, 151, 172, 194; in Popper, 156, 159, 189, 190, 195, 197; problem of application, 77, 81. Falsificationist ethic, 14
Fawcett, W., 166n
Feigenbaum, E. A. *see* Cyert, R.
Feigenbaum, E. A. and Feldman, J. (1963), *148*, 134n
Fellner, W. (1949), *40*, 13, 32n, 38n
Ferber, R. (1973), *62*, 58n
Fetter, F. A. (1915), *62*, 47n; (1920), *62*, 48n; (1923), *62*, 48n
Feyerabend, P. K., 155n, 158n, 198, 203n (1970), *125*, 124n, 182n, 198; (1974), *178*, 159n; (1975), *204*, 203n
firm, theory of: Chamberlin on, 33; classical theory of, and real business, 137–8; economic behaviouralism as research programme for, 129, 169–70; and falsificationism, 9; Machlup on, 25, 195–6; MSRP applied to, 16–39, 45, 68n, 129, 167–71, 195–6; neoclassical programme for, 17–18, 27–8, 33,

171; orthodox theory of, 194; situational determinism as research programme for, 22–3, 30, 129
Fischer, Bobby, 146
Fisher, F. M. (1971), *178*, 173
Fisher, Irving, 51, 164, 172 (1892), *62*, 47n, 51
forecasting, 143–4
formalism, 139; formalist revolution, 160
France, Anatole, 213n
Frankian losses, 69
Franklin, R. J. and Resnik, S. (1974), *178*, 174n
Frege, Gottlieb, 68n, 72n
Friedman, Milton: his conventionalist methodology, 9–10, 12, 195; monetarist views, 71n, 104n, 164, 175; his form of falsification, 109, 123, 149, 159, 174–5; on maximisation of returns, 161, 169n; permanent income hypothesis, 164 (1953), *40*, 9n, 12n, 109n, 123n, 149, 169n; (1957), *178*, 174–5; (1970), *108*, 71n, 175n; (1971), *108*, 71n; (1974), *204*, 202n
Furubotn, E. G. *see* Ekelund

Gaitskell, Hugh, 163
Gale, David and Nikaido, Hukukene (1965), *125*, 116
Galiani, F., 166
Galileo, 186
Gayer, A. D., 163
German historical school of economics, 68
Gordon, D. F. (1965), *178*, 160
Gould, J. and Kolb, W. L. (1964), *148*, 130n
Gouldner, A. W. (1971), *178*, 157n
Gramm, W. P. *see* Ekelund, R. B., Jr
growth theory, 142, 164, 172, 174, 194, 199, 215
Growth of Knowledge theories: applied to history of economics, 65–9; positive and normative, 78–9; and Keynesian economics, 83; *also mentioned*, 89
Gruchy, A. G. (1947), *62*, 47n
Grünbaum, A. (1973), *178*, 156n, 173n
Grünberg, E., 172n

Haberler, G. (1930), *125*, 115n
Hadley, A. T. (1893), *62*, 47n
Hague, Douglas *see* Harrod, Roy
Hahn, F. H. *see* Arrow, K.
Hall, R. L. and Hitch, C. H. (1939), *148*, 137
Haney, L. (1914), *62*, 48n
Hanson, N. R., 67, 155n (1958), *108*, 76n, 80n

hard cores: in behaviouralism, 170; in classical theory, 162, 164; different models with same, 77; in imperfect competition, 27, 167; in Keynesian general theory, 95, 161, 162, 164; in Kuhn's apparatus, 158; in Lakatosian MSRP, 14, 16, 67, 70–2, 79–81, 117n, 156–8; in marginal utility analysis, 48–50; in maximisation of returns hypothesis, 161–2; in metahistorical research programme, 176–7; in neoclassical theory, 22, 162; in neo-Walrasian school, 86, 106–7; in oligopoly, 32; orthodox, 51, 53; in perfect competition, 23, 167; in pure monopoly, 26; Ricardo's, 165

Harrod, Roy, 163, 164, 174

Harrod, Roy and Hague, Douglas (1963), *125*, 118n, 120n

Hawtrey, Charles, 163, 216–17
(1919), *218*, 216–17

Hayek, F. A., 23, 89, 95
(1948), *40*, 23n, 90n

Heckscher, Eli, 111n

Heckscher–Ohlin theory of trade, 111–15, 119, 120, 124

hedonism, 47, 48, 50, 52n

Hempel, C. G. (1942), *40*, 18n; (1915), *178*, 173n

Hesse, Helmut (1973), 158n

heuristic *see* positive heuristic

Hicks, John; on criteria, vii; indifference curves, 52; IS-LM apparatus, 71n, 160, 162n; Growth of Knowledge theories, 72, 73; on economic models, 74–5, 77; general equilibrium pricing process, 116; *also mentioned*, 149n, 172
Nafplion Colloquium paper, 207–18
(1932), *218*, 215; (1939), *178*, 167; (1959), *125*, 118n; (1965), *218*, 172n, 208n

hidden hand *see* Invisible Hand

Higgins, B. (1939), *40*, 25n

Hitch, C. H. *see* Hall, R. L.

Hodd, M. (1967), *125*, 120n

Holt, H. G., Modigliani, F., Muth, J. F. and Simon, H. A. (1960), *148*, 139n

Houthakker, H. S., 172

Hufbauer, G. C. (1970), *125*, 122n, 123n

Hume, David, 155
Political Discourses, 1752, 160

Hutchison, T. W., vii, 129n
Nafplion Colloquium paper, 181–205
(1938), *40*, 7, 181n, 201n, 204; (1964), *204*, 187n; (1968), *178*, 163, 197n

hypotheses *see* assumptions, auxiliary

indifference curve analysis, 52, 54, 115

interdependence theory of pricing *see* price

intuition, 43, 52n, 109, 120, 195, 196

Invisible Hand, 91, 166, 176, 213; *see also* automatic self-righting

Jacobian matrix, 120

James, S. F. and Pearce, I. F. (1951/2), *125*, 121n

James, William, 47, 48
(1890), *148*, 131

Jevons, Stanley, in the marginalist revolution, 47n, 165, 211; Law of Indifference, 75n; *also mentioned*, 213
(1865), *178*, 166; (1871), *218*, 211n

Johnson, H. G., 172
(1972), *204*, 200n

Jones, R. W. (1956–7), *125*, 111n, 115n; *see also* Caves, R. E.

Jorgenson, D. W., 141
(1963), *148*, 141n

Kahn, Richard, 164n

Kahneman, D. and Tversky, A. (1973), *148*, 134

Kaldor, N., 28
(1935), *40*, 29n; (1938), *40*, 29n

Kant, I. 9, 150n

Katona, G. (1951), *148*, 147n

Kelley, H. H. (1965), *40*, 39n

Kemeny, J. G. (1959), *204*, 188n

Kemp, Murray C. (1969), *125*, 117n

Keynes, J. M.: Keynesian revolution, 65, 68, 81–7, 92, 107, 160–5, 208–9; an analysis in macroeconomics, 30, 84n, 104, 215; as a research programme, 82, 85, 105–6, 161–2, 163–5; general theory: not a 'hardened' programme, 85n; directed against Marshallians and Pigou, 87, 163; denies automatic self-righting, 91, 93, 216–17; effective demand failure, 93, 97, 101–2; Keynesian model, 94–5, 103–4; propensity to save, 100; unemployment equilibrium, 100; price theory, 105; consumption function, 161; as a general equilibrium theory, 161; novel aspects of, 162; applied to policy-making, 164; now a special case, 165; not a general theory (Hicks), 209n; belongs to monetary economics, 216–17
and the classics, 82–3, 87, 88, 90–1, 94–7, 98–100; and the neoclassics, 83, 84–6, 93, 94, 95–8, 103–5, 164–5; monetarist–Keynes debate, 202; and Hawtrey, 216–17
(1930), *178*, 164, 216–17; (1933), *178*, 163n; (1934), *108*, 84n, 85n, 87, 91, 94, 95, 105, 163, 164, 216–17; (1973), *178*, 164n

Keynesians, 86, 94, 104n, 163, 202; American, 85; British, 85n

Keynes, John Neville (1955), *179*, 159
Kindleberger, Charles, 124
 (1962), *125*, 124n
Knight, Frank: defence of orthodox hard
  core, 51; on the limitations of econo-
  mics as a science, 52; *also mentioned*,
  163, 201
 (1921*a*), *62*, 52n; (1921*b*), *62*, 52n;
  (1924), *62*, 52n; (1925*a*), *62*, 52n;
  (1925*b*), *62*, 52n; (1931*a*), *62*, 51n,
  52n; (1931*b*), *62*, 55n
Koch, S. (1963), *63*
Kolb, W. L. *see* Gould, J.
Koopmans, L., 174
Kornai, J. (1971), *148*, 141n
Krauss, R. M. *see* Deutsch, M.
Kristol, I. (1964), *204*, 183
Krupp, S. R. (1966), *179*, 171n, 172n
Kuhn, T. S.: 'internal–external', 30n, 60n;
  structure of scientific revolutions, 44,
  149, 152; the Kuhnian revolution, 65,
  68; Keynesian revolution as, 83–4,
  164; predictive failure in physical
  science, 113–14
 paradigms, 149, 157, 160; term defined,
  152; applicability of, to economics
  questioned, 149; applied to science,
  153–4, 185; to economics, 160; mature
  and immature sciences, 183, 189–91,
  193
 Lakatos and, 155, 158–9, 182, 198n;
  Kuhn on Lakatos, 182n, 198–9;
  Lakatos on Kuhn, 198–9; Popper on,
  155n; Feyerabend on, 182n
 also mentioned, 67, 88, 170n
 (1957), *179*, 159n; (1959), *125*, 116;
  (1961), *125*, 114n; (1962), *179*, 149n,
  152n; (1968), *204*, 183n; (1970*a*), *63*,
  44, 114n, 152, 153n, 154, 190n; (1970*b*,)
  182n, 189n; (1971), *40*, 30n
Kuhnian losses, 69, 75, 84, 157n
Kunin, L. and Weaver, F. S. (1971), *179*,
  149n, 153n
Kuznets, Simon, 83n

Laidler, D. (1974), *204*, 202n
Lakatos, Imre
 and MSRP: designs Nafplion Colloquium as test for, in economics, vii, 43, 65;
  urges appraisal not advice, viii, 155;
  bases method on sequence of theories,
  150; intended it for history of natural
  sciences, 2n, 185; thought it perhaps
  'too elaborate', 44; allows for extra-
  scientific influences, 60–1; belief in
  rational reconstruction, 66, 177; on
  empirical success, **78**; budding research programmes, 194–5; prescriptions, 195, 197; or criteria of adequacy,

198; his methodology compared with
  Popper's, 155–6, 196–7, 200; controversy with Kuhn, 155–9, 182,
  198–9
 on problem-shifts, 119n, 156; internal
  and external history, 157–8; a rare
  reference to economics, 193–4; distinction between science and social
  sciences, 199
 use of terms: positive heuristic, 117n;
  ad hoc, 123; naive falsification, 151;
  mature and immature sciences, 183,
  193
 (1963), *108*, 81; (1964), *179*, 158; (1968),
  40, 2n, 14n, 117n, 118n, 119n, 194n;
  (1970), *40*, 2n, 14n, 124n, 182n, 193,
  194n, 199n, 215n; (1971*a*), *40*, 30n,
  109n, 150n, 151n, 157n, 158n, 193,
  197n; (1971*b*), *40*, 14n
Lakatos, I and Musgrave, A. (1970), *179*,
  151n, 152n, 153n, 155n, 156n, 157n,
  158n, 159n
Lakatos, I, and Zahar, E. (1976), *63*, 44,
  159n
Lammer, C. J. (1974), *63*, 61n
Lancaster, K. (1957), *126*, 111n
Lange, Oscar (1945–6), *204*, 181n
Latsis, S. J., vii, 43n, 54n, 67n, 68n, 109n,
  147, 149n, 181n
 on theories of the firm, 11, 16–18, 22, 25,
  27–30, 33, 34–9, 45, 129; indictment
  of traditional theory, 167–71; applies
  Lakatosian prescriptions, 159n, 167–
  70, 195–6
 Nafplion Colloquium paper, 1–41
 (1972), *63*, 44n, 45, 58, 60n, 67n, 68n,
  129n, 159n, 167n, 168–70, 195n;
  (1974), *179*, 152n; (1976), *40*
Lausanne school of economics, 87
Layton, W. T., 163
Leibnitz, 153
Leijonhufvud, Axel, vii, viii
 disequilibrium interpretation of Keynes,
  71, 94–103, 161–2, 164
 Nafplion Colloquium paper, 65–108
 (1968), *108*, 65n, 85, 95n, 96n, 104n;
  (1969), *108*, 85n, 104n; (1973*a*), *108*,
  71n, 87n; (1973*b*), *108*, 72n, 93n, 101;
  (1974*a*), *108*, 77n; (1974*b*), *108*, 77n;
  (forthcoming), *108*, 67n, 77n, 80n
Leontief, W. W., the Leontief paradox,
  110, 113–15, 118–24
 (1953), *126*, 113; (1956), *126*, 111n;
  (1964), *126*, 119n
Lerner, Abba, an instance of parallel discovery, 115–16
 (1932), *126*, 115n; (1933), *126*, 115n;
  (1953), *126*, 116n
Le Roy, E. (1899), *40*, 9

limit-price theory, 33–9
linear-programming, 131, 133, 138, 143
Lipsey, R. G., 151n
  (1963), *204*, 200n; (1966), *179*, 151n, 173, 200n; (1971), *179*, 200n
Loasby, B. J. (1971), *179*, 170n
LSE school of economics, 87

McCulloch, J. R., 165n
MacDougall, G. D. A. (1951/2), *126*, 121n
McDougall, William, 46, 47
Machlup, Fritz: defends conventionalist methodology, 9–12, 195–6; on economic actions and reactions, 25; prediction, 171–2
  (1946), *40*, 9n, 25n; (1952), *40*, 9n, 11n, 12n, 28n, 35n, 38n; (1955), *40*, 9n, 171–2; (1956), *40*, 10n; (1967), *40*, 10n, 11n, 25, 28n; (1974), *179*, 170n
macroeconomics: and the coordination problem, 88; criterion for appraisal of, 93; Keynesian, 30, 81, 85n, 92, 104, 160, 165–6; micro-foundations of, 103–7; monetarist, 70–1, 84, 104n, 194; Pigouvian, 215–16; pre-Keynesian, 163–4; Wicksell's rocking-horse and, 73–4
Magee, B. (1973), *179*, 151n
Maloney, 43n, 56n
Malthus, T. R., 207; theory of population, 177
March, J. G. *see* Cyert, R.
marginal efficiency: of capital, 161, 162; productivity theory of wages, 172; utility, 47–8, 51, 54
marginalist revolution, 45, 46, 50, 68, 86–7, 160, 161, 212–15; and operations research, 139; MSRP apparatus for, 161; 'internalist' account of, 165, 167; and behaviouralism, 170n, 171; *see also* catallactics
market systems, 88; automacity of, 91, 96–7, 160, 176; in imperfect competition, 140, 167; in perfect, 167, 168; Keynes's theory of, 93, 162; in neoclassical and behavioural theory, 170; Ohlin and, 117, 122; theory of, 208n
Marschak, Jacob, 83n
Marshall, Alfred: theory of the firm, 23n, 27; imperfect competition, 26; supply and demand model, 77n, 160; demand curves, 174; Marshallian theory and Keynes, 91, 96, 105; and Walras, 107n; *also mentioned*, 173, 200–1, 207, 215n
  (1890), *40*, 23n; (1919), *40*, 23n, 33n
Marshallian school of economics, 87, 93–4, 95, 105; research programme, 167
Martins, H. (1972), *179*, 149n

Marx, Karl, 157n, 207, 213; and Ricardo, 212
Marxian economics, 58, 188n; research programme, 167n, 197, 201; revolution, 211–12; Marxism, 211; Marxists, 200n, 202
  Das Kapital, 1867, 211n
Masterman, M. (1965), *108*, 83n, 152n
mathematical economics, 77n, 82, 113–14, 160, 191; game-playing, 79; mathematical solutions in Marshallian theory, 91; general equilibrium theory, 103; and factor proportions theory, 116, 124; computational mathematics, 132–3
maximising behaviour postulates, 67, 75n, 80n, 107, 161; maximisation-of-returns hypothesis, 169n, 212; *see also* profit maximisation
Meade, James, 163
Medawar, P. (1967), *63*, 59n
Menger, Carl, and the marginalist revolution, 165, 166, 211, 213; *also mentioned*, 201
  (1871), *218*, 211n
Menger, Karl (1973), *108*, 76n
mercantilism, 91, 92; neomercantilism, 207
methodology: aggressive and defensive, 152, 155; alternatives, of economics, 1–14; Friedman's 'as-if', 159; Kuhnian, 149–54, 185, 189–90; nineteenth century, 159; normative, 150, 155, 181; Popper's, 149–52, 159, 185–9, 201. Methodological criteria, 191, 198; dualism, 5; individualism, 161; monstrosities, 187; questions in economics, 181–5; *see also* apriorism, conventionalism, falsification, MSRP
microeconomics: decline of interest in, 59n; and the Great Depression, 163; and macroeconomics, 92, 103–7; neoclassical, 171, 195–6; pre-Keynesian, 164; resistance to psychology, 52–3; revolution in, 30, 215
Milhaud, E. (1896), *41*, 9
Mill, J. S., 160, 166, 212
  Principles, 1848, 166n, 212
Minabe, Nobuo (1966), *126*, 111n
Minhas, B. S., 119, 120
  (1962), *126*, 119n; (1963), *126*, 119n
Mises, L. von, apriorism methodology 3–5, 201; rationalistic approach, 4, 6; simplified model, 7; antipsychologism, 12, 24; a die-hard individualist, 213
  (1922), *218*, 213n; (1949), *41*, 3–4, 24, 212n; (1959), *218*, 213n
Mishan, E. J. (1961), *63*, 55n
Mitchell, Wesley, 46n
  (1910), *63*, 47n; (1937), *63*, 47n

models: in anatomy and physiology, 76n; in Cambridge capital controversy, 174; econometric, 77; Keynesian and classical, 82, 95; and neo-Walrasian, 104–5; in *General Theory*, 85n, 94–5; monetarist, 70–1; planning and development, 138; perfectly competitive, 196; product cycle, 122; Samuelson's, 112, 116–17; a ship model, 98–103; Sraffa's, 194; *also mentioned*, 75

Modigliani, F., 38, 39, 164; and the Sylos postulate (1958), *41*, 34, 36n; *see also* Holt, H. G.

monetarists: and Keynes controversy, 70–1, 194, 202; monetary economics and *General Theory*, 216; 'new quantity' theory, 84; neo-Walrasian model, 95, 104

monopoly, 23–6, 35; monopolistic competition, 17, 26–30, 167

Morgenstern, O. (1965), *204*, 184n; *see also* Neumann, J. von

Morphy, Paul, 146

Morrall, John F. (1972), *126*, 119n, 120n, 121n

MSRP (methodology of scientific research programmes): as a tool for economics, vii, 2–3, 14, 43–5, 54–5, 59–61, 65, 70, 81, 124, 150, 167, 176–7, 195, 198; unit of appraisal, 14, 56n, 155–6; structural features, 14–16, 70, 80, 86, 90, 117n, 118, 155–7, 176–7; normative and positive statements in, 61–7, 78, 151; an internalist methodology, 73n, 74; and Kuhn's paradigms, 157–9; novel facts in, 120; anomalies and, 109; competing programmes, 70–2, 77, 83n, 87n, 105, 170; controversies in, 69; applied to demand theories, 49–50, 54, 56, 58; to growth theory, 215; to Keynesian economics, 162, 164; to natural sciences, 159n; to neoclassical theory of the firm, 10, 12, 16–68; to Ohlin–Samuelson programme, 115, 118–19, 123; to Ricardian system, 165–6; Veblen's attempt at, 47
    see also hard core; Lakatos, Imre; positive heuristic; progressive and degenerating programmes; protective belt

multiple-exit situations, 16, 19–23, 31; *see also* single-exit

Musgrave, Alan (1973), *204*, 198n, 199n; *see also* Lakatos and Musgrave

Nabarro, Sir Gerald, 200n

Nagel, E. (1961), *179*, 175n

natural sciences: and social sciences, 1, 5, 43–6, 65–8, 171, 176, 181n, 183–4, 185–9, 199; mature and immature,

183, 185, 187, 189–93, 197; *see also* economics, physics

Naya, S. (1967), *126*, 120n

neoclassical economics, 8, 68; or orthodox, 83; or pre-Keynesian, 86; or neo-Walrasian, 86, 95; assumptions, 111; economic man, 12; empirical tests, 174; growth models, 106, 107n; hard core, 22, 27, 35, 80n, 162; heuristics, 31, 32; positive heuristic, 22, 33; and Keynesianism, 85–6, 164; Marshallian school of, 93; maximisation, 13; microeconomics, 4, 10, 16, 195–6; oligopoly theory, 31, 34–5; partial equilibrium analysis, 5n, 10; policies for Great Depression, 163; and psychologism, 17; research programme, viii, 10, 17–18, 171; resurgence of, 84; schools of 93, 96; and situational determinism, 26; synthesis, 85, 93, 95–7, 98–104, 105n; theories of investment, 141; theory of the firm, 11, 16, 17, 27, 45, 68n, 167–70, 195–6

Netherlands, economists and government planning, 138, 139n, 140n

Neumann, J. von and Morgenstern, O. (1955), *204*, 184n

Newell, A. and Simon, H. A. (1972), *148*, 136n

Nicols, A. (1947), *41*, 30n

normal science, 153, 158, 190

normative: methodology, Popper's, 152; and descriptive theory, 74; and positive aspects of theories, 66, 78–9; of MSRP, 67, 150, 155, 157, 170; of economics, 172, 175, 181–2; of confusion between philosopher and historian, 182

novel facts, definition, 110n; prediction of, as criterion of progressiveness, 78, 109–10, 119, 156, 158; in Ohlin–Samuelson programme, 120, 123; in Keynesian, 162; in Ricardian system, 165; none produced by behaviouralism, 170; economists and, 176; in metahistorical programme, 177

O'Brien, D. P., 149n (1970), *179*, 165n; (1974), *204*, 193n

Ohlin, Bertil: theory of commodity trade, 110–13, 117–18, 120; factor-proportions model, 111n, 117, 118, 120, 124n; interdependent theory of pricing, 112, 113, 117, 118n, 120, 124n; the Ohlin tradition, 124; *see also* Heckscher–Ohlin
    (1933), *126*, 115, 117n, 118n, 121; (1967), *126*, 110n, 111n, 112n, 117n, 118n, 120n; (1974), *179*, 163n

Ohlin–Samuelson trade theory, 110, 114, 115, 118, 119–21; research programme, 123–4

oligopoly, 28, 31–3, 141, 142, 169; and limit-price, 34–7; Chamberlin's model, 28, 32–3; Cournot–Bertrand model, 31; Stigler's model, 39n

operations research, 138–40, 146, 147

optimal solutions, 133, 135, 139–40; optimisation, 140, 170

orthodox economics: assumptions, 168; automatic self-righting presupposition, 91–2, 194; and General Theory, 94; attempt to synthesise Keynesians and, 98; Laws proclaimed by, 188n; a microeconomic theory, 163; and unemployment, 162–3

Osborne, D. K. (1964), 41, 39n

paradigms, Kuhn's, 149; definitions, 152–3, 160; in history of science, 152, 153–4; and of economics, 160; and MSRP, 157–8; applied to Keynesian revolution, 164; to marginalist, 165; profit-maximisation as, 170n; Cambridge capital controversy as war of, 174; and radical political economists, 174

Pareto, Vilfredo, 12, 172, 213
  (1909), 41, 6n, 9

Parry, C. E. (1921), 63, 50n

Pashigian, B. P. (1968), 41, 39n

Patinkin, D., 164, 202–3
  (1956), 108, 106; (1972), 94, 203n

Pearce, I. F., 121
  (1959), 126, 121n; see also James, S. F.

Phelps-Brown, E. J., 183n, 190, 202
  (1972), 205, 183n

physics: classical and quantum, 153, 157; neoclassical economics compared to quantum, 172; see also economics, natural sciences

Physiocrats, 68, 176, 209

Pigou, A. C.: Keynes and, 87, 163, 164n; his welfare macroeconomics, 125–6
  (1912), 218, 215; (1920), 218, 215; (1925), 215, 201n

Pinson, A. R. A. see Zaltman, G.

Pitts, G., 133

plutology: Hicks's, 75, 216; Marshallian, 93–5

Poincaré, H., 9, 155–6
  (1902), 41, 9n

political economy: flow of wealth in Adam Smith, 210–11; distribution in Ricardo, 212; and Keynesian models, 104; Pigou's revival of, 215; radical, 160, 174; social character of, 213

Popper, Karl: demarcation criteria, 190; falsificationism, 8n, 149, 151–2, 156, 159, 194–7, 199n, 200–1, 203; an internalist methodology, 73n; Lakatos and, 150, 155–6, 195–7, 200–1; 'logic of the situation', 18, 23; concerned with natural, not social sciences, 185, 201; accepts Newtonian revolution in economic theory, 186–9, 194; rationality principle, 6–7; scientific decision and political choice, 203
  (1945), 41, 18n, 23n, 186n, 187n; (1957), 41, 8n, 18, 186, 188, 202n; (1962), 179, 151n; (1963), 41, 14n, 15n, 202n; (1965), 179, 151; (1970), 205, 186n; (1972), 179, 151n, 169n; (1974), 205, 185, 203n

positive heuristic: defined, 54, 117n; the normative hard core, 16; in demand theory, 49, 50, 54; in factor-proportions model, 118; in Keynesian revolution, 161, 162; in limit-price theory, 38; in metahistorical programme, 177; in neo-Walrasian theory, 86, 167; in Ohlin's trade theory, 117, 124; Ohlin–Samuelson programme, 123; in Ricardo, 165. Negative heuristic, 117, 123; defined, 117n

pre-Keynesian economics, 86, 91, 92, 94, 96–7, 102, 105n

presupposition: use of term, 72, 80; internalist, 74; in Keynes revolution, 81, 85, 87, 90n; in Adam Smith, 91

price: Chamberlin's theory of, 30; in general equilibrium theory, 99, 110–12; in General Theory, 105, 162; limit-price, 33–9; monopoly, 32; Ohlin's 'mutual interdependence', theory of, 112, 113, 117, 118n, 120, 123, 124n; in perfect competition, 23–4; in pre-Keynesian economics, 96–7

problem-shifts, 50, 124, 166; progressive, 119, 165, 166

procedural rationality: a concept of psychology, 130, 131, 146; applied to problem situations, 132–7; economics and, 137–44, 147–8; in chess and business, 145–6

product cycle model, 122

product differentiation, 28, 29–30; homogeneity, 37, 210–11

production and distribution in economic revolutions, 211–12, 215

profit-maximisation: an alternative assumption to, 24; in classical analysis, 131, 137, 139–40; in Cournot and Fellner, 13; in imperfect competition, 140–2, 167; perfect, 23, 27, 167; in limit-price theory, 36–8; in neoclassi-

profit-maximisation *(cont.)*
cal theory of the firm, 11, 167-9; as a paradigm, 170n; in real business, 138; in Stigler's oligopoly model, 39n
progressive and degenerating research programmes, 68, 75n, 158, 176, 193; theoretical and empirical changes, 15, 60, 156; criterion of progressiveness, 109–10, 158; in positive theory, 78; in normative, 79; symptoms of degeneration, 84n, 156, 165–6; problem of identification, in economics, 60–1; in science, 158. Progressive programmes: Keynesian, 162, 163–4; disequilibrium interpretation of, 164–5; neo-Walrasian, 95; degenerating programmes: Marshallian and Austrian, 167; Marxian, 167n; neoclassical theory of the firm, 27–8, 30, 170–1; orthodox theory, 58–9
degeneration and hard cores, 79; and stagnation, 84, 95
protective belt: function in research programmes, 15, 22–3, 61, 70, 156–7; shifts between hard cores and, 69n; competing theories fought out in, 70–1; and Kuhn's 'normal science', 158. In economic theory, 53; Keynesian, 164; marginalist, 161; metahistorical, 176; neo-Walrasian, 86; perfect and imperfect competition identical, 167
proto-sciences, 189–90
Providence, 89, 93
Ptolemaic system, 68, 207

quantity theory of money, 95, 123, 160, 163–4, 175, 194

Rapaport, A., 133
Rapaport, A. and Wallsten, T. S. (1972), *148*, 134
rationality: rationalistic approach to social sciences, 4, 6–7; rational choice, 133–4, 137, 143–4; and decision-making, 17, 21, 26, 48, 141n; and degenerating programmes, 85; and the economic man, 53; limits to, in man, 148; rational and irrational, 131–2; in situational determinism, 129–30. Classical models of, 143; future models, 147; *see also* procedural and substantive rationality
Ravetz, J., on mature and immature sciences, 183, 185, 191, 193; appraisal of economics, 190–3
(1971), *205*, 183n, 184n, 190–3
research programmes *see* MSRP
revolutions: in science, 207; Kuhn's structure of, 44, 65, 84, 149, 152–4; Popper's

Newtonian, 186, 188, 194, 200; in economics, 68, 149, 160, 207–15; counterrevolution, 84, 164; *see also under particular schools of economics*
Ricardo, David: theory of comparative cost, 110, 112, 121n; accumulation of capital, 165; value, 211; rent, 211; emphasis on distribution, 211–12; Ricardian system as research programme, 165–6; as a minor revolution, 211; *also mentioned*, 188n, 207, 215n
Robbins, Lionel, 3, 8, 12, 188n
(1932), *41*, 3n, 201; (1935), *63*, 52n; (1971), *126*, 115n
Roberthall, Lord (1959), *205*, 202
Roberts, M. J. (1974), *205*, 184n, 189, 192n
Robertson, D. H., 164
Robinson, E. A. G., 163
Robinson, Joan, 163, 174
(1933), *41*, 13, 30; (1963), *108*, 77
Robinson, Romney (1956), *126*, 115n
Rothchild, K. W. (1947), *41*, 25n
Rotterdam School of Economics, 139n
Ryan, A. (1970), *179*, 149n

Samuelson, Paul: factor-prices research programme, 115–17, 118, 119, 123, 124, 172; factor proportions model, 118, 124; a falsificationist, 174; and Ohlin's trade theory, 112–13, 114; price theory, 30; simplified model, 8
(1945), *126*, 124n; (1946), *108*, 83n; (1948), *179*, 167, 176; (1948), *126*, 115, 116n, 118n, 120; (1949), *126*, 115, 116n, 118n; (1951–2), *127*, 118n, 120; (1953–4), *127*, 112n, 115, 116, 118n, 123n; (1960), *127*, 119n; (1963), *41*, 12n; (1964), *205*, 201; (1966), *127*, 116n, 118n, 119n, 124n; (1967), *41*, 26, 30
Say's law, 165
science *see* economics, natural sciences, physics
Schilpp, P. A. (1974), *179*, 151n, 152n
Schultz, T. W., 163
Schumpeter, J. A., his term 'Vision', 71, 157n
(1954), *179*, 157n
Sen, A. K. (1970), *179*, 175n
Senior, Nassau, 3, 160, 201n
Shove, G. E. (1942), *108*, 94n
Shubik, M. (1970), *63*, 58n
SRP (scientific research programmes) *see* MSRP
Sidgwick, Henry, 165
Simon, H. A., viii, 67n; on the widening scope of economics, 57; economic behaviouralism, 129, 130, 147–8, 169

Simon, H. A. (*cont.*)
Nafplion Colloquium paper, 129–48
(1957), *148*, 147n; (1959), *41*, 18n;
(1963), *63*; 57n; (1967), *63*, 57n;
(1969), *41*, 17n, 18n, n; *see also* Chase,
W. G.
Simons, H. C., 163
single-exit situations, 12, 16–17, 19–23, 25,
31–2, 33, 168, 170; *see also* multiple-
exit
situational determinism: as a research programme, 16–18, 30, 68n, 129–30, 147,
167; in multiple- and single-exit situations, 19–20, 33; origin of phrase,
168n; in monopolistic competition
and oligopoly, 28, 31–3, 39n; in neoclassical economics, 26, 35, 38; in
perfect competition, 27–8, 30
Slichter, S. H., 163
Slutzky, E. V., 52n 172
(1972), *63*, 52n
Slutzky–Hicks–Allen indifference curve, 52
Smith, Adam: as origin of neoclassical research programme, 17, 23, 160–1, 194;
founder of 'classical' revolution, 209–
11; Invisible Hand analysis, 91, 176;
Smithian research programme, 166;
also mentioned, 125n
Wealth of Nations, 1776, 23n, 209–10, 211
social sciences *see* economics, natural
sciences
Soelberg, Peer (1967), *148*, 136
Sraffa, Piero, 194
(1926), *41*, 26n
Stamp, Josiah, 163
Stalinist research programme, 197
Stein, H. (1969), *179*, 163
Stewart, Ian, 43n
Stigler, George (1940), *41*, 38n; (1950), *63*,
55n; (1957), *41*, 23n; (1964), *41*, 39n;
(1965), *63*, 55n, 56n; (1970), *63*, 55n,
56
Stockholm school of economics, 87, 163n
Stolper, W. F. and Samuelson, P. (1941),
127, 115n
Stuart, H. W. (1896), *63*, 48n; (1917), *63*,
48n
substantive rationality: definition, 130–1; a
theory of best solutions, 133, 138;
failure under uncertainty, 140–2,
143–4; shifts from, to procedural,
146–7
Suppe, F., 157n
(1974), *179*, 153n, 155n, 157n, 158n
Sylos-Labini, P., limit-price theory, 33–9;
Sylos postulate, 35–9
(1956), *41*, 33n, 34n, 35n, 38n
Sylos–Bain model, 35n, 37
target planning, 138, 140n

Taussig, F., 163
Teich, M. and Young, R. (1973), *179*, 158n
tenacity, principle of, 151, 152, 176, 194
testability, 56, 58, 80n, 157, 159, 166, 169,
173, 177, 181n, 186, 187, 189, 196–8,
199, 201, 202; alternative tests, 175n
Theil, Henri (1958), *148*, 139n
theories: as blinkers, 208, 209, 218; clusters
as units of appraisal, 155–6, 171, 177;
corroboration of, 169, 170, 171;
criteria of, 109, 174, 175n; in economics and physical sciences, 76–7,
78; facts and, 155, 166n, 172, 173–6,
207–8, 216, 218; general, 209; history
and, 217; language problems of, 81;
longevity of, 199; and models, 70–2,
77; policy and, 163, 164; rejection of,
109–10, 124–5, 151, 176, 199n, 208;
tests for, 198, 200–3; *see also* falsifiability, falsification
Tinbergen, J. (1952), *148*, 138n
Tobin, J., 71n
Tobin, J. and Dolbear, F. T., Jr (1963), *63*,
58n
Towse, R., 149n
Triffin, R., 30
(1940), *41*, 30 n
Tugwell, R. G. (1922), *63*, 49n, 51n;
(1924), *63*, 49n
Tversky, A., 133; *see also* Kahneman, D.

Uhr, C. G. (1973), *179*, 163n
uncertainty, 134, 135, 142–4, 203; *see also*
expectation
unemployment: as a problem in economic
theory, 88; in classical and Keynesian
cosmology, 99; equilibrium, 94, 100,
162; an external factor in Keynes, 90;
in neoclassical synthesis, 96; dis-
regarded by neo-Walrasians, 106; in
post-war Keynesian economics, 164
United States: economics *versus* psychology
controversy, 44, 45–8, 130; economists
and business firms, 137–8; Great
Depression, 88; industry and limit-
price, 38n; Leontief paradox, 113–14,
122, 124
utility, 52; analysis, 53, 55, 145; expected,
174; marginal, 47–8, 53, 54; maximisation, 131, 174; tests for, 134;
theory, 56, 172, 215; theory of value,
166

value, theory of, 54, 84n, 211; labour, 110,
120, 165, 211; marginalist subjective,
45–7
Veblen, Thorstein: research programme,
47–8; pecuniary logic, 53
(1932), *63*, 47n

verifiability, 151, 171–2
Vernon, Raymond, product cycle model, 122
(1966), *127*, 122n; (1970), *127*, 122n, 123n
Vienna Circle, 73n, 151
Viner, Jacob, on importance as criteria for theory, 56–7; comparative cost, 115n; an advocate of Keynesian policies, 163
(1925), *63*, 48n, 57n; (1955), *127*, 115n

Wallsten, T. S. *see* Rapaport, A.
Walras, L.: supply-and-demand model, 77n; neo-Walrasian economics, 86–7, 92n, 94, 167; a progressive programme 95, 104; and Keynesian programme, 96, 103–7; leader of marginal revolution, 211
(1874), *218*, 211n
Walras–Cassel theory, 111n
Walter, Ingo (1968), *127*, 121n
Ward, Benjamin, 160
(1972), *179*, 160n, 168n, 172, 175n
Watkins, J. W. N., 6, 12n, 19n
Weaver, F. S. *see* Kunin, L.
wealth, 209–10; flow of, 210; theory of, or plutology, 215

welfare economics, 175–6, 213; Pigou's, 215
Wells, Louis T. (1969), *127*, 122n; (1972), *127*, 122n, 123n
Whitley, R. (1974), *180*, 149n
Whittaker, A. C. (1916), *63*, 47n
Wicksell, Knut, 73, 164, 167, 213
(1896), *218*, 213n
Wieser, 201n
Williams, John H. (1929), *127*, 122
Williamson, O. E., 170
Winch, Donald, 149n
(1970), *63*, 50n
Wolfe, A. B. (1924), *63*, 48n
Worland, S. T. (1972), *180*, 174n
Wrong, Dennis H. (1961), *108*, 91n

Yale, 203
Yamey, B. S. (1972), *41*, 39n
Young, R. *see* Teich, M.

Zahar, E, definition of 'novel fact', 110n
(1973), *127*, 110n, 123n, 159n; *see also* Lakatos and Zahar
Zaltman, G., Pinson, A. R. A. and Angelmar, R. (1973), *63*, 55n